Joyriding

A Practical Manual for Learning the Fundamentals of Masterful Driving

By Kenneth L. Zuber

THE HELIOS INSTITUTE
3433 West 192nd Street
Homewood, Illinois 60430

ISBN 0-9660004-0-4

Printed in the U.S.A.

10 9 8 7 6 5 4 3 2 1

Illustrations: Gregory J. Kenney

*This book is dedicated to everyone
in the past, present and future who did,
does, and will love driving.*

The following named people were fundamental to the genesis and completion of this book.
Warm and heartfelt thanks to:

Jerome P. Baron

Benjamin C. Bogue

Joakim Bonnier

Joseph Campbell

Dennis J. Day

John H. Klancnik

Angela Kouzins

John C. Sorrentino

Janet Mae Yates

Mitchell L. Zuber

VERY SPECIAL THANKS TO:
Jean C. Yates

The following named people helped me obtain photographs for this book by giving their time, effort, often their automobiles, and sometimes themselves.

Warm thanks to:

Anonymous

Anonymous

Phillip Armstrong

George & Jacquie Balaschak: TLC Carrossiers, Inc.

Robert Del Sarto

Peter & Heather Donnelly: The Chicago Land Rover Club

Peggy Dusman: American Automobile Manufacturers Association

Jerry E. Federspiel: Executive Director, Indiana State Police
        Youth Education and Historical Center

Don Gowler: President, Delorean Midwest Connection

John Guerrieri

Lynda Guerrieri

Bruce Henderson

Susan Lane

Raymond L. Marion

Jerry & Roberta Matejovsky

Lori Millen: National Highway Traffic Safety Administration

Charles T. Miller

Rick Miller: Rick Miller Photos

Allan Mottson

Jerry Murawski

Coung Nguyen

Patrick G. O'Rourke

Alice Preston: General Manager/Curator, Brooks Stevens
        Automobile Collection, Inc.

Rob & Debbie Pulsidski: ARTGO

D. Randy Riggs: *Sports Car International*

Peter Sachs: The Klemantaski Collection

Milton Smazik

Mal Tallungan

John L. Thornton

John Wazorick: President, Windy City Chapter, American Truck
        Historical Society

John F. Weinberger: President, Continental Autosports

Photographs taken for this book are by:

John Holmstrom, Holmstrom Photography

John H. Klancnik

Matthew Rubinberg, Matthew Rubinberg Photography

Kenneth L. Zuber

Thanks to the people who posed for photos: Allan, Arfan, Asema, Bobbie, Brad, Bruce, Carol, Cuong, Danielle, Jamar, Jean, John, Ken, Lisa, Mike, Milt, Niki, Pat, Phil, and Sara.

Table of Contents

1 Chapter One

Joyriding

A Personal Introduction from the Author

You're driving an automobile that can do 100 miles per hour. Not just on the speedometer — that can be anything from 75 up — but an honest 100 by stop watch. You are at the beginning of a five-mile straight stretch of concrete, so you stick your foot into it, hit and hold the 100 mark. Ahead of you there is a parked car, white, low and mean looking. As you pass, the fellow behind the wheel guns his engine and starts after you. You keep your foot hard down, and well before you've covered a mile, you hear a brutal scream, a roar that sears your eardrums, a whoosh, and the white car has passed you. Another quarter of a mile and he's out of sight.

That, gentlemen, is acceleration. Let us have no nonsense about how fast your car is away from the lights; never mind the time you spun the wheels in second gear on dry concrete. The man in the white car spotted you 100 miles per hour and a running start and almost blasted you off the road when he went by you within a single mile.[1]

The two paragraphs you have just read were written by the legendary automotive writer, Ken W. Purdy. They describe the awesome capabilities of a particular car. In the quotes which follow, Mr. Purdy describes the awesome capabilities of a man — a *driver.*

Tazio Giorgio Nuvolari was unique: indisputably he was supreme in his own sport, better than any other man who had ever lived. Nuvolari was a racing automobile driver so fabulously skilled that lesser men were hard-pressed even to understand how he did the things they watched him do.

"I tell you honestly," a contemporary said, "in a match race with the devil himself I would bet all on Tazio."

Rules of form were revised for Nuvolari. If his car were as fast as anything else running and stayed together, he would probably win. If it were 10 miles an hour slower, still he might win. He once beat nine of the best cars in the world, and beat them

1. Ken W. Purdy, "The Big White Cars" *The Kings of the Road*, Bantam Books (New York, 1954), p. 67.

twice in the same race, driving an Alfa that was 20 miles an hour slower. That was in the Grand Prix of Germany, held on July 28, 1935.

The German Mercedes-Benz and Auto Union cars of the 1930s were the fastest racing machines the world had seen to this day. The German Grand Prix of 1935 was supposed to be a private contest between the four Auto Union entries and the five from Mercedes-Benz. The Auto Unions would do 180 mph, the Mercedes were 5 mph slower, and Nuvolari's Alfa-Romeo was 20 miles an hour off the pace. The German cars were handled by some of the world's best: Rosemeyer, Von Brauchitsch, Stuck, Geier, Fagioli, and Caracciola and Varzi, the only two drivers automobile men ever attempt to compare with Nuvolari — *il maestro, il campionissimo.* The course was the Nürburgring, a mountain circuit, fourteen miles to the lap, 175 curves — a driver's course.

In ten laps Nuvolari moved his obsolescent Alfa-Romeo through the pack from sixth place to first. Still leading in the twelfth lap, Nuvolari came in for fuel. An Auto Union had just refueled in forty-nine seconds. It took Nuvolari's excited crew two minutes and fourteen seconds, and when he came screaming onto the track again he was back in sixth place. The Germans in the crowd relaxed. But in the next lap, the thirteenth, Nuvolari raced past four cars with absurd ease and lay an incredible second to Von Brauchitsch's Mercedes. The Mercedes pit gave their man the flat-out signal and he responded — indeed he broke the Nürburgring lap record. But he was over-revving his engine and wearing down the thinning tread of his tires to do it. Inevitably the big red car appeared in his mirrors, grew bigger and bigger until, halfway through the last lap, a rear tire blew out and Nuvolari blasted past to win by thirty-two seconds. It was the greatest individual triumph in the history of automobile racing.[2]

He could slide a car through a curve at 150 mph with the front wheels six inches from a fence at the beginning of the bend and the same six inches from it at the end. No one has ever bettered his fantastic judgment of a car's balance: its speed sideways as well as forward, and the exact amount of weight resting on each of the four wheels as the load shifted from side to side and front to back under braking, turns and acceleration.

The little man's career is full of examples of his weird art. In 1935 the Grand Prix of Monte Carlo was driven in a heavy rain. One car broke an oil line in the middle of a double bend, dumping an enormous quantity of oil on the already rain-slick pavement. The next car through crashed. The second crashed. No. 3 crashed. No. 4 piled into him and No. 5 repeated. Nuvolari was sixth and he hit the corner with his foot well down. He not only steered the car through the oil, slamming the wheels from side to side faster than the eye could follow, but he never touched one of the five cars stacked up all over the place.

"Nivola" won his last race, the Monte Pellegrino, on April 10, 1950, driving an 1100-c.c. Abarth. He was 58 years old. At one point in the running of this race he had one wheel spinning in empty air over a precipice, but he brought it back. He would not consider such a trifle notable.[3]

Running in the 1930 Mille Miglia — he won this insanely dangerous 1000-mile road race two times — he was behind Achille Varzi, his great rival. Varzi was well

2. Ken W. Purdy, "The Marvel of Mantua" *Ken Purdy's Book of Automobiles*, Playboy Press (1972), p. 60.

3. Ken W. Purdy, "The Flying Mantuan" *The Kings of the Road*, Bantam Books (New York, 1954), p. 58 and p. 65.

ahead, and Nuvolari knew that if Varzi saw him coming he would never catch up. It was night. Nuvolari switched off his lights. He drove over the winding roads of Italy for sixty miles, howling along in the blackness flat-out, his mechanic sitting beside him stiff with fear, until he was just behind Varzi. He threw on the lights then, rode past, and won.[4]

Another man, one of my uncles, boasting about his driving ability, once said, "Give me a car that will accelerate like I want it to and brake like I want it to, and nobody will pass me on the road!" Hearing this as a teenager and relatively new driver, I was impressed. Years later I realized what he had really said. Nobody could pass him on the road if he could have a magic car. Nuvolari never had a magic car!

My uncle had made a common mistake. He had imagined that the abilities of his car were his own. A car has power and speed. It has handling, braking, and accelerative abilities. These are the very things a driver uses when driving. He develops a very close relationship with these things. He can easily begin to believe that the car's abilities are his. From there, it is a short psychological step to believing that driving a fast car means he is athletic, driving a beautiful car means he is good looking, driving an expensive car somehow entitles him to respect, driving a four-wheel drive vehicle means he is rugged and strong, or driving a sporty car means he is a dashing hero.

The truth is that no driver has three hundred horsepower. In fact, no driver has even one horsepower. No driver can accelerate himself down the road from zero to sixty miles an hour in 6.5 seconds. No driver, no matter how much he wishes or believes it, really is that black stallion rampant on the yellow field of the Ferrari emblem.

Cars are cars, and people are people, and driving is driving. What matters about you as a driver is your driving ability. Your driving ability is what gets you respect behind the wheel. Your driving ability is what entitles you to take the lives of your passengers in your hands. Your driving ability is what gives you pleasure and pride as a driver.

A poor driver can make the world's greatest car look clumsy. He can make it go slowly and uncomfortably. He can make it bounce and jerk. He can get into the way with it, cut off people with it, and generally mess up traffic with it. He can get tickets with it. He can embarrass himself with it. He can crash with it. He can even kill people with it.

A good driver can take an ordinary, low performance economy car and make it look really good. He can maneuver through traffic with grace and style. He can keep up a good pace safely regardless of traffic, terrain, or weather. He can give his passengers the feeling that they can trust him completely, and he can win for himself the emotional rewards of a good performance. In any vehicle, under any conditions, he can be proud of his driving!

Driving is More Than Transportation

If we could be "beamed" everywhere, would we still drive? Yes, because driving is not just another way to get somewhere. It is not only for convenience that we drive, nor for freedom, nor to make a living, nor for independence. The love we have of driving goes far deeper than those things.

CONTROL: Driving *means* controlling. The feeling of being in control is a basic human need. When we do not feel at least some control, we are afraid. If our feeling of not being in control con-

---

4. Ken W. Purdy, "The Marvel of Mantua" *Ken Purdy's Book of Automobiles*, Playboy Press (1972), p. 62.

tinues long enough, we begin to lose our feeling of self worth. We feel not just afraid, but worthless. Say to almost any driver that he drives poorly and you have attacked a very basic part of his self esteem. Feeling in control makes us feel good about ourselves and the rest of the world. It makes us better people. Driving gives us a feeling of control.

All by itself, physical control of an automobile can give great pleasure. The child delight of "making it go," the feeling of applying perfectly balanced power coming out of a precisely rounded corner, making an absolutely seamless shift in a stick-shift car, coming to a sure, smooth stop on an ice-covered downhill slope, making the exhaust roar with your right foot, feeling the engine and brakes respond to your feet on the pedals, holding the wheel in your hands, sensing the g-forces of stopping, turning, and accelerating, these are all part of the fun of driving.

Control is why the driver is respected. Just like the captain of a ship or the pilot of an airliner, the driver of a car is respected for the knowledge and skill he must have to control his vehicle regardless of weather, traffic, or any other factors. He is respected because his ability at control has earned him the right and the honor of being responsible for the very lives of his passengers. This trust is probably the main reason a driver's license has become the certificate of adulthood in developed countries.

Control of a car means grace, balance, safety, and efficiency. These are the things a great driver achieves. They are the reasons he is respected and admired. Throughout history the excellent sailor, or horseman, or flier, or chariot driver has been admired because mankind has always loved speed and power and the person who can control them. The person who challenges the forces of nature and comes to terms with them seems to master them. He is always admired. He is a hero. That is why sea captains, race drivers, and astronauts are such glamorous figures. They are heroes because they can control.

All of us humans need to feel in control, and all of us humans need to feel that we are heroes. I believe that these two, great human needs are the reasons for the strong love humans have for cars and driving. They are why, in spite of inconvenience, expense, and the maddening frustration of daily, rush hour traffic jams, we humans cherish our cars and continue to drive.

THE HERO JOURNEY: Think about a tractor semi-trailer rig. Think about its power, its size. Think about the pounding of its diesel exhaust under acceleration. Think about its huge tires whining as they gobble up the miles.

We respond emotionally to big trucks. We can't help it. Even when they are just parked, big trucks excite us. Why? Big trucks are designed, built, bought, and used for only one purpose —rolling along the open road. Big trucks symbolize the romance of the open road, and we humans respond to that romance.

The romance of the open road is the reason we take pictures of our car when we are on a trip. The romance of the open road is what captures our imagination when we see a car with license plates from a state a thousand miles away moving along the highway. The romance of the open road is why we buy souvenirs. It is why we leave those bumper stickers shouting, "SEE THE COLOSSAL CAVE OF THE DINOSAURS!" on the car. Those bumper stickers are much more than advertising. They are symbols of adventure. They tell the whole world that we have experienced something far beyond the ordinary and that we are richer for it. We are special. We are not just people from Los Angeles, New York, Phoenix, or Atlanta. We are people who have actually been inside the Colossal Cave of the Dinosaurs. We are proud of that, and we want all the ordinary people on the road and at the motel and back home to know it.

The romance of the open road is why those squashed bugs all over the windshield and front end of the car are not just dead bugs to be cleaned away. They are a badge of something, just like the bumper sticker, just like the heavy grime all over a car which has obviously just finished a long trip through snow, rain, dust, or mud. International rally and off-road racing cars and trucks are displayed at automobile shows with the dirt from their latest victory still on them. Why? The dirt is proof of their heroic adventure and safe return. Racing cars stir the romance of the open road in our souls, even when they are displayed on flat tires in museums, even when they are old and slow by today's standards. Obviously it is more than tremendous power, fiendish speed, and glorious noise that excites us. These cars raced. They have been out there. They have risked all and won, and they are back. They are veterans of battle, of adventure, of triumph! They have taken the hero journey! They and their drivers are heroes, and all human beings respond to heroes. It is basic psychology and age old truth. We all love heroes, and we all need to see ourselves as heroes: brave, strong, honest, true, good, and triumphant!

Cars and driving are perfect metaphors for the great hero journey. When we drive, we are trying to satisfy that fundamental human longing to be heroes. When we drive, in our most private souls, we are heroes!

When we go on a car trip, something deep inside us does take the great, mythic, hero journey. We do what heroes have done since before their stories were told. We leave the familiar to go on a quest: to slay a dragon, to gain wisdom, to prove ourselves, to get a job, to see the Grand Canyon! We see different places. We meet different people. We learn about different customs. We have adventures. We must use our knowledge and skill to survive. We learn about ourselves and the world. Finally, we return in triumph, having survived, having come back with stories, souvenirs, and truths. We are heroes!

Let us truly be hero drivers then. Let us always honor driving and never disgrace it. Let us control. Let us not blame others, or rationalize, or tell tall stories. Let us drive honestly, bravely, wisely, admirably. Let us heap glory upon ourselves through our wonderful driving! Let us try to make each and every drive a hero journey!

MOST COMPLEX PSYCHOMOTOR ACTIVITY: Driving has been called the most complex psychomotor activity we humans do. A psychomotor activity is one in which both the mind and the body work together. In other words, while higher mathematics, philosophy, etc., may be extremely complex mental activities, driving has been considered the most complex thing we do using our minds and bodies together, the most complex thing we do as total beings. Being truly excellent at the most complex thing you can do using all of yourself is an achievement of which you can be justly proud any time, anywhere, in any company!

Driver Education

Driver education must not only acknowledge, but place high value on the genuine and positive human passions which underlie the obvious love people all over the world have for driving. Driver education must stop its doomed efforts to teach students that their longings for freedom, control, and heroism are wrong. Instead, driver education must use these passions as the strong foundations for learning to drive well.

Driver education must realize that nobody learns to drive because he wants to be safe. People learn to drive because they want to drive. People learn to sky-dive because they want to sky-dive.

"I hate finals week."

People learn to weld because they want to weld. People learn to climb mountains because they want to climb mountains. All these students must learn safety techniques. The sky-divers, welders, and mountain climbers will learn safety eagerly because it will allow them to do the things they want to do. These sky-divers, welders, and mountain climbers will become proud of their knowledge and skill in safety. They will wear their safety savvy as a badge of honor. They will enjoy being looked up to as wise "old pros," people who do it right!

Driving students, on the other hand, will tend to reject the safety training offered them because it is offered as if it were the highest goal of driver education, instead of a vital basic needed to master and enjoy driving. Education must never hold back, but always push forward.

Driver education should expose the false and teach the true. It should teach the simplest, best techniques which build real skill and genuine confidence quickest. It should encourage enjoyment and growth. It should promote a love of excellence in driving. Its goal should be mastery as the result of desire, discipline, study, understanding, and hard practice. It should produce drivers who consider themselves driving hobbyists, lifelong driving students, who will eagerly pursue greater understanding and mastery for decades. Driver education must always honor driving. It must never trivialize the most complex psychomotor activity. Driver education must understand and teach that the reason to drive well *is* to drive well! Safety, courtesy, easing of congestion, etc., will all result if most drivers want to drive well and work at it because they believe in it and enjoy it.

They say, "There is no substitute for experience." They are right. They also say, "Practice makes perfect." Once again, they are right, but only if the right things are practiced. Your on-the-road experience and practice will be much more valuable if they are based upon the concepts in this book.

The concepts in this and other books will become more meaningful and useful if you re-read them after you have had considerable driving experience. In fact, reviewing the basics is always valuable. When reviewed through experienced eyes, the basics deepen and broaden in meaning and value. They lead to new understandings, new discoveries, new possibilities, and higher levels of mastery. Theory and practice work together. Base your practice on sound, well-understood theory and use your experience better to understand the theory.

I believe that it took me about 100,000 miles (roughly ten years of normal driving) to become a decent driver. My father gave me an idea about how to work the clutch and shift gears in his 1941

6

Chevy. I guess I found out just about everything else I know about driving on my own. I studied the laws. I read books. Luckily, I seemed to understand aiming from the beginning. I watched traffic. I tried to understand traffic and fit into it. I read about and practiced parallel parking and skid control, etc. After I had become a decent driver, I taught driving, raced a sportscar, and read more, and thought more. The more I did, the more I learned and the better I got.

It is obvious to me that for the most part I taught me how to drive. It may not be so obvious to you that *you* teach *you* how to drive. You have the primary responsibility for learning the basics. You have the sole responsibility for learning all the rest.

With driver education you should be able to become a decent driver in much less time than I needed. Perhaps you can become a good basic driver in only 30,000 miles or three years. Perhaps in only 10,000 miles or one year! Who knows? The keys are how much *you* care and how hard *you* work on the proper things in the classroom, in the training car, in your own car, and even when you are not driving. How good do *you* want to be?

You alone are responsible for your driving for the rest of your life, not the driver ed. teacher, not the policeman, not the courts, not your parents. You yourself must learn. You yourself must control. You yourself must work. You yourself must progress. You yourself must care, for you alone must suffer the costs, the embarrassment, the pain, the guilt of your driving errors, and you alone can enjoy the rewards of your driving excellence: the control, the fun, the freedom, the respect, the heroism, and the glory!

Hobby

Why ride a horse, or sail a boat, or fly an airplane? Why ski, or surf, or skateboard, or ride a motorcycle? Why do any sport or hobby activity which is centered on controlling or driving something?

Fun, of course!

What is the fun?

Control — in any sport or hobby which is about controlling something, the fun must be in the controlling. Sometimes people say that speed is the fun of skiing, etc. Pure speed, in and of itself, is meaningless in terms of fun. Consider the difference in fun between experiencing a speed of 300 mph in a jet airliner (nothing) and experiencing a speed of 50 mph skiing down a mountainside (very exciting). Speed without control is terrifying! However, speed gracefully achieved with perfect control is truly an exultant thing. Control of a vehicle at speed *is* fun. The main thing though is always control!

A person tries one of these controlling or driving activities because he thinks it should be fun. He finds it is fun. The movement is fun. Whatever control he achieves is fun. He gets a feeling of personal satisfaction in achievement. Therefore, he tries the activity again. He finds that he is getting more control and having more fun. His personal satisfaction in achievement increases.

The more he does the activity, the better he gets at it. He has more fun and gets more personal satisfaction. He is learning and growing. It feels good. He cares more and more about the activity. He begins to see that there is much more to his sport/hobby than the basics he has mastered. He wants to get really good. He studies more. He takes advanced courses. He gets better equipment. He finds a whole new world of learning and achieving and enjoyment. The better he gets, the more possibilities he sees for improving. There is no limit to learning and improving. He

wants to get better and better forever!

He begins to study the history and lore of his hobby/sport. He gets interested in the construction and maintenance of his equipment. Perhaps he even gets interested in equipment design or manufacture. He may even teach his beloved sport/hobby.

Driving probably starts out as fun for most of us, but it rarely ends up that way. We get into rush hour traffic jams every day. We have to drive people places when we don't want to. We get tickets and have accidents. We have to pay so much to drive, own, and maintain cars. We have to deal with so many bad drivers on the road. We lose the passion we had for driving when we started doing it. We get self-satisfied with whatever basic abilities we have, and we get lazy. We rationalize our mistakes and blame others for our problems. We think we are experts, even though we have never gotten to the higher levels of the hobby. Most drivers do not even master the fundamentals, and it is not much fun doing something at which you are not very good.

I want driving to be one of your hobbies for the rest of your life! I want you to care, and study, and try, and learn, and improve, and enjoy more and more for as long as you drive. The more drivers have this hobbyist's dedication, the more motor travel will get safer, and faster, and more efficient, and more enjoyable. *Do not let the passion die!* Do not get bored and self-satisfied without ever getting to experience the real heart and soul of driving, the real fun, the real control, the real satisfaction, the real accomplishment, the real heroism!

If possible, drive a car that is fun. Some cars are new. Some cars are old. Some are fast, some are slow. Some are big or small or capacious, etc. Some are beautiful. Some are ugly. A few can be fun. Try to drive one of those, if you can. It helps so much to have a car which encourages you to drive well and which rewards you for doing it.

Engage in some other hobby which relates to cars and driving. Go racing, rallying, slaloming, hill-climbing, off-roading, ice-racing. Get interested in stock cars, monster trucks, open-wheel race cars. Go to a high performance driving school. Go to car museums and car shows. Collect and/or show cars yourself. Restore cars. Get and read books about cars and drivers and driving and automobile mechanics and people who made their living with cars. Get interested in automotive safety. Get a job which deals with automobiles and/or driving. Share your knowledge with others. Collect automotive art, or car badges, or radiator caps, or hood ornaments, or license plates, etc. Any and all of these things will probably help keep you interested in driving and in improving your driving.

PERFORMANCE: You're good. You're very good! Because you care and because that caring made you study, and practice, and work *very* hard, you are *very* good! Then, one day, you are absolutely great! You do EVERYTHING perfectly! In fact, on that day, you *cannot* make a mistake, and you *know* it! You are doing what you do best far better than you have ever done it before. You are doing what you do best even better than you thought you could!

The psychologist Maslow calls this rare and wonderful phenomenon a "peak experience." It is the experience of functioning at the highest level possible, being the very best you can be!

Others may be thrilled by your performance. Others may honor you for it. Others probably helped make your performance possible, but *YOU DID IT! You* were perfectly in control! *You* soared far, far above the ordinary, far above the excellent! *You* got possibly 100% performance from yourself, and it felt so good! A peak experience is a transcendent performance you'll cherish for the rest of your life, should you be lucky enough to have one.

Tazio Nuvolari routinely raced a car better than his competitors. Babe Ruth's World Series home run past the flagpole in Wrigley Field was thrilling!

Al Jolson, called the greatest entertainer of the twentieth century, had a standard line to begin his performances. After all the other great stars had performed, after the audience had already seen an excellent show, after the audience should have been satisfied, Al Jolson would come out and declare, "You ain't seen nothin' yet!" Then he would deliver on that promise.

When "Satchel" Paige, the legendary baseball pitcher from the old Negro leagues finally got his chance to pitch in the majors, he was 42 years old. The first three batters he faced all got on base through a combination of a hit, a walk, and an error. In the very first inning of his first major league appearance, 42 year old "Satchel" Paige faced loaded bases with nobody out.

What did he do?

He turned to his teammates on the field and said, "You can all sit down now, because I'm going to strike the next three men out." then he did it!

Were any of those performances a peak experience? Only the people who did them might know. Regardless of that, though, they were great performances, and performing is what life is all about. Doing it! Doing it as well as you possibly can! Putting 100% effort into your own hero journey! Performing is simultaneously the greatest challenge and the greatest reward you can give yourself! Performance is the celebration of excellence!

Every drive is a chance to perform. Every drive should echo a peak experience in driving. That peak experience need not have happened yet. It may never happen, but each and every drive can relate to an ideal performance given in the past or sought in the future. Each and every drive must be connected to that great drive. Each and every drive goes to build up a record, a kind of driver's biography. Each and every drive is a piece of your life's work as a driver. Try to make each performance a gem. Make that biography of yours something worth reading, something full of great performances and successes! Heap glory upon yourself, and leave the world a better place because you drove through it!

GETTING READY: Drivers getting into race cars are already dressed in their flame resistant coveralls, underwear, socks, and shoes. They get belted into the seat. They make sure everything is adjusted correctly. They put on their helmets and gloves. While doing these things, they think about racing.

This procedure of getting physically ready to race, the little ritual of getting into the car, helps them get mentally ready to race. Every time you get physically ready to drive a car, get mentally ready to drive a car. Make a little ritual of getting into the car, adjusting everything, buckling up, and starting the engine. While doing these things, think about driving. Decide that this drive will be a good experience, that it will be fun, that you will learn something, that you will perform well, that this will be one more excellent performance in a decades long record of excellent performances!

Never take a mile or two to warm up when driving. Always drive beautifully from the instant you begin.

A great driving record will not come through luck alone. It will come from dedication, discipline, and work. If you care enough about yourself and your driving, if you care enough about the hero inside you, you will develop the discipline to work hard on this wonderful hobby of driving!

DON'T WASTE YOUR CHANCE: Most people in the world today still do not own cars and drive

them daily. Most people in the world still can only long for such blessings. They yearn for the freedom! They hunger for the control! They languish among impossible dreams of glorious automotive hero journeys!

What would those millions of people think about the multitudes of drivers in developed countries to whom driving has become a chore, a bore, a waste of time? What would they think of all those drivers who complain about traffic and all the fools on the road and yet do nothing to ease the flow, or raise the standards, or set a shining example? What would they think of all those drivers who excuse their own embarrassingly poor driving performances by rationalizing instead of working every day to improve their skills? What would they think of all those drivers who waste miles, and roads, and money, and cars, and precious time? What would they think about all the drivers who throw away their daily opportunity for fun and fulfillment, who throw away their daily opportunity to perform on hero journeys?

They who dream of driving while you have to do it would be thunderstruck! They could not believe that any sane human being could ever tire of such a challenging, entertaining, rewarding, uplifting experience as driving. They would be angered that people given the opportunity to drive every day could waste that opportunity. They would be right!

An opportunity missed is missed forever. Missing an opportunity is not just missing a chance to progress. By default it is taking a step backward. Missing an opportunity to grow and to perform and to enjoy is a lessening of the value of your life and of yourself!

Do not waste your chance for freedom, control, self-expression, and mythic heroism! Do not miss your chance to perform! Drive beautifully! Drive with full attention, full enthusiasm, full commitment to excellence! Build a glowing record of fine driving! Realize what an opportunity you have and make the most of it! Make each and every one of your drives a hero journey! Make each and every one of your drives a *JOYRIDE*!

The Other Side

Everything has at least one other side. Find and examine as many sides of a thing as possible. Then put all your information together. You may discover truth. You may gain understanding. You may even achieve wisdom!

For a long time many people have tried to link wisdom with driving, mostly unsuccessfully. Linking wisdom and driving is probably the main goal of driver education. So far in this chapter I have tried in a broad, general way to explain the positive side of driving. I hope I have succeeded. I hope you are inspired. However, to get a real understanding of driving and to be able to link wisdom with it, we must explore, understand, and accept the other side, too.

The other side of driving is death… disfigurement… dismemberment… paralysis… brain damage. The other side of driving is pain… suffering… embarrassment… guilt… regret. The other side of driving is the desperate but impossible wish for another chance! The other side of driving is danger! Every time you get behind the wheel, death gets into the passenger seat. Any drive may end suddenly in agony.

Remember a time when you were barefoot and stubbed your toe. Remember that pain. Remember the pain when you hit your finger with a hammer. Remember pain that was so bad you cried. Remember bad cuts and scrapes. Remember bad burns. Remember pain. Imagine pain so bad it would make you faint. Pain is part of the negative side.

Now add panic to your understanding of driving. Imagine yourself staring at the raw end of a broken bone sticking right through the skin of your leg. Imagine a half gallon of your blood soaking into your clothes and dripping into puddles around you. Imagine waking up in a hospital bed and realizing that you are alright after the crash only to be told by some doctor you have never seen before that you no longer have your legs!

Imagine the guilt and anguish. Imagine how you'd feel when you met the parents of the little boy you killed! Imagine how you'd feel at the trial. Imagine your brother or girlfriend or mother and father struggling not to cry when they see you in a hospital bed with a circular, metal frame screwed into your head. Imagine feeling phantom pains in arms or legs you no longer have. Imagine learning to walk all over again on artificial legs. Imagine your parents crying and screaming when they have to identify your cold, dead, broken body in a morgue.

Think about having to sit in a wheelchair for the rest of your life. Imagine having to be fed and needing the food wiped off your face after every meal. Imagine not being able to control when you urinate or defecate. Imagine speaking slurred and slowly through a twisted and drooling mouth. Imagine your face burned half away. People will either look away quickly in shock, or stare. Strangers will actually walk up to you and ask how you got that way. Imagine that it is a major struggle for you just to lift a glass of water to your lips. Imagine your normal, thinking, wishing, dreaming head attached to a useless body, a body which cannot move itself, a body which cannot even feel!

Many of your friends will leave you. People do not like to be around sick, injured, or dying people. Your family will have to stay with you, unless they put you in a home somewhere. Your family will have to give up their time and money, etc., to take care of you. They will have to pretend they are not too tired. They will try to believe that they don't mind. They will tell people how brave you are, how you suffer so courageously, how cheerful you stay, what a strong person you are.

You'll be strong and brave and cheerful and try hard. Sometimes you'll even do wonderful things, but sometimes, late at night, in bed all alone, you'll remember how things used to be: school, friends, sports, dancing, dates, music, plans, driving, coming and going as you please. Then you'll cry silently. You'll cry and cry and cry remembering how it used to be and how awful it is!

"It can't happen to me." People actually believe that! "It always happens to the other guy."

To everybody else *YOU* are the other guy! Think about that! It *can* happen to you. It *can* happen to me. It *can* happen to anybody! Believe it! Believe it as much as you believe that you are yourself!

Then do something about it. Do not just accept the danger. Minimize the risks. Mountain climbers, test-pilots, race drivers, etc., look for the risks, try to understand them, and then do whatever they can to eliminate or minimize them. Foolhardiness is not courage. Foolhardiness is foolhardiness. Minimize the risks of driving by studying safety, by thinking safety, by having the safest car you can, by driving as safely as you can, and by using safety equipment properly.

The Story of Helios and Phaëthon

The story of Helios and Phaëthon is a Greek myth. To me, it is a story about driving. It shows both sides of driving — the glorious and the dangerous. It tells the truth. It leads toward wisdom. Enjoy it. Remember it!

Helios was the Greek god who drove the chariot of the sun across the sky every day, supplying the earth with heat and light energy. All mankind depended upon that energy, as did the rest of the animal kingdom, and the trees, and the grass, and the crops, and the flowers, etc. The gods themselves

depended on the sun's energy, and Helios was the only being able to drive the chariot of the sun. Helios alone had the knowledge, the strength, the courage, the experience, the understanding, and the carefully developed sensitivity needed to control the great chariot and its marvelous horses. Not even Zeus, the chief god, could drive that awesome chariot.

Obviously, Helios was a very important and highly respected god. He was more important than the greatest king. He supplied energy to the world! Added to that, he was a great hero. Daily, he drove those colossal horses over a tricky and dangerous route at thrilling speed, carrying the blazing sun!

Phaëthon was a teenage boy. One day he and a few friends were idling away some time. They began talking about their fathers' jobs. "My dad is a lawyer." said one. "My dad makes sandals." added another. Each boy in turn told what his father did for a living. Finally, it was Phaëthon's turn. Phaëthon had never known his father. However, his mother had once told him that the god Helios was his father. Phaëthon pointed up at the sun in the sky and said, "There, there's my dad!"

Naturally, none of the other boys could believe such seeming nonsense. Imagine saying that the majestic god Helios was your father! They laughed derisively. They taunted Phaëthon. They jeered him. They sneered. They mocked viciously.

Phaëthon fought back, but it was useless. He went home embarrassed, angry, hurt, and wanting to get even.

At home, Phaëthon once again asked his mother whether Helios really was his father. She repeated that Helios was Phaëthon's father, but that she had no proof.

Dejected, Phaëthon sulked and thought — and thought, and thought. He needed proof. Finally, he got an idea. He would travel east. He would find and climb the great mountain on top of which was the temple of the sun. He would talk to Helios himself. He would get proof. Then he would show those guys.

Phaëthon's journey east was long and tiring. He had to cross several countries. He had many adventures along the way. Finally, he found and climbed the mountain of the sun. The higher he climbed, the more trouble he had in seeing, because the brilliant, yellow light from the temple, the burning light of the sun itself, shown brighter and brighter. At last, after great effort, Phaëthon reached the temple and found the throne room, the brightest place of all. As his eyes adjusted to the brilliance, he was able to see Helios himself sitting on his shimmering, golden throne, himself aglow with dazzling, yellow light.

The radiant god asked the boy's business.

Phaëthon gave his name and that of his mother. He told his story and finally, all atremble, asked whether Helios really was his father.

The god answered that he was indeed Phaëthon's father. Phaëthon explained that he needed proof for his friends. Helios asked immediately, "What do you want?" Gods, you see, were allowed to prove things merely by fulfilling requests.

It took Phaëthon not a second to answer. What did he want? What would any teenage boy want from the god who drove the chariot of the sun? "Sir, I'd like to drive the chariot!"

Helios knew what it was to drive the fiery chariot. He knew that he was the only being, human or god, who could do it. He did not want to send his son into such danger. He pleaded with Phaëthon to change his mind, to ask for anything else.

Phaëthon refused even to consider any other request. He wanted to drive the ultimate chariot. Already he could see himself racing across the sky, controlling those fierce and mighty horses! He imagined his friends looking up at the sun and seeing *him* driving the great chariot! He would wave to them. He would wave majestically, a wave that said, "See me. See Phaëthon, son of Helios, driving the chariot of the sun!" What joy that would be, what glory!

Just like humans, the gods had to live by certain laws. The same law which gave gods the right to prove things by granting wishes forced them to grant exactly the wish wished. The deal had been done. Nothing could persuade Phaëthon to change his mind. Helios *must* let Phaëthon drive.

Helios prepared the boy for the drive as well as he could. He tried to remember and explain everything he knew about driving the chariot. He explained the route. The ascent was so steep that even with their tremendous power, it was all the horses could do to move the great load up into the sky. He made it clear that the trip across the sky held much challenge, too. The track was so narrow and so high that the very spirited horses might easily get spooked and break away into a rush of uncontrollable speed. Finally, the descent might well require the greatest skill of all. Helios knew that it was all he could do to hold back the great load on the steep, downhill slope.

The time came. Smiling, Phaëthon waved to his father, then slapped the horses' backs with the reins. He cracked the whip. The horses strained against the weight. Their hooves stomped and slipped in the dust. Slowly, the great cart began to move.

Amazingly, Phaëthon managed to drive the chariot up into the sky. The path leveled. The view was magnificent. Phaëthon couldn't believe his luck, his joy. What an experience. What a thrill.

After a while, he actually did see his friends look up at him. He waved. They waved back in astonished embarrassment at seeing Phaëthon driving Helios' great chariot. Phaëthon's joy was complete.

Just at that moment, the horses caught their second wind. They wanted to run a little faster. They surged and struggled against the driver. Phaëthon reined in. He yelled commands to slow. He screamed, "Whoa!" The horses did not respond. Indeed they ran even faster, until they spooked and bolted into a wild frenzy. Their manes and tails streamed in the wind. Their huge muscles pumped hooves like pistons onto the path which smoked and chipped. Lather blew back off the horses' necks. It splattered on Phaëthon's face and sizzled on the sun. The horses' nostrils flared wide open. Veins stood out on their faces. Their wild eyes rolled in terror!

The chariot began to buffet and sway, then to bounce and swerve. The grease burned off the axle, and the wheel hubs began to smoke.

Phaëthon threw away the useless reins and huddled down in the front of the chariot, whimpering and hiding his face.

Nothing could stop the horses now. The chariot careened more and more out of control. It went farther and farther off course, alternately brushing the stars and swooping down toward earth.

The chariot caught fire. Soon Phaëthon was burning. In moments, Phaëthon's soaring glory had turned into raging panic!

Each earthward swoop of the chariot burned a vast scorch on the earth. Soon all of creation was wailing and screaming for help. It seemed the end of the world!

Finally, Mother Earth herself begged the gods for help. Zeus struck the chariot with a thunderbolt, shattering it. The horses fell into the sea. The dead, flaming body of Phaëthon fell into the mysterious river Eridanus.

2 Chapter Two

In the Cockpit

Enjoying a museum with race cars in its collection, visitors look at the outside form of the cars first. They look at the colors, the number, the general shape. Those who understand such things examine the suspension, the drive system, and the power plant. Most end up staring into the cockpit. They ponder the gauges, the pedals, the gearshift lever — the steering wheel. They are fascinated by the safety harness and roll cage which armor the driver and the seat from which he operates the controls with wonderful skill!

Perhaps these visitors imagine the thrills, the joy, the pride, the glory of driving beautifully. Perhaps they begin to sense the indescribable feeling of control, of unity with the cosmos which the race driver, fired by the human longing for excellence, may achieve when drifting the car through a corner perfectly, balancing it at the very limit of adhesion with sensitivities and skills fine tuned by study, practice, and experience — challenging the laws of Nature herself!

Perhaps they think these thoughts and feel these feelings as they stand peering into the very cockpit in which Richard Petty, or Michael Andretti, or even Tazio Nuvolari sat when he *controlled* this car — *drove* this car to victory!

Is not *any* driver's seat, to the non-driver, a place of awe, surrounded by gadgets of all sorts, which *only* the *driver* understands and can operate? Is not the driver's seat an honored place, reserved for someone with very special knowledge, for someone worthy of great respect? Is not the driver's seat a fearsome place of heavy responsibility?

Should not *your* driver's seat, *your* driving compartment, be taken very seriously? Should not the cockpit in which *you* hold the responsibility for life and death help you drive the best you can?

You bet your steering wheel it should. It should fit you well. It should be clean and efficient.

GETTING BEHIND THE WHEEL: Get into the car — on the driver's side. Sit behind the wheel. Close and lock the door. Now, adjust the seat.

Opinions vary about exactly how to sit behind a steering wheel, and in the end, you will have to figure out your own best position in each vehicle you drive. The cockpit's size and shape will affect your seating position, as will the proportions of your own body. Seat designs and means of adjustment vary a great deal, as do pedal placement, and steering wheel location and angle. Gearshift and parking brake controls also come in several styles and locations. However, certain guidelines about how to sit behind the wheel can be given.

You should be able to see over the steering wheel and parked windshield wipers. You should also be able to reach and operate all the controls easily. You should never have to force any part of your body into an unnaturally stretched or cramped position to reach or operate any major control.

Always sit as high as practical. A high seating position makes the car seem smaller and more manageable, while a low seating position makes it seem huge and clumsy. A high seating position will give you the best chance to see where you are going and where you want to go. It will make it easier for you to watch traffic, notice hazards, and see signs, signals, pavement markings, and road conditions. It will give you a good feeling of alertness and command.

Some car seats have height adjustments. Most do not. Therefore, in most cases, if you need to sit higher, you'll have to use an extra cushion. If you do, make sure it *does* give you a lift. A rather thin but crush resistant cushion may raise you higher than one which looks tall but squeezes way down when you sit on it. If the cushion is thicker at one end, put that end toward the rear of the car seat. If the big end is at the front, the cushion will raise mostly your legs, pulling your feet away from the pedals. Sometimes any extra cushion at all under you will pull your feet away from the pedals. If that happens, try putting the cushion behind your back. This will move you forward, improving your vision, but leave your feet near the pedals. If one end of a cushion to be used behind your back is thicker, put that end at the bottom. Finally, you may need to have one cushion beneath you and another behind you.

You should always be able to push the pedals down to the floor. This is the normal and proper way to operate the clutch pedal (stick shift cars only). It is necessary for the accelerator (gas pedal) as well.

The brake pedal will not normally go down to the floor. However, in the very unlikely event of total brake failure, it will. In a partial failure or in certain extremely severe stopping conditions, the brake pedal will go lower than normal. In any case, you should be able to push the brake pedal as far as it might go. If you can reach the toeboard with the tip of your shoe, you have more than enough leg reach. Because it has thickness of its own, no pedal can ever go down that far (Figure 1).

Avoid resting your left foot under the brake pedal. A foot there, especially a foot wearing a stiff, heavy shoe, can halt the pedal's downward movement before the brakes are applied hard enough to stop or slow down the car within the available distance. Faced with this situation, a driver may not realize what is wrong and just keep pressing harder and harder on the brake pedal. This will not help. Similarly, a driver may understand the problem but believe there is not enough time to release the brakes momentarily so he can remove his foot and restore normal pedal travel. This will not help either. Not only feet, but almost anything on the floor like a purse, book, tool, pop can, or even a twisted floor mat, can lodge under a pedal. Keep the floor clear, and keep your feet out from under the pedals. The best place for your left foot is planted firmly against the toeboard, bracing you and giving you more feel for the car.

Driving barefoot may or may not be legal in your state. Changing to barefoot driving affects your adjustment to the car just as changing between very stiff or heavy and very soft or light shoes does. Any of these changes can make fine pedal control difficult until you get used to it. This is also true for overshoes.

Driving barefoot or in extremely light, thin soled shoes will shorten the reach of your leg and foot. If you do not readjust your seat, this may force you to use your toes more than the stronger, more efficient balls of your feet. Heavy work boots and overshoes make your feet seem bigger, and you may bump them into the pedals or even step accidentally on more than one pedal at a time. Extremely loose shoes are an obvious hazard. High heeled footwear can make driving difficult.

Metal trim on pedals can be dangerous,

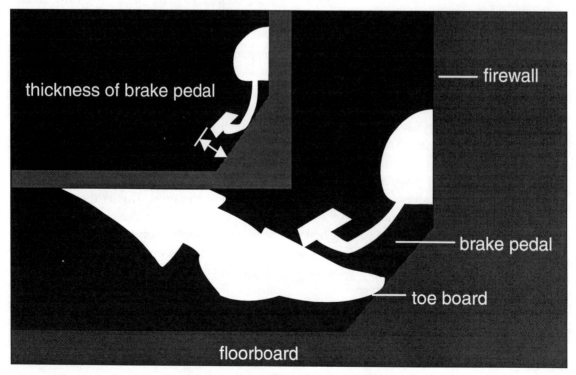

thickness of brake pedal

firewall

brake pedal

toe board

floorboard

Figure 1

because metal gives little grip. The same is true of pedals on which that rubber pedal pad has come off or worn through, exposing a metal surface which becomes slipperier as it is polished by use.

Wet shoes, particularly the rubber soled kind, and wet feet can easily slip off wet pedals. Grease, oil, water, snow and ice, even fresh dog droppings or french fries, can cause slippage, especially on metal.

LEARNING HOW TO SIT: A comfortable, well-supported driving posture keeps you erect and alert, allowing you to maintain control and enjoy driving. A slouching, cramped, or stretched driving posture tires you and actually makes it harder to drive.

Do not test a driver's seat by sitting on it for only a minute or two. A good driver's seat is not one that makes you want to curl up and take a nap as soon as you sit on it, but one which allows you to get out of the car feeling free of aches and stiffness after driving all day. A good driver's seat should not remind you of either a plank in the bleachers or an overstuffed reclining chair. It should be a solid structure designed to support your body firmly in a comfortable, natural sitting position from which you can operate the car's controls most efficiently. It should hold your body erect in corners with side support. It should be firm enough to allow you to feel the forces acting upon the car. It should not mask them.

Kinesthesia is the perception of position and motion through nerve endings in the muscles, tendons, and joints. It is critical to car control. You must be able to feel the car's acceleration, deceleration, cornering forces, and grip on the road to drive. You get these kinesthetic feelings through your body from the seat, steering wheel, pedals, and floor. The larger the area of your body in contact with the car, the more kinesthetic information you will receive. The more you receive, the better you will be able to control the car precisely, smoothly, and beautifully, especially in severe conditions.

Sit back in the driver's seat. Do not slouch or force your head into an unnatural position against the head restraint. Firmly tuck your buttocks well back into the crotch of the seat.

Tuck your buttocks firmly into the crotch of the seat.

Sit up straight. Then relax, letting your back and shoulders make as much contact as possible with the seatback. Let your upper legs lie on the seat cushion. Brace your left foot on the toeboard to the left of the pedals, and *let the seat support you!*

Use your safety harness. Let it hold you erect and alert in the seat. Adjust it snug, making your body almost a part of the car. That way, you will get more and better feedback from the car about its relationship with the road and about the results of your control inputs.

To steer with maximum efficiency, you need to give your arms freedom of movement. Sitting very near the steering wheel will not allow this, making steering awkward. Moreover, sitting very near the wheel will invite you to use it as a support rather than a control. The idea is *not* to use the steering wheel as something to lean on or to hang from. You should use the steering wheel from a solid base in the driver's seat. You should feel rooted like an oak tree, riveted in place like a steel girder. With the trunk of your body anchored securely in the driver's seat, you should extend your arms and legs to operate the controls with grace and mastery.

If you find yourself holding the bottom of the steering wheel all the time, you are probably sitting too far from it. When sitting too far from the wheel, holding it properly can be uncomfortable and tiring.

Sitting too far from the steering wheel.

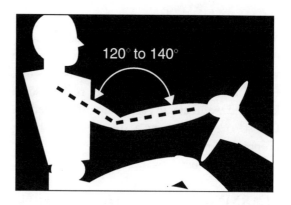

Finally, turn the steering wheel as shown.

One way to check the distance you sit from the steering wheel is to sit properly supported by the seat and reach your arm straight out to the wheel. Extend your arm fully, but do not pull your shoulder away from the seatback. When you are sitting in this position, your wrist should rest upon the top of the steering wheel.

Your back should remain completely in contact with the seatback. The driver below is siting much too far from the wheel.

Another way to measure proper distance from the steering wheel is to check the angle made by your upper and lower arm when you hold the wheel properly. (The angle should be between 120 and 140 degrees.)

The extreme slouch posture, currently popular with teens, is modeled by a clown. Need we say more?

The steering wheel should not block your view of the instruments.

The best angle for the steering wheel itself is near vertical, with the top farther from you than the bottom. The more nearly horizontal angle, often seen in buses, is less efficient, but does offer support for a driver's hands and arms.

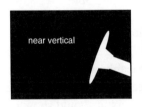

When you buy your own car, and if you will be its only driver, you may want to custom tailor its cockpit especially to fit your body by adding such items as: custom seats, a custom steering wheel, competition safety harness, and/or very securely attached, well-made pedal blocks with a non-skid surface. If your left foot does not reach the toeboard, you might want to install a "dead pedal" for it. A dead pedal is a solidly built up platform on which to rest your foot, adding to your comfort and kinesthetic sense.

SAFETY HARNESS: Use it. Tuck your buttocks well into the crotch of the seat, and sit up straight. Wear the lap belt as low as possible over your hips. Adjust it to fit quite snugly. Do not let the lap strap slip up over your abdomen. In case of a crash, you want to be held by your hips, the strongest structure in your body, not by your belly. The shoulder belt should also be adjusted snugly.

Safety harness systems vary, so to make sure you are using yours correctly, read the owner's manual for your car or ask for help from a *very knowledgeable* driver. When you put on the harness, make certain

Illustration by Julie Beaupain.

that no part of the webbing is twisted. After getting harnessed up, check the belts' fit and readjust as needed.

Some seat belt inertia reels do not lock except automatically in a crash. These never allow a driver truly to feel securely belted into the car. They can sometimes be made to lock (for testing purposes) by ending a stop with an extremely hard lurch. Before trying this, make sure of your clearance to the rear and warn your passengers.

Adjust the safety harness only *after* you have adjusted the seat. Moving the seat forward after adjusting the harness is almost impossible. Moving the seat backward after adjusting the harness will leave the belts much too loose. NEVER WEAR THE SHOULDER BELT WITHOUT THE LAP BELT!

Wearing the lap strap *over* a coat or very long shirt, sweater, jacket, sweatshirt, etc. will restrict the movement of your upper body, shoulders, and arms. Therefore, always open coats and flop them over the lap belt. Let other long clothes flop over the lap belt.

When transporting small children be certain they are correctly anchored in properly installed child seats, etc.

> *There was a cool guy from Kentucky*
> *Who thought he was so very lucky*
> *That he never wore belts*
> *With the natural results*
> *That he ended up dead as a ducky.*

ADJUSTING THE MIRRORS: Adjusting the mirrors is one of those funny things about driving — seemingly little tasks that take a great deal of practice to learn and never really stop causing difficulty.

Always take enough time and care to adjust the mirrors correctly. It is best to adjust mirrors on a relatively long strip of straight, level road. Curves and hills make adjusting mirrors difficult at best. Be sure your seat is adjusted before adjusting your mirrors.

While adjusting the mirrors, try to sit in a normal driving position. Avoid sitting extremely tall and erect, because after you drive a very short distance, your body will settle into a normal driving posture, and you'll find that the mirrors are much too high.

ADJUSTING THE INSIDE MIRROR: The job of the inside rearview mirror is to show you the scene directly behind the car. It's your main mirror. Always make sure it is adjusted to give you the best view you can get. Never be satisfied with a view which is cut off, crooked, lopsided, too high, or too low.

Hold the mirror by the frame to avoid getting your fingerprints all over the glass. Move it so that its top frame lines up with the top frame of the back window. Because of your particular size and the shape of your particular car, you may find it better to line up the bottom frame of the mirror with the bottom frame of the back window. In any case, the idea here is to get the height adjusted properly — to establish a baseline which allows you to see all the way back to the horizon.

Once you have the height right, move the mirror sideways until you can see straight behind the car without leaning. The sides of the mirror may line up with the sides of the rear window frame. They probably won't.

What should you see in the mirror? If there is a car directly behind yours, it should show up in the middle of the mirror. If there is nothing but road behind your car, the middle of your lane should show in the middle of the mirror. If you need to, twist way around and look out the rear window to see just exactly what is directly behind you. Then adjust the mirror so that that object appears in the middle of the mirror. *Remember, the view through the mirror should make sense to you just as the view through the windshield does.* You should be able to see a great distance back just as you see a great distance ahead.

Mirror all adjusted? Okay. Now check it. Sitting in a normal driving position, look straight ahead at least one block, just as you would while driving. Then move your eyes to look at the mirror. Don't lean over. Don't duck. Don't stretch. Just look at the mirror and see whether you can still see properly through it. If not, continue readjusting and rechecking until you can.

You should not see a lot of the roof, back seats, or your face in the mirror. Nor should you see only one rear window side frame.

The illustration shows a good inside rearview mirror adjustment.

Not too high or low and centered

Once you have achieved a good adjustment, do not give it up easily. For example, waiting at a stop light, you may look up at the inside mirror, see that the vehicle behind yours is off center, and be tempted to move your mirror. Before you do, though, double check. Is it your mirror that is wrong, or is the vehicle behind yours actually out of line? Another reason for thinking that your mirror is wrong when it isn't is that you have slumped over and are no longer sitting squarely in the driver's seat.

In the illustration above, the car's rearview

mirror cannot possibly be adjusted properly, and you can tell that from *outside* the car!

In many cars, tall drivers find that the inside rearview mirror is mounted almost exactly at their eye level, blocking a very important part of their forward vision. However, many mirrors can be adjusted up and at least partly out of the way before adjusting them for proper rearward vision.

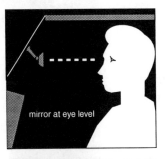

mirror at eye level

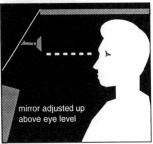

mirror adjusted up above eye level

When examining a car before buying it, tall drivers should check the position of the inside rearview mirror carefully.

FIELDS OF MIRRORED VISION:

In Figure 2, the shaded area is the field of vision given by a correctly adjusted inside rearview mirror.

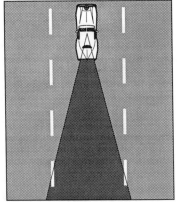

Figure 2

Figure 3 adds another shaded area showing, the field of vision given by the outside mirror adjusted as it *usually is.*

The darkest portion is the area of overlap.

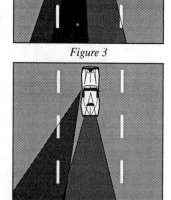

Figure 3

Figure 4 shows the fields of vision given by a properly adjusted inside mirror (lighter grey area) and *properly* adjusted outside mirror (darker-grey area).

The proper

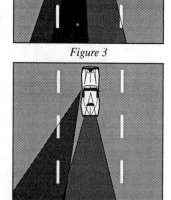

Figure 4

adjustment of the outside mirror, seen in Figure 4, nearly eliminates the large area of wasteful overlap and adds valuable vision along the left side. Still, the faulty adjustment, shown in Figure 3, despite its obvious shortcomings, is widely used and even taught as standard. Why?

Two bits of *imagined* security — First, the view through the outside mirror adjusted as in Figure 3 is comforting. It is merely a picture

back along the road similar to the one seen through the inside mirror. This comforting view actually deprives a driver of valuable information about the situation immediately to his left rear. Most drivers are not bothered by this, because they do not realize that there is so much more that can and should be seen.

The second bit of imagined security given by this incorrect adjustment is that the driver can see some of his own car in the outside mirror. This, he believes, gives him a reference point from which to judge the nearness of vehicles approaching and passing from his left rear. In truth, though, with this adjustment once a car passing from the left rear gets near enough for the reference point to be of any value, the car is no longer visible in the mirror.

ADJUSTING THE OUTSIDE MIRROR: *Do not* use the side of your car as a starting point for adjusting the outside mirror. Instead, remaining seated in a normal driving position and without leaning over, ducking, etc., find the object you see closest to the left side frame of the inside mirror. This may be a tree, bush, part of a house, part of a parked car or truck, a fire plug, sign-post, almost anything that doesn't move. Then adjust your outside mirror so that this same object can be seen at its extreme RIGHT edge.

Once again, do not lean over to see this. You should be able to look at the inside mirror, see the

Figure 5

object, whatever it is, then, almost without moving, look at the outside mirror and see the same object. There should be only slight overlap and certainly no gap between the ranges of the two mirrors (Figure 5 on previous page).

Your mirrors are now adjusted to be of maximum use to you. Because the outside one is not aimed back down the street but more across it, it will at first be a little confusing to you. However, as you use it and get used to it, you will realize that it is not necessary to see way down the street in your outside mirror. You can already see that in the inside mirror.

Test it. When you have progressed to driving in light traffic on a four or more lane road, drive in the right lane and watch a car coming up to pass you in the left lane. You will be able to see the car in your inside mirror when it is far to the rear.

 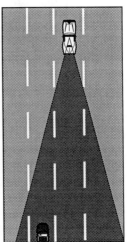

As it approaches, it will move to the left side of the mirror.

 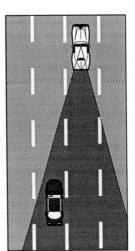

Then its front end will move off the left side of the inside mirror onto the right side of the outside mirror. You may be able to see the side of the passing car in the inside mirror while you see its front end in the outside mirror.

  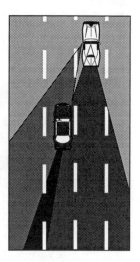

Next the passing car will move completely out of the inside mirror and completely into the outside mirror.

  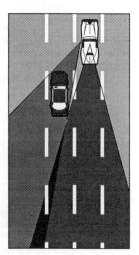

Finally, as its rear fender is moving out of the outside mirror, the passing car's front fender will be just coming into your left peripheral vision — you'll be able to see it out of the corner of your left eye. *(See photos and illustration at top of next page)*

24

  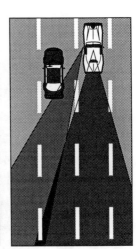

If your car has an outside rearview mirror on the right side, adjust it just as you did the one on the left side. It should pick up where the inside mirror leaves off and extend your vision to the right.

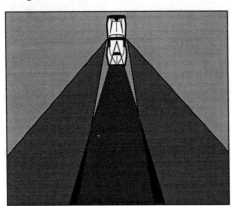

Never settle for having your mirrors less than perfectly adjusted. When you need them in complex and fast moving situations, they should tell you exactly what you need to know.

BLIND SPOTS: When you are driving, the fields of your normal forward vision and all your mirrored vision *do not* add up to a full 360 degrees. All the places you can't see from the driver's seat without making a special effort are *blind spots*.

One blind spot has already been mentioned. It is the one caused for tall drivers in many cars

by the inside rearview mirror. During certain maneuvers, like a right turn or curve on an uphill section of road, even a short driver can be blinded by the rearview mirror. Looking to the right and up to see the road, he will see only the mirror.

Outside mirrors can also cause blind spots. Indeed the large, rectangular, west coast mirrors used on trucks cause very large blind spots. Truck drivers must lean back and forth to look around them in driving situations like crossing intersections.

Cargo and passengers' bodies can block your vision. So can any of the posts that hold up the roof of the car. The hood, the dashboard, the window sills, the fenders, and the rear deck lid of a car make it impossible for its driver to see some things near the car: fire plugs, stumps, large rocks, low fences, curbs, small animals, children, bumps and potholes in the pavement, debris on the pavement, and the pavement itself. In rare instances, the car's top can block a driver's view of traffic signals. Sunvisors can also block a driver's view.

While all these blind spots do exist and can cause accidents, what people usually mean when they talk about their blind spot is none of them. The standard, well known blind spots are the areas on a driver's left and right which he cannot see without actually turning his head and looking over his shoulder at them. *Mirrors do*

not cover them. Peripheral vision (side vision) does not cover them.

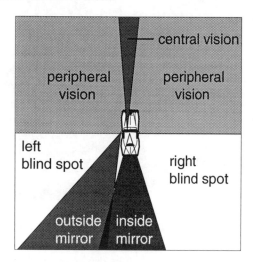

Check your blind spot every time you move your car sideways more than a couple of inches. When the driver on one side of you starts squeezing you because his lane is blocked, or because his lane ends, or because in confusion he suddenly thinks your lane is his lane, you should not just move over without checking your blind spot. You might be putting the squeeze on the guy next to you. When avoiding debris or pot holes or leaving a little extra room next to a hazard means you'll have to get close to or cross the lane line, don't just move over. Check your blind spot. When you change lanes, enter the expressway, pull over to the curb, or pull out of a parallel parking space into traffic, check your blind spot.

Which blind spot should you check? Check the blind spot on the side toward which you are moving. If you are going to move toward the left, check the left blind spot. If you are going to move toward the right, check the right blind spot. *Always check the blind spot on the side from which you could either get hit or hit somebody else.*

Check your blind spot every time your lane moves on the pavement, or the pavement moves your lane.

 OR

(Above, left) Left turn bay moves your lane to the right. Car in right lane may not move right but continue straight ahead.
Or, (above, right) Left turn bay moves your lane to the right and the lane line just gives up. Car on the right may easily try to continue straight ahead.

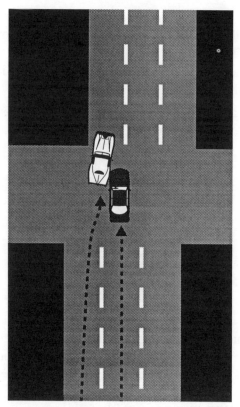

Many drivers assume their lane is always straight ahead.

Check your blind spot whenever there is a funneling down of lanes or traffic.

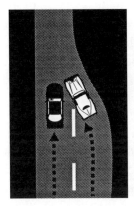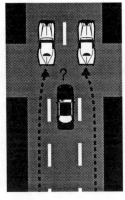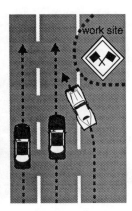

A good driver has such a strong *habit* of checking his blind spots that he can't just put a car into motion without checking them — without *knowing* what is *all around* his vehicle. He has been surprised by things he didn't see because he didn't check his blind spot or checked it too long ago. He has seen other drivers surprised by things they didn't see because they didn't check their blind spot or checked it too long ago. He has even surprised other drivers by being in their blind spot when they didn't check it or checked it too long ago. He knows how very quickly things can happen, how very quickly the traffic pattern can change. He knows that even in very ordinary, normal circumstances, a space that was clear a moment ago may not be clear now.

Even in the middle of a field, he will probably check at least his left side blind spot automatically before moving his car forward. Indeed, he may very well check both blind spots because he will probably have no idea what may be approaching from any direction.

However, in stop-and-go traffic, on an extremely crowded, urban expressway at rush hour, he will not check his blind spot(s) every time he resumes forward motion. In those circumstances, there is virtually no chance of his getting into the way of anyone in those places. He will, however, remain aware of the traffic on both sides of his car and check those vehicles whose blind spots he is in for turn signals, etc.

A good driver knows when he is in another driver's blind spot because he knows where his own blind spots are, or because he can't see the other driver's face either directly or in any of the other driver's mirrors.

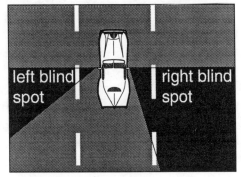

If my blind spots are here, his must be, too.

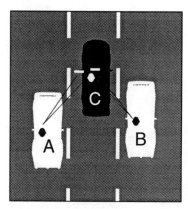

A. can't see C.'s face directly or in his outside mirror.
B. can't see C.'s face directly or in his inside mirror.

A good driver putting his car into rearward motion does not check his blind spots in addition to his mirrors and ahead. He just uses his eyes directly to check 360 degrees plus around the car. (See "Doing It Backwards," Chapter 6.)

REMEMBER: You must turn your head and look over your shoulder to check your blind spots. To avoid surprises you should make sure everything ahead is okay. before checking your blind spot. (Good, long following distances help.) A blind spot can easily be big enough to hide a good sized truck!

CLUTTER: Some drivers hang fuzzy dice, graduation tassels, baby shoes, air fresheners, dream catchers, garters, scarves, neckties, and all sorts of other things from their inside rearview mirror. This stuff is probably meant to be handy (neckties), useful (air fresheners), or decorative (all the rest). In fact, it blocks the vision of these drivers. It also tells anyone who notices it that these drivers can't be bothered with the small details of driving — like seeing traffic.

Other drivers prefer to keep their stuff on top of the dashboard. There it doesn't block their view directly, it merely reflects into the windshield to create distracting, confusing ghost images which often do obstruct vision. It also falls off the dashboard when the car goes around a corner or accelerates hard. When that happens, the driver may even try to pick up whatever fell while still attempting to control the car. Of course, this behavior has caused crashes.

Still other drivers keep all that litter behind or attached to the sunvisor. Those who put loose material up there cannot pull down the sunvisor to block out the sun. The others, the ones who have learned that lesson, use rubber bands to hold the clutter to the visor. This, they think, is much better, because the visor is still useable against the sun. However, as time passes, the weight of all the things hanging up there loosens the sunvisor, and it begins sagging, and later, flopping in front of these drivers' eyes at all the wrong times.

Finally, some drivers choose to keep all the junk on the shelf under the back window where, again, it blocks their view and, in an accident, will fly forward toward their heads.

Plain old dust can be a real problem. A great deal of grit can collect on the floor of a car during a hard winter. When the first beautiful, warm day of spring comes, and the driver opens all the windows to enjoy the weather, the dirt blows into his eyes.

There was a man in Chicago who drove, or tried to drive, with a small compass stuck to the windshield directly in front of his face, exactly at his eye level!!

Drivers are seen with pets riding on their laps or shoulders. What happens when quick, evasive steering is needed?

Sometimes little children are allowed to sit on the laps of adult passengers and drivers. Crash! The child is padding between the adult and the steering wheel or dashboard.

3 Chapter Three

Fire It Up

You are sitting behind the steering wheel of a car. The seat and mirrors are adjusted. You are belted in securely. The doors are locked. *You* are about to drive a car for the first time!

So far, you have moved levers, pushed buttons, etc. You have touched and forced parts of

the car to your will but, until now, the car has not been running. It has not been alive. It has not *required* your control. The things you've done to it have been ordinary and one-sided, like using a bread knife, a baseball bat, or a hand towel. The car has just sat there, accepting whatever you

did to it. It has not *responded*.

Things are about to change. You are about to fire up the engine. You are about to turn a key that will change a complex collection of parts into an almost living thing, a breathing, fuel burning, waste producing machine capable of doing work using its own power, a machine requiring your constant supervision, a mindless machine which will do exactly what you tell it to do whether or not your commands are appropriate.

What a moment! Enjoy it. Think about it. Driving is a rite of passage. It's a mark of adulthood. It's a great responsibility. It's a very challenging activity which offers a lifetime of pleasure and pride obtained from doing a very difficult thing with good judgment and grace. It is an activity which keeps giving new opportunities for study, growth, and achievement.

Here, take these keys.

KEYS: The ignition key will probably have the larger, more square head. It may not work in the door locks. If both sides of the ignition key's blade are the same, you can put it into the ignition switch either way.

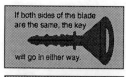
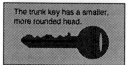
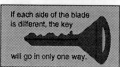

The other key if there is one, is for the remaining locks on the car: trunk lid, rear hatch, tailgate, glove compartment, perhaps the doors.

Slide the ignition key into the ignition switch. Never force it. Push it gently and let it align itself in the slot. Don't turn it yet.

Before you do that, you must know a few things about the car's transmission.

THE TRANSMISSION: We all know what the car's engine does. It makes power by burning fuel. The car's transmission, as its name suggests, transmits that power from the engine to other parts which eventually get it to the wheels. (See Ch. 21 on the mechanical operation of the automobile.) The transmission lets the driver control the car's primary direction of travel. By selecting the proper gear, he can use the engine's power to move the car either forward or backward. He may also choose a gear which keeps the engine's power from reaching the wheels at all, allowing the car to stand still even though its engine is running.

The internal combustion engine (the kind used in nearly all cars) can run only so fast before it breaks. On the other hand, if it runs too slowly, it cannot produce power. No matter how fast or slow the car itself moves, the transmission allows the engine to run in a speed range where it is comfortable and can produce power. It does this by providing a choice of several forward gears: first, second, third, fourth, etc. By selecting the appropriate gear, the driver matches the engine's power output and speed with the car's power needs and road speed.

Since the forward gears in a bicycle's transmission perform the same function as those in the transmission of a car, taking an imaginary bike ride may result in a better understanding of what a car's transmission does. For simplicity, use a three speed bike and compare it with a three speed automobile. Riding a bicycle, *you* are the vehicle's engine. *You* supply the power, and just like the internal combustion engine, which can run only so fast and make only so much power, you can pedal only so fast and so hard.

Suppose you are cruising along at about twenty m.p.h. in third (high) gear. So long as you maintain your speed, you are comfortable pedaling and pleased with your rate of progress along the road.

Stop. Now try to start up again in third gear.

It is very hard to get going again, because it is very hard to pedal. It might even be impossible to get going. You might not be able to pedal hard enough.

What should you do? Shift the transmission into first (low) gear. This gear ratio will allow you to pedal more times than third gear to make the bike travel the same distance. Because you pedal more times to travel the same distance, the pedaling is easier. Because the pedaling is easier, you have the strength to move and accelerate the bike.

Keep accelerating in first gear. What happens? Pretty soon you find that even though the bike is not travelling at a very high speed, you can't pedal any faster.

Then what?

Shift to second gear. What happens? You find yourself pedaling slower, but still travelling at the same speed, because second gear lets you pedal fewer times than first gear to move the bike the same distance. Because you pedal fewer times to travel the same distance, you can now pedal faster again and make the bike go faster. However, there is a price to pay. Because you pedal fewer times to do the same work, that is, to move the bike the same distance, you have to pedal harder.

Now get up more speed and shift to third (high) gear. Exactly the same thing happens again. You find yourself pedaling slower but still travelling at the same speed, because third gear lets you pedal fewer times than second gear to move the bike the same distance. Because you pedal fewer times to travel the same distance, you can, once again, pedal faster and make the bike go even faster. However, once again, there is that price to pay. Because you pedal fewer times to do the same work, that is, to move the bike the same distance, you have to pedal harder.

Got it? Every time you shift to a *higher* gear, you trade power for vehicle speed, that is, you get to pedal harder but more slowly for a given road speed. Therefore, by pedaling faster, you can make the bike travel faster.

Every time you shift to a *lower* gear, you trade vehicle speed for power, that is, you get to pedal faster but more easily for a given road speed. Therefore, although you can't make the bike travel at maximum speed (you can't pedal fast enough), you have more power to get moving, accelerate, carry a passenger, and climb hills.

It's exactly the same with a car. If you try to force the engine to get the car moving from rest with the transmission in third (high) gear, it probably will not be able to push hard enough, and it will stall, die, stop running.

Put the car's transmission into first (low) gear though, allowing the engine to turn more times for the distance the car will travel, and the engine will be able to run more easily. Therefore, it will be able to supply enough power to put the car in motion and accelerate it. Just like first gear on the bicycle, first gear in the car gives you maximum power at low vehicle speed from a fast turning engine.

Accelerate in first gear. What happens? Just like with a bike, pretty soon you find that even though the car is not travelling at normal driving speed, the engine is running very fast.

Then what?

Shift to second gear. What happens? The engine runs slower to maintain the same car speed, because second gear lets it turn fewer times than first gear to move the car the same distance. Just like with the bike, because the engine turns fewer times to move the car the same distance, you can increase the engine's turning speed and thus make the car go faster. However, just like with the bike, you pay a price for the higher vehicle speed. You lose some power. In second gear, the car has less "get-up-and-go" than it had in first.

Accelerate again and shift to third (high) gear. Now what happens? Once again, the engine runs slower to maintain the same car speed, because third gear lets it turn fewer times than second gear to move the car the same distance. Because the engine turns fewer times to move the car the same distance, once again, you can increase the engine's turning speed and make the car go even faster. However, just as before, you pay a price for the higher vehicle speed. You lose more power. In third gear the car has hardly any "get-up-and-go."

That's all there is to it. With either a bike or a car, the lower the gear, the more and the more easily the engine has to turn to move the vehicle a given distance. Therefore, the lower the gear, the more power the vehicle has to start off from rest, accelerate quickly, or carry heavy loads and climb steep hills, but also the lower the gear, the slower the vehicle must travel.

The higher the gear, the less and the harder the engine has to turn to move the vehicle a given distance. Therefore, the higher the gear, the faster the vehicle can travel, but the less power it has to start from rest, accelerate, carry loads, and climb hills.

An automatic transmission chooses the appropriate gear for conditions all by itself. The driver of a car with an automatic transmission,

after deciding whether he wants the car to move forward, backward, or stand still, merely places the gear selector in the proper position, lining up the lever itself and/or the pointer attached to it with the correct letter or number on the gear indicator.

The car you will soon drive probably has an automatic transmission. (If you are going to drive a stick shift car, see Ch. 22 on how to operate a manual transmission.) Take a look at the gear indicator. It looks something like Figure 1.

D stands for Drive. In drive, the car will move forward. The transmission will take care of all shifting among first, second, and third gears.

R stands for Reverse. In reverse, the car will move backward.

N stands for Neutral. In neutral, the flow of power is stopped at the transmission. However, in neutral, the car is free to roll just like a ball, toy car, or shopping cart. Therefore, the car can be pushed and towed in neutral.

P stands for Park. In park, just as in neutral, the car cannot move under its own power. In fact, it can not move at all. The transmission is actually locked. The car *must not* be pushed or towed in park.

In D2 or 2, the transmission is prevented

Figure 1

from shifting into third (high) gear. It can use only first and second.

In D1 or 1, the transmission is prevented even from shifting into second gear. It must stay in first (low) gear.

If the idea of an automatic transmission is that it shifts for itself, why does it offer these extra choices (D2 or 2 and D1 or 1), and when should a driver use them? When climbing up a hill, when moving a heavy load, or when moving a heavy load up a hill, a driver may wish to prevent the transmission from shifting into high gear because he knows the engine would be overworked if that happened. He might use D2 or 2. More severe versions of the same situations would call for D1 or 1 so that the transmission could not shift out of low, and maximum power would always be available.

Most often, though, these gears are used when driving *down* hills. When a driver takes his foot off the gas pedal of a car in a lower gear, the car slows down faster than it would in a higher gear. Because of this "hold back," drivers use lower gears to help control downhill speed, save brakes, and increase safety. Coming down a rather mild, fairly high speed hill, a driver might use D2 or 2. Coming down an extremely steep hill, a driver should use D1 or 1 for maximum "hold back". In the mountains, truckers use low gears for power to go uphill and for "hold back" going downhill. A heavily loaded rig, kept in too high a gear going downhill, can burn up its brakes and run away out of control.

Some automatic transmissions were designed to have only two forward gears. Other automatics have four or even five forward gears.

You may come upon unusual arrangements for automatic transmission gear selectors and gear indicators. For example, many cars built during the nineteen fifties used push buttons.

A part called a neutral safety switch prevents any car with an automatic transmission from being started normally unless it is in either neutral or park. This is because the car could begin to move all by itself if the engine were started with the transmission in any other gear.

One morning a man went out to the garage and tried to start the car. It wouldn't start. The night before, his wife had left the transmission in drive when she parked in the garage.

Without checking, the man jumped out, opened the hood, and began crossing wires to start the car. It started all right. Then it ran through four hundred dollars worth of storm windows and the back wall of the garage.

Stick shift cars do not really need neutral safety switches, and until recently they did not have them. Starting a stick shift vehicle with a safety switch requires you to hold the clutch pedal down to the floor while turning the key.

THE IGNITION SWITCH: The ignition switch on the car you are about to drive probably looks similar to one of these.

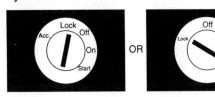

When the switch is in the "lock" position, the engine is off, the electric power to the engine is off, the gear selector and the steering wheel are locked in position, and the ignition key can be taken out of and put into the switch. In many cases, a little push button must be used to release the ignition key for removal.

When the switch is in the "off" position, the engine is off, the electric power to it is off, but the gear lever and steering wheel are free to be moved.

When the switch is in the "on" position, the electric power to the engine is on, the engine is probably running, and, of course, the gear lever and steering wheel can be moved.

When the switch is in the "start" position, the electric power to the engine is on, and elec-

tricity is sent to the starter to start the engine. You turn the switch to the "start" position and hold it there until the engine begins to run. Then release the switch (key), and it returns to the "on" position, where it remains until you turn it to the "off" and "lock" positions.

The "acc." stands for accessories. With the switch in this position, electric power can flow to the radio, cigarette lighter, etc., but not to the engine or starter. In other words, you can use the radio and other accessories even though the engine is not running. The headlights, four-way-flashers, etc. can be used with the ignition switch in any position. Remember that a car's electricity comes from a battery, not a wall outlet. Leaving any electrical accessory operating for any significant length of time while the engine is not running will drain the battery of its charge. If drained (discharged) enough, the battery will not have enough power to start the car. Watch this carefully in cold weather.

GAS AND CHOKE FOR CARS WITH CARBURETORS:

Should you feed some gas when starting the car? It depends. If the car has been running and is warmed up, it should start with just a turn of the key. If the engine is cold (after hours of not running), most likely it will need some gas. If the temperature is cool or cold and the engine has not run for several hours, it will probably need you to set the choke before it can start. In most cars, you set the choke by pushing the gas pedal all the way to the floor and releasing it.

Some older cars may require the accelerator to be pumped up and down several times before the engine will fire. Some cars start well if the accelerator is held down part way.

Knowing when and how much gas to use in starting a car is one of those things that you never really perfect. The car, the gasoline, the weather, the engine's state of tune, etc., all affect the balance required to fire the engine. It takes

time, practice, and familiarity with the car you drive. It is a good idea to read the owner's manual for your car to see what the manufacturer recommends as a starting procedure.

GAS FOR CARS WITH FUEL INJECTION:

If your car has fuel injection instead of a carburetor, starting should be simpler. There is no choke as such, so you needn't worry about that. Usually, you either push the gas pedal about one quarter of the way down or you don't touch it at all, whether the car is hot, warm, cool, or cold. (See your owner's manual.)

FIRE IT UP:

Okay. All set? Transmission in park or neutral? Key in the ignition switch? Gas fed or not fed as you think proper?

Turn the key and "crank her up!" The first sound you hear is the starter working. The second should be the sound of the engine firing. When the engine fires, let go of the key. Holding it in the "start" position once the engine is running can damage the starter.

When the ignition key is turned to the "start" position, a small gear on the end of the starter engages with a big gear (flywheel gear) on the back of the engine. Then the starter gear turns the flywheel gear, which turns the engine, inducing it to start. After the engine starts, and the key is released, the starter gear disengages from the flywheel gear. The flywheel gear keeps turning as long as the engine is running. Therefore, always make sure the engine is *not* running before you turn the key to start it. Sometimes people sit in a car with the engine running. Then, when they get ready to drive away, they forget and turn the key. The starter gear tries to engage with the flywheel gear. Because the engine is running though, the flywheel gear is already turning — at a different speed from the starter gear. The two can't mesh. A terrible shriek comes from under the hood as the flywheel gear thrashes the starter gear. Repeated enough, this mistake will break the starter.

For the same reason, if you try to start the engine, but it doesn't start, or starts and dies, wait a second or two until you know the engine has stopped turning before you hit the key again.

After starting the engine, let it idle a few seconds to warm up. Make sure it is running smoothly before you begin driving. Remember when you pushed the gas pedal in the carbureted car to the floor to set the choke? You also set the fast idle, so the engine will run rather fast. Shifting gears when the engine is running at high idle is rough on automatic transmissions. Moreover, driving off with a high idle can lead to unwanted and possibly unexpected spirited acceleration, or uselessly spinning wheels stuck in snow, mud, ice, etc. Finally, letting an engine run so fast just doesn't feel right. A quick jab on the accelerator may slow down the idle. If it doesn't, let the engine run fast a while longer and jab the accelerator again. This can be tricky. In very cold or wet weather, until the engine is pretty well warmed up, it may not be able to move the car unless it is running quite fast. Slowing it with this gas pedal trick may just make it die when you try to begin driving. You will have tricked yourself. You'll have to start the engine again. You may have to drive with the high idle for a while until it switches off by itself.

Don't be impatient. A car is a machine. It can't be forced, or begged, or bribed. It doesn't know anything about love, or loyalty, or being late. You, the thinking, feeling, adaptable partner in driving must plan ahead, keep up the car, be sensitive to its idiosyncrasies, and use your head and skill to control clumsy situations.

PREPARE TO DRIVE: Take the time you need to set up the cockpit. Start the engine and let it warm up. Prepare *yourself* for driving. Don't make a big ceremony of it, but don't just jump into the car, fire it up, and take off in a scatterbrained exhibition of sloppy, illegal, unsafe, impolite, just plain ugly driving either.

Develop a routine, and let each activity needed to get the car ready to be driven get *you* ready to drive it. You have to make sure the seat and mirrors are correctly adjusted, lock the door, buckle yourself into the safety harness, start and warm up the engine, and maybe plan a route anyway. Just be aware of these things as you do them. Let yourself unite with the car. A good thing to do is to start the engine first, then do all the adjusting, etc., while it is warming up.

Let your mind and emotions adjust to changing from a student, sister, doctor, baby-sitter, boyfriend, sports player, employee, engineer, father, pedestrian, adult, or teenager into a driver. Set yourself up to meet the challenge of driving, to learn, to enjoy the mental exercise of adapting to ever-changing conditions by using your knowledge, perception, experience, skill, and good judgment. Get ready to enjoy the feel of the car, the physical act of controlling it. Prepare to do with beauty and grace the most complex psychomotor activity done by humans. Prepare to make yourself feel good!

4 Chapter Four

Drive It

A LEARNING AND PRACTICE AREA: A clearly marked training car with dual brake pedals is readily identifiable by other roadway users and easily controlled by the instructor. Therefore, unlike an ordinary automobile, it can operate safely in practice areas which are much less than perfect.

Much too much less than perfect are parking lots. They should be avoided as places to begin or practice driving at almost any cost. When in ordinary use, they are extremely difficult places in which to drive, because they offer very poor visibility and their traffic is unpredictable. When they are deserted, parking lots provide vague and skimpy longitudinal guidelines, which are nearly useless to a true beginning driver. A beginning driver must be provided with clearly defined road edges and readily visible, easily used traffic lane boundaries to mark his path. The obvious longitudinal guidelines of a good practice course will show up correct and incorrect steering inputs immediately and indisputably.

School driving ranges frequently have very narrow lanes and short straightaways. These force students to look down just in front of their car to stay on course. This can easily get the students into the *habit* of looking near the front of the car all the time. This habit can delay or even prevent their learning to aim and steer properly, let alone watch traffic.

In short, to learn anything at all of value about getting used to and controlling a car, a student driver needs to drive on a real road.

Because a student driver should do plenty of practice on basic car control techniques, and because he will probably have to do it with non-professional help from relatives and/or friends, he should know something about picking a practice driving area.

The place in which you do your beginning driving should be relatively free of traffic. It should be familiar to your instructor. If it is not, he must check it out and get used to it before you drive, so that he does not accidentally allow you to drive into a situation for which you are not ready. You should not find yourself suddenly having to drive across or turn onto a busy street. You should not have to do any maneuver you have not yet learned. You should not be forced by traffic and/or terrain to operate two or more car controls quickly and perfectly at the same time.

The area should not contain any one-way streets upon which you must drive. One-way streets, especially when mixed with two-way streets, can cause lane choice problems and a great deal of confusion about proper turning paths. This confusion puts needless stress on both the student and the instructor.

The area should accommodate patterns of all left turns, all right turns, and a mixture of the two without forcing the car onto any busy streets.

The streets should provide good to excellent visibility far ahead on straightaways as well as at curves, corners, and intersections. The road should be predictable, not full of blind areas and possible hazards. In this regard, hilly areas can cause much frustration.

Long straightaways are necessary to learn straight steering, to relax upon between turns, and to give adequate straight ahead aiming distance when coming out of turns. Long straightaways also make crossing intersections, pulling over, pulling out, starting and stopping much easier and safer by providing long sight lines.

Intersections with stop and yield signs should be avoided if possible. Pressure to take one's proper turn there can stress beginning drivers too much. Areas in which spectators may be found, especially spectators acquainted with the student driver, can cause needless stress.

The time of day and part of the week can make a huge difference in whether an area is good or bad for a beginning driver. For example, consider a small, quiet, residential neighborhood with an elementary school in the middle of it.

DRIVE IT! Okay. The car is in a suitable area. You are ready. The cockpit is arranged. The engine is running and warm. There is only one thing left to do now — drive it. Take charge of the car. Make it do exactly what you want it to do. It will, but it must be given clear commands. It cannot and will not respond properly to hints or suggestions. In learning to drive, first get used to how the car reacts to your inputs, and then try to make those inputs perfectly appropriate under all conditions.

You'll make mistakes. You made mistakes learning to eat with a knife, fork, and spoon. You made mistakes learning to tie your shoes, and learning to catch a ball, and talk, and walk. You'll make mistakes learning to drive, and you'll learn from them. Your teacher will try to prevent your mistakes, but he will also expect and explain them.

Make the car go. Make it stop. Steer it. Feel what it does. The first part of actually learning to drive is to get the feel of the car. Make it do things and see and feel its responses to your inputs with the accelerator, brake pedal, and steering wheel. Then react to its actions and reactions and learn to cooperate with it to control it. Once you have that foundation, you will be able to learn all the other skills of masterful driving. Remember, though, that no matter how skillful a driver you become or how complex a driving situation may be, your major means of controlling the car will always be only the gas pedal, brake pedal, and steering wheel.

Of course, you have to *know the rules of the road thoroughly, understand them, be able to apply them easily and quickly, and obey them.* You also have to watch for traffic. At this stage, however, your teacher can take care of most of the checking for traffic and looking for trouble, making sure that you notice it too.

USING THE BRAKES: The very first control you'll have to use is the brake pedal. Operate it with your right foot only. There are several reasons for this.

First, if you intend to drive a stick shift car, your left foot should be reserved and trained for using the clutch pedal.

Second, the idea that keeping your left foot ready, just above or lightly touching the brake pedal, will cut your reaction time and allow you to stop more quickly, is noble but impractical. After hanging for some time in this position, your left leg will get tired and let your left foot rest on the brake pedal. This will light your brake lights. Since you have no intention of stopping, this will confuse drivers following you. It will also cause slight extra wear on your brakes and engine. Finally, it will waste a little gas. Therefore, when the situation calls for unusual readiness to use the brakes, release the accelerator and cover the brake pedal with your *right* foot. (Hold your right foot just above the brake pedal, ready to use it.)

Third, as a new driver trying to brake left-footed, you will quickly begin thinking subconsciously about slowing and stopping only as left foot activities. Then you will begin to rely on the firm, positive slowing and stopping action of the brakes and forget all about releasing the gas pedal when you want to slow down or stop. You will push both pedals. This will make it difficult to slow down or stop. In an emergency, even an experienced driver trying left foot braking will most likely press both pedals as far as they go.

There are left foot braking techniques used in racing, rallying and pursuit driving, even in stick shift cars, but wait to learn those things until you are a serious racer, rally driver or police officer.

Push the brake pedal with the ball of your foot, not your toes. Avoid using just the very edge of the brake pedal.

THIS — use ball of foot

NOT THIS — do not use toes

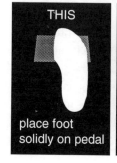

THIS — place foot solidly on pedal

NOT THIS — don't use just the edge

To get the feel of using the brakes, you'll have to use the brakes. To use them, you'll have to have the car in motion. Let's get moving.

SELECTING GEARS (SHIFTING AN AUTOMATIC TRANSMISSION): If your car's gear selector lever is mounted on the floor, there will be some kind of button on it. That is just another safety measure. To get the transmission out of park, you must press the button. You must also press the button to shift into park, reverse, D2, and D1. In other words, you can shift only between neutral and drive without using the button. To select any other gears, you'll have to press it.

You can shift only between neutral and drive without pushing the button.

If your car's gear selector lever is on the steering column, you'll have to pull the lever toward you before it will come out of park. You'll have to pull it toward you any time you would have to push the button on the floor-mounted selector lever.

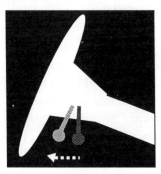

Before moving the lever though, step on the brake pedal. Remember, once you take the automatic transmission out of park or neutral, the running car is ready to move. With the transmission in drive, or reverse, or D2, or D1, if you do not hold the car with the brakes, it will move.

Press the brake pedal. Shift to drive. Feel the transmission lurch the car as it shifts into gear. Check the gear indicator to make sure that the transmission is in the gear you want. Hold the car with the brakes until *you* are ready to move. Then, gradually release the brake pedal. The car will begin to move very slowly. Remember, you needn't feed gas to make the car go. On the other hand, once the car is in motion, it has momentum. It *will* coast. It *will not just stop dead* if you don't keep feeding gas.

THE ACCELERATOR: Use your whole right foot to operate the accelerator, keeping your heel on the floor as a pivot point. Do not try to use your tip-toes for extremely delicate control. It doesn't work. Trying to use your toes means that instead of pivoting just your foot on the floor, you will have to swing much of your leg from at least your knee. Obviously, you'll get finer control (less jumping and lurching) by using just your solidly supported and easily pivoted foot than by attempting to point toes out at the very end of a swaying foot attached to a dangling leg.

Neither should you keep most of your foot flat on the floor and work the very bottom of the accelerator with your toes. The poor leverage given by this system tends to cause the car to lurch and bounce each time you press the pedal.

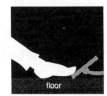

Finally, toeing the top of some gas pedals will do nothing but pivot the pedal itself. This can be a problem for very short drivers, especially when trying to back up.

Just as with the brakes, the only way to get used to using a car's power is to use it. The response of one car to pressure on its accelerator can be very different from that of another. Some cars accelerate rather slowly. Others can easily roar off in great clouds of stinking rubber smoke. Still others will cough and stumble. All can be made to lurch, though, so try the accelerator gently and carefully.

Push the pedal, and the car goes faster. Just like that. You might want to giggle. You might get goose bumps and feel shivers up and down your spine. A tiny motion by you sets a great machine to work. It's like pushing the button that fires a space craft into the heavens, or throwing the lever that sets a ferris wheel or merry-go-round in motion. It's that delight mankind takes in control, in achieving. It's the spontaneous joy and the undeniable truth of control at the moment when man and machine interact. It's that wonderful, giggly feeling you get when, fearful after waiting and wishing for so long, you finally try something for the first time, and it works! Enjoy it, and let it become the basis for a positive attitude toward driving and striving to drive beautifully for the rest of your life!

USING BOTH PEDALS SMOOTHLY: Strive to learn to use both pedals smoothly. It will take a lot of practice to build the habit of always being smooth, so don't be discouraged easily or try too

hard for instant perfection in this.

Avoid snatching your foot off the brake pedal and lurching the car when putting it into motion. Instead, take the tiny amount of time needed to *ease off* of the brake pedal. Then don't shove the gas pedal and make the car jump, but ease down on it. If quick acceleration is required, mash down on the accelerator, but only after easing the car into motion. Quickness and efficiency can be achieved with grace. Jerkiness is not necessary. Jerkiness is hard on the machinery and the passengers.

While it is rather difficult to release the accelerator with a jerk, applying the brakes can be done harshly or softly. You can decelerate quickly without being rough. Finally, just to add the cherry on top of the ice cream sundae, just as the car comes to a standstill, ease up on the brake pedal a bit. This is tricky to learn but very worthwhile. It avoids that lurch just as the car stops and marks you as a driver who cares about his passengers and his car, and a person who takes pride in his driving ability.

AIMING: Steering is done by your hands using the steering wheel. Aiming is done by your brain using your eyes. Before your brain can tell your hands what to do with the steering wheel to place your car in exactly the right position, your brain must see and know exactly what the right position is. Your eyes must show your brain where you want the car to go.

You must *force* your eyes to show your brain the path you want the car to follow. It is almost certain that without training and practice your eyes will not give your brain the information it needs to be able to steer the car easily and well. Without training and practice, your eyes will tend to look too close in front of your car. They may try to line up a fender, hood ornament, etc. with the road edge, lane line, etc. They may try to aim at a point as if you wanted to throw a ball or a dart, etc.

To aim, your brain needs to see the path you want the car to follow. Show your brain that path! Show your brain a LANE. Learn to see LANES. Learn to separate out and aim along your LANE. The following illustrations show the concept of LANE.

Lanes have *both length and width*. To give your brain the information it needs to aim, show it *both length and width*. Use your eyes in a way close to those shown in these two illustrations below. Looking from close ahead to far ahead where the arrowheads point will give your brain the idea of length between boundaries, of length and width, of LANE.

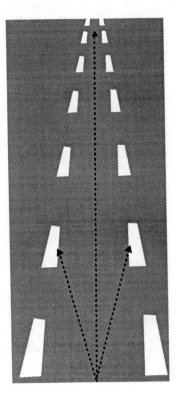 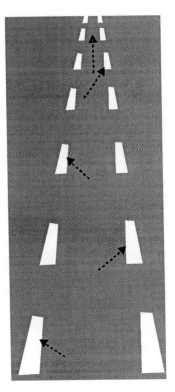

The car will go where you look. Therefore, *look where you want the car to go!* The road will help you if you let it. The apparently converging but actually parallel lines formed by the road edges, road shoulders, curbs, sidewalks, rows of trees, bushes, poles, etc., the center line, and the dirty area in the middle of the lane all guide your eyes along your intended path. Let them by aiming far ahead while seeing far out to the sides.

The driver of the car at the bottom of the illustration to the right wants to go straight ahead on his side of the street, between the center line and the parked cars (shaded path). Therefore, he looks (aims) about a block ahead along his intended path (toward the arrowhead, K). When he looks up ahead toward the arrowhead, he sees the center line and the row of parked cars (B, C, and J) forming parallel lines in front of him, marking the sides of his LANE, guiding him toward his goal.

Yes, he has to see the parked truck (A), the oncoming cyclist (I), the playing children (E), the stop sign (F), the stop bar (G), the pedestrian (H), and the intersection (D), but before he can deal with obstacles, hazards, and traffic continuously and well, he must be able subconsciously to aim and steer his car perfectly.

To aim and steer, he must look quite far ahead, toward where he wants to go. If, for example, he looks no farther forward than perhaps line (L), he will not see those parallel lines pointing the way. He will find it difficult to drive straight, as if he were trying to walk straight looking only at his feet.

Suppose our driver has just gotten his driver's license. He doesn't have half a million miles of driving experience under his seat belt. He is unsure of himself. He is quite concerned about keeping his car where it belongs and not hitting anything. As a result, he might start watching his hood and front fenders. If he does, he will see no further ahead that line (M)!

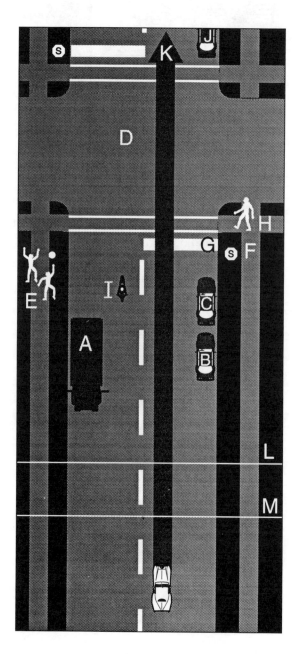

He might want to use the curb on the right as a guideline or make sure he stays well away from it. Therefore, he might begin staring at the curb or lining up his right front fender with it. If he does, his car will begin moving toward the curb, because the car goes where its driver looks.

He might worry about crowding or straying across the center line. He might therefore try to line up his left front fender with it. If he does, his car will crowd or even stray across the center line, because the car goes where its driver looks.

Our driver might want to make sure of clearing the parked cars (B&C) and so watch the relationship of his right front fender with them. If he does without looking away soon enough, he might crash right into those cars.

He might try to be especially careful to give the approaching cyclist (I) wide clearance. Therefore, he might glue his eyes on the cyclist. If he does…you guessed it. If he does, he will drive toward the cyclist and at least scare himself, to say nothing of the cyclist.

If a driver looks at anything too long, he will tend to steer toward it unconsciously. Because the car goes where he looks, besides watching traffic, a driver must, from time to time, aim the car by looking far ahead toward where he wants to go. Even an experienced driver, if he looks at something too long and gets very close to it, can find it difficult or even impossible to avoid hitting it.

ALWAYS AIM THROUGH SPACE: Trying to force two cars to occupy the same space at the same time always results in a crash. Likewise, trying to force a car to occupy the same space already occupied by a tree, a post, a house, or a pedestrian always results in a crash. There is a lesson here for us. It is that we must always drive our cars through unoccupied (empty) space.

No kidding! How obvious!

Yes, that's obvious. What is not always so obvious is *how* to do it. To drive through a space, one must aim through that space. The problem is that there is nothing in an empty space — nothing at which to aim. The eye is automatically attracted to *something*, anything, not nothing. It is so much easier to aim at some object: a car, a post, a tree, a person, than to aim at a space. Still, a driver must aim at space.

The following example actually happened. A driving student who lived in a large apartment building got into the training car, adjusted everything, and found herself in the situation illustrated below.

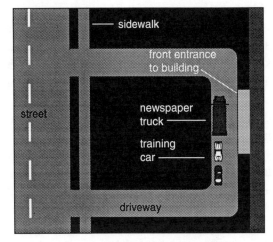

First, she backed up. That was good. Then she tried to drive around the newspaper truck. That was good. However, its big rear bumper, made of heavy, diamond plate steel, was quite near the car. That wasn't so good, because the student became very concerned that she might hit the bumper and damage the training car. Therefore, she watched that big bumper very carefully, too carefully. She forgot to aim for the space through which she wanted to drive and watched only that big, solid bumper. Because she watched it so hard, she automatically aimed at it. She didn't want to aim at it. She didn't realize she was aiming at it, but she was. Because she was aiming at it, she did not turn the steering wheel far enough toward the right. As a matter of fact, once she got hooked on looking at that darned bumper, she forgot to steer at all. She just sat there inching the car closer and closer to the bumper and watching it. She leaned her own body away from the truck as if that would pull the car away from it. It didn't.

The instructor stopped the car, explained the situation, and had the student turn the steering wheel full right and inch past the truck.

Then a new problem arose. The car had passed the dreadful bumper all right, but now it was very close to and headed directly at the front entrance of the apartment building. Once again, the student became over concerned with an object, the front door of her building, and forgot to look, aim, and steer toward space. She attempted to steer away from the doorway, but kept looking (aiming) at it. The car got closer and closer to it. Once again, the instructor stopped the car and explained. He had the student cut the wheels full left and move the car neatly away from the building.

Then, of course, the car started heading back toward the side of the newspaper truck. Once again stress took over. The tired, nervous student driver concentrated on the side of the truck as the training car moved ever closer to it. One final time, the instructor stopped the car and explained. The student looked, aimed, and steered toward the space ahead of the car and finally pulled away from the congestion and out into the street.

In each case, what the student driver should have done was to aim toward the space through which she wanted to drive. She should have looked at the bumper, doorway, and side of the truck to check her clearances, but focused her attention mainly on aiming toward and seeing the car move through the space — THE LANE.

Look where you want the car to go. Look at objects to locate them. Then aim where they aren't. When close to objects, look at them only to check clearances. Then aim toward the space through which you want to drive. Check your clearances as carefully and as often as you believe necessary, but keep aiming toward space!

See the traffic in adjacent lanes, the parked cars, the hedges along the sides of the driveway, the sides of the garage door frame. Decide whether your car will fit. If it will, aim at the space between the objects.

Rarely, a student driver can try too hard to look where he wants the car to go. He can begin staring at some point far ahead. While aiming this way is exactly right for throwing a ball, it is exactly wrong for learning to steer a car. To steer a car, especially to *learn* to steer a car, you need to see a *lane*; you need to see road edges, shoulders, center line, lane lines, curbs, ruts, the dirty stripe in the middle of your lane, sidewalks, rows of trees or hedges, strings of parked cars, etc., all the parallel lines that point the way. If you stare at only one point, all these things will disappear from your vision. Even the front end of the car may disappear, robbing you of one more bit of useful information — like taking the sights off a rifle. You'll have nothing to guide you but a distant point. The car will wander around most of the time and travel a true course only by accident. *Do not stare!* Relax and *see*. Move your eyes. Aim and see. See and aim.

The faster you drive, the farther ahead you must look and aim. As your car keeps moving forward, you must keep looking and aiming farther ahead.

Finally, you cannot tell that your front wheels are pointed straight ahead by looking at the steering wheel. The illustrations show why.

In each case above, the steering wheel seems straight. The front wheels are pointed straight ahead in only one case.

Another reason why the steering wheel can tell you nothing about the position of your front wheels is that, especially in older cars, the steering wheel may be crooked when the front wheels are pointed straight ahead.

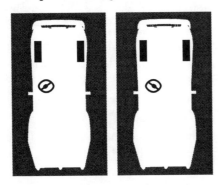

The only way to know whether the front wheels are pointed straight is to let the car move. If it moves straight, the wheels *must* be pointed straight.

REVIEW OF AIMING: *The car goes where you look, therefore, aim along a lane which goes through the space through which you want to drive.* Remember: a lane has *both* width and length!

HOLDING AND TURNING THE STEERING WHEEL: Imagine the steering wheel is a clock face.

Hold the wheel at either ten o'clock and two o'clock or nine and three.

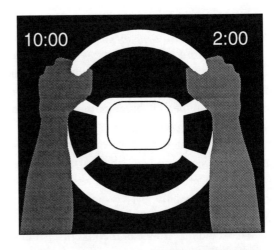

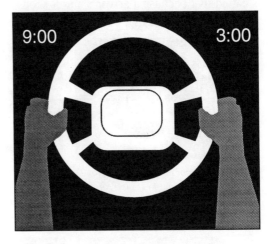

Both of these positions are good. They allow you comfort and the best control of the steering wheel. They help you sit straight to see well and stay alert. They feel good. They make you look good and feel in control.

Don't keep moving your hands on the wheel. Keep them at ten and two or nine and three. Don't saw at the wheel. Move it only when necessary and only as much as necessary. Don't hold the bottom of the wheel. It's a little too relaxing, and you really do not have good control down there. Never hold just one side of the wheel, for example, only eight, nine, or ten o'clock. If you do, you will unconsciously keep pulling down on that side of the wheel, driving in a series of long swerves. For the same reason, don't hold either the top or bottom of the wheel

with one hand and one side of it with the other. Don't steer by using the spokes. Grip the wheel gently for the most feel of the car. If you hit a pothole, drop a front wheel off the pavement into a soft shoulder, run only one side of the car through a deep puddle at high speed, hit a sharp bump, etc., the steering wheel can be wrenched from your hands. Always hold the wheel as if you mean it, but remember that a gentle grip gives more car feel. *Never steer with your wrist*!

If you absolutely must use only one hand, *hold* the wheel at twelve o'clock. Habitually using only one hand to steer can leave the unused hand unready for quick reaction on the steering wheel, horn, wiper switch, etc. In cars with air-bags, keep your hands no higher than 9 and 3, and do not drive with one hand—especially at 12 o'clock. Keep your hands inside the car unless you are giving a signal. The roof and outside mirror will probably stay on the car all by themselves.

The standard American method of operating a steering wheel is called hand-over-hand steering. It's called that because a driver using it keeps crossing one hand over the other as if he were pulling a rope. It works like this.

From this straight ahead position, begin left turn by pulling wheel down with left hand.

Release grip of left hand and continue turning with right hand.

Cross left hand over right. Release grip of right hand and continue turning with left hand.

Left hand continues turning.

Left hand releases grip and right hand continues turning.

Right hand continues turning.

If more turning is required, cross left hand over right again and continue the process.

To straighten out, reverse the process.

Right hand guides wheel back toward the right.

Left hand continues as right hand releases grip.

Right hand crosses over left and continues guiding wheel right until car is going straight.

Right turns are just the reverse of left turns.

Standard European steering technique avoids crossing the arms at the top of the steering wheel. The right hand stays on the right side of the wheel, and the left hand stays on the left side of the wheel. The technique works like this.

Once again turning left, the left hand pulls the wheel down while right hand releases grip.

As left hand finishes pulling down, right hand grips wheel and pushes up.

As right hand finishes pushing up and releases grip, left hand takes over and pulls down.

The process continues until the wheel has been turned enough. Straightening out is the opposite of turning. The hands never cross.

With either the American or European method, the first stroke at the wheel can be lengthened by repositioning the hand before beginning the turn.

Before a left turn the left hand can be repositioned from 9 or 10 o'clock to 12 o'clock for a longer stroke.

Indeed, both hands may be repositioned.

Curves and fairly mild turns can be made without taking either hand off the wheel.

Keeping your hands in the same place on the steering wheel gives a reference for straight. Do not change hand positions on the wheel or let go of it unless necessary.

In the past, drivers in automotive thrill shows used to drive with only their right hand on the wheel. Their left hand was holding onto the window frame for support in violent maneuvers.

Today, they hold the A-pillar with their left hand.

There are many proven methods of operating a car's steering wheel. Use the one which makes the most sense to you, and feels the most comfortable to you, and gives you the best control over your car. Regardless of which steering method you use, by far the most important factor in steering is *aiming*! *If your eyes tell your brain what it needs to know, it will make your hands steer the car properly.*

Turning the wheel back to the straight ahead position gives you full-time, positive steering control. It is best. However, in gentle, street driving, it is permissible to let the wheel straighten itself with appropriate, gentle control from the hands through which it is slipping.

Keep your hands on the outside of the steering wheel rim. It is unnecessary to put them inside it. Girls who do that will eventually break a finger nail on a spoke. Everybody who does it risks having his hand slip off the wheel and/or jamming a finger in an emergency maneuver. Do not steer using the spokes of the steering wheel. Use the rim.

Do not look at the steering wheel. Keep your eyes on the road. The only thing looking at the steering wheel while you are using it can do is confuse you.

Anything in your hands: cigarettes, pens, handkerchiefs, etc., will make wheel handling clumsy. Hand lotion and french fry oil will grease the wheel, making it slippery. Gloves should have leather or plastic surfaces with which to grip the wheel. Mittens are not recommended.

Clipping the apex.   *Photo provided by Rick Miller Photo.*

5 Chapter Five

Perfect Placement

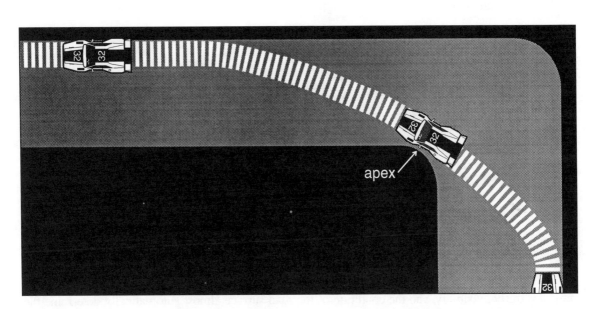

apex

The car in the illustration above is being driven by an expert race driver. It is taking the perfect racing line through the corner. Because its driver is so skillful, the car will take the same perfect line lap after lap. It will approach the corner from the same place on the track. It will decelerate at the same point. It will begin turning at the same point. It will begin to accelerate at the same point. It will clip the same apex and drift (tires partially sliding, partially rolling) out to the same point at the outside edge of the track lap after lap. It will travel at virtually the same speed lap after lap.

Perfect placement, it's efficient and beautiful. It prevents the race driver from getting into trouble by being in the wrong place at the wrong time. It is the solid basis, the known starting point from which he can deviate to pass and be passed. It is the standard from which he can adjust to changing track, car, weather, light, and traffic conditions.

Perfect placement is also the solid foundation the *beginning* driver needs to build so that he can tackle various road, vehicle, weather, light, traffic, and legal conditions successfully. For the road driver, just as for the race driver,

perfect placement is efficient and beautiful. It prevents trouble from being in the wrong place at the wrong time.

On the street, perfect placement is the result of achieving skill at basic car control. It is obtained by knowing, understanding, and applying the laws regarding proper positioning, by practicing the skills of seeing, planning, aiming, steering, accelerating, maintaining speed, and braking, and by sensitizing oneself to and using kinesthetic feedback from the car.

However, mere proper placement, even perfect placement, is not enough. Perfect placement must be achieved with smoothness, balance, and a feeling of control. The car should not jump when put into motion. It should not bounce when being stopped. It should not follow a hooked or ragged course in turns nor slow down in the middle or at the end of them. The car's speed should always be slow enough *before* entering a turn. It should increase naturally, automatically exiting. Car speed should always be appropriate, and all control inputs should be perfectly correlated to car speed. All vehicle movements should have a balanced feeling of positive control.

Following are some illustrations of straight line perfect placements:

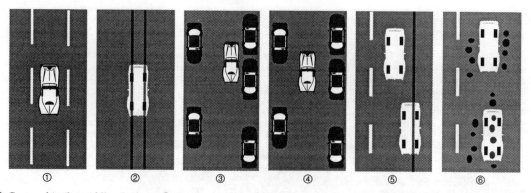

① *Centered in the middle of a lane;* ② *Centered in ruts;* ③ *On the right side of an urban or suburban side-street;* ④ *In the middle of an urban or suburban side street;* ⑤ *With tires not on a seam in the pavement;* ⑥ *With tires away from rows of holes or bumps.*

On side streets, the road width, number and type of parked vehicles, amount of pedestrian and vehicular traffic, visibility, and the condition of the road surface almost automatically determine the best lateral position for your car. For example, on a narrow side street with lines of parked vehicles on both sides, but no oncoming traffic, it is probably best to drive in the middle of the street. This position allows more space on *both* sides to see and provides clearance for possible hazards in and between the parked vehicles or coming out of alleys and/or driveways.

Except on *very* narrow side streets, swerving in and out among the parked cars to provide clearance for oncoming traffic is both clumsy and needless and should be avoided. (See illustrations at right.)

Look for, pick out, and keep a lane for yourself between the line of parked cars and the middle of the street.

How do you know four cars will fit next to each other on a side street? You watch how the car ahead of yours fits between the oncoming cars and those that are parked. Here, the vehicle ahead of yours fits easily between the oncoming car and the parked cars.

When a car is coming toward you between lines of parked cars, check its width against the size of the open space next to it to determine whether another car (yours) will fit. Here, there is plenty of room to drive between the oncoming car and the parked cars.

In all this, remember that cars come in various widths. When in doubt, slow down. When in greater doubt, chicken out, that is, yield. When driving through narrow spaces or moving over, remember: always aim up the lane — through the space!

At intersections on two-way side streets, the best place to be is always the right side of the street.

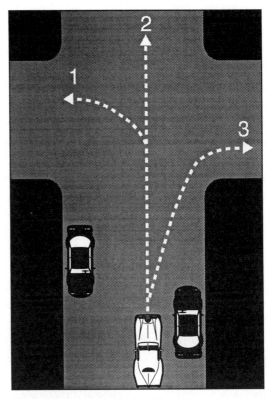

Figure 1: Whether turning left (1), going straight ahead (2), or turning right (3), it is always best to be on the right side at two-way side street intersections.

Being on your own side of the street at intersections prevents conflicts with other traffic coming straight at you (① below), turning right into your street (② below), and turning left into your street (③ below).

Conflicts avoided automatically by being on your own side of the street at intersections.

TURNING: Though turns have three parts: beginning, middle, and end, think of them as units, as graceful sections of a graceful process. *Plan* and *execute* turns so perfectly that nobody

53

riding with you can notice any transition from a turn's approach, to its beginning, to its middle, to its end, to its blending into the following straightaway. The beginning and end of each turn connect to straightaways. If you don't connect the turns to the straightaways in your head before you begin turning, you'll never be able to connect them properly on the road. Neither will you be able to connect the three parts (beginning, middle, end) of a turn on the road if you don't connect them in your head first. Visualize the complete turn with its approach and departure before you make it. That way, at any point during the turn, you'll be able to compare where your car is actually going with where you know it should be going and make any needed adjustments easily, smoothly, immediately, and unnoticeably.

When turning, just as when driving straight, see the space through which you want to drive. *Look where you want the car to go.* It *will* go there. *In turning, the most important thing is to see and know exactly where you want the car to end up BEFORE you start the turn.* Always look far along the lane you will end up in *before* you begin to turn. Always use your eyes to aim *before* you begin to use your hands to steer.

You wouldn't start jumping over a puddle without first seeing the other side and aiming at it. You wouldn't begin cooking unless you knew what you wanted to make. If you cook milk, eggs, flour, sugar, baking powder, butter, vanilla, pecans, and chocolate chips in the oven, you will not end up with pizza. *Know* exactly where you'll finish every turn *before* you start it.

PERFECT PLACEMENT FOR TURNS: For race driver and street driver alike, where and at what speed a turn is begun are determined by the location of the turn's apex and its end point, and how these two points line up with the car's position as it approaches the turn. The illustration below shows the paths a race

car and a street car would take to turn left at the same corner.

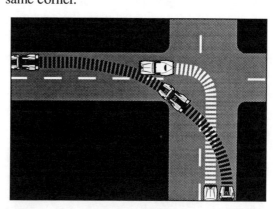

For the race car, the streets would be blocked off and free of all but race traffic. The rules would be the race rules and the laws of physics. The race driver would want to get through the corner as efficiently as possible (quickly, smoothly, safely). Most important, he would want to finish the corner at the highest possible exit speed to achieve the highest possible speed over the greatest distance on the next straightaway. Because he would be allowed to use the whole width of the road surface, he would take the standard racing line shown above. Very basically and with the adjustments obvious in the illustration, he would widen or straighten the corner as much as possible.

To do this, he would stay as far right as he could before the turn, next to the right curb. He would use the apex of the curb to his left as the apex of his turn. (Actually, he would use a point just past the curb's true, geometric apex.) Finally, his end point would be close to the right curb of the new street, at the end of a smooth arc which would allow maximum speed and acceleration out of the corner. By seeing and lining up his end point and apex, he would determine where his beginning point *must* be. (Actually, a top line racing driver probably would not rely only on driving around the corners, but would walk the track to study them carefully.) In any case, he would visualize his path through each corner before turning into it. He would never start turning with the idea that he could fix things as he kept going through the corner. His mental image of exactly how he wanted to drive through the corner would be as complete as possible *before* he did anything with his steering wheel.

A driver attempting to follow the racing line, approaching the corner from the proper position along the right curb, and paying attention *only to the apex*, would probably start turning too early and at too high a speed. He would take much too long and gentle an arc toward the apex only to find when he got there that his speed was much too high and most of his turning still had to be done.

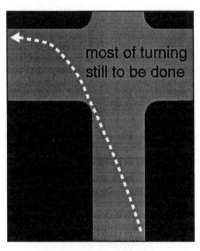

He would have to slow down a lot to keep the car on the road at the end of the turn. Even if he could make the needed adjustments and keep the car from hitting the curb at the end of the turn and rolling over, he would still have made a very inefficient (slow, erratic, unsafe) turn which felt unbalanced and frightening. He would have had to do most of his turning at the end of the corner. Therefore, he would have had to slow down most of the way through the turn, instead of accelerating and would have started on the straightaway at a much slower speed than he should, making the whole lap slower.

If he started the turn too late, he would be unable to hit the apex at all. Just as when he started turning too early, his car would end up off the road at the end of the turn.

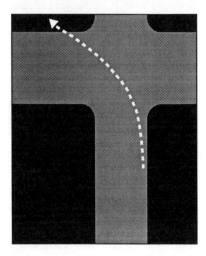

Before a race driver can *take* the best line through a corner, he must *see* that line. *If his eyes see the turn correctly, his hands and feet will control the car correctly.*

Going through the same corner just turned by the race driver, the street driver has different needs and goals. Despite that, he, just like the race driver, must see and plan the turn *before* using his steering wheel. Of course, he wants to get through the corner in the most efficient manner (quickly, smoothly, safely), but the rules and priorities are different for him. He *must* begin and should finish his left turn just as far left as is legal on the two streets so that he *cannot* cut across traffic. He *must* stay on the right side of the street except at the very middle of the turn. He *must* drive in traffic lanes. Therefore, he must be much more concerned with seeing LANES than with seeing end points and apexes. For the street driver, the end or aiming point is merely a place well ahead in the new lane — a place which allows him to see and get oriented to the new lane. The apex merely marks the entrance to that lane, as a gate marks the entrance to a driveway.

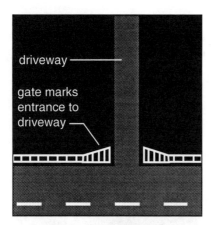

Before turning left into the driveway illustrated above, the driver should look up the driveway. That gives his brain a clear picture of where he wants to go. Next, he should look at the entrance. That gives his brain a clear idea of where the apex of the turn is. Then, looking across the entrance into the driveway (new lane), the driver can easily plan a perfect turn. He will almost automatically know the point from which to start turning and how fast to go. Before he is even halfway through the turn, he will have a clear idea of exactly how to steer and speed up to end the turn perfectly. He will always have plenty of time to steer and accelerate smoothly. Likewise, he will be able to begin rechecking traffic early.

Turning should be done in the corner, not in the old or the new lane.

THIS	NOT THIS

Turn is square, and car goes straight up driveway;

Turn is much too wide. It starts too early, ends too late, and marks a poor driver.

As you can see, your general concept of turns

should be more square than round.

The street driver must use much less speed than the racer and he must start turning much later: that is, make a much sharper (more square) turn.

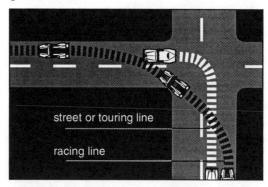

street or touring line

racing line

However, the bad results of starting too soon or too late because he has not lined up the end point and apex of his turn with his approach position will cause the same kind of problems for him as for the race driver. *Both* of them *must* use their eyes to place the car perfectly before, during, and after the turn.

PERFECT PLACEMENT FOR LEFT TURNS: Start your left turns from as far left as you can be legally.

On a two-lane two-way street.

In a left turn bay.

On a one-way street.

As you approach the corner, get an early idea of where the new lane must be by looking out your *driver's side window*. This will pre-program your brain and help it slow the car down to the proper speed. This step is *routinely ignored,* but it is CRITICAL to making really good turns. It gives your brain an overview of the entire turn and its connections to both straightaways.

Re-check traffic. (Checking traffic when approaching intersections is covered in detail in Chapter 7.) Then look out your *driver's side window* again to find *exactly* where your new lane is. Visually separate it from the rest of the street. Find an apex for the turn.

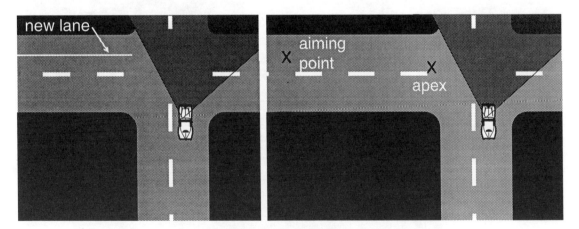

Because you can't see them through the windshield look through driver's side window to locate the new lane and the turn's apex and end point.

Use driver's side window to locate the new lane and the turn's apex and end or aiming point. The aiming point in this photo is no closer than just even with the pick-up truck parked on the right. The apex, which marks the entrance to the new lane, is in the middle of the street just off the end of the stop bar.

Drive to the point from which you must start the turn. Locate this point by keeping an eye on the apex, while sighting up the new lane to or beyond the aiming point, still using the driver's side window.

Do not look ahead through the windshield just in front of the car or at the intersection itself trying to figure out how far to go before turning. This cannot and will not help you turn. If you do it, you'll be driving blind, guessing at where you want to go.

Just as soon as you actually start the turn and can see that the car is beginning an arc which will take it *around* the apex,

aim straight down the street in your *new lane* well beyond the turn's end point, still looking through the driver's side window. Then wait and watch as the *new lane* moves into view through your windshield.

At this point in the turn, your work is done. All you have to do is keep aiming (looking far and near ahead in the new lane and keeping track of where its left edge is) and eventually unwind the steering wheel.

The center line and the sides of the parked cars will point the way you want to go, just as they do when you are driving straight.

During the turn, you may shift the focus of your eyes back and forth between a point far ahead in your new lane and the turn's apex. That's fine. You will be seeing a *lane.* You will be seeing *LENGTH,* which is *exactly what your brain needs to aim!* Looking back and forth along the new lane ensures that your car will go *around* the apex and that the whole turn will be seen as a unit and made in one smooth sweep.

The car and its front wheels must get pointed straight down the new street at exactly the same time. Therefore, you must begin straightening the steering just before the car points straight down the new street.

If you wait until the car is pointed straight, it will be impossible to straighten the steering before the car turns too far, and your turn will come out like this.

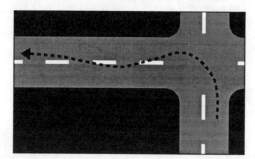

Remember, if you are aiming and planning correctly, there will always seem to be plenty of time to straighten out, and you will never even have to think about getting your wheels straight at the right time. It will happen automatically. If you do have to rush to straighten out or your turns look like the one above, you are not aiming far down your new lane when you start turning, and are trying somehow to line up the hood and/or front fenders with the street by looking down in front of the car when you are finishing the turn.

Looking at the far curb is no good either.

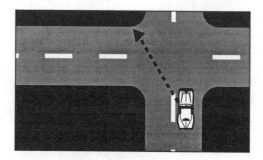

It cannot tell you where the apex is and will only draw you toward itself and off the proper line for your turn, necessitating a hook back into line.

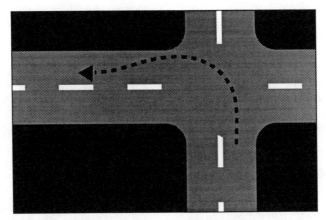

Concentrating on the apex also can force the car to turn too wide.

Finally, finish your turn with natural, confident acceleration out of the corner with the car exactly in the middle of the new lane or slightly toward its left edge. If you are aiming correctly, this will happen automatically.

In review then, locate your new lane (see it as a separate strip of road), line up your turn's new lane and apex with your approach position to determine your beginning point and speed, make an overall plan for the whole turn. Then begin your turn by aiming at its apex. Remember, the apex is the turn's pivot point. Your car's rear wheel must clear it. As soon as the car is definitely moving toward the apex, aim at least half a block ahead in your new lane. Recheck and maintain the proper alignment of apex and end point. *In simplest terms, before you start a turn, look into your new lane across the apex. Your brain will then control the car properly.*

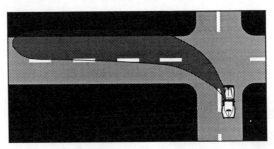

If you use your eyes properly, your hands and feet will automatically perform the physical actions required to drive through the corner properly. The car will travel nicely through the corner, making no hooks and needing no late slowdowns. In fact, if you do make a mistake, your correct aiming techniques will let you (actually force you) to notice it and correct it before it can get large.

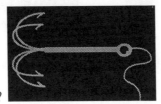

Do you know what this is?

It's a picture of a grappling hook. You know, in the movies, the hero, private investigator S.A. (for Strong And) Handsome, has to rescue the lovely Miss P. (for Perfect) Angel. She is being held in the castle hideout of the evil V.B. (Very Bad) Guy. Strong And Handsome has to climb the castle wall. He takes his trusty (rusty?) grappling hook and throws it over the top of the wall. He tugs the rope to set the hook and climbs up to his Perfect Angel.

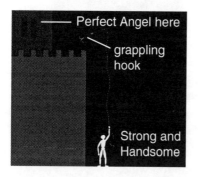 

Think of your eyes as a grappling hook. Throw them around the corner, set them, and pull yourself and the car around the corner toward them. Like this.

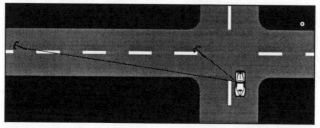

Never, never try to plan and make a turn by looking just ahead of where your car is. IT WILL NOT WORK!

You'll notice that most left turns are quite similar. On most side streets and many major, urban streets, you'll begin turning when the front end of your car is roughly the width of a traffic lane from the lane into which you want to turn.

Starting Point on side street.

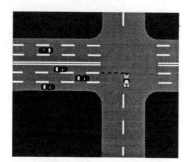

Starting Point on major, urban street.

This starting point allows plenty of room to accommodate oncoming left turners.

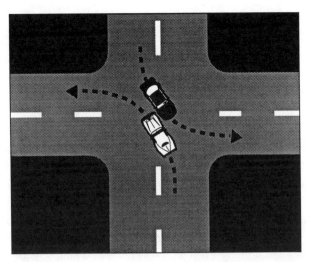

Turning left too soon and too fast because you are concentrating too much on just the apex or trying to beat an oncoming car can cause trouble. Because you turned too soon and too fast, you'll have to tighten your arc and slow down late in your turn. On major streets, that can confuse and block any following driver. It can also cause him to follow in your clumsy path.

Starting a turn too late on a major street because you are looking at the far curb or right down in front of your car can cause you to slow down late, change your line, and get into trouble with the car behind yours like this.

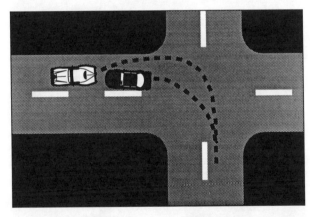

Perfect placement for two cars turning left from adjacent lanes is

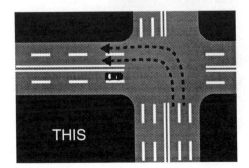

The driver on the right should make a good, square left turn, leaving enough room for the car on his left. If he doesn't, the driver on the left will have to do one of two things. Either he must force the driver of the car on the right to make a good, square left turn by keeping slightly ahead of him as he himself makes a good, square, safe, and legal left turn, or he must yield to accommodate the other driver's selfish sloppiness.

PERFECT PLACEMENT FOR RIGHT TURNS: The aiming techniques and geometry of right turns are much the same as those for left turns. The law requires a right turning driver to begin and end his turn in the lane nearest the curb. He should be able to begin his right turn just a few feet from the curb and end it the same few feet from the curb with no hooks, jerks, or late decelerations.

Preparing to make a right turn, pre-program your brain by looking far into the new street and finding your new lane as early as possible. Re-check traffic. Then locate the end point and apex to determine where you must begin the turn. For a standard, urban right turn, use the point at which the front end of your car gets even with the curb on the street into which you are turning as your starting point.

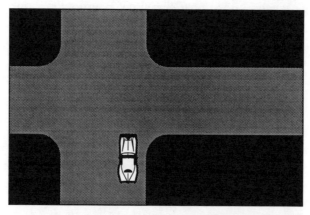

Beginning point for average right turn.

Where curbs have very long radii, just follow the curb, starting to turn where it does.

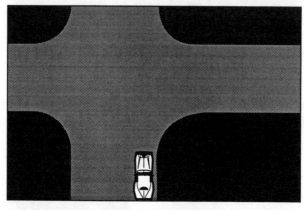

Starting point for right turn when curb has long radius.

Where curbs have extremely short radii, let the front end of your car pass the curb on the street into which you are turning before starting to turn.

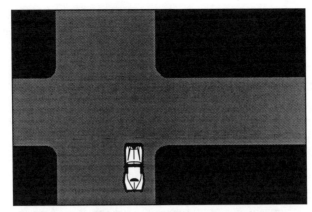

Starting point for right turn when curb has short radius.

Drive to your starting point at a low enough speed. Then begin turning, looking toward and past the end point to keep your bearings. Accelerate as you straighten out again.

In urban areas, many times lines of parked cars and trucks will make it impossible to see the end point of your right turns until you are well into them. How can you aim? Look at the place where you *know* the end point must be even if you can't see it and then aim beyond it. See both the curb apex and the left rear fender of the car apex and let your brain blend them into one imaginary apex somewhere between them.

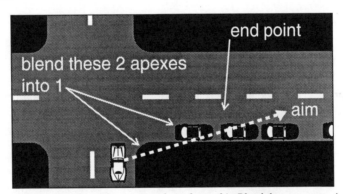

Look where you know the end point is and aim beyond it. Blend the two apexes into one.

On very congested, urban streets, begin right turns very late and make them extremely square.

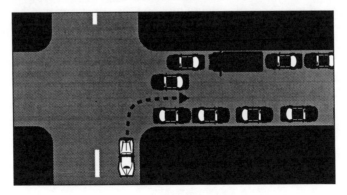

SPEED IN TURNS: Excluding factors like weather, driver skill, etc., speed is determined by the line your car must take through the corner. *Always* get down to a speed at which you *know* you can make the turn *BEFORE* reaching the corner. Accelerate coming out of the turn.

HOW FAR TO TURN THE WHEEL: Never worry about how far to turn the wheel. That will came naturally. Just make a few turns with the grappling hook technique and you won't even have to think about how much to turn the wheel. You'll just do exactly what is required for each turn by see-ing how the car heads toward where you are aiming.

CURVES: When rounding a curve, many times you don't have to do hand-over-hand steering. Just swing the wheel over a bit, keeping both hands in place on it. Then swing it back. By not moving your hands on the wheel, you always know where the straight ahead position is and can straighten out with perfect precision.

On curves, look alternately far and near through the curve to grasp its entire sweep. This is basi-cally the same thing you should do when making a turn. Before using the steering wheel, see and know exactly where the end, middle (apex), and beginning are.

Either before entering it, or as soon as possible in the middle of it, check the end of the curve to see where it is, what is there, and where the road goes after that. Does the road straighten out or go the other way? Is there a cross street, stop sign, traffic, a road blockage...

FINAL NOTES: People who ride with driving students when they practice driving tend to accept very sloppy turns in the mistaken belief that they are as good as can be expected from a brand new driver. That is *wrong*! If the eyes are being used properly to aim, virtually perfect turns will result with surprisingly little practice. If improvement is slow and/or laborious, the eyes are being used improperly, and continued practice will serve only to set and reinforce very bad eye habits which may handicap the student driver throughout his entire driving life!

If approach and entry speed into turns is too high, the student driver is probably focusing much too much on the apex.

Steering wheel movement should *not* have to be rapid at the end of a turn to catch the car before it turns too far. If it is, once gain the eyes are at fault. The driver is not aiming far enough along the new lane. If his turns are planned correctly, it will seem to the driver that there is always plenty of time to do everything, especially straighten out the steering.

In basic concept and in eye use, the racing turn and the street turn are the same. Poor turns are so common in street traffic because very slow speeds mask their inadequacies and render them tol-erable.

6 Chapter Six

Doing It Backwards

Photo courtesy of Indiana State Police Youth Education & Historical Center

When you drive straight forward, your passengers are not aware that you are continually making small steering corrections. At least they shouldn't be. The car should seem to move in a perfectly straight line along the road. It should be the same when you back up. Your passengers should remain unaware that you are continually making small steering corrections.

Just as with steering forward, the most important thing about steering backward is how you use your eyes to aim the car. When steering forward, you look far ahead along the lane through which you want to drive. When steering backward, you should do the same kind of thing. Look way back behind the car — half a block, a block, more. See all those apparently converging lines pointing the way. *See* the space through which you want to drive so that you can *aim* and *steer* toward it.

To do this, it is very important to get your body into a posture from which you can see very easily straight back behind the car to the horizon or to the point where something blocks your view. Most backing problems are seeing problems. They result from poor backing posture. POSTURE IS THE KEY TO BACKING UP. In a good backing up posture, you are twisted so far around to the right that you can see just about as well through the back window as you see through the windshield when you drive forward.

GETTING TWISTED: Start getting into the proper posture by leaning over onto your right hip and turning your entire body toward the right. In a good backing up posture your upper legs should point more or less toward the middle of the dashboard, not straight ahead.

Not This;   *But This*

Next twist your back and pull your shoulders well around to the right. Then twist your head around to the right so you can look squarely out the back window. If you are not tall enough to see over the driver's head restraint, you will probably have to lean over and look between the front seats. Use your right hand to hold your body in position. Put it on your seat cushion, the passenger's seat cushion, or best, if you can do it, behind the passenger's seatback.

Test your backward driving posture. If with just a slight extra effort, you can look out the left rear side window of the car, you are twisted far enough around.

Very short drivers may be unable to do this side window trick because their vision can be blocked by the driver's head restraint.

It is very unlikely that you will achieve a comfortable backing posture which allows you to see well and control the car on your first try. It will take a while. Keep trying. The first time you get ready to back up, it is a good idea to shift to park before trying to find a good backing posture. That way you will not have to keep pressing the brake pedal or worry that the car will move while you twist and stretch and check your posture again and again.

This driver (below) is not twisted around far enough to get a good look through her back window.

Her view will be similar to this.

She will be able to see only one side of the alley through which she is backing. Because she will be able to see only one side of the alley, she will be able to aim at only one side of the alley. If she aims at one side of the alley, she will steer toward that side. She will find it difficult and frustrating to back up or to learn to back up in a straight line. Her poor backing posture will make it impossible for her to see her intended path (LANE) and aim along it. Her eyes and neck muscles will ache, because she will try to do all the twisting necessary to see with just her head and eyes, not her whole body.

BACKWARD STEERING: With the car stopped straight (car and wheels both pointing straight ahead), put your left hand at twelve o'clock on the steering wheel. Keep it there! *Do not let go of the wheel or move your hand around on it.* Do any necessary steering by moving your *hand and the wheel together.* That way you'll always have the twelve o'clock position as a reference point. You'll always know where the middle is. You'll know whether you've turned the wheel toward one side or the other and how much. Whenever you bring your hand back to the twelve o'clock position, you'll automatically straighten the wheels, and the car will go more or less straight in whatever direction it is pointing. If you move your hand around on the wheel or try to toss or spin it like a ship's wheel, you'll lose this valuable reference point.

Keep your right hand off the wheel! If you put it on, you will automatically begin using it to help steer. Once you use your right hand to steer, you'll move your left hand off the twelve o'clock position and lose your reference point. Moreover, putting your right hand on the steering wheel will force your body to twist back toward the left and make good rearward vision harder for you. Then, instead of looking straight back through the rear window and steering straight, you'll begin looking through the right corner of the rear window and steering toward the right. Keep your right hand off the wheel!

FEET: When you are backing up, your right foot should be on or just above the brake pedal. You will need to feed gas when backing uphill and when a hole or bump keeps the car from beginning to move backward by itself after you have released the brakes. In most backing situations, though, your foot should be near or touching the brake pedal, controlling speed and ready to stop the car instantly. Don't allow the car to decide how fast you go. You're the driver. You decide. Very short people may have to use their *left* foot to operate the pedals when twisted around to back up. This allows them to stay twisted so they can see and still reach the pedals.

WHICH WAY IS WHICH? When backing up, it is easy to get confused about which way is left and which way is right. What happens is that when you turn yourself around to look out the back window, you put *your* right side on the *car's* left side.

The best thing to do is just forget about left and right. Think only of *this way* and *that way*. Think, if I turn the wheel this way, the car will go this way, and if I turn the wheel that way, the car will go that way.

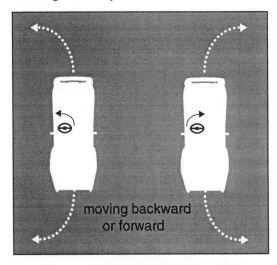

moving backward or forward

To the car, left and right are always the same. Travelling forward or backward, if the steering wheel is turned toward the car's left, the car will go toward its left. Travelling forward or backward, if the steering wheel is turned toward the car's right, the car will go toward its right.

DOING IT. Back up a few times. See how the car responds to your steering inputs. Don't try to analyze too much, and don't be afraid to steer. That's how you'll learn. Just be ready to stop the car if you do make a mistake.

Don't look close behind the car to aim. Don't try to aim by lining up some part of the car with some part of the road. See the rear window frame with your peripheral vision while you aim far back behind the car. If the car does begin moving toward one side, don't start looking (aiming) at that side. Look (aim) where you want the car to go. Check side clearances as necessary, but *always aim* at the space through which you want to drive. If you do get confused about which way is which, NEVER try to figure it out by looking forward! That will confuse you even more!

When preparing to stop, don't coast back the last few feet (or yards!) looking forward. Really embarrassing accidents happen that way. Check forward just before stopping. Then keep looking backward until the car is stopped.

Plan ahead. When you know that the next thing you will do is back up, make sure to stop the car straight. After checking your mirror, just aim far ahead and make sure the car is rolling straight before you bring it to a halt. That way the car cannot start backing crooked because it is not lined up with the road or because the front wheels are not pointed straight ahead.

Actually, whenever you stop, you should stop straight. It looks good. It shows that you care about your driving. It prevents you from sending false information about your intentions to other drivers through inappropriate wheel position. It prevents you from starting off from a green light, etc., with your front wheels pointing the wrong way.

Some drivers always pull the steering wheel toward the left just as they start to back up. If you find that even though you have stopped the car straight, it never begins moving backward without also moving toward its own left, or that you always seem to have to correct just as you begin backing, make sure that you are not pulling the wheel left just as the car begins to move backward.

Avoid leaning or hanging on the steering wheel. Sit and lean on the seat. Hold yourself in position with your right hand. Steer with your left hand.

Try to see the need for corrections as early as possible. Then try to make the corrections as early as possible. If you let the car go way off to one side before starting to correct, you'll have two problems. One, you'll have to turn the wheel a lot to correct. Two, because the car is pointing way over toward one side, you'll be tempted to aim where the car is pointing instead of aiming where you want it to go.

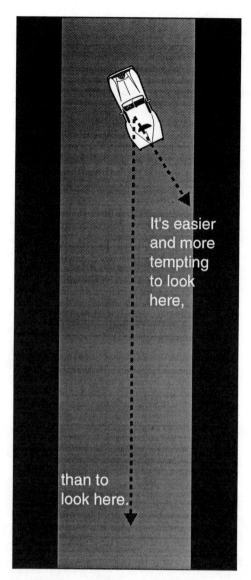

It's easier and more tempting to look here,

than to look here.

Both of these problems can confuse you and make learning harder. Finally, avoid making needless corrections. Sometimes students try too hard. Just let the car go and watch whether or not it is going where you want it to go. Correct its course *only* if it *needs* correction. Remember: you can always stop the car.

Very short drivers may have difficulty seeing over the car's rear sill, especially when backing over a short uphill section of an otherwise level road like an entrance to an alley or driveway.

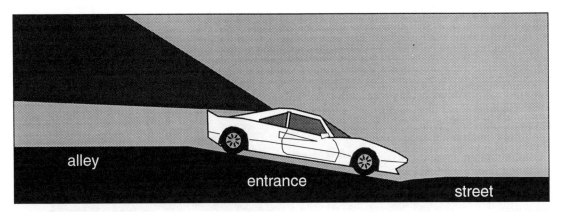

These drivers must compensate through higher seating positions and/or extra care in aiming when they *can* see.

Find road before rear of car goes too high to see over.

If the angles involved are sharp enough, any size driver can have difficulty.

YOU ARE NOT ALONE: There is traffic to watch. When you are backing up, you do not have *any* right of way. Besides that, you'll be moving quite slowly when backing, much more slowly than traffic moving forward. Therefore, traffic can approach and overtake you very quickly. You can find yourself in the way very suddenly. When backing up, just as when driving forward, don't just aim your car, check traffic. Know what is happening *all* around the car, near and far, and check for blind areas. Take a look through the windshield every few seconds while you are backing up, just as you check the rearview mirror periodically when you drive forward. Never allow a car to begin moving backward without first checking traffic in *all* directions.

If you maintain a good backing up posture, aim *far back* along the path through which you want to drive, and control car speed, in a short time you'll be able to back up easily.

WHERE TO DO IT: The best place to learn backing up in a straight line is an alley, an *extremely* long driveway, or a *very* narrow road. The narrowness of these places lets you notice almost immediately when the car begins going off course. On a wider road, it is much easier to get way off course before you notice it. After you have mastered backing in a narrow road, try it on a wider road where you actually have to pick and maintain a lane.

THE SERPENTINE: When you can back the length of a city block in a straight line easily and repeatedly, without noticeable steering correction, while keeping aware of *all* related traffic, you are ready for the serpentine. While backing up and monitoring surrounding traffic, swing the car easily and slowly from side to side at your instructor's command. Regain the middle of your lane (or the middle of the alley, etc.) and make the car continue straight down the middle.

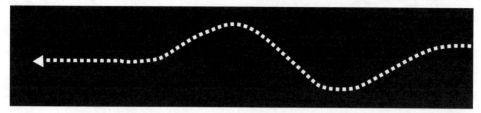

Practicing changing lanes may be even better.

A very wide alley or a very quiet street is a good place to do these maneuvers. A quiet, dead-end street can be excellent. Keep away from intersections. Be certain to check traffic in *all* directions throughout the maneuver, especially before changing lanes. Monitor side clearances. Remember not to move your hand around on the steering wheel. Forget about which way is right and which way is left. Just go this way and that way.

CHECKING FRONT END CLEARANCE: When turning backwards, the car takes a different path from the one it takes when turning forward. That's why one backs into a small, parallel parking space. In a forward turn, the front wheels lead the way, and the rears follow a bit later, cutting slightly closer to the turn's apex. In a backward turn, the car pivots on the rear wheels while the front wheels swing wide around them. Therefore, when turning while backing up, a driver must *always* remember to check that there is clearance for the front end of his car on the *outside of the turn.*

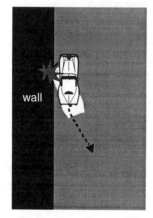

Backing away from a wall.

Backing out of an angle parking place.

Backing into a parallel parking place.

When performing close maneuvers like those illustrated above, it is easy to forget that you are *always driving in traffic*. Remember to check frequently in *all* directions for vehicles and pedestrians.

Good performance in these backward serpentine and/or backward lane changing exercises shows that you can make the car go backward in any direction you want any time you want. It proves that you look and aim at the space through which you want to back, that you have no doubts about which way to turn the steering wheel, and that you can recognize a lane and straighten out in the middle of it while backing. Finally, it gets you ready to make backward turns.

BACKWARD TURNS: Backward turns are necessary to get into or out of driveways, angle and perpendicular parking spaces, many garages, etc. Backward turns can be used in turning the car around. They lay the groundwork for learning to parallel park. Because they require proper aiming techniques, they work to cure improper aiming habits in forward turns.

Because alleys are readily available in many areas; because backing into and out of them is probably legal, whereas backing around street corners probably isn't; because alleys provide long straightaway sightlines along which to aim when straightening out after a turn; and because alleys are narrow enough to show up mistakes early, they are excellent places to learn and practice backward turns.

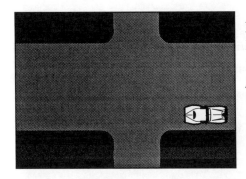

BACKWARD RIGHT TURNS: On the right side of a lightly travelled side street, find an alley with no vehicles parked near it. Check your inside rearview mirror. Pull up *past* the alley, allowing yourself a little distance to lead into the backward turn, so you have time to figure and aim. Stop straight. Stop with the right side of your car about the same distance from the curb it would be if you were going to make a *forward* right turn.

Shift to reverse. Switch on your right turn signal. Check traffic *all* around the car.

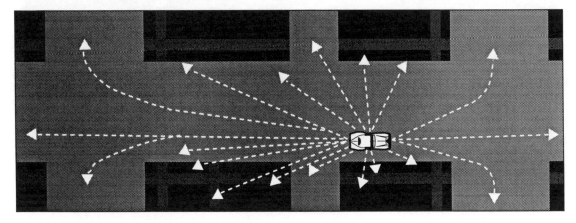

Remember, when you back up, your vehicle moves slowly. Traffic going forward travels much faster. Therefore, it can approach and overtake you in a surprisingly short time.

Check for anything moving in the next block, even blocks ahead and behind. Check for traffic at the intersections ahead and behind. Check all along *both* sides of your street and behind for movement like cars pulling out of parking spaces or driveways and approaching cyclists.

Check close to the car, too. Check into *both* alleys. Look for pedestrians, cyclists, etc. on the sidewalk you will cross and anywhere else near the car. They can get into your way from any direction.

Perform these checks while sitting in or getting into your backing up posture, with the car ready to go. One sweep of your eyes should cover the entire area.

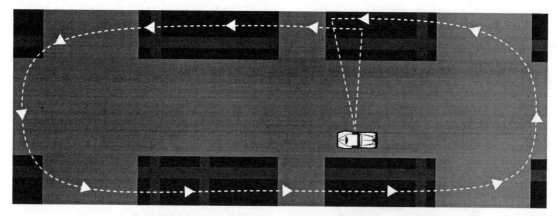

Sweep your eyes 360 degrees plus in either direction.

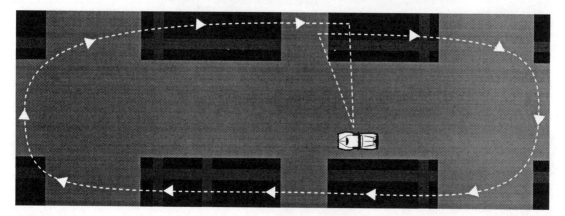

Then back up. Aim straight back while moving straight back. Locate the turn's end point and apex just as in a forward turn. Use them to determine the starting point for your backward turn. See and know where the car will end up *before* you begin the turn.

Plan the turn.

Remember, your car must clear the apex. You may not be able to see the apex from your position in the car.

In that case, locate the near edge of the alley, the edge around which the car must move, and judge from that where the apex must be.

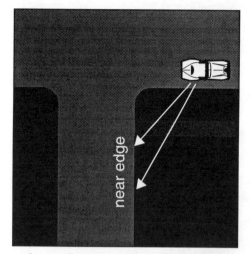

Locate alley's near edge and judge by that.

Trying to aim by using the alley's far edge or curb will not help. If you base your turn on those, you'll swing much too wide (THE CAR GOES WHERE YOU LOOK.)

Aiming at far edge will not help.

Getting the car turned properly into the alley will require you to crank the steering wheel almost all the way to the right. Don't bother guessing how far to turn while you're trying to learn. Just turn the steering wheel until it won't go any farther. In general, begin turning just when your car's rear bumper approaches and passes the apex.

Begin turn when your rear bumper is just about opposite the apex.

Time your wheel turning so that you have turned all the way at about the time your right rear wheel is passing the apex.

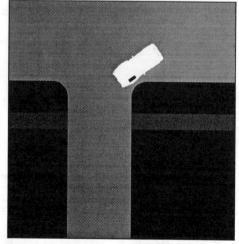

Finish turning wheel as right rear wheel passes apex.

In most cars, the rear wheels are just behind the rear seat and/or just beneath the c-pillar.

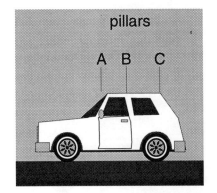

Aim through the right rear side window of your car down the middle of the alley.

As the car keeps turning backwards, wait for the middle of the alley to seem to move across out of the right rear side window into the back window.

Get ready to straighten out. Keep aiming near and far along the length of the alley (1/2 block, 1 block back). Let *both* edges of the alley define a long lane for you and straighten the steering so that the car continues straight up the middle of the alley (lane).

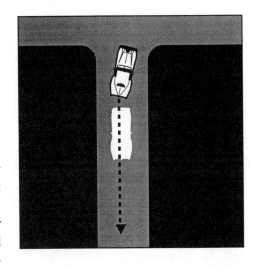

Just as in forward turning, straightening the steering should never need to be rushed. If it is, you are not aiming correctly.

The point of this exercise is not JUST to get the car backed into the alley SOMEHOW and stop. That isn't much of a trick. The point of this exercise is to make perfect backward turns; i.e., get into the alley in the proper place (begin the turn properly), straighten out again and keep backing straight down the middle of the alley (finish the turn properly). These are the things that show you have full control when turning backward, set you up for parallel parking, etc., and polish your forward turns.

With a lot of practice, it is possible to make passable forward turns even though you look at (aim at) all the wrong things, or aim too close in front of the car. However, making good backward turns by trying to steer away from obstacles at which you are looking or by looking right down behind the car is nearly impossible. You must aim at the space through which you want the car to go.

The farther around the corner the car gets, the farther back you'll be able to see. The farther back around the corner you can see, the farther back you should aim. When you get into a position to see 1/16 of a block back, aim 1/16 of a block back. When you get to where you can see 1/8 of a block back, aim 1/8 of a block back, etc.

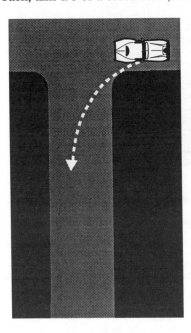
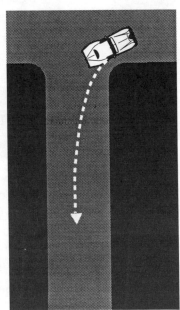
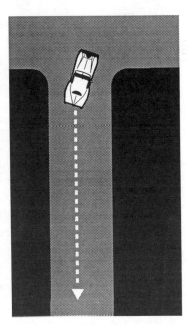

PROBLEMS: Beginning a backward turn, the driver must monitor his car's progress into the alley. However, once the turn is well begun, his attention must shift to finishing the turn. He must look and aim far down the alley — *throw out the grappling hook*. What can happen, though, is instead of throwing the grappling hook far back down the alley, the student driver will just keep watching the rear end of his car turn. He will not look to see the alley coming into view through the rear window. He will keep looking out the side window. The car will keep turning too long. It will turn too far. It will turn past the middle of the alley toward the edge, toward a garage, a garbage can, a utility pole, a fence, etc.

Car has turned too far because driver has not aimed far back.

Then the driver will keep looking (aiming) at the obstacle and trying to steer away from it. He'll get very confused about which way to turn the steering wheel and find that he CANNOT make the car move away from the obstacle. The car will just keep closing in on it. The driver will get frustrated. DON'T HAVE THIS PROBLEM! Don't get hypnotized and just keep watching the car turn! Aim at the space through which you want the car to go! Throw that grappling hook as far down the alley as you can and pull yourself and the car through the turn. Aim at the end

point of the turn up in the alley through the right rear side window and keep aiming at the end point when it appears in the rear window.

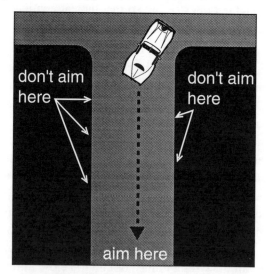

Sometimes driving students will try to compensate for letting the car turn too far by straightening the steering too soon instead of aiming properly. This makes them miss the middle of the alley on the outside.

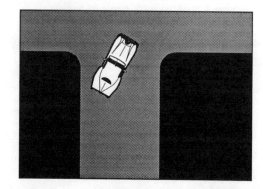

The answer is still the same. Throw that grappling hook way back down the alley and pull yourself through the turn with your eyes.

If you do decide to try to make a good turn out of either of the above illustrated misses, remember to aim for the space way back there through which you want to drive. Check side clearances and remember that the front end will swing *toward* whichever side of the alley you are already too near.

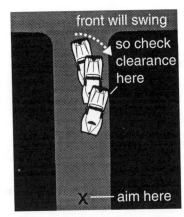

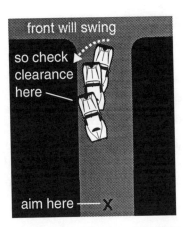

STEERING WHEEL TECHNIQUE WHEN BACKING AROUND CORNERS: Putting your right hand on the wheel to help steer will automatically twist your body toward the left, making it harder for you to see and aim. Don't use your right hand unless unusually heavy steering effort is required by your vehicle. Nowadays, virtually all cars have power steering and effort is light. Therefore, in general, when backing use the technique of "palming" the wheel. Make sure to keep your fingers together, *including your thumb.*

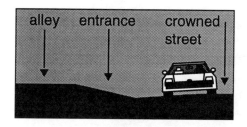

alley   entrance   crowned
street

SOME FINER POINTS OF TECHNIQUE: Because the street is crowned and the entrance to the alley is most likely uphill, you may find that you have to do some pretty fine speed control using both the gas and brake pedals.

First the front end of the car will have to climb up the crown of the road. You may need gas. Next the car will roll down hill off the crown of the road. You may need brakes. Finally the car will have to climb up into the alley. You may need gas again. The key is to take it easy.

By the way, who's been watching traffic while you've been straining to make the car go where you want it to go?

Probably your instructor —

As you develop skill at turning backward, take over more and more of the work of checking traffic. You'll notice, as you achieve greater skill in this maneuver, that there seems to be much more time available for checking traffic.

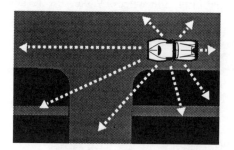

Just before swinging in, recheck all around the car including sidewalks you'll cross

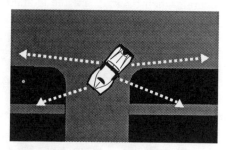

Many drivers recheck street and/or sidewalk traffic while waiting for car to get turned into alley.

If delayed at any point, recheck everything.

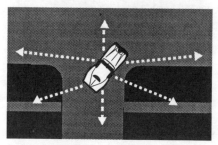

BACKWARD RIGHT TURN *OUT* OF AN ALLEY OR DRIVEWAY: When you have mastered making backward turns into an alley, try a backward turn *out* of an alley. The first thing you'll probably notice is that when you are backing out, it is harder to check traffic. In some situations, like the one illustrated below, you may have to back more than half the length of your vehicle out across the sidewalk before you can be completely sure about sidewalk traffic.

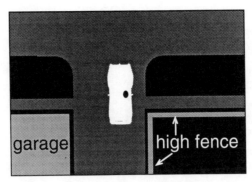

Never assume that any area into which you can't actually see is clear! Never put responsibility for safety on sidewalk users! A blind person will not see your car even though you have stopped with your back bumper just even with the near edge of the sidewalk before creeping out.

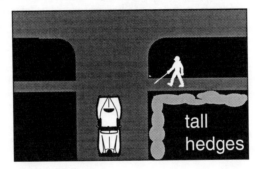

A severely hearing impaired person, surrounded by street noise, may not hear your horn signal or automatic back up alarm. A dog won't understand it.

What about a child? Never assume the sidewalk user will turn out to be an alert adult. It could be a child running or riding a bicycle fast. It could even be a child running or turning a fast moving bicycle blindly into the very alley out of which you are backing!

While creeping out of the alley and checking sidewalk traffic so carefully, don't forget to check road traffic, too. Sure, you'll check road traffic before you actually back into the road, but will you figure that just like that kid running or riding that bike on the sidewalk, a car or truck driver, or even a bigger kid riding a bigger bike faster on the road, could be preparing to turn into your alley just as you back out of it?

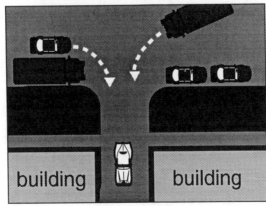

Check near and far in *all* directions.

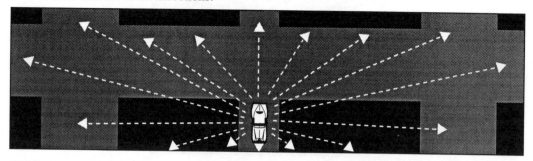

While checking traffic, plan your turn. Make sure you know exactly where the car will end up BEFORE you begin turning. Locate the one and only lane into which you want to back. Pick it out from the others and aim along it. Often you will have to imagine your lane, because it will not be painted on the street or lined up with seams in the pavement. Keep checking traffic while you make your turn. Use all the checking and car control techniques you learned backing into the alley.

SUCCESS: It's not good enough just to back out of the alley and end up somewhere. The point of the exercise is perfect backward turns into the street, including ending up backing straight down the middle of the proper lane.

BACKWARD LEFT TURNS: Many drivers twist their bodies toward the right when backing to the right and toward the left when backing to the left.

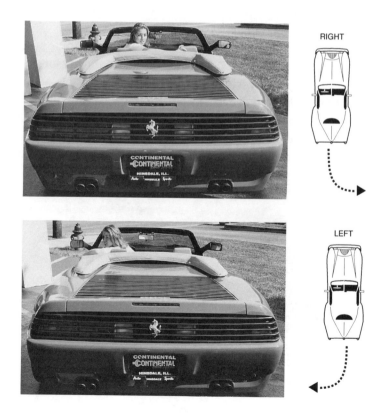

RIGHT

LEFT

While this seems natural and sensible, it can be inefficient and dangerous. A driver twisted toward his left to make a backward left turn will tend to focus primarily on the apex. He may easily ignore the right side of his car and everything beyond it. He may forget to check whether there is clearance for his right rear fender.

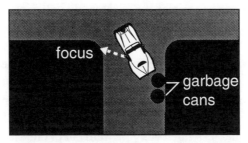

He may forget to assure clearance for the outward swing of his right *front* fender.

He may even forget to check traffic *all* around the car, even directly behind!

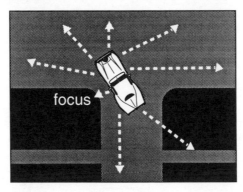

However, a driver using the standard backing up posture can easily check traffic with the habitual 360 plus degree sweep of his eyes.

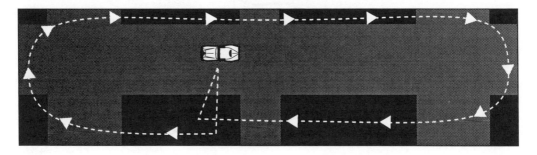

He cannot forget about his right rear fender. He will tend to remember his right front fender. He can see and plan his intended path. Drivers who have great difficulty twisting their bodies and very short drivers who can't see because of the head restraint might have to twist left to begin backing left, but they should *make sure to check all areas that require checking* by twisting back to the right as needed. They should try to finish the turn in the standard backing posture for better control.

Many times the clumsy and less safe backward left turn (turning backward *across* traffic) can be avoided altogether. Planning ahead may allow you to make a backward *right* turn instead.

When practicing backward turns, you'll have to make several (perhaps many) in succession. That means you'll be pulling forward out of the alley. Remember to make proper forward turns. Do not forget about aiming well ahead along your new lane. You may be tempted to look close to the front of the car and at the curb,

because you do not intend to go far forward. Do not! You *could* unlearn your good forward turns. Remember to check the rearview mirror before you stop after pulling back onto the street. Nobody will expect you to pull out of an alley or driveway and stop immediately!

A perfect backward left turn into the correct lane on a street is the hardest backward turn to do. Try it last, after you have mastered the other backward turns. Once you have learned to turn backward into an alley or driveway, turning backward out of one onto a street should be fairly easy if you make sure to twist far enough to see well and you aim along a real or imagined *lane*.

MASTERY: Once you have done most any maneuver perfectly three times in a row, you have learned it. Future mistakes will come from lack of attention. Don't rest on your laurels. Build solid habits. Each time you do any maneuver, try to make it perfect, something both you and your instructor would be proud of, something beautiful!

7 *Chapter Seven*

Looking for Trouble

Once upon a time, in a very large city, there lived a little boy. His name was Kenny. Kenny lived in an apartment building on a city block full of apartment buildings. Between these buildings were double width walks or gangways.

One afternoon, Kenny was riding his scooter home and enjoying its speed as he rounded the *blind corner* from the front sidewalk into the gangway between his building and the one next door. Suddenly, there appeared, exactly in Kenny's path, a man walking toward the street.

There was nothing Kenny could do. It had all happened too fast. Kenny crashed into the man. His scooter's front wheel ended up on top of the man's left foot.

Scared, Kenny backed his scooter away and scooted home as fast as he could. A few days later, Kenny happened to see the man again. His left foot was in a cast!

Several years after that, Kenny, now living on the outskirts of that same very large city, was trying out his first two-wheeler. Kenny rode the length of his driveway and out into the street, where he was T-boned by another bicyclist. The other boy took the blame for the accident. He said that he had been riding with his *eyes closed*!

Kenny survived many more crashes, grew up, and got a job teaching driving. That was when he remembered the two crashes described above and understood their lesson. Not only does a driver have to *keep his eyes open*, he has to *look for trouble in order to avoid it*.

Chapters 4 and 5 of this book explored the basic technique for aiming and steering an automobile. This chapter tells the basics of how to look for trouble; i.e., check traffic.

At the earliest stages of learning to drive, you are concerned almost completely with managing the car. Your teacher does a lot of the monitoring of and making sure about traffic for you. As your skills develop, your teacher puts more and more of the responsibility of looking for trouble on you.

STRAIGHT AHEAD: Generally, steering straight ahead at relatively low speeds becomes quite easy quite quickly. The next step is to learn to look for trouble, a step many drivers never take.

Driving straight on a side street, you aim up a lane which extends about a block ahead. Look for trouble at least that far ahead. Try to see everywhere in the area between the buildings on one side of the street and the buildings on the other side of the street for at least one block ahead.

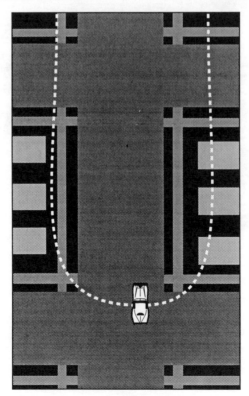

Don't look off to the sides only way up ahead near your aiming point, and certainly don't just aim at a distant point in your lane. Let your glance move all over a deep and wide area in front of your car.

LOOKING AROUND: Your brain does not see everything the same way. It does not give the same importance to or even focus your eyes on everything in your field of vision. Instead, your brain lets your eyes jump around, focusing on points of interest. For example, movements and bright colors attract your eyes. If you let your brain allow your eyes to work as they should (don't stare at the road in front of your car), they will automatically break the large area ahead into several smaller areas surrounding the various points of interest. This idea is suggested in the illustration below.

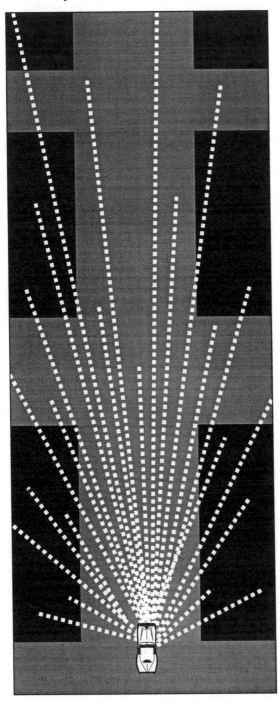

Your brain will put together the information from each of these smaller sections into an overall view of the entire broad and deep area ahead of your car, giving you an integrated understanding of the total scene in front of you.

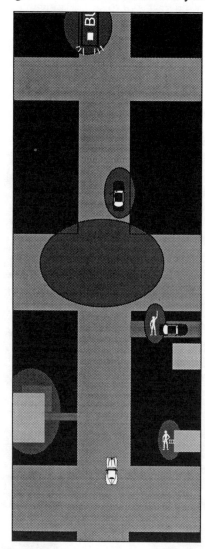

If you were actually driving through the simplified situation shown above and letting your eyes work properly, they would be attracted to the man on the ladder close ahead on the right, the huge and magnificent house on the left, the woman doing something at the open trunk of the car in the driveway ahead on the right, maybe the intersection straight ahead, the

open door on the car parked at the beginning of the next block, and the flashing red lights of the stopped school bus about two blocks ahead. In the illustration, the shaded areas contain these points of interest, noticed immediately by your brain. The area not shaded contains all the rest, the left over, uninteresting stuff. As you drive along, keep rechecking this area for things you may have missed and for new situations.

Consider the consequences to your driving of what you see in the areas containing the things you do notice.

The big, beautiful house on the left is lovely to look at but has nothing to do with your driving. There are no people, animals, cars, toys, tools, etc. near it. Disregard it immediately.

The man on the ladder is painting the window frames on the front of his house. He is an adult. He is occupied at the top of a ladder. Nobody else is around watching or helping him. It seems very unlikely there could be any conflict here. Moreover, right now, as you are about to pass his house, he is quite a long distance off to the right. There just isn't enough time left for him to get into your way. It is now safe to disregard him.

The woman by the car in the driveway seems to be either loading or unloading the car's trunk. She is an adult. She seems to be alone, but a child or a pet could easily be hidden by the car. You are not yet close enough to the situation to make a final decision about it. Let it go for now and check it again later.

Meanwhile, look ahead toward the intersection, the parked car just beyond it, and even farther ahead toward the school bus. See whether there have been any changes in any of these areas. Scan for new possible hazards. This keeps you aware in plenty of time about future driving problems. Being aware of problems early gives you enough time to see them in detail, analyze them as they develop, and handle them smoothly and easily.

If you dealt with only one problem at a time, you'd have to drive very slowly and in only the most basic of driving environments, because you'd seldom know what was ahead. You'd be like the fellow in a canoe with a bad leak in it. He was so concerned with bailing water out of the canoe that he didn't notice the waterfall ahead until just before he went over it. Knowing everything that is in a wide area far ahead as well as near ahead allows you to watch the *entire* driving scene *develop* ahead of you and plan a safe and graceful course which takes into account *all actual* and *most potential problems*. That allows you to select an appropriate speed and leaves you time and space to see and deal with hazards which do show up suddenly.

A driver who looks mostly close ahead of his car usually must deal with only one situation at a time. He is like the ball in a pinball machine, bouncing around erratically from one bumper or flipper to another — accelerating, decelerating, stopping, starting, and jerking around. His driving is erratic and unpredictable. It is unpredictable because he is confused. He is confused because EVERYTHING ALWAYS seems to come at him so SUDDENLY — apparently out of nowhere. He sees things only ONCE, when he is already close to them. He sees only fully developed situations one after another. However, a driver looking near and far ahead and near and far to the left and right sees things several times from several angles as they develop in the area other drivers think of as nowhere. Because he watches situations develop, he always seems to have more than enough time to deal with road and traffic conditions. His speed is always appropriate. His driving is graceful, safe, and efficient. He is rarely surprised.

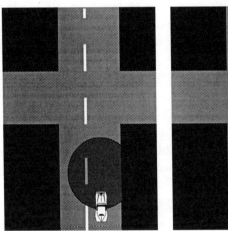 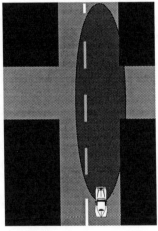 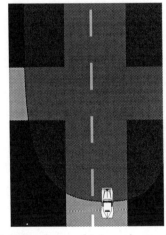

A driver who sees this or even this is always being surprised.   *A driver who sees this is rarely surprised.*

Now, recheck the lady by the car trunk. From the other side of the car, a small child is running toward her. Will the lady notice and control the child?

Yes, she does.

The only remaining question about this situation is whether there may be a pet animal or another child still hidden by the car.

You are still some distance from the situation. You are still unsure about it. You know that you may have to slow down or even stop quickly. Check your inside rearview mirror to see whether anybody is close behind you. It is probably also a very good idea to "cover the brake"; i.e., remove your foot from the gas pedal and place it over the brake pedal ready to use the brakes.

Recheck the lady, child, and car.

No change.

Recheck ahead quickly. The intersection, parked car, and school bus are all unchanged and still safe distances ahead.

Once more, check the lady, child, and car in the driveway. You see that just as you begin passing this situation, it has resolved itself. The lady and the child are both moving toward the house, and you can see that there is nothing else on the far side of the car.

Notice that all this checking and rechecking have allowed you to use your time and distance most efficiently. If you had just kept watching the situation in the driveway as you neared it and it developed, you would have known nothing else. You would not have known that no new threat was developing near ahead of you, to your left, or to your right just beyond the driveway. You wouldn't have known whether anybody was following close behind you. Finally, if you had kept looking off to the right for such a long time, you might very well have steered off toward the right.

INTERSECTIONS: Unlike the man on the ladder, the huge, beautiful house, the lady at the rear of the car, the car parked ahead with its door open, and the school bus lights, intersections may not catch your eye automatically. Many times you have to hunt for them. Look for breaks in the lines of houses, or trees, or parked cars on your street. Look for street name signs, one-way signs, stop signs, yield signs, etc. ahead. Look for the street pavement actually spreading sideways into the grass, forming an intersection. Look for vehicles parked at right angles to your street, corner houses, hedges, etc. Look for vehicular and pedestrian cross traffic and cars turning off of or onto your street. Even a mail box can alert you that an intersection is ahead.

Why bother so much about finding intersections? At an intersection, one street with all its traffic crosses another street with all its traffic.

That guarantees conflict situations. Intersections are where the action is.

A second reason to find intersections is that they serve to break up the road into shorter, more manageable sections. As in our illustrated example, a driver sees and considers things beyond the next intersection, but his attention is focused mainly upon the block in which he is driving. When he is just about to cross an intersection, he must focus his attention mainly on that intersection. When a conflict situation exists just beyond the intersection, a good driver slows down a little more to give himself more time. This allows him to split his attention between the known conflict and the intersection. Once past the intersection, he focuses his attention mainly on the new block in which he is driving. However, he knows that at the end of this block, too, his attention will be required by another intersection which he may already have noticed. *Intersections are different from other situations and stand out as natural break points, punctuation marks along the road.*

Before you can drive across *any* intersection, you must *know* that your car can get across it with no risk of getting hit from either side, or of hitting anything coming from either side.

Sometimes this is easy. The intersection is wide open. There is little or nothing to block your view. You can look far off toward the left and right twice and be sure the intersection will be clear before you even get near it. Therefore, you can cruise across it in complete confidence without slowing down at all. Most often on side streets though, you can't. Houses, fences, trees, bushes, hedges, tall weeds, hilly terrain, odd intersection angles, parked vehicles, road work crews, and so on limit your view. You have to slow down to be able to see everything you *must* see *before* entering the intersection.

CHECKING INTERSECTIONS: First, locate the intersection. Then, while you are still a good distance back (as much as half a block), and, while still continuing to check situations on your current block, start getting ready to cross the intersection.

Check the inside rearview mirror, because you will probably have to slow down.

Check ahead beyond the intersection. Do you see anybody coming toward you who might turn left in front of you? Is there a potential conflict situation just past the intersection? Is there some kind of road blockage just beyond the intersection?

Check left. What do you see there? Probably not much from this far back.

The corner building usually blocks your vision. Nonetheless, check that area to get the basics of the situation. Make sure that there really is an intersecting street on the left side. Look for pedestrian and vehicular traffic currently in that area. Children playing near the intersection might move into it as you approach. A car might make a right turn into your street and come toward you. You want to see it as early as possible.

At this point you may also be able to notice other obstacles to your vision in addition to the corner building. You may even discover spaces between vision blocking objects. As you approach the intersection, you can look through these spaces to get more information.

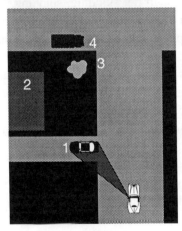

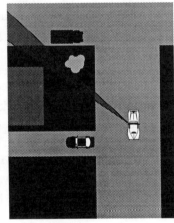

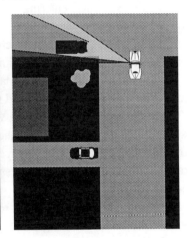

I. Car in driveway (1) blocks vision between house (2) and bush (3) and van (4).

II. From this position driver can see between house and bush.

III. From this position driver can see between bush and van and, of course, still to the other side of the van.

Look left before looking right to establish a pattern in which you get information from the left side of the intersection first. Because we drive on the right half of the road, you will encounter traffic from the left side of the cross street before you encounter traffic from the right side. In other words, you can hit or get hit by something coming from the left before you can hit or get hit by something coming from the right. Obviously, however, if visibility is much better to the right than to the left, look right first.

After your first check to the left, check right. Look for the same kinds of things you looked for when you checked left. You may be able to see just a little bit farther down the cross street to the right than you could to the left because your car will have moved closer to the intersection.

Check ahead again, still looking for the same kinds of things as before and *still making sure that your car is in the proper position on the road — AIM.*

Recheck left. Because your car has now moved closer to the intersection, you'll be able to see farther into the cross street.

Recheck right.

Remember to make sure you have a clear path beyond the intersection before committing yourself to crossing.

Recheck left and right and maybe left and right again BEFORE entering the intersection. You must *know* that you can get across safely or stop *before* you enter the intersection. Remember, you cannot make your car either accelerate or stop instantly when you see danger coming close. You and your car *both* need time to react. When visibility is extremely bad, you will have to keep checking both sides and ahead as you let your car creep across the intersection, while your foot covers or actually presses the brake pedal.

Turning at an intersection requires even more time and checking than just driving straight through one. You need to locate the lane into which you want to turn, regulate your speed, and place your car accurately to begin your turn. You begin this while still checking for intersection traffic.

Just as with most other driving situations, with intersections, don't expect to see and understand everything all at once. First, notice the situation. Then, as you approach it, keep adding to your knowledge of it with repeated checks and rechecks. Watch it develop. Build an understanding of the total situation including your part in it and effect on it. Remember, just as you watch and react to the actions of others in traffic, they watch and react to your actions.

Frequently, driving students will begin looking toward the left and find that they can see only very little there. Instead of being satisfied for the time being with that basic information and checking other areas to get more information to add to it, knowing that they will look left again and again to recheck, they just keep looking left until they *can* see the total situation there. When they finally do finish looking left, they find to their surprise that they have arrived at the intersection in the wrong position on the road (too far left), moving much too fast, and knowing nothing about what is happening on the right or ahead. If there *is* a problem on the right or ahead, there's nothing THEY can do about it. It's too late. Though not skidding, spinning, or flying, their car is completely *out of control*! The only hope of preventing a crash rests with the *other guy*!

Sometimes, finding that their first looks to the left and right provide so little information, students decide that it would be more efficient to wait longer before beginning to check the intersection. It isn't, but they try it. They find that when they *do* finally begin looking left, they must get the whole picture there in one very long look. Just like the students described above, they find that they are entering or even *leaving* the intersection with only a fraction of the information they need, no time to get it, and certainly no hope of doing anything about any problem.

It is much safer and smoother to keep checking and rechecking. Not only that, slowing down earlier to take the time to see everything actually allows a driver to clear an intersection at a higher speed. Remember, *speed must always be based on visibility*! Kenny didn't know that when he ran his scooter over his neighbor.

THERE'S A LOT TO DO BEFORE ENTERING AN INTERSECTION, AND IT TAKES TIME.

- Identify the intersection
- Check traffic behind you
- Begin checking traffic to both sides at intersection
- Monitor conditions on the block in which you are still driving
- Check conditions beyond the intersection
- Control car speed (based on visibility)
- Control car position (aim)
- Be certain intersection is safe to cross or turn into

LEAVING THE INTERSECTION

- Accelerate across
- Begin rechecking conditions ahead
- Check inside rearview mirror

As you approached and began crossing the intersection, you continued monitoring the car with its door open, parked on the right just past the intersection. You saw its driver close the door. You also saw a puff of smoke come from the tailpipe when the driver started the engine. Nothing else is going on near the car.

Now, looking into the car you see that the driver is stretching over toward the middle of the car, looking at himself in the inside rearview mirror as he combs his hair. You know that he will not move the car. It is safe to pass.

Check for any other close dangers and return to your regular scanning of the entire scene ahead. The school bus has unloaded, switched off its red lights, and resumed forward motion. It is moving toward you at a moderate speed. There will be plenty of sideways space for you to pass each other. Might the bus stop again before reaching you? It could. Where are the children who got off the school bus? A small group is heading toward one house. Are there other children going in other directions? Is any child crossing the street? It seems not. Are there any new hazards?

Everything else on this block appears to be trouble free. Locate the next intersection and begin checking the block beyond it. The things you see two or more blocks ahead on side streets are too far away to be hazardous now, but they may become conflict situations later. Seeing them early and watching them develop preprograms you to deal with them. Since you already know they are ahead, you merely keep rechecking them while looking for other trouble and dealing with more immediate concerns as you move along the road.

Keep scanning the entire scene, checking and rechecking near and far ahead and near and far to the left and right. Allow your eyes to work. Try to see everything that might be important to your driving for at least a block ahead between the buildings on one side of the street and the buildings on the other. See points of interest, moving things, blind areas, details. Check your mirror. Let your brain put all these together to give you a clear concept of the entire broad and deep area ahead of and all around your car.

8 *Chapter Eight*

Son of Looking for Trouble – Traffic

Traffic is *not* some evil thing sent by a demon to make your life miserable. Sometimes it does seem that way, but traffic is neither evil nor special. Traffic just *is*. Traffic is part of driving like the road, your car, the weather, the laws, etc. Drivers drive through traffic, and that is all there is to it. Even race drivers drive through traffic.

There is more to do in traffic, but that is not an excuse to let your driving get sloppy. The aiming and looking techniques, the perfect placement, the dead solid car control you began mastering on the side streets are the basics of good driving form. They are the foundations upon which to build more driving skills and get more satisfaction from your driving. They must not be given up in heavier traffic. Having tenuous control over your car will *not* make your traffic driving easier. Moving at the wrong speed will *not* make your traffic driving more efficient. Being in the wrong place at the wrong time will *not* make your traffic driving more fun. Being unpredictable will *not* make your traffic driving safer.

Traffic should not lessen your smoothness or your safety, or, in relative terms, your efficient progress. *Traffic should not be an obstacle to your control. It should be a stage from which to show it off*!

Driving well in traffic means making it look easy. Your car should glide gracefully through traffic. In fact, most of the time your car should run where the worst traffic isn't, where the congestion isn't. Hazards should be seen and controlled long before they develop into emergencies. Your passengers, lucky people, should sit comfortably and chat happily in total ignorance of your masterful driving performance. Indeed, other drivers riding with you should wonder why every time you drive, traffic is so light, so easy. Smooth, graceful, efficient traffic driving is not caused by lack of traffic, but by focused attention, effective search patterns,

accurate analysis, careful vehicle placement, and perfect timing.

THREE IMPORTANT FACTS ABOUT TRAFFIC: First, *traffic moves*. If it isn't moving, it isn't traffic.

Second, traffic is not just everybody else on the road. *Traffic is you too*. While you see everybody else as traffic, everybody else sees you as traffic.

Third, because traffic is about moving, and because you and your vehicle are part of traffic, *the way you drive affects traffic movement*.

Your driving can make traffic move better or worse. Your driving *does* make traffic move better or worse. There can be no question about it. Because traffic moves and because you are part of traffic, the way you drive your car makes traffic better or worse for everybody every moment you drive.

Does your driving add to the delays, confusion, unpredictability, and danger of traffic? Does your driving add to the stopping, starting, and the general disorder, or does your driving promote safe, quick, efficient traffic flow?

TRAFFIC ATTITUDES: To many drivers, traffic means traffic jams. Traffic means red lights, j-walkers, being cut-off, fighting for space. Traffic means getting trapped blocking other cars and trucks at intersections. Traffic means hundreds of vehicles creeping a few feet at a time between long periods of waiting.

To a very few drivers, traffic is a normal part of driving. It is a challenge to meet successfully. It is a place to learn, a chance to *perform*.

Many American drivers seem not to think about traffic at all. If they do think about it, they seem to believe that it is beyond control, certainly beyond their control or even their influence.

These drivers are like grazing sheep in a herd. They just go along with the random running and stopping, pushing and shoving of the group. They never wonder whether anybody is in charge, or whether there is a plan, or whether things could be better. They do not understand traffic. They do not try to understand traffic. Therefore, they cannot even think about improving traffic *flow*. They have no feeling of control, no feeling of working as a team to accomplish some end. They just follow the guy ahead — like sheep.

Other drivers seem to think of traffic as a brutal contest of threatening and forcing fools out of their way. Lacking true understanding of traffic, they drive on raw nerve. They believe that grabbing a momentary advantage for themselves by inconveniencing and even endangering others is "beating traffic."

It isn't. It is just making everything worse for everybody. There is such a thing as avoiding or "beating" traffic, slipping through holes that don't exist for anybody else, but it is not being a bully or a slob. It is usually such a graceful thing that other drivers do not even notice it.

Some drivers drive in fear. They do not love driving. They do not think of traffic, or snow, or parking lots, or mountains as honest challenges to their skill, knowledge, and character. Actually, they believe that they are somehow separate from traffic and superior to other drivers. They do not understand traffic flow and do not want to. They accept that old defensive driving idea that one should consider every other driver a madman trying to kill him. These drivers proudly sacrifice cooperation, efficient traffic flow, control, safety, grace, fun, and their own rights for their arrogant, private concept of maturity and good citizenship, a concept they foolishly believe will, in some magical way, solve all driving problems. They do not watch traffic to see the results of their way of driving. They do not see the delays, confusion and danger their defensive driving causes.

A few drivers think of traffic as a game in which *everybody* is supposed to win. They do not fear traffic. They do not fight traffic. They do not blame traffic. They drive through traffic safely and efficiently with skill, confidence, and style. They know that they have to cooperate with their fellow drivers. They try to see them as teammates. They see traffic in terms of *flow*.

They watch traffic not just for occasional trouble, but to learn. They watch how the actions of other drivers affect traffic flow. They watch how their own actions affect traffic flow. They get very good at not getting caught up in messy traffic and not causing any messes. They learn to drive through traffic in a way that the average driver would find absolutely amazing.

They drive in a safe, efficient, masterful way that improves traffic flow for everybody. They drive so that everybody gets through faster, and safer, and more easily — so that everybody wins.

These drivers point the way to the future. They are doing the only thing that can improve traffic. More money for more roads, police, and courts will not do it. More laws and restrictions and quotas will not do it. Good intentions will not do it. Experiments in traffic engineering or driver training that trivialize driving will not do it. Drivers who enjoy driving, who consider it a life-long hobby, who pay full attention to driving can improve traffic by being aware of *traffic flow*, by watching it and learning about it, and by cooperating with *all* their fellow drivers to promote it so that everybody wins.

TRAFFIC FLOW: Traffic moves, but it does not move like an army marching in straight ranks and perfect step. Traffic moves in lanes marked on streets, but it also moves in alleys, and driveways, and parking lots, and across railroad tracks. It moves on sidewalks and along roadsides. It turns and changes lanes. It starts and stops and speeds up and slows down. It parks. It breaks down. It crashes. It gets heavier and lighter. It cannot be regimented. It is made up of thousands of different people in thousands of different vehicles and on thousands of different feet going thousands of different places for thousands of different reasons in thousands of different states of mind.

These people must know and follow the rules of the road and cooperate with each other so that each can do what he must do in the total flow. Some need to park. Some need to pull out. Some need to get through. Some have plenty of time. Some are in a hurry. Some are happy. Some are angry. Some have brand new cars in perfect running condition. Some have junks. Some have sports cars or motorcycles. Some are walking. Some are running for buses. Some are driving trucks. Some are riding bicycles very well. Some are riding bicycles very poorly. Some are paying attention. Some are not. Some are nervous. Some are confident. Some are sick. Some are drugged. Oh it goes on and on and on. Some are not even human. Dogs and raccoons and buffalo can never be expected to know, let alone follow, traffic laws.

However, traffic does flow. It does not always flow in the same way though. It flows one way in morning rush hour, another way in afternoon rush hour. It flows differently on weekends. It flows differently on weekend nights. It flows differently on different roads, and on different parts of roads, and on different kinds of roads. Holiday flow is different. Christmas shopping flow in commercial districts is very different. Add rain, or fog, or snow, or ice. They all cause other differences in flow.

LEARNING TO DRIVE IN TRAFFIC:
When first driving in traffic, you will feel awkward. You will not know how to fit into the flow. You will not even see the flow. You will be quite pleased just to get along safely.

With experience, you will get used to driving in traffic. You may not enjoy it, but you will no longer feel out of place, in the way, clumsy, or as if you'll get run over. You will feel a part of traffic.

That is as far as most drivers go in learning about traffic. They learn enough and experience enough to be able to function in traffic. Then they forget all about learning any more about it. They never try really to understand traffic. They never think to try to do something about traffic. They complain.

Well drivers, traffic *can* be better. *You* can make it better. *You* can ease the flow so that everybody gets through easier, safer, and faster. *You* can set an inspiring example of excellent driving. *You* can get great satisfaction from being a *really* good driver.

You can, but you have to want it, and you have to work at it. You have to keep watching and analyzing traffic flow and traffic flows. Watch individuals, too. See how the maneuvers of other drivers add to or take away from the flow. Then check what effect your driving has on traffic flow. Watch your mirrors not only before maneuvers, but after them, too. See the chaos *you* cause. When other drivers inconvenience or endanger you, think about whether you do the same thoughtless and dangerous things to others.

Many thousands of miles of observing and thinking about traffic flow will allow you to understand a great deal about it and learn how to improve it. More and more you will be able to time your maneuvers and signals in ways that not only keep you clear of trouble, but actually make more space and faster, easier, safer flow for other drivers.

You will learn that you can *use* traffic, too. By understanding the dynamics of traffic flow, you will be able to predict how the normal flow of traffic will, at certain times, provide golden opportunities for your lane changes, turns, etc.

By watching the traffic carom, you will be able to position your car in just the right place at just the right time to benefit from the traffic flow. You will be able to use traffic just as a football running back uses his blockers. Traffic will actually run interference for you — sometimes.

A word of caution here, it is easy to outslick yourself. *Never rush* to take advantage of some wonderful opportunity. If it can't be done smoothly, really beautifully, don't do it. Never take anything for granted. Never assume that surrounding drivers will understand or even notice what you are trying to do until it is too late. This stuff is supposed to be graceful. It is not supposed to get you traffic tickets or ambulance rides. Your driving should relieve congestion, stress, and danger, not cause them. If you are taking advantage of traffic (using your blockers) properly, your slick maneuvers will frequently benefit traffic flow.

Probably the most amazing thing you will discover by studying traffic and traffic flow is that you can actually control the behavior of other drivers for the benefit of all. Your car's position and speed, your timing and use of its signals, and the timing of your maneuvers automatically cause other drivers to behave in certain ways. Drive so that you cause traffic to move in such a way that dangers are avoided and traffic flows freely. "Do unto others as you would have them do unto you."

Do not fear traffic. Do not fight traffic. Do not blame traffic. Study it. Understand it. *Perform in it*! Go where you want to go without getting into anybody's way and without getting blocked or endangered by others. Think of driving in traffic as a team sport in which the goal is to achieve maximum *flow*. Think flow. Work for flow so that everybody wins! Watch, and learn, and improve. Keep getting more and more satisfaction from your driving for the rest of your life!

WHO DRIVES YOUR CAR ANYWAY? In a sense, your brain drives your car. It decides whether your car should stand still, begin moving, move forward, move backward, speed up, keep a steady speed, slow down, turn left, turn right, continue straight, stop. It also decides, controls, and checks when, where, how, and how much.

To make all these decisions and judgments and to perform these control functions, your brain needs a lot of training and experience. It needs to know a great deal. It needs to know traffic laws, basic applied physics, weather, traffic movements, how people act, and how to control an automobile. It needs to be able to analyze the interaction of traffic, including your car, and predict the possible, probable, and unlikely.

The better trained and the more experienced your brain is in these things, the better it can drive your car. There is one more thing it needs, though — current information. It gets this mostly through your eyes. The more complete, accurate, and timely this information is, the better your brain can drive your car.

Using your eyes to get correct, complete, detailed information to your brain in plenty of time is extremely important to driving. It is a complex and fascinating skill which you can improve as long as you drive.

SEEING WHERE TO AIM: Regardless of traffic, the basic job of driving is following the road — following *your lane* on the road. Before you can aim and steer up your lane, though, you must see where it goes.

Remember how in turning you must always see and know exactly where your car will finish the turn *BEFORE* you begin turning. It's the same with driving in lanes. You must be able to see where your lane goes *BEFORE* you can aim and steer through it.

Your lane may not simply continue in a straight line, especially in cities. It may move sideways. It may merge into another lane. It may turn. It may even end with little or no warning.

Here are illustrations of some common lane irregularities with arrows to show the traffic flow problems they create.

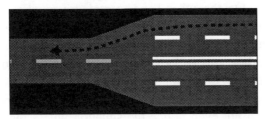

Right lane ends.

Often right lane driver does not see 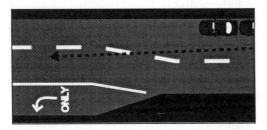 sign and is surprised when he has to merge left. Many right lane drivers merely follow the road, never realizing that they are changing lanes.

This right lane driver does not notice his lane moves over and he changes lanes without realizing it. Often he is merely following the traffic ahead, which has done the same thing. By changing lanes without realizing it, the right lane driver can force the left lane driver into the empty left turn bay.

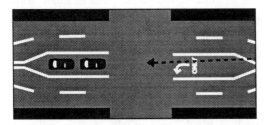

This left lane driver cuts through empty left turn bay, then faces left turn bay with cars in it.

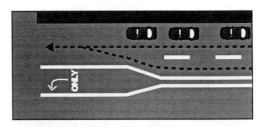

Here the city has placed *all* the responsibility on the drivers by allowing parking up to the point where the left turn bay is full width. This has, in effect, eliminated the right lane. At the point when the left turn bay becomes full width, there is only one lane for straight through traffic.

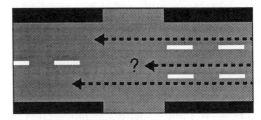

As this one-way street crosses the intersection, the middle lane just ends.

The white car entered the left turn bay properly and was cut off by the grey car which entered the bay improperly by cutting through the island.

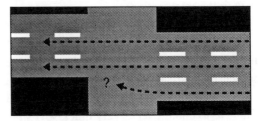

As it crosses the intersection, this whole one-way street moves over.

Let us analyze one of the lane situations shown above.

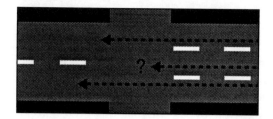

Just past the intersection, this one-way street changes from three lanes to two. The sudden ending of the middle lane affects aiming, steering, and traffic flow. The drivers in the left and right lanes will probably just continue straight ahead, but what about the driver in the middle lane?

First, he must see and understand the situation — his lane ends. He must change lanes to the right or the left. Which?

If he is familiar with the intersection, he will decide and plan ahead of time. He will probably change lanes a block or so before the intersection. This will give him the advantage of being settled in the through lane well before the intersection. He will not have to struggle at the last moment to change lanes. He will also be able to choose the through lane which better suits his needs beyond the intersection. He might have to turn left or turn right or park in the next block. Finally, by changing lanes early and getting out of the way, he will not add to the problems at the intersection. He will contribute a good deal to smooth, safe, easy traffic flow through the intersection.

Suppose he is not familiar with the intersection. Unless he is paying careful attention to aiming, he will see the situation at the last moment. He will have to find a space available *right now* in either the left or the right lane. He will have to change lanes very quickly. His lane change probably will not be graceful.

Suppose he cannot find a space. He will have to slow down or even stop and wait to be

let into a lane, cut off someone, or continue between lanes until somebody lets him change lanes. Any of these will result in inefficient traffic flow and perhaps in horn blowing, rude gestures, or an accident.

On the other hand, a real driver who is unfamiliar with the intersection will be paying attention to aiming. He will see the problem earlier. This will give him much more time and space to deal with it.

Many drivers in the left and right lanes will not even notice the situation unless they get crowded, cut off, or hit, etc. Because there is no obvious problem with their lane, they assume they can just sail ahead in blissful ignorance.

Real drivers in the left and right lanes will see that the middle lane is ending. They will watch the traffic in it and time their movement through the intersection to allow space for lane changes in front of or behind their car, whichever is best for flow. They will also take into account the traffic following them. Making room for a lane changer only to get hit in the rear is not a slick maneuver.

Changes in lanes cause traffic flow problems and accidents. Seeing where your lane and all the other lanes go as early as possible gives you time and space to aim and steer properly. It also gives you time and space to see and understand any traffic flow problems caused by the lane irregularities. This lets you plan and time your passage and/or maneuvers to move traffic easily and efficiently. Knowing exactly where you are and exactly where you soon will be in traffic is vital!

Get your aiming information primarily from the road, not the rear end of the car in front of you. See what is painted on the street. Aim far ahead: a block, two blocks, half a mile, etc. Actually *see* your lane continue off into the distance from where you are in it right now. Look for your lane through the cars ahead, over them, even under them. In heavy traffic, look next to them, too.

See the lane lines, but do not rely completely on them. There are other clues. Look for road signs that warn of changes in lanes ahead. Watch traffic flow far ahead, too. Notice slowdowns and lane changing ahead especially at intersections. Be alert for intersections where left and/or right turn bays may move the lanes. If one intersection on your street has lanes that move around a left turn bay, expect the next intersection to have them, too. Never just assume that your lane keeps going straight forever!

Fog and rain, especially at night, can make it very difficult to see the lane lines. Snow and slush actually cover up the lines. Cars and trucks can cover the lane lines, too, if their drivers do not take care to look for and use the lines. By following the car ahead or assuming the lane will go on straight ahead forever, some drivers drive over the lines instead of between them. This wears out the lane lines at the most important places. Don't wear out lane lines.

On rare occasions, in tricky conditions (snow, for example), knowing where the lane lines are and trying to keep between them can be wrong. When nobody else knows where the lane lines are, and everybody is just following the car ahead, it may be best to join the parade. In these conditions, drive in the correct position only if you can do so without getting in the way or confusing other drivers.

Traffic driving is so complex that you may not be aware that you are aiming. You are, though. Do it right.

ROAD SURFACE AND CONDITION: Look at the road surface not only to find out what is painted on it. Check the type and condition of the road surface.

Is it concrete? Concrete is usually tan in color, like a concrete sidewalk. It normally gives the best traction.

Asphalt pavement is black or gray. Asphalt's surface is smoother than that of concrete; therefore, it gives less traction. It is more likely than concrete to be "slippery when wet."

Gravel may be packed down or loose. It may even be treated. Loose gravel is much more slippery than well packed gravel. Gravel roads may have loose gravel along their edges and between the ruts packed down by passing traffic. Gravel gives less traction than pavement because the pieces of gravel act as rollers under the tires.

Dirt roads are not gravel. They are dirt.

BUMPS: Is the road surface bumpy? Bumps make the ride uncomfortable and wear the car's suspension. Bumps also reduce traction because the tires touch the road surface only part of the time. The tires tend to skip from the top of one bump to the top of the next. They may not touch the road between bumps.

The reduced traction caused by bumps is most noticeable in fast curves and in hard stops.

ROAD CAMBER: Think of road camber as the sideways slope of the road surface. A flat curve is said to have no camber. A curve which slopes *upward* toward its outside edge is said to have positive camber. A curve which slopes *down-*

ward toward its outside edge is said to have negative camber.

  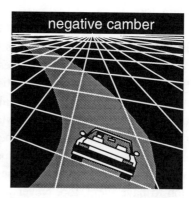

Banked curve

A positively cambered or "banked" curve helps a car hold the road. The turning car is pushed *into* the upward slope of the road. A negatively cambered curve tends to throw a turning car off the road. The turning car is pushed *away* from the road surface. Negatively cambered curves are rare, but they do exist even on superhighways. They can be troublesome when made slippery by rain, snow, etc.

Does the road have a crown? Most roads are crowned. They are higher in the middle than at the edges.

 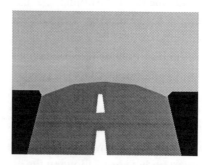

The crowning is for strength and drainage. Except on curves to the right, crowned roads are *negatively* cambered. Very slippery conditions are made more challenging by very high crowned roads.

Ruts are worn into a road surface by the tires of vehicles passing over it. Shallow ruts of the kind you see on well worn expressways add four different cambers to each lane.

Ruts also fill with water from rain, melting snow, etc. Deep ruts in ice or hard packed snow can be very difficult or even impossible to leave.

Notice camber changes and surface irregularities like: cracks, potholes, ruts, bumps, patches, etc. Hitting potholes can damage tires, wheels, etc.

Look for debris on the road and alongside it. You will find dead animals, clothing, truck tire treads, car parts, gravel, tools, furniture, pieces of wood, broken glass, etc. Just when you think you have seen it all, you will notice something new and amazing in the road.

Do not trust the driver ahead to see and maneuver around potholes and debris. He may not see them in time. He may not see them at all. If he is driving a truck, he may straddle a piece of debris which is too tall for your car to straddle. Keep a good following distance and see all these things for yourself in plenty of time.

Rain, snow, ice, slush, puddles, sand, gravel, mud, oil, wet leaves on the road all reduce traction. In cold areas, salt may be used to melt snow and ice off the roads. After its work is done and the road is dry, this salt can leave a light colored residue which surprises unwary drivers with its reduced traction.

ROAD SIGNS: Most drivers drive mostly to the same, old, familiar places over and over again. They drive to work. They drive back home. They drive to school. They drive back home. They drive to Aunt Susan's house. They drive back home. They get to know these routes very well. They get to know which roads to take and where to turn. They get to know where the hills, and curves, and bumps, and potholes are. They get to know the speed limits. They get to know where the traffic is bad and how to avoid it. They even get to know where the police check for speeders.

On these familiar routes, drivers do not need the help of road signs, so they stop looking at them. Then they stop looking *for* them. Then they get into the habit of not looking for them.

This habit causes drivers not to see road signs even when their help *is* needed. Drivers miss street name signs, route signs, road construction signs, lane ending signs, no passing signs, etc. When they do see these signs, they do not see them early enough. Their reactions have to be very quick, their maneuvers hastily planned and clumsily executed. Their driving is less predictable and much less fun. Their business trips, vacations, visits, etc., are more dangerous.

Think of road signs as a valuable early warning system.

The curve illustrated above goes uphill to its apex, then it goes downhill. A driver driving through this curve cannot see what is in the road beyond the hillcrest.

Suppose this particular curve is part of a sportscar race track. The racers, of course, know which way the road goes beyond the hillcrest. They may have looked at a map. They may have walked the track. They may have driven through that curve many, many times at very high speeds. *They know where the track goes.* What they need to know is whether the track ahead is clear. If a car has spun and is blocking the track, the driver taking the curve at his car's limit of adhesion is in trouble.

The people in the picture are corner workers. One of their jobs is showing flags to approaching race drivers to let them know track conditions ahead. If the corner worker shows no flag, the track is clear. If he shows a yellow flag, there is something wrong ahead. The driver may not pass another racer and should take it easy. If the corner worker *waves* the yellow flag, there is something seriously wrong ahead. The driver may not pass and should be ready to stop if needed. A yellow and red striped flag means there is oil or something else on the road surface ahead. A white flag means that there is a slow moving vehicle ahead: an ambulance, a tow truck, a fire truck, a crippled race car.

These flags are an early warning system. Think of road signs as an early warning system. Try to build the habit of seeing them. Consider the value of knowing ahead of time the information given by signs like these.

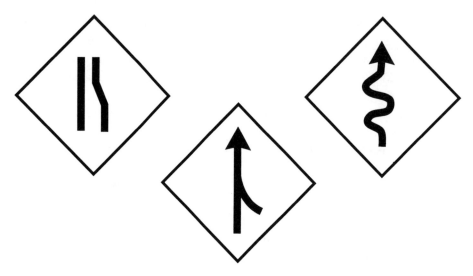

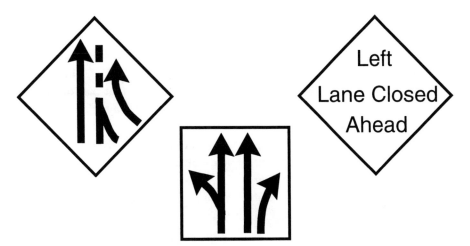

TRAFFIC SIGNALS: Because traffic signals tell traffic when to stop and start, they affect the way traffic flows. Traffic which is stopping for a red light flows very differently from traffic moving at a steady speed. Stopping traffic and steadily moving traffic each flow quite differently from traffic starting up on a green light.

For example, think about trying to change lanes in each of these types of traffic flow. In steadily moving traffic, the spaces stay about the same size and tend to keep their positions relative to us. In stopping traffic, the spaces shrink rapidly and stop catching up to us from the rear. In traffic which is starting up on a green light, the spaces can open and close rapidly and appear and disappear in positions ahead of, next to, and behind us. Because traffic flows differently, we must drive differently.

Never assume that you will automatically see all traffic signals in plenty of time. Never merely follow the car ahead trusting its driver to see the traffic signals and react properly in time. *Look for traffic signals*! They are a separate and important part of the traffic scene.

Seeing traffic signals *early* adds to your understanding of the traffic situation ahead. It also allows you to choose a convenient and safe time to check your rearview mirror before slowing and/or stopping. Check your rearview mirror even when approaching green lights. They

change. Decide *right now* that yellow lights mean *stop unless you'll get rear-ended*! Real drivers don't "make" yellow lights!

Complex traffic conditions just before intersections can cause drivers to lose track of traffic signals. Drivers get so involved in watching so many other things that they forget all about the traffic signals. This can cause smashed cars and flowing blood. Know the *total* traffic situation!

As you approach traffic signals, keep rechecking them for changes. Suppose, for example, you are in a moving line of cars turning left on a green left turn arrow. Never simply follow the car ahead or just aim and check traffic. Keep checking the green arrow, too. It may be green for the driver ahead of you and off or yellow or red for you. Know what color the traffic signals is. Do not assume. Do not guess.

It's simple responsibility. You are in charge of your vehicle. You are responsible for it, for where it goes, for when it goes, and for the people in it. Do not assume or follow, *know*!

Traffic signals turn green, too. When trying to make a right turn on red, for example, drivers can get so busy checking traffic and looking for a space into which to turn that they do not notice when the red light changes to green.

SECTIONS OF ROAD: Intersections, hills, curves, traffic signals, railroad crossings, etc.,

break the road ahead into sections. In city driving, the block you have just entered will get most of your attention. However, in normal conditions, it should not get *all* of your attention. Keep glancing far ahead to get clues about what will be happening and where the road will be going farther ahead and even farther ahead. Remember, the idea is to see things developing over time, not to arrive suddenly upon full blown situations. Seeing situations develop over time will give you a much better idea about exactly what is happening and what you should or should not do about it.

VEHICULAR TRAFFIC: Not all vehicles in traffic are cars, trucks, or buses. Motorcycles, bicycles, motor scooters, horse drawn wagons, snow plows, tractors, tricycles, big wheels, skate boards, street sweepers, baby buggies, etc., are all seen in traffic. Even wheel chairs and unicycles may be seen in traffic. It is very easy for people not to see things they do not expect to see. Drivers must see as much as possible, so expect to see ANYTHING!

How is the vehicular traffic moving over all? Is it fast, slow, excited, relaxed, clumsy, etc.?

How is each individual part of vehicular traffic moving? Are vehicles going straight, changing lanes, pulling into traffic, parking, turning left ahead of you, turning left across your path, turning right into your path, signalling, not signalling, speeding, stopping, skidding? Is a driver forgetting all about traffic because he is looking for an address or a parking place? What is happening on the side streets? What is behind you? Is there a semi-trailer truck behind you? Is it right on your rear bumper? Is there a motorcycle behind you? Nothing? What about traffic near you in adjacent lanes? Do you see turn signals flashing or brake lights? A jam up ahead in the lane next to yours means that drivers in that lane may soon need to enter your lane.

PEDESTRIAN TRAFFIC: Remember that not all pedestrians are healthy, sophisticated, responsible adults and teenagers paying attention. Some are sick, deaf, blind. Some are from a completely different part of the world. Some know the right-of-way rules. Some do not. Some are children. Some are elderly people. Some may not know how to drive and therefore may not realize what problems you, as a driver, may have in seeing them or being able to control your vehicle. Some are working. Some are playing. Some are drunk or drugged. Some are confused. Some are rushing. Some are shopping, trying to catch buses, etc. Some are on the sidewalk. Some are crossing the street. Some are j-walking. Some are j-running to buy ice cream from a truck. Some are getting into or out of cars. Some are slipping and even falling on the ice. Some are being arrested. Some are wearing bright, easy to see colors. Some are wearing dark, hard to see colors. Some are out in the open. Some are behind posts, trees, bushes, cars, vans, etc. Some are on ladders. Some may be approaching your stopped car from the side or even from behind. These can get into your way suddenly just as you begin to move.

Human pedestrians can be just about anywhere, doing just about anything. Understand that. Expect that.

Some pedestrians aren't even human! They are dogs, cats, pigeons, cows, frogs, squirrels, deer, raccoons, etc. What can you expect a frog to know about traffic?

BLIND AREAS: "The car just came out of nowhere!" So often a driver says something like that right after a crash. The truth is that the car certainly did *not come out of nowhere.* Cars do not come out of nowhere. They come out of factories. What really happened was that the car came into view suddenly or unexpectedly from *behind* something. The car came out of a *blind area.*

Blind areas are the *other* places, the places you should see but can't. They are the places *behind* things, the places blocked from your view by the things you do see.

That's the problem. People naturally tend to focus their attention on the things they *do* see. In fact, they focus their attention on only a few of the things they see. They get used to picking out the main things in any view. For example:

Above is a picture of a car. There are other things in the picture, but we know that the car is the subject of the photograph. We tend to focus our attention on the car, not the building, the open garage door, the driveway, the plants, etc. We do not care about those things, because this is *obviously* a picture of an automobile. People subconsciously assign values to the things they see and pay attention to the things they think are the most important.

Only rarely is what is *behind* something else important to us: when we are playing hide-and-seek; when we are looking for something lost; and when we have reason to believe that we may be attacked or ambushed, as in walking through a forest in a war zone.

When driving, you are not playing hide-and-seek, nor looking for something lost, but you *can be ambushed*! When driving, you must always ask yourself, "Could there be something behind that, could something come out from behind that?"

You must learn to know automatically every time your view is blocked. Because of the way we are used to seeing, this is not always as easy as you might think it is.

Above is a picture of a car, but the girl has blocked our view. We know instantly that our view is blocked, but what about this picture?

Is our view blocked here? Most people would say, "Of course not! This is another picture of a car." What if we walk past the car toward the house in the background?

YEeeooowww!

AMBUSHED!

Is our view blocked here?

Each vehicle blocks our view to some extent. Think of each vehicle as a blacked out area on the picture.

Look at the areas that are not blacked out. Look into the cars. Look through the cars. Look over, under, and around the cars and trucks. Sometimes you can even see between the parts of a tractor/semi-trailer truck.

Is your view blocked here?

Our driving path is clear. There are many parked vehicles along the curbs, but they are no threat. Parked vehicles cannot get into our way.

The truth is that there are many blind areas here, but the way we are used to seeing keeps us from noticing them. We see cars and trucks and think no more about them. Parked cars and trucks cannot get into our way.

One problem is that we cannot see into all of the parked vehicles. We cannot be sure that no vehicle is occupied, that no door will open into our path, that no vehicle will pull out into our way.

The rows of parked vehicles also block our view of the sidewalks and small lawns. Might a dog be there, hidden from our view? Might it run into the street from between the parked cars? Might there be children playing on the lawns, hidden from our view? Might one of them run into the street from between the parked cars?

Many an urban driver would feel completely relaxed and absolutely safe cruising down this street at 30 m.p.h. — the legal limit, until some kid ran out in front of his car and he hit him.

"He came out of nowhere! I didn't see him until it was too late! Oh, I feel terrible! I'm so sorry! The kid just ran right in front of my car. I'm so sorry!"

Don't be ambushed! *Learn to recognize blind areas*!

Think about blind areas. Train yourself to look for them when you are driving. You will be amazed at how many blind areas there are, and how many you find, and how you keep finding new ones.

There are two kinds of blind areas. The first and most easily recognized is the kind in which your view of the path ahead or into which you are turning is blocked. For example:

Hill blocks view ahead.

Overhanging bushes and trees block view around curve to right.

Weeds to left, though low, still block view of road.

A right turn into the alley beyond this construction site would be blind.
Even a left turn would be at least semi-blind.

The second kind of blind area is the one in which something could cross your path from behind something else. For example:

Leaving this alley, we can see only straight ahead. The buildings on each side create large blind areas. What is happening on the street, the sidewalk? Will a truck or bicycle turn into this alley?

What's at the other end of this viaduct? Might somebody even be standing between the pillars in the middle?

What danger might lurk just past this gate?

The buildings in this alley overlap each other. What might come out from the walkways and driveways between them? What if a garage door is open? What might be to our right past the garage? What might be to our left past the fence?

What might be blocked from our view by this parked bus?

PREVENTING AMBUSHES: How does a driver control blind areas? How does he drive through or past them safely? First, he must recognize them early. The earlier a driver recognizes a blind area, the better his chances are to observe it, to understand it, and to control it. Recognizing a blind area early, a driver can use his time and constantly changing position to get a great deal of information about the blind area. As he approaches it, he can observe the blind area from several different angles, at several different times, with several different glances. For example:

This truck creates a blind area ahead of it and to its right. From far back you can see a little bit to the truck's right. Look there for anything which could move to a position under or in front of the truck. Look to the left of the truck for possible ambushes ahead of it. Look there for side streets, alleys, parked vehicles, pedestrians, etc. Look under the truck for feet, small animals, wheels on bicycles, baby buggies, cars, etc. Also look for shadows and movements.

From here you get a different view under the truck. From here you can also look into a truck's mirror. If the light is exactly right, you will be able to see into the cab of the truck. You will be able to see whether or not there is a driver in the truck. You may even be able to see what the driver is doing: looking back at you through the mirror, looking down as if he is doing paperwork, or eating a banana!

From here you can see better just in front of the truck and get still another view under it. Remember that someone could be standing or walking just where your view is still blocked by the truck's left front wheel and tire.

The last look.

Remember that all these checks of the parked truck must be separated by continued checks of the rest of the traffic scene. *NEVER LOOK AT ONLY ONE AREA FOR A LONG PERIOD OF TIME!*
A parked truck can easily block your view of several cars parked in front of it.

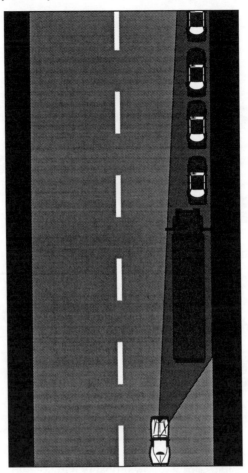

Where there are lines of parked vehicles like this, check the sidewalks when you can see, before you get next to the cars.

Look for pedestrians on the sidewalks who might disappear behind the parked cars and trucks only to walk into the street just as your car is passing. Look through the cars to see toward the sidewalk.

Look between the parked cars and over their hoods. Look under them as much as possible. It is much more difficult to see under low vehicles like cars and transit buses than high ones like trucks and school buses. You may be able to see under one car if you are far enough back.

But when cars are all lined up like this, it is almost impossible to see under them.

Look into parked cars. Look for people in the cars. See what the driver is doing if you can. A driver looking at you through his mirror or window probably will not pull out or open his door. A driver looking into his inside rearview mirror as he combs his hair will not pull out or open his door. Beware when you can't tell what the driver is doing. He is the one who might pull out or open his door.

In this picture, the fence and trash bin block our view of the parking lot to the left. The garage on the left and the bushes on the right ahead block our view of the intersection, including the sidewalk.

Lines of stopped vehicles create blind areas just as lines of parked vehicles do. Here our view to the right is blocked.

Look for alleys and driveways blocked from sight by vehicles, bushes, buildings, etc. Look for individual blockages like the van, cars, etc., (below).

Check the open spaces between them.

LOOK FOR HOLES: From here this intersection looks blind to the left.

However, just a short distance farther up the road, when we recheck to the left, we find this space between the trees and the bushes.

Here we can see through the trees where the road curves to the right.

These kinds of spaces are just like the spaces we find under trucks, and between cars, etc. By looking into these spaces we can get information about areas which would otherwise be totally blind. Learn to look for these spaces and use them to get early clues. In the winter you may be able to see through bushes or hedges which are full of leaves in summer. In the situation shown below, our minimum checks should include: to the right of the big old Mack truck, under it, into it, between it and the dump truck, and under, inside and to the left of the dump truck.

Recognizing blind areas is a very special skill, a very special way of seeing and of thinking about what you see while driving. Learn to know every time your view is blocked. Most drivers haven't a clue.

The skills of recognizing and dealing with blind areas are extremely important to driving well. Learning and using them will go a very long way toward making your driving smooth, safe, efficient, and rewarding. Learning, using, and developing these skills are fun, too. You can't help but feel good when you quickly and easily identify and control dangers that most drivers do not even realize might exist.

It keeps getting better. You learn this way of seeing and thinking — this way of LOOKING FOR TROUBLE, and you notice more and more and drive better and better! It's like getting extremely good at baseball, or the piano, or art, or mathematics. It's a whole new world far beyond the ordinary! It's beyond safety and efficiency and economy. It's one important part of being great at doing the most complex psychomotor activity that ordinary humans do — DRIVING!

Finally, think about the phrase "blind areas". A "blind area" is a place into which one cannot see.

CANNOT SEE! Like being blindfolded — would you drive a car blindfolded?

DO NOT CREATE BLIND AREAS WHERE NONE EXIST NATURALLY: We are taught to keep our eye on the ball. We must concentrate on our reading. We learn to stare at the T.V. screen. Rarely are we expected to see a wide variety of details in a broad area and to understand their interrelationships.

Have you been to a three-ring circus? There was too much happening all at the same time. There was a completely different act going on in each of the three rings. There were spotlights of various colors shining and moving on different parts of each ring. The roustabouts were doing all kinds of work in the dimly lit background. Off in a corner, some clowns were fooling around. Above it all the brass band thundered. The audience responded to different things in different rings. Peddlers moved through the audience. You tried to cope with your sticky cotton-candy and pay attention to your father as he directed your attention to whatever he thought particularly important at the moment. Too much all at the same time!

Driving in traffic can be that way.

Most likely, you were not taught to see everything all at the same time. You were probably taught to keep you eye on the ball, pay attention to your book, and watch a T.V. screen. Most drivers were. Therefore, it is very easy for people to spend their entire driving lives seeing very little because they limit their vision artificially without realizing it. Some simply follow the car ahead like this.

Others may feel very well informed because they keep track of a few vehicles near them like this.

Never be satisfied with this,

or even this,

when you can have this.

Use your eyes! Give your brain all the pertinent information you can get for it. One day your life may suddenly depend on that information!

PERIPHERAL AREAS: Peripheral areas are *not* blind areas. Peripheral areas are in plain sight, but they are off to the sides. They are places like gas stations, alleys, driveways, parking lots, and front yards. Because they are off to the sides, they are just as easy to ignore as blind areas.

Check gas stations more than once as you approach them.

Often gas stations contain blind areas. There can be a lot of traffic going into and out of gas stations. The same is true for parking lots, especially drive-ins and grocery stores. Do not ignore alleys and driveways. Look for them! See what is happening on lawns and sidewalks. You can be ambushed from a peripheral area in plain sight. Don't be.

MIRRORS: Check your mirror(s) at least every five seconds. Yes, that often! Know what is behind your car because it matters. It matters every time you change lanes, every time you stop, every time you slow down. It matters every time you see something which might force you to slow down, stop, or change lanes, especially if you are forced to slow down, stop, or change lanes suddenly. It matters *after* every turn, *after* every lane change, *after* every merge.

Knowing what is happening behind your car gives you a true picture of your traffic situation. *Traffic is not all ahead of you.* There is traffic *behind* you, too. Knowing the total situation, having the most details about it, lets you handle any situation better.

Too often, drivers notice a situation ahead, watch it develop, decide what to do about it, and *then* check their mirror(s), only find out that the following traffic makes their escape plan impossible. Check your mirror(s) *before* making a plan. That way, your plan will fit into the total traffic pattern.

Every time you see trouble ahead, check your mirror(s) immediately. Avoid getting rear-ended. Avoid cutting off people.

As soon as you see any potential problem ahead, check your mirror(s) so you can understand the whole situation. As soon as you see a problem on your right front, check your left rear. As soon as you see a problem on your left front, check your right rear. Look for safe places to escape the problem. Look to see whether you will be boxed in next to or behind the problem.

THE OVERALL TRAFFIC SCENE IS MADE UP OF DETAILS: Where to aim, road surface and condition, road signs, traffic signals, sections of road, vehicular traffic, pedestrian traffic, blind areas, peripheral areas and mirrors added together form the overall traffic scene through which you drive. Do not be fooled by the phrase "overall traffic scene." It *does not* mean a *general* idea about a broad and deep driving scene. It means a *very specific* idea about a broad and deep driving scene. It is made up of details —details that matter. Think details. Look for details. Just as a six inch deep blanket of snow is made up of billions of snow flakes, the overall traffic scene is made up of many significant details.

Details! Details! Details! Imagine you are following a car which has confused you by slowing down too much at two intersections in a row. Drivers usually have reasons for slowing. Get some details. The driver seems to be very busy looking around. The car has out-of-state license plates. There is a good chance that the driver is looking for a street or an address. If he finds it, he may suddenly turn or even pull over to park.

The traffic story is written in the details. A broken tailpipe is dangling under that white Ford station wagon ahead of you. The green Toyota next to you seems to be in a hurry. The driver of the good looking old Buick convertible is shaking his head and left hand in time to the music on his radio. That bicycle ahead and to the right is a little wobbly; the rider seems unsure of himself. The bus behind you is close.

Your brain will put together whatever information you give it to form your overall traffic scene. Give it skimpy and unimportant information, and it will give you back a skimpy picture full of gaps — a dull story which will let your mind wander. Give your brain as much of the best information you can, and it will give you back a remarkably complete, well integrated, easy to use, four dimensional mental videotape of the traffic scene. (The fourth dimension is time.) You will enjoy a constantly changing story which will fascinate you every time you drive.

Add up the details and you will seem to know everything about traffic. You will cruise gracefully through and around really rough traffic with little *apparent* effort. Being really good is making the difficult look easy.

THE OVERALL TRAFFIC SCENE CHANGES: The overall traffic scene is like a fascinating videotape, not a photograph or a painting. The overall traffic scene changes — constantly. It changes because you are moving through it, and it changes because many of the things in it are moving, too. A pedestrian walks to the curb, stops, looks at you, waits for you to pass, or runs in front of you. A child drops a school book as he crosses in front of you. Then he notices his loss and runs back to get the book. A car is standing still at the curb, then it is pulling out into traffic ahead of you. Another car is going along smoothly ahead of you. Suddenly, it pulls over to the curb. A turn signal is flashing. Then it is not flashing. A traffic light is green. Then it is yellow. There was nothing behind your car. Now there is a big truck almost touching your rear bumper. The light changes to green and the car ahead of yours accelerates away briskly, then stops quickly. The road is dry where you are now, but icy at the intersection.

The details change. Never look at anything significant in traffic only once. Keep rechecking the changes. Watch the situations *develop*. Be ready for new details and new situations.

Concentrating on one problem or one area will ruin everything by shutting out your overall traffic scene. Without constant rechecking of all significant areas, your big picture will become a big blind area surrounding one small spot of understanding. You will lose track of everything but the one small area you are watching. Meanwhile, in all the unseen areas, there may be hazards preparing to ambush you. If you concentrate on one area or one detail, your car is *out of control*! *You are driving blind*!

If your traffic driving is just a jumble of hazards rushing at you one after another, you simply are not seeing anywhere near enough. You are concentrating on only the most obvious situations too long, after noticing them too late. You are missing most of what is happening. You should always see much, much more than the things that force you to react to them.

If you use your eyes properly, traffic will make sense. All parts of it will be related in order of importance, time, and space. Your speed will always be correct and your driving will have a graceful rhythm. If there is not a flowing rhythm to your traffic driving, your seeing habits are bad.

Seeing well in traffic will give you control. Control will give you time. You will have time to keep track of traffic; time to check blind and peripheral areas; time to aim; time to look for new problems ahead and mixed in among the old ones; time to check road conditions, signs, and signals; time to get the details and understand the changes.

You will even know exactly the right time to take your eyes off the road to check mirrors, blind spots, gauges, etc. You will have time to figure out each situation and decide the best thing to do about those situations you *do* need to

control. For each situation, you will automatically adjust your speed and path if needed. You will check your mirror in plenty of time when you think that you might have to stop suddenly. You will get eye contact with pedestrians and other drivers whenever possible. (Many situations are resolved automatically when the people involved look each other in the eye.) You will warn people at just the right time with a friendly honk of your horn. You will never just keep approaching a clumsy or dangerous situation hoping that nobody will do the wrong thing and cause you to crash. You will not have to trust strangers to save you. You will be in control!

Remember, *steering is not driving*! Many driver's license holders concern themselves mainly with steering. These are the people who will tell you how easy driving is. They go along thinking that they are great drivers when actually, most of the time they are not driving at all. They are steering (rather poorly), following the car ahead, and staying ignorant of most of the potential conflicts that wait to ambush them. One day, a hazard does not take care of itself. These great "drivers" crash and sob, "He came out of nowhere. I'm so sorry!"

PUTTING THE CHANGING DETAILS ALL TOGETHER: Using your eyes to get the constantly changing details of traffic to your brain at the right time is a big job. You will develop your own systems and techniques. A good example of how to use your eyes properly when driving is given on pages 90-97 in Chapter 7 of this book. Following is another much shorter one.

Suppose that you are turning a corner into a new street. A whole new world is about to appear through your windshield. During the last half of the turn, as you straighten the steering and accelerate back up to cruising speed, see as much of the new scene as possible. Let your eyes roam quickly, broadly, and freely over as much of the scene as you can. Look near and far, right and left. Allow your eyes to pick out the details ahead that matter to your driving. Take an instant to aim. Make sure that your turn is ending perfectly (as planned). Steal a glance at the inside rearview mirror. In a moment you will have a very good idea about exactly where you are in the overall traffic scene and what you will need to watch as you continue forward.

As you drive on, and your view keeps changing, keep rechecking all the places that matter. Get more details by seeing things from different angles at different times as you approach them. Add more and more information to your file on each significant part of the traffic scene. Get the most information about the most important areas, but skip none. watch situations *DEVELOP* with several quick glances while staying alert for new ones. Your eyes need only an instant to see. Do not weld your eyes on one area, trying to get its whole story in one long look.

See what is there. Years ago, when American cars were really big, many American drivers did not see the few, small, foreign cars in traffic. They were looking for big, American cars. Today, many American drivers fail to see motorcycles. Be open-minded. See what is there, not what you expect to see.

Finally, how much should you see?

9 *Chapter Nine*

Maneuvering

Whenever your car is in motion, you are maneuvering it. You maneuver it in traffic, around curves, through snow, onto expressways, and so on. The kind of maneuvering covered in this chapter, however, is the kind that usually involves low speeds, close clearances, sharp turns — stuff like: angle parking, pulling over, pulling out, turning around.

Some people, who do not understand driving, judge drivers on just such maneuvers. A new driver can really impress these people simply by backing straight down a long driveway or by parking between the lines in a parking lot.

On the other hand, there are the brutes and the beasts who drive... Well, they don't really *drive*, do they? They seem to be too lazy even to try. So what if they run over the curb? Who cares if they ram the bumper of the car ahead or behind or both when backing into a parking space? Park between the lines in the parking lot? Why bother?

Close maneuvers *are* part of driving and can be done gracefully and easily. No one should consider himself a good driver unless he can do them well. Neither should anyone consider himself a good driver *only* because he can do them well. In close maneuvers, as in all areas of driving performance, the keys are knowing what to do and how to do it and *caring enough to pay attention to what you're doing.*

PULLING AWAY FROM THE CURB: Pulling into traffic from the curb *is* a lane change. You need to signal. With the signal on, the car running and in gear — ready to go, look through the windshield. Before you check ahead for traffic left and right and near and far, pick out the path you will follow. Visualize it. Check it for bumps and holes, etc. Have an idea whether it takes a long, easy angle or makes a couple of short, sharp curves. In other words, just as in planning a turn, *know* where your car will end up and how it will get there *before* you start the maneuver.

Once you have picked out your path, check up ahead for traffic. Check whether anyone is pulling out of an alley, driveway, or parking space ahead and coming toward you. Check for cyclists, j-walking pedestrians, etc. Even check whether anyone is turning into your street up ahead at the next intersection. If there is a problem ahead, wait. Then start checking all over again.

If there is no problem ahead, check your inside rearview mirror next. You may have to look through the windows of the car(s) parked behind yours. See whether anything is coming from behind you. If there is something approaching, how far back is it and how fast is it coming? Can you see anyone else pulling away from the curb or out of a driveway, or an alley, or turning from a cross street behind you? Is there a driver in the car parked behind yours? Is he moving his car? Is he preparing to move his car?

If there is a problem behind you, you'll have to wait and start all over again. If not, check your outside rearview mirror. The area shown by this mirror *must* be clear for you to move. It must have no traffic in it and no traffic entering it from behind. If there is a problem here, once again, you'll have to wait and start over.

If there is no problem, check your left side blind spot. Check whether anyone is turning left out of a nearby driveway, alley, or cross street. Is a pedestrian, animal, or cyclist approaching your vehicle from this area? On one-way streets, is anyone pulling out of a parking space in this area?

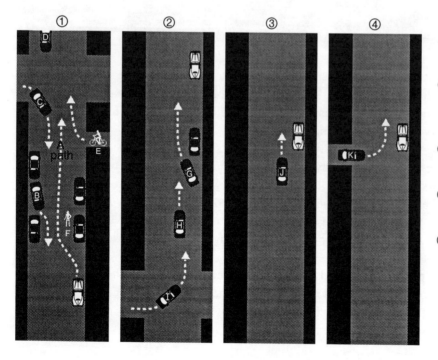

① Check Ahead
Find Path (A), Check
Traffic (B, C, D, E, F)

② Check Inside Mirror
Check Traffic (G, H, I)

③ Check Outside Mirror
Check Traffic (J)

④ Check Blind Spot
Check Traffic (K)

Everything okay?

Good. Look forward quickly. Quickly remember the path you picked out. Pull out as you recheck ahead for new problems.

He who hesitates after making all the checks is asking to get hit or go through the whole procedure again. That's why it's important to pick out your path first and to do the traffic checks in the proper order; near and far ahead (through the windshield), far behind (through the inside mirror), near behind and to the side (through the outside mirror), very near behind and far to the side (blind spot). That way you make the best use of your time. You don't *waste* time figuring out where and how to go *after* you have checked traffic. You keep adding more and more information, working closer and closer to the car until you know you are clear all around and actually start to pull out.

Once you have pulled out, check the inside rearview mirror again. Is everything back there still alright? Did you miss something? Is a car coming faster than you thought? Is what you missed right on your tail? Did you cut it off? Remember, *you* decided to pull out. Therefore, it was your responsibility to pull into traffic without getting into anybody's way.

When pulling out of a parking space just beyond an intersection, it is a good idea to check your *right* side blind spot, too.

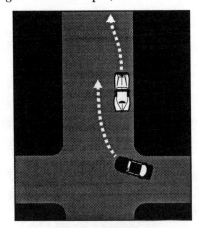

A car coming around the corner can get into your way quite quickly.

When pulling out of a parallel parking space from behind another parked car, you may have to back up to get enough room to clear the rear end of the car ahead. Take a lot of space when it is available. You're backing up anyway, and a lot of space will make pulling out so much easier.

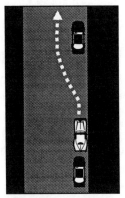

This is so much easier...

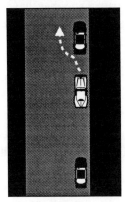

...than this.

When backing up to get this space, never just assume that everything is clear and safe behind your car. Never just peek at your mirror(s). Twist around into a proper backing up posture and check to both sides before moving the car.

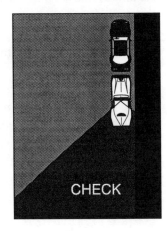

137

Remember Kenny from the chapter about looking for trouble? Once upon a time, he was hit by a car. Kenny and his mother were j-walking across the urban street on which they lived. While they were standing between two parked cars, another car pulled into the space behind the car to their left and hit it. It rolled forward very slowly, just enough to touch Kenny's left leg lightly. At about age six, Kenny thought it was really neat to have been "hit" by a car. Still, he knew better than to tell his mother. He knew she'd get all excited. He knew she'd take him to the doctor. He knew she'd give the driver of the car that had hit the parked car a great deal of trouble.

The point is that in moving your car just inches you can touch somebody and injure him, or scare him, causing him to injure himself. Consider an elderly person who gets scared when your car begins to move. He thinks he might get hit or crushed. He stumbles and falls. In falling, he hits his head on your car. He gets paralyzed. Big lawsuit! Lots of guilt! Even when moving just inches, KNOW what is near and/or approaching your car!

If you have backed up close to the car behind yours to get space, don't waste it! Cut your wheels all the way NOW. Don't forget to shift into drive. Check traffic as above. Pull forward. See whether your car will clear the one ahead. Because it takes time to check this clearance, recheck over your left shoulder (your blind spot and beyond to the rear) before actually pulling out of the parking space. You may have to check your forward clearance several times. Look over your shoulder after each clearance check. Many times you will have to recheck traffic ahead, too. On extremely narrow streets, you may have to check the clearance for your left front fender. (See illustration on right.)

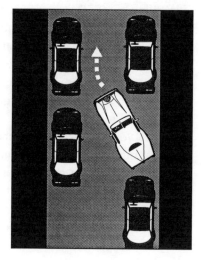

There may be a truck parked right behind your car. In that case, your inside rearview mirror will be of little use to you. You'll have to rely heavily on looking over your left shoulder several times as you *creep* out of the space.

PULLING OVER TO THE CURB: First, pick out your spot. Everything you do in pulling over to the curb depends upon your *knowing* exactly where you want to park: when to release the gas pedal, when and how hard to press the brake pedal, when and how much to steer, when to check the mirror and blind spot, when to signal. Never pull over "somewhere over there." Pick out the exact spot you want. See and know just where it is *before* you start pulling over. Check your spot and the path to it for holes, debris, toys, children, animals, etc. Then pull over. Because you are slowing down, you must know what is behind you. Check your inside mirror. Because you are moving over toward the right, you must know what is behind you to the right. Check your right blind spot.

Pulling over to the curb *is* a lane change, so signal. Remember, though, that signalling to pull over *can* be more confusing than helpful to other drivers. If oncoming drivers think you are signalling to turn right into a cross street, they may turn left in front of you. (See illustration on right.)

Drivers waiting to turn right into your street may pull out in front of you.

In the middle of the block, following drivers may think you are signalling to turn right into an alley or driveway and react inappropriately. Notice how you react to a right turn signal given in the middle of the block. A stop signal given with your arm and hand might show your intentions to following drivers better than a right turn signal. Be very careful about when, how, and even whether you signal when pulling over to the curb.

Whenever you give a signal, try to time it so that its meaning is clear. Remember that you cannot give a properly timed signal until you can see where you want to go.

Once you have pulled over, how do you know whether your car really is near the curb? You don't just keep going until you run into the curb and then move away a little. Hitting curbs is rough on the curbs, the tires, the steering, the suspension, the passengers, and your pride. You don't get out of the car and look. That's embarrassing and needless. You don't lean over into the passenger seat, open the door, and look. That's also embarrassing and needless.

Many streets have gutters between the curbs and the actual road surface. Often the joint between the gutter pavement and the street pavement is uneven or broken. If you try, you can feel when your right front tire goes over the uneven joint.

Once you feel the joint, you know exactly where your tire is. Then, depending on how wide your tire is and how close it is to the edge of your car, with a little practice, you can figure out whether to stop or get just a little closer to the curb.

The bottom of the curb forms a line where it meets the street or the gutter. Look at it while stopping or just after you have stopped. If you are parked properly, it will cut into your hood just a little to the right of center.

Get used to where it should be. If you cannot see your hood, you can still use this method. Find the right place on the top of your dashboard and use that.

Another good method is just to line up with the car in front of your parking space. Line up both sides of the two cars. Put your own body right behind the other car's steering wheel. This works well if the car ahead is about the same width as yours and is parked correctly. Naturally, it will not work at all if there is no car parked ahead of yours.

Always make sure your car is parked straight. Don't try to do this by looking at the curb or at anything else near the car. Just look way up ahead as if you were driving along, then drop your eyes to the hood. You'll see immediately whether your car is parked straight.

FORWARD PARALLEL PARKING: If a parallel parking space is long enough, you do not have to back into it. You can pull in forward. Do all the same things you would do just to pull over to the curb and get your speed *way down*. You need time to figure. Turn in very sharply at just about the time your own body is passing the front end of the car behind the parking space. Make the best use of whatever space you have. Try to get the front end of your car as close as possible to the curb in the shortest distance possible. Then line up with the car ahead of the space. Take plenty of time and make as many clearance checks as necessary.

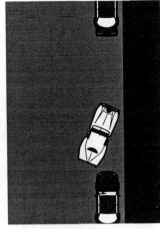
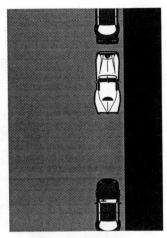

Turn in very sharply when your body passes front end of car behind space;

Get as close as possible to curb in shortest distance possible;

Line up with the car ahead.

Trying to line up with a car much wider or narrower than yours takes a good deal of practice. You must adjust your judgments for the differing widths.

TURNING AROUND: To turn your car around, you can drive around the block, use an alley or driveway, make a u-turn, us a cul-de-sac, make a three point turn, or use a parking lot.

Simply *driving around the block* is frequently the easiest and safest way to turn around. It can even be the fastest.

There are four ways of turning around *using an alley or driveway*.

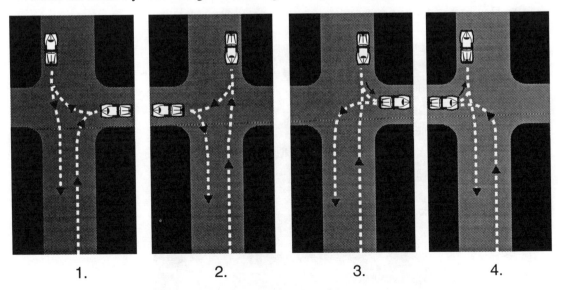

Because they involve backing to the left and backing across at least two traffic lanes, the methods shown in illustrations 1 and 2 are more clumsy and less safe than those shown in illustrations 3 and 4.

When *making a u-turn*, the car just seems to keep turning and turning. This makes u-turns sort of fun. U-turns are also sort of dangerous. Because the car turns so far in so little time and space, u-turns require a tremendous amount of checking, careful planning, and perfect timing.

You have to check everything behind, to the left, and ahead before making a u-turn. This check must include people and vehicles that *might* move into your path as well as those that will. The driver making the u-turn in the illustration below has at least five potential conflicts to see.

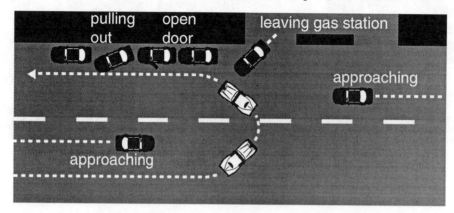

You have to plan the turn carefully, knowing that the car can turn around in the space and time available. If there is any traffic at all, timing is critical! It must correlate perfectly all elements of a 180 degree turn and 180 degrees of traffic. The timing and planning must predict the positions and actions of every traffic element ahead, behind, and to both sides for the entire duration of the turn.

Finally, the driver must monitor *EVERYTHING CONSTANTLY* and be ready to react to the unexpected without getting into someone else's way.

Laws tell drivers where u-turns are legal. Obey them and use common sense. If you must do a "u-ey," do it where traffic is very light and space and visibility are best. Don't make a u-turn on a hill or a curve. Don't make a u-turn in an intersection unless allowed by law.

This is a *cul-de-sac*.

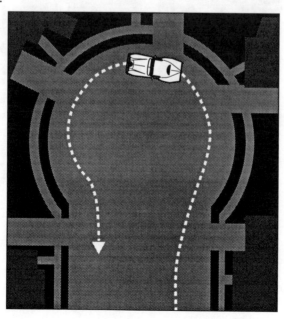

It's a dead-end street widened at the end so vehicles can turn around to get out of the street easily. Using a cul-de-sac is very much like making a u-turn, but a great deal easier.

Plan the entire turn *before* beginning it. Plan to stay along the curb. Keep checking near and far ahead as in driving through any curve. Periodically check quite far ahead through the driver's side window. At about the half way point, recheck the end point of the turn and check the street for other approaching traffic. Keep an eye out for traffic in the driveways, on the sidewalks and lawns. Just as with u-turns, always turn left.

Vehicles parked in the cul-de-sac can make careful planning very important.

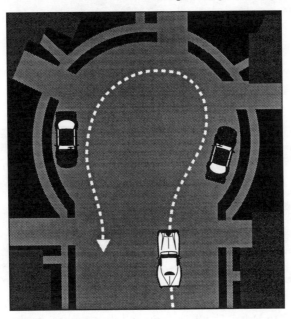

THREE POINT TURNS: Where there are no blocks to go around and no alleys, driveways, or parking lots to use, drivers make u-turns and *three point turns*. They make three point turns in relatively narrow dead-end streets and on two-lane, country roads.

Three point turns are similar to u-turns. You begin them in much the same way. However, because the street is not wide enough to allow a complete turn about in one sweep, you have to back up in the middle of a three point turn.

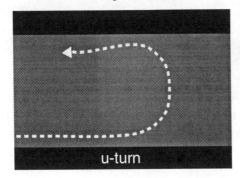

u-turn

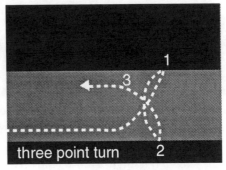

three point turn

Preparing to make a three point turn, place your car's right side quite near the right edge of the road or the right curb. Then, with the transmission in Drive, your steering cut all the way to the left, and your left turn signal on, check traffic everywhere ahead, behind, left, and even right, before you begin.

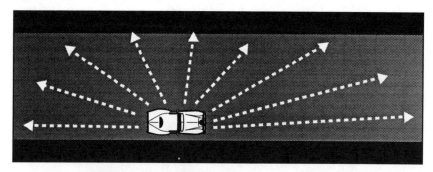

Then, move the car forward in a sharp turn to the left. Get your front wheels close to the curb or edge of the road at point one. Shift to Reverse. Cut the steering all the way back to the right. Check *everywhere*.

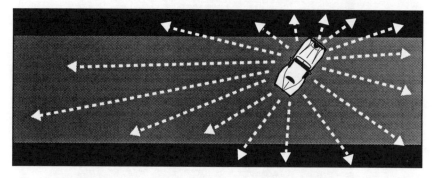

Looking through the back window, back up to point two. Once again, do not hit the curb or drop off the edge of the road. Shift to Drive. Cut the steering all the way back to the left. Check mostly where you want to go, and way back toward the right for approaching traffic which might try to pass in front of your vehicle.

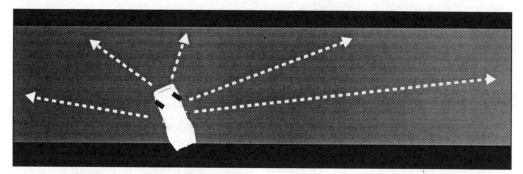

Then go. If the right front of your car will go near the road edge or curb as you finish the three point turn, you can easily pay too much attention to this area and forget to aim along the lane in which you should end up. If you do that, you will keep turning too long and end your turn way out in the middle of the street. You might even end up on the wrong side of the street with traffic coming at you. Aim! Check your right front as much as needed, but aim too.

As you pull away after your three point turn, check the inside rearview mirror.

PLANNING: As usual, pick a good spot in which to do your three point turn. Don't do it near a hill or curve. Approaching drivers may not be able to see your car blocking the road until it is too late.

Check along the edge of the road for low obstacles like fire plugs, stumps, large rocks, etc. When you back up, you will not be able to see such obstacles and may back into them. Some drivers have even backed right *over* them!

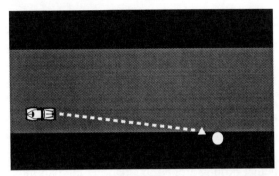

Pick your spot. Look for low obstacles along the right edge of the road. Drivers have backed right over such obstacles.

Drivers even back into things they *can* see, things like sign posts and young trees. They *can* see them, but they don't, because they are rushing to get out of the middle of the road. They may be rushing because they have not taken the time to plan the maneuver carefully in advance, and traffic is bearing down on them.

Out in the country, you may want to use the road shoulders for more space when turning around. As usual, though, think ahead. If the shoulder is clean, well packed gravel, go ahead and use it. With the added space you might even be able to make a u-turn instead of a three point turn. If, however, the shoulder is sand, forget it. It's easy to get stuck in sand. It's also easy to get stuck in mud. Stay off earthen or grassy shoulders when it's raining and after heavy rains or long periods of rain. Be careful of mud puddles and snow too. If the shoulder has tall grass, do you think the grass may be hiding a 2 x 4 with a nail in it, or a lot of broken bottles, or soft earth? If there is a high drop off from the pavement to the shoulder, stay on the paved surface.

Picking your spot on a dead-end, city street can be very interesting because of parked vehicles.

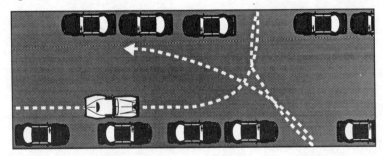

Earlier in this section, you were told to begin a three point turn by turning your front wheels all the way to the left while the car was standing still. That was so you could make the sharpest possible turn. Many drivers, driver education teachers, and driver education textbooks tell you *never to turn the wheels unless the car is moving*. What's the truth?

The truth is that if you turn the wheels while the car is moving, you will not make the sharpest possible turn. You will waste whatever space it takes to get the wheels turned full left. The truth is also that if you turn the front wheels while the car is standing still, you *are* causing extra wear on the steering system, the tires, and the pavement.

There is even more to it than that. In the old days, before power steering, it was nearly impossible to turn the front wheels of some really big, heavy cars while they were standing still. If you moved these cars ever so slowly, though, it was fairly easy to steer them. Thus was born the rule that you never steer while the car is standing still.

Power steering came along, and most people began breaking that rule without bad results. In the end, the easiest way for the driver is to steer while standing still. The easiest way for the car is not to. The choice, as in most areas of driving, is YOURS.

You can ease the strain a little if you ease up on the brake pedal several times when steering while standing still.

Avoid turning around in intersections. It's probably illegal. It's surely clumsy. *Whatever is clumsy is probably dangerous.*

TURNING AROUND IN A PARKING LOT: Whether turning around in a parking lot, parking in one, or just driving out of one, remember that parking lots are less predictable and more confusing than streets. In parking lots there is *always* a great deal to watch. There may be pedestrians milling around all over the place. There may be cars going forward and backward in the right and wrong directions. There may even be skateboarders and/or bicyclists anywhere. Never relax in a parking lot. Be at least as alert as you are on the street.

As soon as possible after entering a parking lot, try to figure out how it is set up. Then, drive down the main aisles to go long distances and turn into the parking aisles to park. *Do not cut across aisles.* It's silly. It makes vision and predictability difficult for you and others.

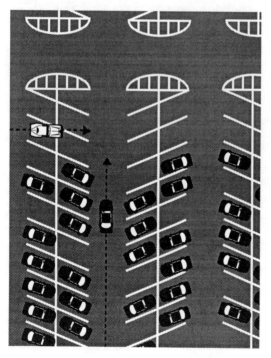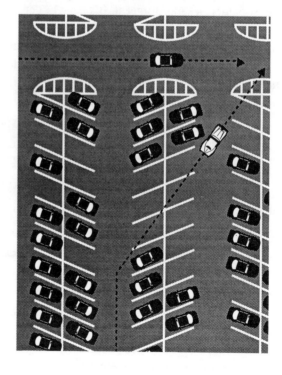

When approaching intersections in parking lots, never be satisfied with checking traffic as you would on the street, but check back down the next aisle, too. Look between and through the parked cars. See who is coming out and heading for the same space you are.

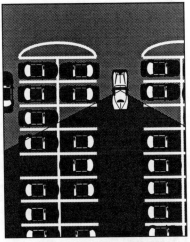

When turning into main aisles, stay on your own side of the road.

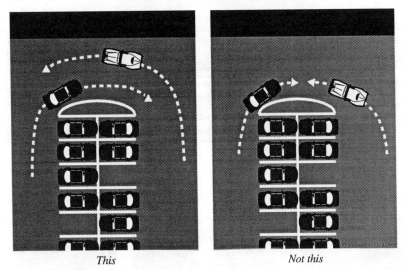

This   *Not this*

When turning around in a parking lot, remember that it was not put there just so you could turn around in it. It has a purpose and an arrangement. Don't drive in and take over. Don't assume that everybody will realize that you want to turn around. Move over, don't assume that anybody will go out of his way to help you turn around. You are the outsider. It's up to you to blend in with what's happening in the parking lot, not the other way around. In fact, some factory and office building parking lots are posted with signs to keep out drivers who want to turn around.

Using a small, empty parking lot can be a quick, easy way to turn around. Simply make a well planned, well monitored u-turn. Plan your turn as early as possible, before entering the lot if you can. Make the turn about the way you use a cul-de-sac. Stick to the outside edge of the parking lot. Always turn toward the left. Because we drive on the right side of the road, u-turns to the right are freaks. They put your vehicle on the inside of the turn instead of the outside. The outside is far more

comfortable, predictable, and safe. The inside will confuse and may surprise other drivers to whom you seem to be doing the maneuver backwards! In short, u-turns to the right are clumsy, less safe, and mark you as an unskilled or, worse, an unthinking driver.

In larger and/or more used parking lots, do whatever makes sense. Drive down one aisle and come back up another as if you were driving around the block. Drive down main aisles instead of parking aisles, etc.

In suburban strip areas where parking lots are crowded together along both sides of the street, pick a parking lot on the LEFT side of the road. This eliminates the problem of making a left turn across a busy street out of the parking lot on the right.

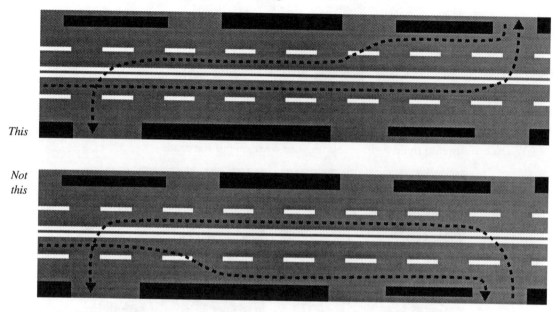

This

Not this

PARKING IN PARKING LOTS: Parking lot aisles are usually set up in one of three ways.

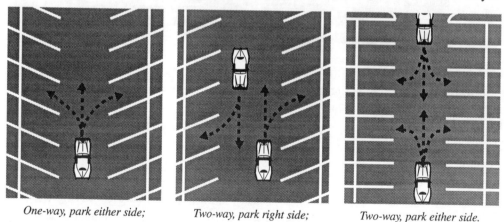

One-way, park either side;   *Two-way, park right side;*   *Two-way, park either side.*

Try to figure out the aisle before you drive into it. Look for signs showing the right way to go. Look for arrows painted on the pavement. See which way the spaces line up (they should open *toward* you).

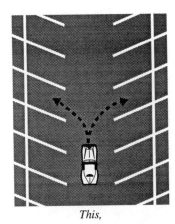
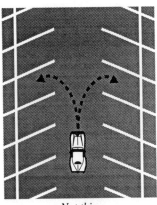

This, *Not this.*

See whether the rear ends of the parked cars point toward you (they should).

If you go the wrong way, you'll probably find it very difficult at best to park, and people going the right way will probably be upset with you.

Once you are driving the proper direction down an aisle, look for a parking space. Scan the line of rear bumpers. Look for a gap, a place where a car isn't. Check through the windows of the car on the nearside of what you hope is a space. Look for the top part of a short car. You won't be able to see its rear bumper in line with all the others, but you may be able to see its upper body in the parking space. If you don't see a little car, check for several shopping carts parked in the space. Double check spaces very near the building entrances. They are probably open because they are for handicapped parking only.

Think you see a space?

Good. As usual, everything you do depends upon where you want to end up.

If you pick a space on the left side, move your car to the right side. If you pick a space on the right side, move your car to the left side.

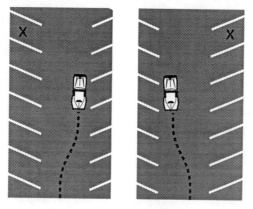

This gives you more room in which to maneuver. Remember, *you are always in traffic*, so check your appropriate blind spot before moving over.

Signal.

Begin your turn into the space late, about when your car's front end is even with the line marking the nearside of the chosen space. (See right.)

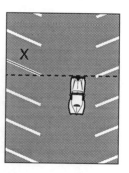

Doing it that way, you'll have the most possible space out in the aisle in which to swing your car around and get lined up with the parking slot. An early or wide turn will put you in conflict with the cars on both sides of your chosen parking slot.

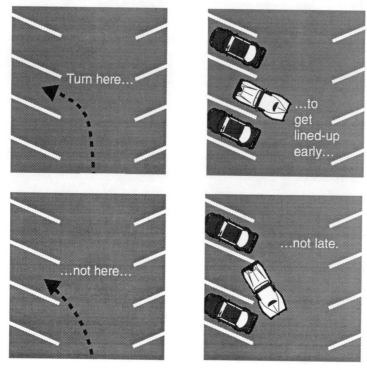

Signal and check your appropriate blind spot before beginning your turn. Check clearances as necessary.

When you park in a slot that butts up against a wall or street or grassy area, it will be harder to stay between the lines and to know when your car gets to the proper angle. This is because once you are part way into the slot, you will no longer be able to see the lines and there will be nothing ahead to give you a clue.

Driver of white car can still aim using lines ahead and other parked cars ahead.

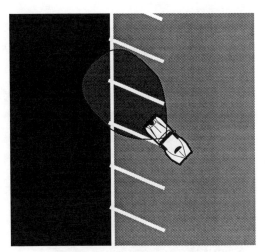

Here he cannot, because of blind spot low in front of his car (shaded area).

To park correctly, pay very careful attention to the location and angle of the line on the nearside of your slot just as you begin turning and can still see it.

If your car has very low mounted fog or driving lights or an air dam under its front bumper, learn not to pull in too near curbs and concrete dividers.

BACKING OUT OF A PARKING LOT SPACE: Backing out of a parking lot space requires you to check and recheck *everything all the time*! Check and recheck clearances on both sides and to the rear. Before backing, check near your car for clearance, pedestrians, shopping carts, posts, and people opening car doors.

Plan and monitor your turn so that you can get your car out of the space and turned without being in conflict with the vehicles on either side of your parking spot or behind your car.

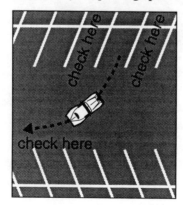

Check and recheck the aisle into which you are backing for vehicular and pedestrian traffic from *both* directions. Keep rechecking this until you are completely out of the parking space. Check that no one else is backing into the same area you are.

When parked near an intersection, you may not assume that no one is coming around the corner.

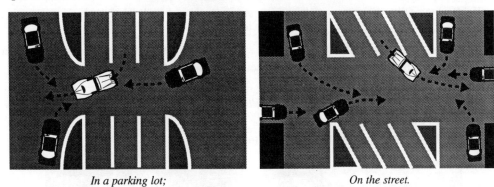

In a parking lot;   *On the street.*

Never just get out of the space. Always place your car in the best position for going forward.

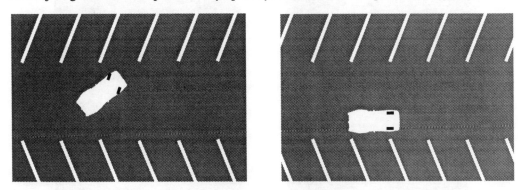

It may seem like too much trouble to get backed out properly and straighten the front wheels, but it isn't. It's so much easier to pull away. You see people in parking lots all the time being too lazy to back out properly, only to struggle to get straight and pull away.

When backing out blind because you are parked next to a van, etc., just follow standard procedure but go unusually slowly and be ready to stop when someone approaching on your blind side blows his horn, or a pedestrian appears suddenly. Likewise, when passing long lines of angle parked cars, especially on the street, be ready to blow your horn at a driver who may not be able to see your vehicle as he backs out into traffic. Check for lit back-up lights and brake lights. Check for movement of rear bumpers. Check for drivers at the wheel.

In review then, there is so much to do when backing out of a parking lot space. Make sure your car goes exactly where you want it to go. Check and recheck clearances as necessary. Keep looking around and looking around for trouble *everywhere*!

In a small vehicle much of this parking lot maneuvering will seem pretty easy. In a large vehicle, though, you'll have to take it all quite seriously.

HOW TO SIT: Many times it is easier to do a good job of backing out of a parking space by sitting more or less facing straight forward and just turning your upper body, head, and eyes way around to both sides over and over again. It may also be convenient to steer with both hands.

UPHILL AND DOWNHILL PARKING: In some areas with steep hills, the police take uphill and downhill parking very seriously. They have probably had experience with driverless cars rolling uncontrollably down hills. They may ticket your car if you do not park it properly. Even if you don't get a ticket, improper hill parking increases your ri$k.

The idea behind uphill and downhill parking systems is to minimize the chances that a car will run away and/or minimize the damage done if one does run away.

WITHOUT A CURB: When *parking either uphill or downhill without a curb*, turn the front wheels all the way toward the edge of the road just after or just as you stop the car. Set the parking brake and shift to park. If the car does move, it will roll *off* the road.

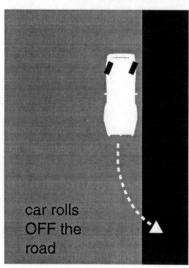

car rolls OFF the road

Uphill

car rolls OFF the road

Downhill

WITH A CURB: When *parking uphill with a curb*, turn the front wheels all the way AWAY from the curb. Shift to neutral. Check behind the car and let it roll slowly backward until the back of the front tire locks in against the curb. Set the parking brake and shift to park.

Don't just release the brakes and crash into the curb. Use the brakes to control the car's speed. Ease the tire up against the curb. The idea is never to *force* the tire into the curb, but to let it roll up against it very smoothly and gently. That's why you use neutral instead of reverse.

To pull out, just follow normal procedure. Shift to drive. Release the parking brake. Signal. Check traffic. Pull out. Remember, however, that your front wheels are turned all the way away from the curb. The car will turn very sharply into traffic. Therefore, do not try for a dragstrip start. Keep your speed way down and work the steering wheel rapidly.

When parking downhill with a curb, turn the front wheels all the way TOWARD the curb. Shift to neutral. Let the car roll slowly forward until the front of the front tire locks in against the curb. Set the parking brake. Shift to park. Once again, the idea is to jam the front tire up against the curb so the car can't run away.

To pull out, *do not* follow normal procedure! Remember that your front wheels are turned toward the curb. If you try to drive away, either you will be prevented from moving by the curb, or you will drive right up over it.

NO, don't just turn the front wheels straight again before pulling out. That puts a strain on the tires, the pavement, the curb, *and* the steering mechanism.

What you do is back up a foot or two before pulling out. This action frees the front tire from the curb. Then straighten the steering either while you back up or after you have stopped backing and pull out normally.

PARKING BRAKE USE: Driving students often ask whether to apply the parking brake before or after shifting to park. Before. Indeed when possible, with the transmission in neutral and the parking brake applied, release the service brakes and let the car settle against the parking brake. Then shift to park. When preparing to pull out, shift out of park first. Then release the parking brake. This will keep the weight of the car mainly on the parking brake, not on the parking gear.

So what?

PARKING WITH CURB

UPHILL	DOWNHILL
pick spot	pick spot
signal	signal
check inside mirror	check inside mirror
check appropriate blind spot	check appropriate blind spot
stop	stop
turn wheels away from curb	turn wheels toward curb
shift to neutral	shift to neutral
check behind car	check ahead of car
ease front tire into curb	ease front tire into curb
set parking brake	set parking brake
shift to park	shift to park

PULLING OUT WITH CURB

UPHILL	DOWNHILL
shift to drive	shift to reverse
release parking brake	release parking brake
	back up and straighten front wheels
	shift to drive
signal	signal
check traffic	check traffic
pull out	pull out

155

You've probably been in a car when the driver had let the car settle against the parking gear either before applying the parking brake, or later when preparing to pull out by releasing the parking brake before shifting out of park. The driver found it difficult to shift out of park. There may even have been a noise when he finally *forced* the transmission out of park. Enough said? It's just easier on the car to keep the weight off the transmission.

Always set the parking brake hard! If you put it on lightly and find that you can drive off with it applied, it cannot have done very much to hold the car in place.

Parking brakes are operated by cables under the car. In the winter these cables can get covered with slush. Then they can freeze solid, especially when the temperature falls during the night. If the cables freeze with the parking brake on, you won't be able to move the car in the morning.

DON'T DRIVE OVER THE CURB: This one will really separate the men from the boys, and the women from the girls, and the sheep from the goats, and the wheat from the chaff. It will separate the real drivers from those who should be passengers.

You are coming out of a side road, an alley, or a driveway, especially a parking lot driveway, and you want to turn right onto the street. You're checking traffic all over the place. Then, just as you are ready to turn right, you realize that you do not know where the curb is. You are too close to it to see it.

You have no idea how high it is or whether there is a big ditch in front of it. Will you embarrass yourself by driving over a curb or through a ditch and over a curb and dropping onto the street, dragging the rear end of your car over the curb? Not if you remember this little trick.

Because you know that you will not be able to see the curb or ditch when you are close to it and ready to turn right, check it when you *can* see it, when you are still thirty or fifty feet back from it. Place the car a few feet from it *then* and *stay* in the same line as you approach the road and check traffic.

10 Chapter Ten

The Lane Change

Ah, what a diverse and wondrous thing is the lane change! It is elegant, complex, simple, dangerous. It is a minor redirection. It is a major challenge. It is quick, and it is slow. It helps. It hinders. It exasperates, and it delights. It is a very common part of driving, and it works like this:

ESSENTIALS OF THE LANE CHANGE

WHILE MAINTAINING	PERFORM	UNDERSTANDING THAT
1. Normal forward vision 2. Adequate following distance 3. Control over your car within the traffic flow	1. See the need for a lane change 2. Check rear 3. Decide 4. Signal 5. Check appropriate blind spot 6. Change lanes 7. Set up in the new lane	The reason(s) for and circumstances surrounding any particular lane change will determine how the steps: 1. Change order 2. Repeat 3. Overlap

These steps are explained below.

1. SEE THE NEED FOR A LANE CHANGE: There are many reasons for changing lanes. Included among them are: leaving a lane which ends ahead; avoiding blockages like accidents, double parked or disabled vehicles, road work, and debris; leaving a lane in which traffic is congested or moving slowly; clearing the way for an overtaking vehicle (especially an emergency vehicle); preparing to park or turn left or right; avoiding others who are parking or turning; avoiding any specific hazard ahead; moving into a lane which offers fewer dangers, a better road surface, greater visibility, or a combination of factors providing better control (a more comfortable place in which to drive); avoiding a collision.

The key to lane changing is realizing early enough that a lane change may be needed. Expect traffic to require you to change lanes at any time with little notice. Actively search for conditions which may force you to change lanes. Look far ahead, gather as many bits of information as possible, and predict traffic flow and its effect upon your intended course. This will usually allow you to check following traffic and plan and execute a neat lane change well before you begin running out of time and space.

2. CHECK REAR: *Immediately* after being alerted that a lane change may be required, check the inside rearview mirror, focusing mostly on the lane into which you would like to move. Is any traffic there? How much? You will already have some information about this from your normal, periodic mirror checks, so you can also begin to look for spaces big enough to accommodate your

158

vehicle and see whether they are located close behind or far back.

This might be all you can find out before you must look forward again. Fine! You've obtained a good amount of worthwhile information. Remember, this is the planning stage, the time to *take the time* to get everything set up properly. Remember also that what is directly behind you (in your own lane) is generally of little importance in lane changing, unless it is following closely, approaching fast, or changing lanes, too.

Look *forward*. Check that you are maintaining adequate distance and that no new problems are developing ahead. If you've found no good spaces during your first mirror check, look for a spot just ahead in the lane you want. It may be the only place you can go.

Now, check the mirror again. Find out whether the spaces are catching up, dropping back, or maintaining the same position relative to you. Are they getting longer, staying the same length, or getting shorter? (Note: if many vehicles ahead and/or behind you are changing lanes, they will fill the spaces currently available very quickly. Therefore, if you cannot make rapid, accurate judgments, you may be forced to continue straight ahead and get stuck behind whatever is blocking your lane.)

In extremely heavy traffic, just finding a place to go may take a very long time and require continual mirror checking. always make as many mirror checks as you need! By the way, is your mirror adjusted correctly? Are your windows clean?

3. DECIDE: Gathering more and more information about your position in the traffic flow, you will form a lane changing plan. You will decide whether to take a space available now or wait for another, whether to take a space behind, ahead or, maybe, right next to you. This decision will determine future checking, signalling, and positioning.

Neither rush your decision nor nervously just DO a lane change without knowing and understanding what you're doing. Do not just go through the physical actions of signalling, checking, etc., without thinking. Let your brain control your actions.

4. SIGNAL: The signal is required by law. It *should* be given. It should be timed to indicate as accurately as possible when you intend to change lanes. However, never let fumbling around for the turn signal lever delay you enough to make an otherwise lovely lane change dangerous. If something *must* be sacrificed due to the pressure of the situation, let it be the signal.

Signal when there is someplace to go. If you signal when there is obviously nowhere to go, you will confuse following drivers. Moreover, on a busy, urban freeway, once a car has passed you while your turn signal is operating, all the other passing drivers will ignore it, assuming that you are not aware it is flashing.

Whatever you do, *DO NOT EXPECT A FLASHING TURN SIGNAL TO CLEAR THE WAY FOR YOU!* A good lane change should be able to be completed with *no* inconvenience to anyone *without* a signal! You must find the space and make a neat lane change by yourself! The signal just tells others what you are doing.

5. CHECK THE APPROPRIATE BLIND SPOT: Notice the word "appropriate." Sometimes driving students get confused and check *both* blind spots or the wrong one. If you want to move toward the right, check the right blind spot. If you want to move toward the left, check the left blind spot. You do not need to check the other one. You are moving *away* from that side. You cannot possibly cut off or hit anything on that side. Checking the wrong blind spot is at best useless and time consuming when time is precious. At worst, checking the wrong blind spot is distracting and counterproductive.

Do not plan your lane change by checking your blind spot! In most situations you cannot get enough information without using your mirror(s). You will not have a complete picture of what is happening behind you. Besides, you cannot afford to spend that much time looking backward over your shoulder. The car ahead may be stopping — RIGHT NOW!

The blind spot check is a double check or fail safe mechanism. When you have everything fairly well planned with your mirrors and are almost ready to go, you check the appropriate blind spot. If you see something in it, you cancel or adjust the maneuver. If nothing is there, you continue as planned.

On roads with more than two lanes in your direction of travel, always let your blind spot check include the lane on the other side of the space you want. A driver there might be planning a lane change into that same space, and both of you could try to enter it at the same time.

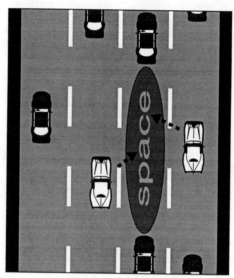

No two objects can occupy the
same space at the same time.

6. CHANGE LANES: *Blend* into the space you've selected. You'll generally have to accelerate to make a smooth lane change. You may have lost some speed unconsciously while making all your checks. You may have had to slow down a bit to wait while the space you picked caught up to you. In addition, your vehicle always must travel farther than the one in front of which you want to change lanes. Yours has to go across lanes as well as forward, while the other has only to move straight ahead. In any case, unless there is an overabundance of space and/or all the traffic is already slowing down, as in making a lane change when approaching a red traffic signal, *do not lose speed while changing lanes, gain it.*

Your car must remain well ahead of the vehicle in front of which you want to change lanes. Sometimes, however, things do not work out quite right. Because he has not yet gained skill at lane changing, a new driver may find both space ahead and time running out while his car stays not much ahead of the vehicle in front of which he has planned to change lanes. Yet he feels committed to the maneuver. In desperation, he may start moving over despite the lack of space. Indeed, he may make things even worse by unconsciously using the brakes to ease the pressure of the situation. The other driver may not notice what's happening in time, or he may believe that he is being crowded out purposely and push back or simply blow his horn. Finally, he might have insufficient space in which to maneuver. In any case, both drivers are in a dangerous position.

Too close but feel committed.

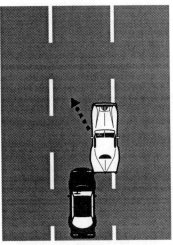

Results when other driver can't maneuver or pushes back OR when you use your brakes.

Always try to keep your wits about you, and avoid these "do or die" situations.

Finally, do not jerk the steering wheel to start the maneuver. Move it smoothly, just a little. Neither should you jerk the car straight at the end of the maneuver. Once you have checked, decided, signalled, and double checked, place almost all of your attention on the new lane so that you can change lanes neatly and straighten the wheels smoothly (aim). A swoop past the center of the new lane and the need to hook back into it show your nervousness or inattention. Violent speed adjustments reveal your poor planning or clumsy execution.

7. SET UP IN THE NEW LANE: Check for immediate hazards. Use the inside mirror to check on the vehicle in front of which you have just placed your car. Get your bearings and consolidate your position in the new lane by adjusting speed and spacing. Resume normal driving activity, and remain alert for another problem to appear before you have time to congratulate yourself on a well done lane change.

SOME MISCELLANEOUS LANE CHANGING THOUGHTS, TECHNIQUES AND TACTICS: When checking your mirror, do not concentrate only on what is relatively near you. In certain instances (usually expressways), there may be a great speed differential between your group of traffic and someone quite a bit farther back who, coming up fast, may decide to change lanes and "blow right past" you and everybody else in your pack at undiminished speed. If you are unaware of his approach, you might begin to change lanes just as he arrives, cutting him off very badly. When circumstances warrant, check far back in *all* lanes for him and avoid the possibility of a serious rear end collision.

When making lane changes to the left, you may use your outside mirror to get information about what is relatively close on that side.

When your only chance to change lanes is to wait for a space a long distance back to catch up to you, watch the vehicles directly behind yours. While you wait, be very careful not to slow down so much or so rapidly that your speed reduction becomes obvious to their drivers. At least one of them, once aware that his lane is slowing down, is quite likely to change lanes into the very space for which you are awaiting before it can reach you.

The wait for a semi trailer truck to pass your car so you can change lanes behind it can seem endless. Make sure that you *do wait* long enough. It is very tempting to begin the lane change just as the truck trailer's rear wheels are passing your driver's door. There may be quite a few feet of trailer *behind* those wheels!

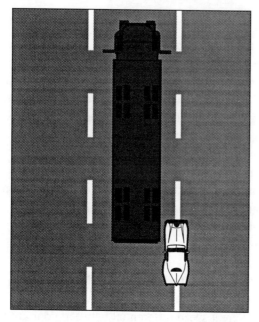

As a general rule, you must be travelling at least as fast as traffic in the new lane to change lanes with any efficiency or smoothness whatsoever. If you are going slower than they are, they and all the spaces will merely keep passing you. You will *never* get your chance. Keep in mind

that it is *NOT their duty to let you in*. It is up to *you* to go where *you* want to go *within* the flow of traffic.

A related problem is the driver who, finding himself balked in his lane, locates a space into which to change lanes, but never bothers to determine whether the vehicle which defines the rear of that space might be travelling faster than his. He merely sees the gap and fills it. For example, he may be moving 45 m.p.h. His lane slows to 40 m.p.h., so he changes lanes and solves his problem. Never noticing, or even caring to notice, that the new lane had been moving at 50 m.p.h., he maintains his 45 m.p.h., cutting off or slowing the car in front of which he has just moved and possibly causing several following drivers balked by his discourteous action to make lane changes of their own.

Do your lane changing well before you get near the problem. Do it smoothly with plenty of time and space. Once you are drawing near or have pulled up behind a left turner, etc., it is usually best to give up the idea of changing lanes. By then, many of the drivers behind you will have changed lanes, almost in a steady stream, and used up virtually all of the spaces. Any maneuvering by you at this point would have to be done very hastily, relying upon violent acceleration, frenzied steering, sketchy information, and harsh deceleration. Especially after you are stopped, unless you see a really large space which you are absolutely certain no one else is rushing to fill, just stay put.

When changing lanes to the right on four lane streets which allow parallel parking, watch those parked cars. One may pull out into the very same space you are heading for in the right lane. The same is true regarding right turners entering your four lane road. Someone may turn into the right lane just as you try to lane change into it.

In general, change lanes one at a time. The consequences of taking more than one lane at a time may be surprises in the blind area ahead, or from the police car behind.

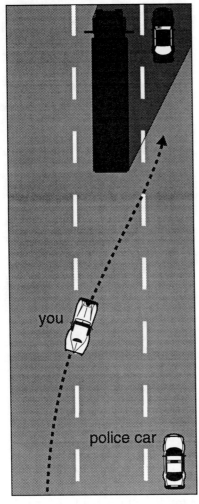

In exceedingly congested (walking paced) traffic, after searching in vain for a place into which to change lanes, you may find it necessary to *squeeze* into the next lane. This is tricky, irritates many people, and can cause front, rear, or side accidents. Try to squeeze into what can develop into a gap in front of someone who seems to be paying attention and might let you in. Never just try to *force* your way into a new lane. The other driver may not notice you or may insist that you stay where you are. Use your turn signals, car speed, and position to demonstrate your intentions. Show the other driver exactly what you are trying to do. You may be able to gesture or even talk to him and request that he let you in ahead of him. While paying so much attention to your rear and side, be careful to watch the car ahead of you in your lane which might stop.

In stop and go traffic, you will be tempted to change lanes in front of a truck because your car can so easily out accelerate it and enter the gap the truck cannot help leaving. This can be a very useful tactic, but do not forget that being directly in front of a large vehicle will seriously limit your rearward vision in future lane change attempts.

It seems that once drivers learn about getting in front of trucks, they overuse the trick. They cut in front of them not only under acceleration as the gap lengthens, but under braking when the gap shortens! Just as the truck can't speed up easily, neither can it slow down or stop easily. *DO NOT* change lanes in front of a truck when slowing down, unless you can leave that truck *plenty* of room.

You are stopped first in line, next to a truck, at a red traffic signal. You need to be in the truck's lane to make a turn in two blocks. After the light has changed and you are certain the intersection is clear (including pedestrians, cyclists, and autos in the blind area in front of and next to the truck), you can easily out accelerate the truck and make an "easy" lane change in front of it. Similar "easy" lanc change opportunities exist any time the lane you want is blocked by anything which makes it impossible for you to cut-off anyone by entering that lane just after passing the obstruction. This type of blockage is provided by unusually slow moving traffic, double parked vehicles, stopped buses, construction, etc. Basically all you have to do is get past the obstruction and move over. Remember, however, that even these "easy" lane changes are not *free*. Always check your blind spot for a bicycle or other small vehicle.

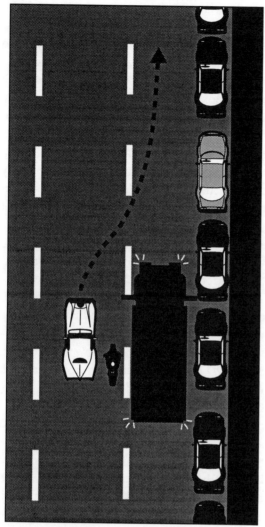

*"Easy" lane change in front of double parked truck
is indicated by arrow. However, cyclist lurks in
blind spot and grey car may pull out.*

On a four lane, urban street, you might be tempted to change lanes around a vehicle which has unaccountably stopped in the middle of the block. Beware! It may have stopped to let a j-walker cross the street. From your position, though, you can't know this. The stopped vehicle blocks your view. You can't see the pedestrian who could enter your path just as you, cruising along at 30 m.p.h. and congratulating yourself on how neatly you avoided an unnecessary slowdown, pass.

When changing lanes to prepare to turn or park, do not delay until the last moment. Observe traffic and make a neat lane change at an opportune time. As your ability at changing lanes develops, you will be able to determine the proper time more easily. When you are unsure, though, it is better to be too early than too late.

Pay attention to the cause for your lane change. A left turning car, or one that is backing into a parallel parking place and blocking your lane, for example, may finish its maneuver and eliminate the need for yours. Sometimes, for example, you will be able to see that no traffic is coming toward the left turner in front of you. This means that he will not have to wait and may be out of the way before you arrive. You may not have to change lanes at all, just slow down a little.

Sooner or later, you will find yourself going for a certain space just as the car immediately ahead or behind yours goes for it. If both you and the other driver are reasonably competent and alert and if everything else involved in the lane changing situation is in order, this probably will not result in a major problem. Ordinarily, whoever is behind will yield.

You should *NEVER* find yourself in a new lane without knowing how you got there. These "automatic" lane changes are typified by the situation in which two lanes merge into one. Drivers in these situations, not realizing that they are merging into another lane, frequently just follow the road, never consulting mirrors or checking blind spots. As far as they are concerned, they are just "following their lane."

Similar circumstances exist at intersections with three lanes approaching and only two lanes leaving. A lane disappears. Its traffic must go somewhere, but many times drivers just head for what appears to be "my lane" with no regard for traffic which they may be cutting off. At other intersections three lanes enter and two exit. Again, drivers switch lanes unknowingly,

oblivious of other traffic. Indeed, many times these drivers never even realize they've changed lanes!

Changing lanes in traffic which is slowing down or stopping is more difficult than changing lanes in traffic moving at a steady speed. Because everybody's speed keeps dropping, you must try to fit your vehicle into a space which keeps getting smaller. The vehicle ahead of the space is slowing or stopped. The vehicle behind the space, though losing speed, is still moving faster than the one ahead, thus closing the space rather quickly. Your problem is to change lanes far enough ahead of the rear vehicle without getting too close to the front vehicle, or the rear end of the vehicle currently in front of you. These factors severely limit your choice of speeds, thus forcing you to time the maneuver perfectly if it is to succeed. Your margin for error is constantly decreasing.

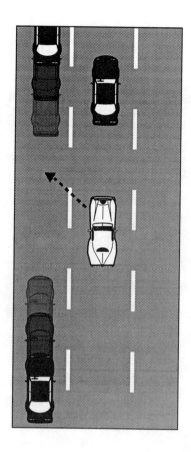

Situations like this can easily overwhelm new drivers. They can overwhelm many experienced drivers. Good lane changing in difficult circumstances takes a lot of skill. Sometimes the situation is so difficult that you are better off not changing lanes at all. Never do an ill-advised or incompletely thought out maneuver to save a minute. You may lose the minute and a great deal more.

John's first traffic ticket was given him quite soon after he got his first driver's license. He was driving his friend somewhere. The friend said to turn at the next cross road. John said, "Okay" and stayed in the right lane preparing to turn right. "No, left!" said the friend. John looked in his mirrors. There was a car close behind him just to the left. "Oh, well" said John, "I'll just cut this guy off a little and make my turn." The guy John cut off a little was a cop! You know what happened next.

Learn and practice lane changing in light traffic at moderate speeds — a lot.

11 *Chapter Eleven*

Parallel Parking

It makes strong men tremble. It makes self-reliant women weep. Is parallel parking driving's greatest challenge?

Of course not! Consider driving through freezing drizzle, and fog, on patchy ice, over unfamiliar roads, alone, at night, through the mountains, while those worn out wiper blades (the ones you meant to replace), smear the wind-

shield. Compared to that, parallel parking is a pleasure, a picnic, a party!

Learning to back into a parking place requires some serious psychomotor work and some uncomfortable twisting. It should not be attempted before one has become skillful at backing around corners (left and right) and straightening out again. However, properly explained and practiced, it will be mastered with surprising ease.

This mastery will prove to the driving student that he has already learned a great deal and is capable of much more. It will fill him with pride. It will ensure that his further student driving challenges will be met with greater confidence. It will provide freedom from undue parking worries, and this will always increase his enjoyment of driving.

There are *so many* methods of learning to park a car. Most involve lining up all sorts of things: bumpers, steering wheels, windows, seatbacks, door posts, etc. Some require not only recognizing but backing the car to a 45 degree angle with the curb. Many even prescribe turning the steering wheel a precise number of turns at specific reference points along the way.

These kinds of methods all endeavor to do the same thing. By prescribing certain actions at fixed check points, they seek to force the driver to guide the car along the *standard path into the parking space*.

Presumably, the student, as he performs these steps, watches their results through the rear window and correlates the observed results with the steps that caused them. Noting the angles and distances assumed by his car, he forms a mental videotape of the proper path into the parking space. Then he gradually throws away most of the prescribed steps and parks by comparing his mental tape recording with what he actually sees behind the car.

In common practice, however, neither the correlation of steps with results, nor the com-parison of mental tape with reality to the rear is mentioned by the driving instructor. The methods are taught as totally self-contained *systems* for parallel parking rather than procedures by which to learn it. However, the teacher in the car *does* consult his own mental videotape of parking and *does* make up for student miscalculations with directions like, "You're doing great, but come back another foot and a half before you turn the wheel," or, "Perfect! But cut the wheels a little more."

The result of all this is that the student never gets a clear mental picture of how to back into a parallel parking space but is left foundering among a lot of "steps" with no thorough understanding of their relationship, proper application, or intended goal.

This chapter presents a simple method by which the student learns exactly what the view through the back window should be. The student driver, by performing the exercises below, will form an accurate mental videotape of this view and be able to park with confidence, compensating, by himself, for his individual miscalculations and for variations among individual parking spaces.

LEARNING TO PARK: Before attempting to learn to back into a parallel parking space, you must be thoroughly familiar with controlling a car in reverse. You must have no question or confusion about which way to turn the steering wheel to make the car go in whichever direction you want (see Backing Around Corners in Chapter 5).

The key to parallel parking is the *standard path into the parking place; that is, the way your car swings over toward the curb and lines up with the front end of the car in front of which you are parking.*

To learn how this should look from behind the wheel, find a car about as wide as yours parked with at least 100 feet of clear space along the curb in front of it, well away from intersections, on a straight street, in a quiet area. Then, checking your mirror, drive past the parked car and stop approximately 100 feet ahead of it. Stop straight on the street not more than about nine feet from the curb.

You have now placed your car in the normal position from which to back into a parking space except, of course, that this space is about 100 feet long and there is no car to mark the front boundary of it, or upon which to base the beginning of your maneuver. At this stage, however, these things are unimportant, unnecessary, even counterproductive.

Now check traffic well ahead, behind, and to the sides. Back up toward the parked car. As soon as your car starts to move, steer to line it up with the parked car. *Do not look at the curb, grass, sidewalk, etc. Aim at the other car. See its whole front end, the entire grille, and the headlights on both sides.* Keep moving gradually over toward the curb and backward until the *entire rear* end of your car is lined up directly in front of the *entire front* end of the other car. Don't rush. Use all the distance you have, and let your coach do most of the traffic checking so you can concentrate on learning the maneuver. Get used to backing up close to the car behind. Finish with your car parked straight on the street, directly in front of and near the target car.

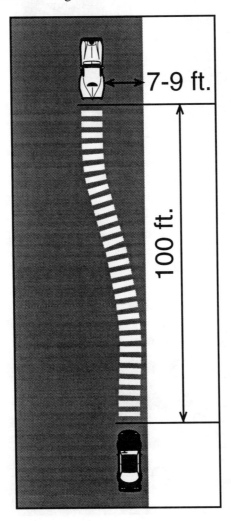

Did it? Terrific! Do it again, and again, and again. Do it until you know it will be perfect every time. Then continue the same maneuver, but instead of starting to move over toward the curb immediately, wait until yo have backed straight back 20 feet or so. When you have mastered the swing over and line up from this shorter distance, cut another 20 feet off your approach, then another 20, and another, changing your path into the parking space as shown in the following illustrations.

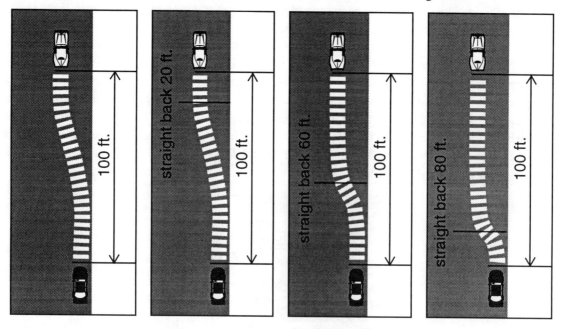

LINING UP YOUR LEFT C-PILLAR AND THE TARGET CAR'S LEFT FRONT FENDER IS THE KEY: At some time during this process of moving the beginning point of your swing closer and closer to the target car, the angle your car assumes relative to the other will become quite acute. Twisting around enough to keep watching the left side (front fender, parking light, headlight, etc.) of the target car will become very difficult. *Do not* give up and let your eyes wander toward the grass, or sidewalk, or the *right* front fender of the target car. *Force* yourself to keep its *left* parking light or headlight in view.

At nearly the same time as this acute angle is encountered, the left side c-pillar of your car will start obstructing your view of the left parking light and headlight of the target car. The c-pillar is the post between the car's rearmost side window and its rear window.

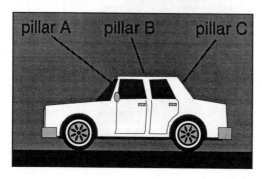

Except in relatively few vehicles (like Jeeps, station wagons, certain hatchbacks, and many cars built during the late 1950s and the early 1960s, etc.), a driver cannot actually see where the rear end of his car or its rear fender tips are. Therefore, he cannot use them to guide his car into a parking space. What he is left with is the back window. However, when the left side c-pillar begins to block his view of the target car's left front fender, the driver is tempted to use another area of the back window — an area further to the right. DO NOT DO THAT! Because all the action in parallel parking happens on the *left side*, watching IT is critical!

Avoid looking too far right by locking in on the left c-pillar and letting it become a convenient guide for parking. Force yourself to watch it swing over and line up with the target car's left side as you turn the steering wheel from hard right (to get the rear end of your car near the curb) to hard left (to swing your front end toward the curb and line up straight in front of the target car). By steering and controlling car speed, line up the c-pillar (usually directly above the left rear wheel and thus an excellent indicator of its path) with the target car's left front fender. *Force* the two into alignment.

The path taken by the left rear wheel, and therefore by the left c-pillar, at this critical point in the maneuver should always be just about the same. *That path is what you need to see, to understand, to practice, and to learn.* That dynamic relationship of c-pillar and left front fender as your car swings over and into line with the target car is the *key to parallel parking*. It is the *most important part of your mental parallel parking videotape. It is how you judge whether or not you are parking properly. Learn how it should look, and you have learned the hardest part of parallel parking.*

View through rear window just before beginning to swing rear end into parking space.

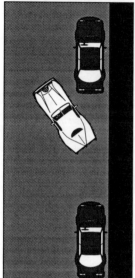

View at about the point of turning steering wheel from hard right to hard left.

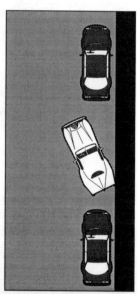

View when wheels must be cut full left.

View when you are in.

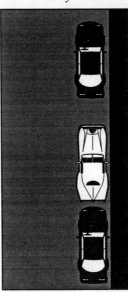

When you can repeatedly begin your swing toward the curb not more than about 20 feet ahead of the target car (less in a short car, a bit more in one of the old dinosaurs of the 1960s and early 1970s) and automatically recognize and easily control that proper relationship of c-pillar and head-light, parking light, or left front fender edge, your parking worries are no more. You know the secret. The mystery is gone. *You* are in control! You need no *steps*, because you have a clear mental video-tape of how to line up the *left side* of your car with the *left side* of the target car.

TURNING THE STEERING WHEEL: Use your left hand only and "palm the wheel." By the time your practice path approximates that used when actually parking, you will be making a drastic change from steering hard right as you back the rear end sharply toward the curb, to steering hard left to swing the front end into line parallel with the curb. This steering will have to be done in very little time over a very short distance. To do this, you will need to turn the wheel rather rapidly. Therefore, you may be tempted to twist forward and use both hands to steer. Don't. Twisting forward can make good vision to the rear nearly impossible, and you *must be able to see where your car is going and where you want it to go to control it.*

Neither should you stop the car so that you can give your full attention to turning the wheel. You must have feedback to know which way and how much to steer. You must be able to tell whether the

car is going where you want it to go. If you stop the car, it goes nowhere. If you stop the car, you stop the feedback and you can tell nothing. The car must be in motion for you to tell whether you are steering it properly. Use brakes and gas to control car speed. However, *do* stop as many times as necessary to check traffic and clearances.

BACKING INTO A REAL PARKING SPACE:

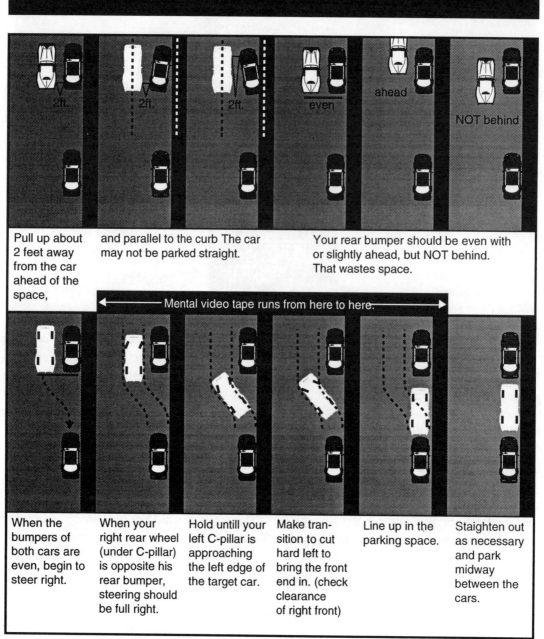

THE PARKING MANEUVER

Pull up about 2 feet away from the car ahead of the space, and parallel to the curb The car may not be parked straight. Your rear bumper should be even with or slightly ahead, but NOT behind. That wastes space.

Mental video tape runs from here to here.

When the bumpers of both cars are even, begin to steer right.

When your right rear wheel (under C-pillar) is opposite his rear bumper, steering should be full right.

Hold untill your left C-pillar is approaching the left edge of the target car.

Make transition to cut hard left to bring the front end in. (check clearance of right front)

Line up in the parking space.

Staighten out as necessary and park midway between the cars.

DETAILS OF BACKING INTO A PARALLEL PARKING SPACE: For simplicity, *all* instructions will be given for parking on the *right* side of the street. Once skill is acquired in this maneuver, it can be transferred rather easily to parking on the left side of a one-way street.

PICK OUT A PARKING SPACE: Try to pick out the parking space well before you reach it. Before you can do this, however, you must know that you are near the house, store, office, etc., that is your destination. If you are familiar with the area, this is no problem. If you are unfamiliar with the area though, it is usually best to find the exact address you want *before* searching for a parking space, unless you can tell from other addresses or the name of the nearest intersecting street that you are *very* close to your objective.

Do not become so absorbed in examining the curb lane for breaks in the lines of parked cars which might prove to be parking spaces that you neglect pedestrian and vehicular traffic, violate driving laws, or become a dangerous, moving road block. In very congested areas, do not be surprised if that space you finally do find is right in front of a fire hydrant.

When you do locate a space, use your mirror(s), avoid sudden stops, and decide whether you can pull forward into the space or must back into it. If possible, at this time, also notice whether the car ahead of the space is standing the proper distance from the curb. Knowing this now will help you avoid confusion later when you are bringing your car into final alignment in the parking space.

If you are not sure that the space is big enough to hold your car, stop next to it and check the size of your car against the length of the space. Once again, however, know what is behind you before stopping.

PLACE YOUR CAR IN THE CORRECT STARTING POSITION: The distance between your car and the one in front of the parking space should be about two feet. If your car is closer than about one foot away from the other car, you may have trouble clearing its rear end later when you swing the front of your car into the space. If your car is farther than about three feet away, the angles assumed in the maneuver will be unnecessarily sharp, and the sight lines needed for precise aiming will be extremely difficult to maintain.

Your car should be straight on the street, not necessarily parallel with the car ahead of the space, which may be parked crooked.

Your rear bumper should be at least as far forward as that on the car in front of the space. Farther forward is alright, because you are going to back up anyway. Behind the other car's rear bumper, though, is no good. In effect, that shortens the parking space, giving you less room in which to maneuver.

When approaching your parking space, begin lining up properly as early as possible. Don't waste space. Don't wait until you are passing the parking place to line up; begin *before* you even reach it. Just ease into position over a long distance. Don't wrestle with sharp turns and large steering wheel movements in a limited space at the last moment. They make accurate spatial judgments and good placement needlessly difficult.

SIGNAL: Signaling that you intend to park is no problem if following traffic is a good distance to the rear. Slow down, illuminating your brake lights; turn on your right turn signal; swoop into the proper starting position; and shift to reverse, illuminating your back-up lights. This combination of movements and signals should make your intentions unmistakable, and following traffic will easily be able to pass you or stop and wait for you to park, depending upon the specific circumstances.

If following traffic is close though, letting

drivers behind know that you intend to park is much more difficult. Use the same signals and movements mentioned above, but remember that there may not be enough time for the driver immediately behind you to realize your intentions and react properly. He must understand the situation in order to react well. To understand it, he *must be aware of the parking space*. If he isn't, no signals or movements will tell him what you intend to do, and he will probably drive up and stop right behind you, blocking your access to the space. The one part of the getting ready to park procedure most likely to call his attention to the space is the deceleration and swoop over into starting position. Make this movement as clearly defined and obvious as possible. It is your best hope of getting the driver behind you to notice the space, figure out the situation, and be able to react in time. If he doesn't see the space, he will still probably drive up and stop right behind your car, blocking you and causing those following him to stop close behind his car, making it impossible for him to back up out of your way or pass you.

If the resulting jam-up is tight enough and long enough, the only way to relieve it may be to give up the parking place or go around the block and try again, since moving up a few feet

to let traffic pass may not work. The driver behind, apparently watching only the rear end of your car, and therefore still unaware of the situation, may merely follow you again.

Always be careful not to signal too early, because, again, if the driver behind you sees only the signal and not the parking space, he may be confused very easily. He may think that you want to turn right into a side street, alley, or driveway and, once more, stop right behind you.

Even giving stop signals by hand may not work. Drivers hardly ever use hand signals any more and usually pay little attention to them, thinking they are merely stretching, arm cooling, or nail polish drying techniques.

On the other side of things, whenever you are driving on an urban or suburban street, remember to be alert for the driver ahead of you to decide to park and try to signal *you*.

CHECK TRAFFIC AND WAIT IF YOU HAVE TO: What you need to look for when checking traffic before parking will vary depending upon the area. Major, urban traffic arteries are much different from suburban side streets. The illustration gives an idea of the kinds of hazards and problems for which you should check before parking.

A. *Driver exiting this car;*

B. *Newspaper vending machine;*

C. D. E. *Children or animal or adult pedestrians;*

F. *Man cutting grass;*

G. H. I. *Traffic approaching from behind (motorcycle H and car I being passed by bicyclist G);*

J. *Parked truck blocks view of alley, driveway, and major street to rear;*

K. *Vehicles coming out of any of these alleys or driveways;*

L. *Vehicles approaching from these intersections;*

M. *Vehicle waiting for you (may decide to pass);*

N. *Car ready to pull out from behind you on a one-way street;*

O. *Driver leaving parked car;*

P. *Pedestrian may go any direction;*

Q. *Clearance far left front on narrow street*

Finally, check how far from the curb the target car is standing, so any needed adjustments to your maneuver can be planned now.

BEGIN BACKING INTO THE SPACE: When all potential conflicts are resolved, assume a proper posture for backing up and start moving into the space. Begin turning the steering wheel toward the right just as your back bumper is passing the other car's back bumper. Control car speed and rate of steering so that just as your right rear wheel (usually directly below the right side c-pillar) is even with the other car's back bumper, you are just finishing turning the wheel full right. A simplification with only slight cost in lost space and wear on the steering

mechanism is merely to line up your right rear wheel with the other car's rear bumper and steer full right before backing.

RECHECK AND PARK: Check traffic as necessary. Remember, the left front fender of your car will be swinging out toward the left. Make sure it has enough space. This is particularly important on unusually narrow side streets, where a parked car on the opposite side of the street might be dangerously close to yours.

Now merely follow the standard path into the parking place, the one you learned and put on a mental video earlier in this chapter. On most streets, at the beginning of the parallel parking maneuver, the front of your car will have to climb up the crown of the road. Therefore, your car will slow down or even stop. Later in the maneuver, the entire car will be rolling down the crown of the road and will accelerate. Control car speed with gas or brakes.

It may be necessary to stop and check your progress and/or traffic several times while parking. Fine. Take your time and keep everything under control. Pay close attention. Keep well twisted and watch how your car is moving over and lining up with the target car. While learning and practicing, you may want to get out of the car and look to see exactly what your clearance is, then get back in and compare what you *see* from inside with what you *know* is outside. Try to avoid scaring the neighbors, though. If they notice you outside your car looking at theirs, they may think you've hit it.

Just before you begin to turn the steering wheel all the way over to the left to bring your car's front end in, check for adequate clearance between your right front fender and the left rear of the car ahead of the parking space. Stop if necessary to make this check and repeat it as many times as needed. Remember, though, that you are only *checking* the front, but *aiming* the rear. *Keep your main attention to the rear.*

If your car has a long rear overhang, this overhang will go into the parking space quite far beyond the left side of the target car.

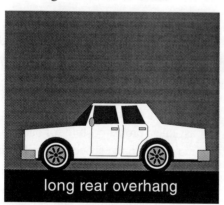

long rear overhang

That is normal. It will swing into line when you bring the front end into line along the curb. Many times the long rear overhang will also move *over the curb* when you're backing into a parking space. Be cautious about high curbs and obstacles near the curb line: fire plugs, sign and parking meter posts, newspaper boxes, light poles, etc. You can hit them.

In very close maneuvering, remember that the left rear corner of your car is the one that would touch the car behind first. As usual, watch *it*, not the right rear corner.

Never waste space, but make good use of all you have.

Having turned the steering wheel full left and backed up as far as possible in the space, you should have the car near the curb and reasonably straight on the street. If your car is in the space and all lined up, but there is still room behind, you may want to use it. If you do, be sure to straighten out the steering before continuing backwards. Otherwise, your car's rear end will move back out into the street again and its right front tire may hit the curb.

If your car ends up much too far from the curb, it is generally better to pull out and try again from the beginning, rather than struggling on, stressing yourself and the car, and possibly never getting parked correctly. If you do pull out

to try again, take the time and effort to get into the proper starting position. Drive around the block if you have to. Beginning badly will just make the whole maneuver more difficult and less gratifying. If you do decide to try again, realize that drivers approaching from the rear and seeing you pull out will expect you to keep going not stop and back up. Therefore, to avoid a rear-end collision, be sure you have plenty of space.

ADJUSTMENT: Maneuvering within the space, remember the path the car followed to enter it — over and straight.

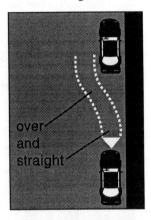

This is the path you will generally have to follow in any further maneuvering — either over and straight backward alternating with straight forward,

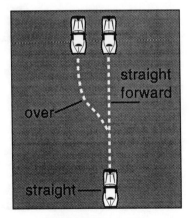

or over and straight backward alternating with over and straight forward.

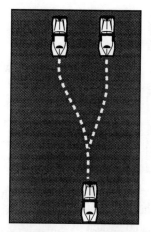

Repeated enough, either of these paths will eventually move your car sideways as much as needed.

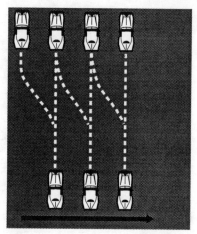 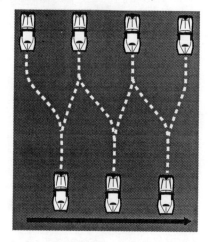

If, after you back into the space, the *rear* of your car ends up too far from the curb, leaving the front even farther from it,

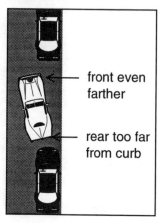

front even
farther

rear too far
from curb

do not use *all* the space ahead to move the front toward the curb. It won't help. The rear will stay too far from the curb.

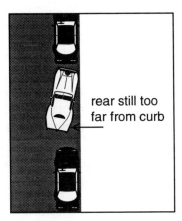

rear still too
far from curb

Then you'll want to use all the space behind the car to get the rear end near the curb, and you'll end up right back where you started.

right back where
you started

If you try it again, you'll just get stuck going back and forth over the same path, never getting any closer to the curb.

Instead, either start over from the beginning, or take your time and repeat the over and straight maneuver as many times as required.

In an extremely short space, be certain to get the right rear wheel of your car quite near the curb. You can then bring the front end in rather easily by using the technique in the following illustrations.

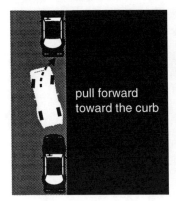

pull forward
toward the curb

back up as
straight as
possible

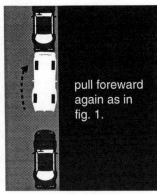

pull foreward
again as in
fig. 1.

Figure 1   *Figure 2*   *Figure 3*

FINAL ADJUSTMENT: Finish parking with your car equidistant from the vehicles ahead of and behind it. That way you cannot block either of them. Moreover, you will lessen your own chances of getting blocked when the vehicle farther from yours pulls out only to be replaced by one that squeezes right up to your bumper, leaving you little room ahead or behind.

Your maneuvering ability in a short parking space will be severely limited by parking extremely close to the curb (one or two inches). It will be nearly impossible to move any way but straight forward or straight backward, because turning the steering wheel will force your right front tire into the curb.

LEAVING THE CAR: Before leaving the car, shut off all switches. A driver who leaves the controls for his air conditioning and radio turned on when shutting down the car, only to have those accessories come on with a roar when he starts up later, shows through this unconcerned attitude a distinct lack of pride in his driving.

Windshield wipers, if not switched off, will sweep the windshield as soon as the ignition key is twisted to the "on" position. Then, if the rain has stopped, and the windshield dried, the wiper blades will grind whatever dust has settled on the glass into it.

Headlights left on will drain the battery. Then the car won't start.

Be very careful about car keys. Do not lay them on the dashboard or seat while you fool around with your sunglasses or something in the back seat, then forget them, get out, slam the door, and lock yourself out of the car. It's a good idea to have at least a spare door key in your wallet.

Before opening the door, check the left side blind spot, looking especially for bicycle riders.

FINAL NOTES: Pay attention! No matter how good you become at backing into parking spaces, you must always pay attention. As soon as your attention slips, your parking performance will suffer.

Sooner or later, you will have to parallel park on a busy street while other drivers wait for you to do it. You'll be nervous. Relax. Take your time. Do it properly. The other drivers will wait — *once.* If, however, you rush, and blunder, and have to pull out again and gain, and nobody can pass you, the waiting drivers will lose their patience.

One last point about parallel parking — fortunately, doing it is usually much easier than reading about it.

12 Chapter Twelve

Traffic Tactics

In general, once a driver understands a traffic situation, he will automatically deal with it properly. The trick to safe, efficient, pleasurable traffic driving is simply *to understand traffic situations in plenty of time*!

Most traffic tactics are just ways of making the best use of available time and distance. They start with proper seeing habits, which provide plenty of accurate, detailed information. This abundant information allows, even forces, precise control of vehicle speed and position. Fine control of speed and position complement already good seeing methods by providing more time and distance in which to recheck developing situations. This allows complete and timely understanding of the interrelationships and consequences of traffic situations and problems, making control undramatic.

Traffic tactics are much more than accident avoidance techniques. They are the smoothers, the givers of grace to traffic driving. They allow the nearly magical early warnings. They give the vitally needed extra moments. Their skillful use is what makes traffic driving look easy for an excellent driver. Using traffic tactics carefully, a good driver can pace his progress through traffic so perfectly that he is almost always in exactly the right place at the right time.

A good driver has time to do everything and does everything in its proper time. For example, there is a great deal that must be done in setting up a turn. Traffic information must be gathered from ahead, behind, both sides and, if possible, well ahead into the new driving path. Road surface and visibility must be considered and managed. Car position and speed must be perfectly controlled to allow time to gather all this information and leave time to plan the arc of the turn. A well timed signal must be given.

If *everything* is *not* done correctly, the turn will suffer. In one way or another it will be clumsy: too fast, too late, too wide, too tight, slowing too late, into the wrong place, into unseen traffic or road problems, etc. These mistakes will often be noticed by passengers, and they must not be thought of as little things that do not matter. They are dangerous mistakes. They show lack of control!

PAYING ATTENTION: Paying attention to driving is not a traffic tactic. However, *it is very likely the single most important factor in good driving. It underlies everything else. It makes everything else possible.* If you are not paying attention, you haven't a chance!

If you are not paying attention, you will not enjoy the satisfaction of perfectly controlling a moving automobile. If you are not paying attention, you will not handle traffic with astonishing grace, you will not see and avoid accident producing situations easily, but you will get

ambushed, and you will get tickets. You will snarl traffic with all sorts of clumsy maneuvers. In short, if you do not pay attention, you will almost never drive well. You will drive safely only when everybody else watches out for you.

"Driving is a full time job." At one time, that was a common safe driving slogan. It is also a fact. Whether you want full time driving enjoyment, full time driving control, full time driving safety, full time driving efficiency, driving must be a full time job.

Beware, though. It is all too easy to agree with this idea and still not do it. Everybody knows that to drive, one must keep his eyes on the road, his hands on the wheel, and his mind on his driving. Everybody knows it, but who does it?

People drive and talk, drive and argue, drive and cuddle and kiss. They drive and think, and worry, and plan, and even daydream. They window shop, they sight-see, they eat, drink, smoke, read, shave, talk on the telephone, put on their make-up, and turn around to the back seat to discipline the children, all the while moving their cars, sometimes only inches from other vehicles, buildings, or pedestrians. People even carry their dogs and children on their laps while attempting to drive. They tune their stereos, listen to music so loud that it must drown out all traffic noises, even emergency sirens, and they gyrate to the music, obviously more involved in the music than in their driving.

Just as people admit that driving is dangerous but do not want to wear seatbelts and drive well, people say that driving is a full time job but do not drive full time. It may be that deep down in their subconscious minds, drivers do not believe that driving is a full time job. It may be that subconsciously they believe driving is something to get done while doing other things, or that driving is just background to other activities.

Driving does SEEM full of gaps, periods of time off. You get into the car, start it, buckle up, shift, check traffic, and back out of the driveway.

Then you shift again, check ahead and behind, and drive down to the corner stop sign. A lot of that is driving, but what about the time and distance between your driveway and the stop sign? That is mostly just moving from one driving situation to the next — apparent time off. At the stop sign, you stop, check traffic, turn right, and move down the road. Then there is more apparent time off. In about three blocks, you see a stop light ahead, so you start driving again. You stop, perhaps checking your inside rearview mirror. Then you wait for the light to change — more apparent time off. The light changes. You look to both sides and go. More time off until you notice a parked police car. Immediately you reduce your speed. You do not know how fast you are going, because you are not driving full time, so you immediately slow down, assuming the worst. That's how it goes. Your driving is made up of driving events scattered along the road at irregular intervals like bumps in the pavement.

Unfortunately for safety, efficiency, and fun, many drivers seem to drive this way. They consider driving to be mostly time off. Much clumsy, irritating, confusing, dangerous driving comes from not paying attention.

Drive it! Drive it as much of the time as you can. Drive it perfectly around corners, gracefully through traffic, safely through parking lots, smoothly onto the expressway. Drive it straight as an arrow when moving straight ahead, not here and there and anywhere — drive it to smooth, almost imperceptible stops, and make smooth, solid applications of power. Drive it dependably through snow. Drive it legally ALWAYS! There's the full time job of driving. There's the life-long hobby of driving.

Yes, *make driving a life-long hobby*! Keep driving something you enjoy, a special activity, a special time to be savored every day for the rest of your life. If you love it, if you look forward to it, if you work on it, you will do it better and better every day. You will automatically take good care of your car and keep up with the latest changes in the laws and drive safely. Your pride in your beautiful driving will never let you take the needless and foolish chance of soiling your record or hurting someone by driving drunk or drugged.

Driving as a hobby is therapy. It is your time to be alone and PERFORM! It takes your mind off worries and pressures. It is positive like laughing, and good music, and sports, and having great ideas, and loving another human being. A man who rides the train or bus to a business appointment about which he is really worried worries all during the trip. When he arrives at the appointment, he is more worried than when he left his house. The good driver who drives to the appointment relaxes and enjoys, and has a break in his nervousness because he drives full time.

Driving full time takes discipline and hard work. However, driving well full time is very rewarding. Not paying attention takes away the rewards and adds many dangers.

Make no mistake, deciding to pay attention and forcing yourself to pay attention are not one-time occurrences. Always, your attention will fade. You will have to force yourself to focus on driving and on driving better. This will happen over and over again and again. Be on guard to notice when your attention slips. Commentary driving (see page 223) is a great help in forcing yourself to drive full-time.

MISCELLANEOUS: There are several other things which are not really traffic tactics, but which are very important in traffic driving.

Know the laws. Law is the basis of civilization. Traffic laws make it possible for urban traffic to move. Traffic laws are the basic instructions for driving safely. It is not sissy to obey the laws. It is common sense.

You can't play the game unless you know the rules. You can't play the game really well unless you know the rules really well. It is not

enough to read the state driving manual once…
or twice … or a few times. It is not enough to be
able to pass a test on the rules of the road while
sitting in a room away from traffic with plenty of
time to think about each answer and even
change your answers if you like. To drive well,
you must have a very good working knowledge
of all the laws and be able to apply them instantly in real road conditions. On the road, you
cannot change your mind and cross out the
wrong answer. You have to know and apply the
correct law(s) NOW! The laws *always* apply,
even in very complex and/or clumsy situations.

Laws supply a framework within which to
drive. Without laws, there are no standards.
Without standards, there can be no excellence,
no achievement, no greatness! Making time by
ignoring the laws is just cheating. There can be
no glory in that. A real driver works within the
laws. He makes time by driving cleverly, not
illegally.

Keep control. Car control is the basis of all
driving. Always aim and steer properly.

Have the best field position. Always get as
many advantages as you can for yourself so
you can keep the best control of your vehicle in
traffic.

You are *always* in traffic: in the parking lot,
in your driveway, even in your garage. *Never,
ever, assume that the way is clear*! *CHECK IT*!

Prepare to drive. *Never* simply jump into the
car and go. Every time you get behind the
wheel, take a few seconds to get properly adjusted to the car, to relax, and to remember that each
drive is supposed to be a joyride. Set out to have
a good, safe time. Set out to learn and improve.
Set out to *perform*! Drive so that when you get
out of the car after the trip, you can give yourself an honest, mental pat on the back for a job
very well done.

FOLLOWING DISTANCE: The reason for
keeping a good following distance is *NOT* so that

you can stop in time if the car ahead stops. Drivers who think that have it all wrong. In fact,
drivers who think that are most often not even
driving! They are playing follow-the-leader.
When the car ahead stops, they stop. When the
car ahead goes, they go. When the car ahead
swerves around a pothole, they swerve around a
pothole. When the car ahead skids, they skid.
These followers, these boxcars in a freight train,
are the same people who will tell you how EASY
driving is. Certainly it is easy for them! They
simply do whatever the driver ahead does. Not
only is driving easy for these elephants in line,
holding the tail of the elephant ahead in their
trunk, it is boring, it is clumsy, it is dangerous, it
is drudgery, it is a battle, because they have no
idea what is going on in traffic. They are not like
the general, who, standing on a hilltop, sees the
entire battlefield: sees where his lines are weak,
where strong; where his army is advancing,
where standing its ground, and where being
pushed back; where his artillery is hitting its target, where it is missing, and where it is needed;
and correlating all this information with other
information about the overall strategy of the war,
the supply lines, reinforcements, medical ser-
vices, weather, and intelligence information
about the enemy's plans, strengths, weaknesses,
etc. These followers are like a soldier in a fox-
hole dealing only with his tiny part of a great
war. The soldier plays an entirely different game
from that played by his general. The general has
the overall view, the overall outcome in mind.
The soldier is thinking only about himself and a
small area around himself. The soldier might
easily believe that the battle is lost, while the
general can see that it is indeed nearly won.

The driver who keeps a good following distance can know the overall situation, like the
good general. He can know where the best flow
will be, and the greatest danger. He can see
problems developing and figure out ways to
avoid them. He can be *in control*. The driver

who just follows right behind the guy ahead and sees only a few cars near his struggles in counter-productive attempts to be first in his little group, while stampeding into the worst flow, the most traffic, and the greatest danger. He is often frustrated by the moves of other drivers. He has other drivers angry at him, but does not know why. He has accidents, but does not know what caused them.

There is a wonderful chess game played in traffic. Play it. Enjoy it. Don't fumble around playing some completely different and unwinable, private game among a few nearby cars. Play the great traffic game in which the goal is for everybody to win through achieving efficiency, safety, cooperation, control, fun, and personal reward.

To play the great traffic game, you must see what must be seen. To see what must be seen, you need a good following distance. *The main reason for keeping a good following distance is to be able to see what is happening far ahead*! If you are too close, you cannot see well, because your view is blocked and/or because you haven't time to use your eyes properly — you must keep watching the brake lights of the vehicle ahead of yours.

Close followers have little idea of what is happening ahead in traffic. Therefore, insignificant slowdowns, tiny ripples in the flow, seem near crises to them. Time after time, they are forced into sudden slowdowns or lurching stops, which are completely unnecessary. When these close followers get tired of this kind of stressful driving, they blame the traffic. They complain that the *other drivers* do not know what *they* are doing.

The accepted proper following distance today is at least two seconds. The two second rule works like this: as you drive along at a steady speed and a steady distance behind the vehicle ahead of yours, pick out some landmark like a large tree beside the road or a signpost,

etc., ahead of the vehicle you are following. When that vehicle passes the landmark, begin counting, "one thousand one, one thousand two…" If you count to one thousand two after you get to the landmark, you are following too close. If you count to one thousand two before you get to the landmark, you have at least a two second following distance. The two second following distance is considered a good *minimum*. In bad conditions, following distance should be increased, and some drivers never want to be closer than three seconds behind.

For greater accuracy in using the two second rule, pick a landmark like the shadow of an overpass or a bump in the road so that you can tell exactly when the car ahead passes the measuring point and exactly when you pass it.

Make a two second minimum following distance a habit. Work and play with the rule until you keep at least two seconds automatically. Keep working with the rule until you feel uncomfortable following any closer than two seconds. Then check yourself periodically.

The two second minimum following distance gives you time to take your eyes off the rear end of the car ahead and see. It gives you time to see the overall traffic scene, to aim, and even to keep track of your speed.

When you are following closely, your view is actually blocked by the vehicle ahead, especially by tall vehicles like vans, trucks, 4-wheel drive vehicles, buses, etc. Stay back and see.

Do not lose following distance. Do not catch up. Either pass or follow at reduced speed.

Look as far ahead as the terrain allows. See eight seconds ahead, or 12 seconds, or 23, or 50, or a minute if possible.

Time how far ahead you look. Pick out landmarks as far ahead as you can see. Time your distance from them by counting, "one thousand one," etc. until you reach them. Get used to looking very far ahead — as far ahead as you can see over, around, and through traffic; from one hilltop to the next or the next; around curves and into the following straightaways, etc. Get used to seeing as much as you can between your front end and the farthest point you can see. Get to feel uncomfortable when your view is blocked. Get your driving to that level of quality at which you seldom let your view get blocked long. Remember, traffic tactics are mostly being always in the right place. Remember also, that the rear and sides must always be included in your overall traffic scene.

TRAFFIC SIGNALS: First, look for them. Because they are normally mounted fairly high, they tend to be easy to see far ahead.

If the traffic signal is red, prepare to stop. Check your inside rearview mirror. Check this mirror every time you know that you will have to slow down or stop. In fact, check this mirror every time you even think that you *may* have to slow down or stop. Check the entire intersection.

Never fix your vision on the rear end of the vehicle stopped or stopping ahead of yours, or on the exact point at which you want to stop. If you fix your gaze there, your brain will do its best to put your car right there. You will tend to stop hard and late — sometimes frighteningly late. Instead, see where you want to stop and then look away. Recheck traffic to the left and right. Then recheck where you want to stop. Recheck traffic to the rear. Then recheck where you want to stop. Recheck the color of the traffic signal, etc. Not staring fixedly at the place you want to stop will let your brain bring your car to a smooth, easy, predictable stop.

When the signal light changes to green as you approach stopped traffic, remember that the stopped vehicles cannot get back up to speed and space themselves out instantly. Keep slowing gently or coasting (while covering the brake) until the gap between your car and the one ahead begins to widen. Then ease back onto the gas. Keep alert for lane changers, turners, and other tie-ups as traffic accelerates away from stoplights.

A yellow light means stop. That is the simplest, safest, best driving rule about yellow lights. "I coulda made it." or "I shoulda made it." or "I'm gonna make it." are not appropriate reactions to yellow lights. When you see a traffic signal change to yellow, your intent should be to stop unless you are very close to the intersection or you will get rear-ended if you stop. With practice, you will get a good idea about how quickly and smoothly you can stop your car at yellow lights. When stopping at yellow lights, try to do all the checks you would do if you were stopping at a red light.

Green lights mean go through the intersection *if it is clear*. Even when cruising through intersections on green lights, check the cross street.

Green lights do change to yellow and red. Expect that. Do not assume that the green light will stay green. On the other hand, do not try to guess when the green light will turn red. You cannot outsmart something which has no brain. Don't try. Just realize that any green light may change. Be ready by knowing what is behind, what is ahead, what is to the sides, and how much traction you have.

When waiting at a red light remember that he green light is not the Christmas tree at the drag strip. You do not just mash the accelerator when you see green. You have to look around before you go. If you can see the light for the cross traffic change to yellow, you know that your light *may* go green, and you can check traffic in preparation for going. If your view is blocked by a truck in the next lane, do not just shoot out, but hang back until the truck (see illustration on right) gets under way, or creep past the

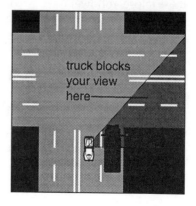

truck blocks
your view
here———

truck until you can see that there is no skateboarder, car, pedestrian, etc. crossing in front of the truck. Then go.

Green arrows for left turns, right turns, and straight ahead as well as yellow and red arrows mixed with regular red, yellow, and green lights at intersections are making traffic signal watching and obeying more and more difficult. Make sure that you obey your own signal. Make sure that your car is in the correct lane to do what you want to do. Remember that a green light is not a green arrow! When making a left turn on a regular green light, YOU MUST YIELD TO ONCOMING TRAFFIC! Remember to keep rechecking that your green arrow is still lit before following the vehicle ahead of yours through the intersection.

RIGHT TURN ON RED: This can be very easy, or extremely difficult, or anything in between. When turning right on a red light, you have right-of-way over *NOTHING*! Make sure you are clear for a good distance in every direction before making a right turn on red. Then make sure again.

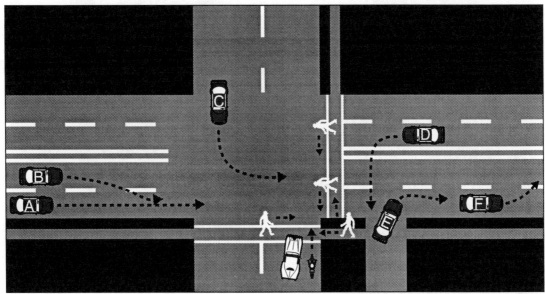

The white car, turning right on red, might get into a conflict with the pedestrians, the bicyclist, and/or cars A, B, C, D, E, F.

Oncoming traffic turning *left* on a green arrow has right-of-way over you. When the left turn arrow ends, the traffic stopped on the cross-street to your left may get a green light and start up quickly.

Be very careful when making a right turn on red when the red light has been lit a long time. The oncoming traffic waiting to turn left in front of you may get a green arrow and start up just as you begin your right turn on red.

STOP SIGNS: Stop signs mean stop. They do not mean go very slowly.

It is easy to be distracted by your passengers, the radio, beautiful sights, searching for street name signs, protecting stray animals, etc. when approaching stop signs. Do not let these things interfere with your skillful handling of stop intersections.

When approaching a stop sign, check the intersection just as if it had no stop sign. Know about all vehicular and pedestrian traffic ahead, to both sides, and behind *BEFORE* you stop. *Know whether cross traffic must also stop.* See who is stopping first, so you know whose turn it will be to go first. When your turn comes, take it.

Too often, drivers approaching stop signs stare straight ahead. They know that they will have to stop and check the intersection before they can go anyway. It may seem like wasted work to check the intersection *BEFORE* they get there, but it is a very good practice. A driver who does not check an intersection until he has stopped at it has far too little information to drive well and is taking chances with his safety and that of others.

Many drivers combine late checking with stopping beyond the stop bar, crosswalk, or stop sign. This leads to surprises.

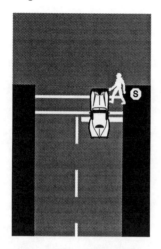 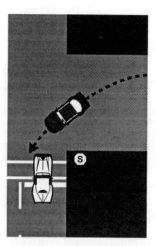

At very busy four way stop intersections, drivers often cooperate.

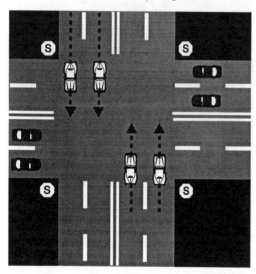 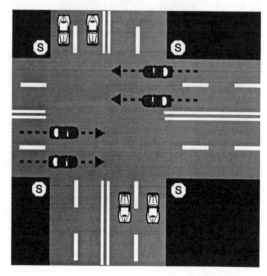

First one street goes; Then the other

This works very well until somebody misses his turn or must turn left. However, the drivers do try to regain the rhythm.

RAILROAD CROSSINGS: Once you have driven for a while, it becomes quite easy to take railroad crossings too lightly. Often the railroad crossings *are* clear when you are not sure they are. This tricks you into relaxing your guard. "The gates aren't down; it must be clear." "The lights are not flashing; it must be clear." "I really can't see, but everybody else is cruising across; it must be clear." "Everybody seems to be in such a hurry. I don't want to get in the way; it must be clear." "I've crossed hundreds of railroad crossings, and they've always been clear." The trouble with taking chances at railroad crossings is that often your first mistake is also your last.

Check railroad crossings the same way you check street intersections. Use several left and right glances between checking the mirror and looking ahead down the road. At railroad crossings just before signalized street intersections, make sure that there is space on the far side for your car *BEFORE* starting across the tracks

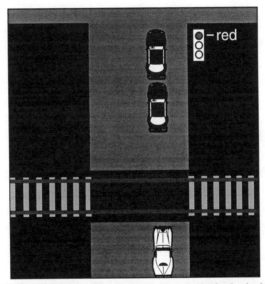

Before crossing the tracks, the white car's driver must check whether there is enough space for his car on the other side of the tracks.

In a stick shift car, always shift to a gear low enough to prevent engine stalling *BEFORE* you start across the tracks. Always check behind the train that has just passed for another one coming from the opposite direction.

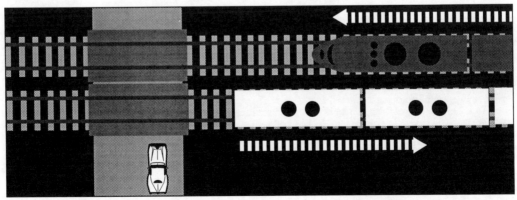

After the white train has passed, check for the gray train before driving across the tracks.

Be very careful at railroad crossings with many sets of tracks, especially when your view is blocked by lines of standing freight cars. Avoid this kind of crossing if you can.

Be *EXTREMELY CAUTIOUS* about crossing tracks when the gates seem to be stuck in the down position. This is illegal and *EXTREMELY DANGEROUS*!

With or without gates, when you look but do not see a train, double check before crossing against a signal. A much smaller railroad section car or a pick-up truck with flanged wheels may be approaching on the tracks. Because you are looking for a train, though, you may not notice one of these much smaller vehicles and go at the wrong time. *Crash!*

Railroad crossings are often bumpy. A good driver f-l-o-a-t-s his car over the bumps. He knows that pounding over the bumps is abusing his car. A good driver does not abuse his car. As you approach a bumpy crossing, check to the rear, slow down, and r-o-l-l over the bumps with the brakes off, then accelerate smartly away to keep from clogging up following traffic. Going over the bumps fast may seem alright to you, because the bumps hit so fast that you cannot feel them all, but your car is getting pounded.

BLIND APPROACHES: When approaching any blind area, your speed must be based upon your ability to see. You must be able to stop in the distance you can see. Tapping your horn is very useful in approaching blind areas, but it must never take the place of seeing. That unseen person may not hear your horn. Covering the brake (holding your foot over the brake pedal ready for instant use) is also a very good tactic in approaching blind areas.

Keep rechecking the blind area over and over in between necessary glances at other parts of the traffic scene and looks needed to aim when turning. This is the only way to negotiate blind areas — always expecting something to pop out at you. It requires almost constant rechecking. It is time consuming. It requires low speed. *Doing it right*, having your car completely under control, *forces your speed to fit conditions*.

An often unrecognized blind approach is the left lane or left turn bay at a red light.

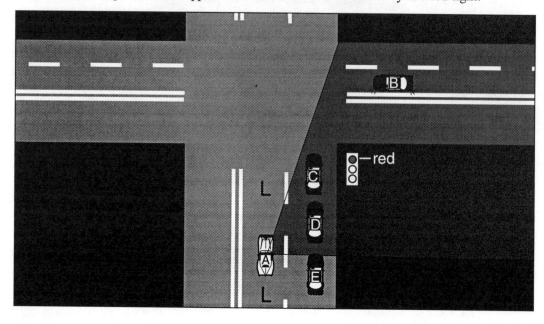

As driver A approaches the red light, his view of car B is blocked by cars C, D, and E. Driver A assumes that lane L ahead of him is clear for his stop. Driver B is planning to turn left. Cars C, D, and E block his view of car A and lane L. He assumes that lane L is clear and cuts short his turn. Thus both A and B try to use lane L from opposite directions at the same time.

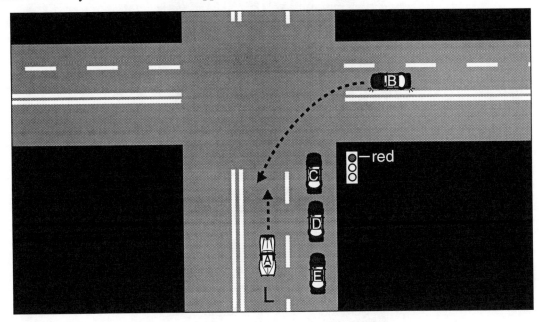

Each thinks the other is wrong.

Driver A should recognize the blind area created by cars C, D, and E. He should approach slowly, checking carefully. When he is sure the way is clear, he should ease far enough forward to be seen by left turners BEFORE they have started their turns.

Driver B should recognize the blind area created for him by cars C, D, and E. He should also approach slowly, checking carefully. He should try to determine exactly where *his* lane is and turn into it.

Both A and B should expect each other to appear out of the blind area.

Another kind of blind intersection approach is this.

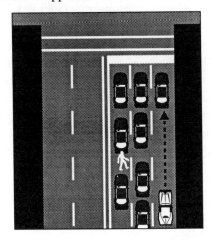

The j-walking pedestrian can come as quite a surprise to the driver of the white car.
Here is another commonly missed blind approach.

Left turning cars B, C, D, and E block driver A's view of oncoming left turners F and G. Obviously, cars B, C, D, and E block car A from the view of drivers F and G.

TURNING: Try to be in the proper lane early before all turns. Before you can get into the proper lane for turning, you must know where you want to turn. In familiar surroundings, this is easy. In unfamiliar territory, search far ahead for route numbers, landmarks, street name signs, etc. Reading a map and/or getting good directions before leaving are good ideas. If possible, know the names of the last few streets you will cross before the one on which you wish to turn.

If it is impossible to be in the proper position from which to make your turn, do not make it. Do as you do on the expressway when you miss your exit — just continue. Then turn around and come back, or find another way to your destination. Some accidents are caused because drivers see where they want to turn at the last second and try to do impossible maneuvers.

Time your signal to turn carefully. Show others exactly where you want to turn. Your speed and lane position also send signals about your intentions. Try not to mislead other drivers with too much or too little speed, etc. Never signal before you know exactly where you want to turn. Find where you want to turn and then time your signal perfectly.

As you approach the intersection, check quickly to both sides as many times as needed. Check ahead as much as needed. Check to the rear.

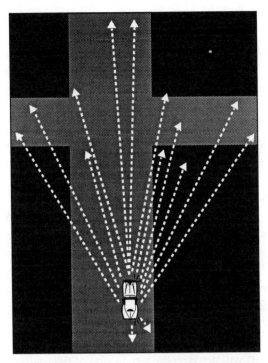

Look for vehicles and pedestrians, traffic signals, road signs, street markings, blind areas, and surface conditions like deep holes and puddles. Know as many details about the developing overall traffic scene as possible.

Check well down the street into which you want to turn BEFORE you begin your turn. *Know the traffic and road conditions on the new street before you enter it.* Looking well into the new street early will also prevent your making those frightening, sudden, late slow downs before turns. Those are caused by staring only at the corner where you want to turn during your approach. Looking well into the new street will also give you the jump on planning your turn. Know exactly where your car will end up BEFORE you start to turn. Proper planning and setting up of your turn will allow easy traffic checks while the turn is being made. Poor turning technique will not; you'll still be trying to figure the end of your turn when you should be watching traffic.

Make a beautiful, efficient, safe, square turn. Check your mirror(s) just after the turn while accelerating into the new street.

All of this takes time. Therefore, once again, if you do everything you need to do at the correct time, your speed will automatically be correct.

EMERGENCY VEHICLES: By aiming far ahead and knowing the overall traffic situation, including what is far behind your car, you will notice the flashing lights of emergency vehicles while they are still far off in the distance. After noticing them early, it is easy to keep track of the lights.

Notice the color of the lights. Red lights are on fire equipment and ambulances. Blue lights are on police vehicles. Some police vehicles may have red and blue lights, or even red, white, and blue lights. Fire vehicles and ambulances may use red with white.

Yellow lights appear on tow trucks, construction vehicles, barricades, street sweepers, snow plows, etc. Yellow lights mark hazards, not emergency vehicles. The yellow and red lights on school

buses flash quite differently from other hazard and emergency lights. Unmarked police cars may show flashing headlights.

Unfortunately, much of what was said above about emergency vehicle lights is no longer true. Always trying harder to be seen, police and fire departments and ambulance companies have added colors. Until now, a police car, for example, may show red, white, blue, and yellow flashing lights all at the same time.

Not only does a good driver work hard at seeing, he listens well too. An alert driver will hear the faint sound of a siren blocks away. Then he will keep listening and looking for the emergency vehicle(s), noticing whether or not the sound seems to be getting closer. When listening, do not be tricked by your car windows. No matter where sounds are coming from, they will sound loudest through whichever window is open. Therefore, when you hear a siren through the open left window, do not assume that the emergency vehicle must be on the left. It may be on the right.

To let an emergency vehicle pass, pull over to the right and stop when possible. It is not always possible. On expressways it is generally not expected. Sometimes, drivers get stuck in left turn bays, and clearly the best thing they can do is just wait where they are.

The thing to remember is that you want to clear an easy, obvious path for the emergency vehicle. If the emergency vehicle's driver is unsure that you know he is there, he will have to drive more slowly. This will delay both of you and make his job needlessly harder on his nerves. Get out of the way *early*, to the right if possible, stop, wave at him if necessary to help him.

Often emergency vehicles will drive on the wrong side of the road when approaching busy intersections to avoid stopped traffic.

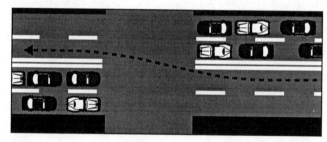

Expect this. Do not be surprised by it.

Something interesting can happen just after the emergency vehicle passes. You begin pulling back into traffic, only to find that the driver who had been behind you is passing you. He stopped first and pulled out first. He couldn't help catching up to you. Make sure to check and recheck your blind spot very carefully before pulling out after yielding to an emergency vehicle. In the same way, you will catch the car which had been ahead of yours. A little alertness and cooperation go a long way.

Remember not to follow close behind an emergency vehicle, and that it is illegal to drive over a fire hose. Finally, remember that a second or third emergency vehicle may approach immediately after the first has passed. Stay alert to this possibility.

FUNERALS: Strange things happen involving funeral processions. For example, you merge onto the expressway and find yourself illegally in the middle of a funeral. An even stranger situation is driving down the entrance ramp only to find that members of the funeral procession are trying to keep you from entering at all.

The most common problem involving funeral processions happens when they are moving through a red traffic signal. Somebody in the procession fails to keep up. There is a big gap in the procession. The drivers waiting at the *green* light think the funeral is past and start through the intersection. Crash!

BEELINES: A beeline is a straight line, a direct path, from one place to another. Driving a beeline would be steering directly at one's goal by staring straight ahead and giving no regard to traffic. This is surprisingly easy to do and happens a lot in parking lots and gas stations. A driver aims at the parking space he wants and drives straight toward and into it noticing nothing else: cars backing out at him, cars which are moving toward the same parking space, pedestrians he nearly hits, etc. In a gas station, a driver drives directly to the gas pump he wants to use without noticing or even looking for cross traffic and blind areas which abound in gas stations.

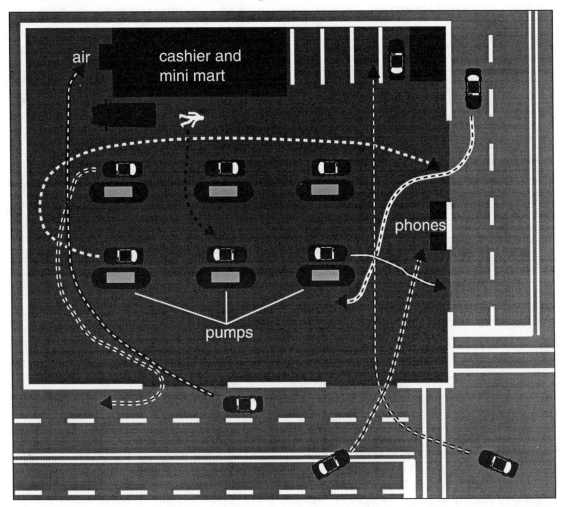

No one is thinking about traffic conflicts in and near this busy gas station. Each is just staring straight ahead and making a beeline toward his goal.

All but one place at which the paths cross are potential accident sites.

Most amazing is that time after time these people are surprised at this and similar places, yet continue to make beelines.

Conflicts, near misses, and even collisions are the results of making beelines when driving. Remember to look for trouble in order to avoid it. When performing what can be difficult maneuvers in complex surroundings like gas stations and parking lots, look for traffic, look for blind areas. Look for trouble.

Drivers make beelines without realizing that they are doing it. Check yourself often. Once you have developed the habit of not making beelines, remember that many drivers do make them. Never assume that because you see another driver or pedestrian, he sees or is even looking for you.

BUS STOPS: It is difficult or impossible to see under transit buses, because their bodies are large as well as relatively close to the ground. A transit bus stopped at a bus stop creates a blind area for drivers passing the bus from behind, approaching it from the front, and crossing in front of it.

 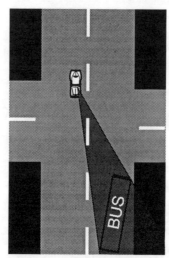 

A transit bus stopped at a bus stop creates blind areas for drivers passing the bus from: behind, ahead, the side

In the same way, the bus creates blind areas for pedestrians near it and crossing in front of or behind it. Pedestrians can easily make beelines to or from stopped buses. When driving past stopped buses, expect people, animals, and vehicles to pop suddenly into view. Drive at an appropriate speed. Cover the brake pedal. Cover and/or blow the horn.

The bus you are passing from behind may be stopped, pulling out, or pulling over to the curb. You have little control over what the bus will be doing when you pass it. However, you should know the relative safety of these three traffic situations. You are safest when the bus is *just beginning* to pull back out into traffic. It can not get into your way, but its movement back into traffic tends to keep vehicular and pedestrian cross traffic from moving in front of it. A bus which is stopping has less tendency to stop cross traffic. A bus which is stopped is the most dangerous to pass because people are more likely to walk, run, ride, or drive into your path from in front of it.

When passing a stopped bus from ahead, expect pedestrians, cyclists, or cars and trucks behind it.

NEVER TRUST STRANGERS: Never, never trust some stranger who may not even know you are there to take care of you. *Control every situation yourself*! Blow your horn. Change speed. Change lanes. Cover and/or use your brake pedal. Do whatever it takes to keep control of *every* situation yourself!

The other guy will probably help. However, the idea is never to risk an accident by *assuming* that he sees you and will do the right thing. He may see you but not see some other important part of the traffic scene and, therefore, still do the wrong thing. He may not be sober, or completely sane, or paying attention.

BLOWING YOUR HORN: Whenever you approach a traffic situation which makes you uncomfortable because you cannot predict accurately what the other guy will do, or because you are not sure that he knows you are approaching, blow your horn. *Make* him notice you.

Tap your horn, do not blast it. Time the sounding of your horn so that the person to be warned has time to react and is not startled at the last moment. However, do not blow your horn so early that the person for whom it is intended will not notice it. Time the sounding of your horn perfectly, just as you would any other signal.

Upon hearing your horn, the other guy may make a rude gesture at you because he knew you were there all the time. That is alright, though, because now you know that he knows.

A horn blast will often freeze a dog in place or send it back out of the way.

Remember that when you blow your horn at one person or group, others in traffic will hear it. Try to avoid confusing other road users.

BICYCLES: As with everything else in traffic, see bicycles early. Be able to recheck them several times before you get near them. Suppose you see a bike rider three quarters of a block ahead on your side of the street. Get as much information as possible about him well before you pass him. How old does he seem to be? Is he riding fast or slow? Is he holding a steady course? Is he weaving or swooping? Is he moving toward the curb when he can between parked cars? (This means he has to move back out again to pass parked cars.) Is he wearing a headset? Is he riding with two hands, one hand, no hands? Is he alone? Is he carrying anything? Is he in danger of being forced into your path by an opening car door ahead, or by someone pulling out into traffic? Does he check behind him when he has to move farther left?

Tap your horn early if necessary. Do not scare him with a loud blast right behind him.

Plan to pass where there is the most lateral (sideways) space for you and the cyclist. For example, pass just as he cuts in toward the curb between parked cars. Do not pass the cyclist just as you are both passing a double-parked car on the other side of the street.

Pass where there is the most lateral space;   *not the least.*

Keep an eye out for the cyclist in your mirror. He will often catch up and re-pass you in heavy traffic. Look for bicyclists anywhere you might look for other vehicles or pedestrians.

WHY DOESN'T HE GO? The other guy doesn't do what you expect him to do, or even what you signal him to do. Why? Perhaps he is not paying attention. Perhaps he is just a bad driver or pedestrian. Perhaps *he* sees something that *you* do not.

Suppose you try to give a driver on a cross street a break by slowing and waving him into line ahead of you, but he does not go. Why? He may have seen that yours is the last car in line, and he is waiting for you to get out of the way.

When the actions of others confuse you, look around. See whether you are missing something.

Rarely, the other guy does not go because he can't until you do. Look at this situation.

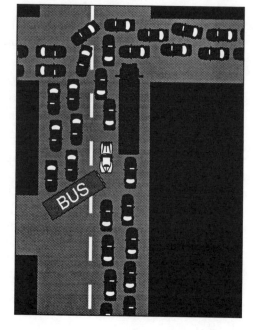

> *You are driving the white car in this traffic jam. Nothing moves at the intersection. Why don't they go? Look around. You hold the key. Move forward. Give the bus behind you room to move ahead so that the oncoming traffic can get past it. The intersection will then be able to clear up and traffic will flow again.*

TAKING TOO MUCH RESPONSIBILITY:
Be careful not to take on more responsibility than you should. In attempting to be courteous, drivers occasionally do incorrect and even dangerous things. For example, drivers sometimes wave other drivers or pedestrians across in front of them when they should not.

In heavy traffic, a stop light ahead has stopped all the dark gray cars. The driver of the white car, obeying the law, has stopped where he does not block the side street. Overcome by a sudden need to be courteous, however, he waves at the driver of the black car. The black car's driver hurries to respond to the kindness offered, and crosses the street... almost. He never gets across because he is hit by the light gray car in the blind area to his right.

The driver of the white car had not checked traffic before "helping" the driver of the black car. He should have been content to obey the law by not blocking the side street. Leaving a space is one thing. Telling someone to use that space is quite another. Signals might have been worked out which indicated that the way had been checked and was clear. However, even those signals can be turned into lies by a car's pulling out of a driveway, parking space, etc., too late to be seen in time by the signalling driver.

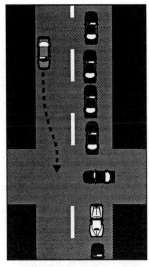

In any case, the driver of the black car should always check for himself unless he is absolutely sure that the white car's driver is telling him that the way is clear. Even then, he should double check for late developments, he should not rush, and he should be responsible for himself. His *best* defense is to try to avoid this kind of clumsy maneuver in the future.

Be very careful about waving across pedestrians, especially children. Children and other non-driving pedestrians may follow your orders without question or hesitation. Children will often run.

DO NOT MASTERMIND: Predict what others in the overall traffic scene will do, but never believe that they will actually do what you predict. "Knowing" what everybody else will do is called masterminding. It happens to you after you have become an experienced driver.

When a driver has driven for years, he has seen the same common traffic situations rerun over and over. He "knows" exactly what will happen in them. He is apt to get caught masterminding. He knows that car X will zig, because, in similar situations all through the years, car X has always zigged. It is the way car X *must* respond in this situation. Well, although it looks like it, this is *not* the same old situation. Car X will *not* zig. It will zag… CRASH!

Cars and trucks in traffic are *not* your toys. Pedestrians are *not* your puppets. You do *not* control them absolutely. Do not mastermind. Be ready for whatever actually happens.

LEFT TURNS AT GREEN LIGHTS: Left turns which are not protected by green arrows are difficult. When planning to turn left at a signalized intersection without left turn arrows, enter the intersection on the green light. *Yield to oncoming traffic.* Drivers have gotten so used to turning on green arrows that they sometimes forget that a green light is not a green arrow. The traffic signal changes from red to green, and they turn left as if the green light were a green arrow — without even thinking about yielding. This causes surprises and collisions.

Do not stop and wait to turn *before* entering the intersection. If you do, and the signal changes, you will have to wait through another complete signal cycle. This will not only delay you, it will delay and anger the drivers behind you.

As you approach and enter the intersection, see where the lane into which you will turn is. See where the entrance to it is. Place your car in just the right spot in the intersection from which to begin a perfect left turn. (See Chapter 5.)

Wait there. Do not creep while you wait. You picked your stopping point carefully so you could make a perfect left turn easily. Do not force yourself into making a clumsy and dangerous left turn by creeping mindlessly past the ideal starting point. For example, giving up the ideal line through the turn may encourage the driver behind you to take it and come into conflict with you.

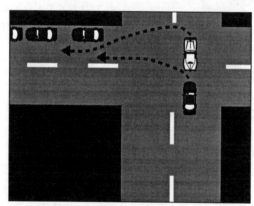

Wait with your front wheels pointed straight. If your wheels were turned to the left and you were rear-ended, your car would be forced into the path of oncoming traffic.

While waiting, move your eyes constantly. Check the oncoming traffic for possible spaces through which to turn. Check the color of the traffic signal. Be ready for it to change. Look to the left at the cross street for pedestrians in the crosswalk and approaching the crosswalk on the sidewalks. Look farther down the block to the left for vehicular traffic and pedestrians in the street. Visualize the path of your turn, that is, aim carefully to the left. Check pedestrian and vehicular traffic to the right as needed.

Keep repeating all these checks while you wait. Waiting to turn left at a green light is a very active task. Drivers often make clumsy and/or dangerous left turns because they do not wait actively. They just sit. When the light changes or a space in traffic becomes available, they are not ready. They are far behind in their planning and scanning.

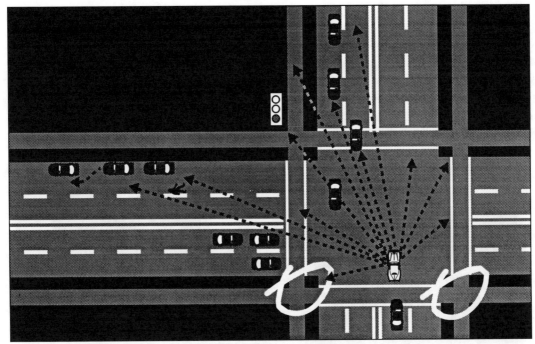

Driver of white car waits actively to turn left at a signalized intersection without left turn arrows. Note that properly checking crosswalk and sidewalk traffic requires looking back over your left shoulder to check the circled area to the left. Driver of the grey car must also check circled area to the right.

One of two things will happen as you wait and keep rechecking everything. Either a space will appear through which you can turn safely, or the traffic signal will change to yellow. Either way, be ready.

Suppose you see a good space through which to turn approaching. *Do not* keep watching the space until it gets to you. Instead, quickly look to the left. Quickly recheck your aiming. Quickly recheck traffic in the crosswalk and farther down your intended lane. Quickly glance at the color of the traffic signal. Quickly recheck right if necessary. Armed with this information, look ahead again to see that the space has arrived and is safe. Then make your turn.

If you just keep watching the space approach, you may not have the chance to use it, because you will have to do all that last second rechecking. If you begin your turn without rechecking left, you might find your path blocked by a pedestrian. Then you might have to stop and become a target for the traffic in front of which you are turning.

Suppose that instead of an approaching space, you see the traffic signal change to yellow. Once again, *do not* watch the oncoming traffic. Do not see whether it is stopping, not yet. Instead, do all the quick checks listed above. Then look ahead to check the stopped or stopping traffic. If the way is clear, turn safely and efficiently.

When an oncoming car turns left, resist the urge to turn left at the same time. Make sure that *your* way is clear, too.

The way is clear for the oncoming car (gray) to turn left. It is not clear for you (white car).

LEFT TURNS ON STREETS WITH FOUR OR MORE LANES: Seeing can be very difficult when making left turns across two or more lanes of oncoming traffic. A large blind area can be created by oncoming vehicles waiting in the left lane to turn or waiting behind left turners. These vehicles block your view of the right oncoming lane.

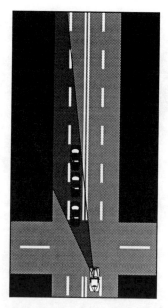

In this situation, *never guess!* Never take a chance. Make *sure* that there is not something that you cannot see coming at you in the oncoming right lane. Look far ahead to see cars enter the blind area. If the last car to enter the blind area comes out of it, and no other car has gone in, the right lane *MIGHT* be clear. However, someone may have moved out of line in the left lane and be coming at you in the right lane.

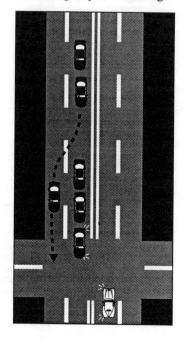

Somebody may even have left a parking spot or a driveway on the right in the blind area and be coming at you in the right lane.

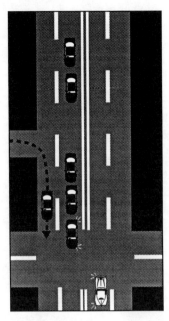

Hills can also block your view and make your turn awkward and dangerous.

Look through car windows, etc. to see. Do not take a chance. *See*. Do not worry about the traffic waiting behind you. *SEE*. If you have to, just wait until the light changes to yellow. Even then, *do not rush*!

When turning left, never simply follow the car or especially the truck or bus ahead. You will not be able to see oncoming traffic, and it will not be able to see you. There may be enough space for one vehicle, but not enough for two. Wait until you can see traffic. While waiting, plan your own turn. When it is clear, make your own turn.

Finally, following the car ahead through a left (or right) turn can very easily lead you into an improper turn.

205

THE HIDDEN CAR: Two cars can look like one. Even though you can see right through it, one car in traffic or parked can hide another car. What happens is that the bottom, top, and posts, and even the driver of the second car, just happen to line up closely enough behind those of the first car, that you can't see them. In this situation,

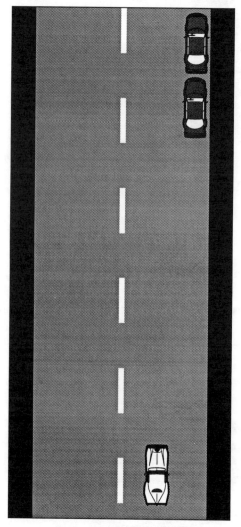

the driver approaching these two parked cars might be unable to see the front car even though he looks next to, under, and right through the rear car. As he passes, thinking there is only one car, the driver of the front car might open his door or even pull out into traffic.

Another example of the hidden car is this.

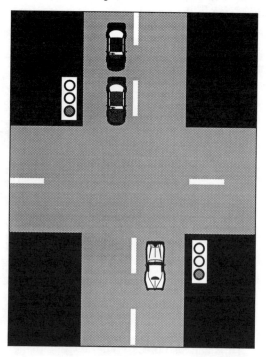

In this situation, the driver of the white car wants to turn left. When the traffic signal changes to green, he yields to the grey car, but, completely unaware of the black car, he turns left in front of or into it.

TAILGATERS: Some few tailgaters are trying to go faster or get past you. The overwhelming majority of these, however, have no grand plan for safely maintaining great speed and gloriously outmaneuvering traffic for super efficiency. They have no understanding of the speed-distance-seeing-control relationship in traffic. They merely push ahead blindly. Often they pass you only to jam in behind a car or group of cars ahead. They pass you and hurry into a clumsy or dangerous situation that they did not even see in their urgent rush.

Most tailgaters, though, are unaware that they tailgate. They think everybody drives that way, or ought to. They follow like boxcars in a train. They do not know any better. They do not understand proper following distance. In fact, if you could show them the overall traffic scene, they would grin as if they had just understood one of the great cosmic mysteries. They do not understand being in control in traffic. They do not even understand their own best interests. They just follow.

The point is that most tailgaters do not know that they are tailgating. They think that they are driving normally. They are watching the rear end of your car. That is why speeding up doesn't work. They just speed up with you. They think that they are going the speed of traffic. That is why your slowing down often has no effect on them either.

What *can* you do to get rid of tailgaters? Slowing down *a lot* may work. In the daytime, try lighting your headlights. Lighting your headlights also lights your taillights. In the daytime, your taillights can be mistaken for your brake lights. Looking at the tailgater *very* often in your inside mirror may catch his eye. He will wonder why you keep looking at him. Sometimes he will drop back a bit. Jamming on your brakes for an instant will work, but is obviously dangerous. Changing lanes and letting him pass can work well. Unfortunately, sometimes he will change lanes with you. A sure, though drastic, method is pulling over to the curb and letting the tailgater go. A strange but probably very effective method would be driving erratically. Slow down, speed up. Wobble around in your lane, wave your arms around, etc. Make the tailgater think you are crazy. He will pass you and be very proud of himself for getting away from a "dangerous" driver. If the police see you doing this, they will *not* get away from you. They will want to talk to you.

Sometimes the fellow behind you is tailgating because you *are* blocking traffic. PAY ATTENTION!

If your car is crippled in some way, use your hazard flashers and stay out of the way as much as possible.

STAY IN LINE: There are safety advantages to being in a moving line of traffic. It's like being part of a freight train. The line of traffic is seen as a unit by pedestrians and other drivers. They treat the line as a unit. They tend not to cut into it from the sides. They just let it pass as if it were a parade.

The driver of the first car has sight and space advantages, but he does not have the advantage of vehicles ahead running interference for him.

Lines of traffic work well in driving through blind areas. Once the first vehicle makes it through, anyone in the blind area will probably be aware that he is in a blind area and expect more traffic behind the lead vehicle.

The negative side of the freight train is that it keeps many drivers from realizing how poorly they see and drive in traffic. As part of the freight train, they blow right past thousands of unseen hazards.

BE PART OF THE GROUP: On multi-lane roads, groups of vehicles can have certain advantages similar to those of lines of vehicles. Groups are easier to see in conditions of poor visibility. They also tend to be seen as having more forward inertia than just one car alone. Therefore, people are less likely to get into the way of groups.

SEPARATE HAZARDS: This is about using space and timing masterfully. It means that you should plan to get to tight or clumsy places when they are most open.

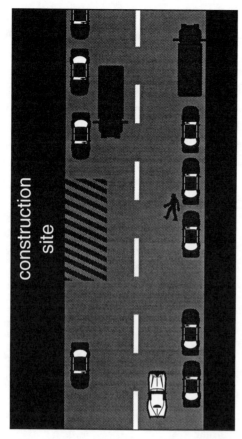

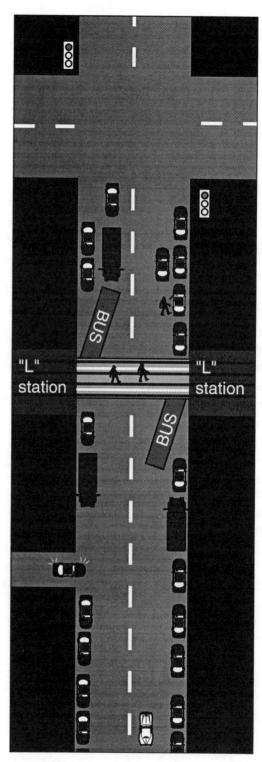

In the situation illustrated above, plan not to arrive at the construction site at the same time that the construction worker (crossing from the right) and the oncoming truck get there. Actually, all three people should plan to be in the area next to the construction site at separate times.

Separating hazards does not mean dealing with only one hazard at a time. It means seeing all traffic as interrelated, then pacing yourself so that you are always at each place at the best time for smooth, safe, efficient, apparently effortless flow. Remember that traffic events do interact with each other and change each other.

SEPARATE OUT COMPLEX TRAFFIC SITUATIONS: Before you get involved in a complex traffic situation (one made up of several traffic events), check traffic beyond it and before it.

The elevated train station ahead is a complex traffic situation. There are two stopped buses loading and unloading. There may be pedestrians crossing the street in the marked crosswalk. The buses block vision severely. Oncoming traffic may try to move through the underpass on your side of the street just as you try to move through the underpass on their side of the street. There may be delivery trucks and delivery men working near the station. There may be pedestrians entering and leaving parked or double-parked cars. Cars may pull out or pull over before or after picking up or dropping off train riders.

Before you get to the situation, begin checking it. Do not concentrate only on it, though. Recheck the space leading to it. There is a car coming out of an alley on your left. It is signalling left. It might pull out in front of you. Get eye contact with its driver, blow your horn, slow down, speed up, etc. Handle the problem in some way so that you can have time to recheck the train station well before you get to it. Check your mirror to prepare for possible slowing down or stopping at the station. Check past the station. See the traffic signal at the intersection beyond the station.

Now that you have a good idea about what is before and after the complex traffic situation at the train station, you can spend time and space dealing with it, without being surprised before or right after it.

See the overall traffic scene. See the interrelationships of traffic situations and events. Then you can handle each part at the proper time, just as if you were cooking a big meal.

When cooking a large meal, you want everything to be ready at the same time. You split your attention among several pots and pans, the oven, the refrigerator, the table, and the sink. By doing everything at the right time, you get the whole meal cooked, but not burned, right on time.

RIGHT TURNS: Yes, right turns are easier than left turns, because you do not have to deal with crossing in front of oncoming traffic. Right turns have their own problems, though. One is visibility to the left.

As long as you drive, bad visibility to the left will make some right turns tricky. Bad visibility to the left will force you to begin making certain right turns before you can be sure that all is clear from the left. Here, parked cars block your vision.

As usual, noticing and planning ahead for blind areas is valuable. Before driving into the situation illustrated above, stop farther back as illustrated here.

From here you have a better angle from which to see between the parked cars and through their windows, as well as the space at the end of their line.

When making a right turn with badly blocked vision to the left, if possible, stop far enough back to get some idea about traffic to the left. Then check ahead and right and move ahead a bit. Recheck left. Recheck ahead and right and move ahead again. Just keep repeating this process as you begin turning right. Do not look only to the left, but do not look only to the right either as you begin your turn. Look both ways with many rapid movements of your head and eyes as you creep into your right turn. The idea is to make a perfect right turn *and* avoid surprises from any direction, including pedestrians in your path.

Keep creeping and looking and turning until you know that you can complete your right turn safely. You may be halfway through your turn before this is possible.

Be patient when making any difficult turn.

While waiting for a space for your right turn to arrive from the left, do not keep watching the space until it does arrive. Instead, after you have seen the space coming, check to the right and ahead. Plan your turning path and check for other traffic.

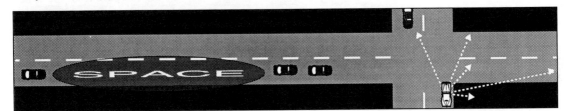

Do not watch space approach, but check ahead and right and plan your turn.

When the space is getting close, look back to the left to recheck it. If the space is good, your checking and planning to the right will allow you to use it. You will look back to the right for a last look and turn right.

Looking only left at the approaching space while waiting to turn right will handicap you. You will not know about traffic conditions ahead and to the right. You will not have pre-programmed your brain to aim properly. As a result, you will miss some opportunities for right turns. You will also make some hasty, unplanned, ragged right turns. You will also start some right turns very late. This will force approaching traffic to slow down because you cannot get up to speed in time.

You decide when to turn right into traffic. You make the decision, you are responsible for it. Traffic should never have to slow down to help you.

Finish most right turns under relatively strong acceleration and checking your rearview mirror.

NEVER "JUST GO": There will be situations in which you can see little or nothing to the sides or rear. For example

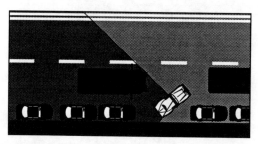

The view to the rear for the driver pulling out is badly blocked by the double-parked truck, yet he must pull out past the double-parked truck ahead.

In situations like this, resist the urge to take a chance and just go, even though you cannot be sure that all is clear (safe) to the rear. It is easy to think that you will never be able to be sure and that all you can do is take a chance and go — *fast* — *NOW!* That is how children think when they run across the street. "If I run fast," they think, "I'll be out there for only a short time." They also run right in front of moving cars whose drivers have no chance to avoid them because they are running suddenly out from between parked cars, or bushes, etc.

Keep creeping and trying to see. It will be nerve-wracking, but it *will* work. One of three things will happen. You will eventually creep into a position from which you can see that the maneuver is safe, or you will creep into a position in which you block traffic, and it will have to let you go, or somebody will notice your problem and wave at you to go. Whichever happens, you will get to go safely.

NOW OR NEVER: A driving mistake very much like going when you are not sure it is safe is seeing an opening and taking it before you have checked thoroughly.

For example, you need to pull out of a gas station or parking lot into a very busy street. Just as you get to the street, you look and see a space. You think that another space may not come for minutes. You are not sure about other traffic. You have not had time to check it properly yet. Because the space is there, though, you decide to take it — right now! You rush into the space. Immediately you find yourself driving right into a problem or a crash in the area you didn't check carefully.

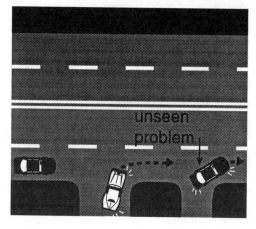

AVOID RUSHING: Rushing is *not* being fast. Rushing is trying to make up time. Rushing is trying to do something very quickly, often by skipping steps.

You may get away with rushing. You may get away with it for a long time. It may become a habit. Sooner or later, though, rushing will get you into trouble.

When rushing or taking chances does get you into trouble, you have no excuses. What can you say? "I took a chance. I thought he'd see me." "I just didn't look." "I was in a hurry." Those things mean nothing when you look with horror at the torn and bleeding, crumpled body of the little girl trapped under your car.

Rushing can make you slower. You can rush right into clumsy situations which will slow you down — situations you would have seen and avoided if you had been driving well.

In cities, rushing by speeding may put you out of phase with timed traffic signals. Instead of making all the green lights, you will get stopped by all the red lights.

To other drivers, rushing can look as if you are trying to push people around. Drivers angered by your apparent trying to take advantage of them may fight back.

Try to plan ahead to avoid rushing. *Never* rush because somebody behind you is in a hurry! He may be late, but if you rush past a blind area and crash, the crash is yours.

Rushing takes the joy out of driving. Rushing makes driving very hard, frustrating, dangerous work. Do not rush, think. Most of the things to which we rush are not worth the trouble. They are surely not worth the consequences of a serious accident. No matter who you are, or who you think you are, the world was here long before you got here, and it will probably be here long after you are gone.

IT *CAN* HAPPEN TO YOU: Believe it! It *can* happen to you! Do your best to make each and every one of your drives a joyride. Never have that sick, faint, feeling people get at accidents.

Imagine the blood, the smashed faces. Imagine the moans, the screams. Imagine the trembling in panic when you find out that you have just killed somebody. Imagine having nightmares of the accident scene for the rest of your life. Imagine the guilt you will feel every day when you remember that you were to blame for a needless death.

Now, on top of that, add the shame, the crushing humiliation of having been drunk or on drugs when the car you were driving smashed, tore, shattered …killed an innocent human being.

MISTAKES: People make mistakes. They do things wrong. They break laws. They take chances. They do clumsy maneuvers. They rush. They don't think.

Expect it. Learn from it. Remember that you do it too, and learn from that. Before you get angry at some driver or pedestrian for making a really bad move, think about whether you ever do the very same thing. If you do it, stop doing it. Get better and better. Make fewer and fewer mistakes. Learn and grow.

Learn from good examples, too. When you see someone do something really smart in traffic, make a point of trying to remember it. Then you may do it when you are faced with the same situation.

SIGNALS: Always time your signals so that they are the most meaningful. Never signal before you know exactly where you want to turn. If you cannot see the place where you intend to turn, how can you show others that place?

When there are several places to turn close together, do the best you can to show exactly which place is the one you want.

Every turn and lane change requires a signal. However, never think that the signal makes a space for you or forces other drivers to let you into line. The signal tells others what you want to do. That is all.

Never approach closely an intersection with your turn signal flashing unless you intend to turn there. This causes crashes.

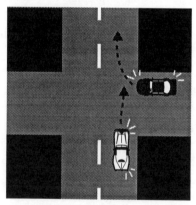

Driver of gray car thinks white car will turn right, so turns right in front of it. White car does not turn.

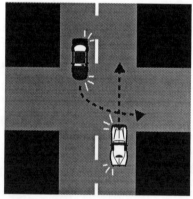

Driver of gray car thinks white car will turn left, so turns left in front of it. White car does not turn.

LOOK FOR OTHERS' PROBLEMS: In watching the overall traffic scene, predict not only your own problems, but those of others, Whether you see the problems of others is a good test. It will tell you whether you are really watching the connected story of developing traffic situations ahead, or just reacting to isolated events.

If other drivers and pedestrians surprise you and cause you difficulty by swerving or stepping into your path to avoid their own problems, you are not predicting their problems. Likewise, if others surprise you with sudden stops, you are not predicting their problems. You are also probably following too closely.

See others' problems behind your car, too. Sometimes speeding up just a bit can create enough space for those behind you to smooth out a rough situation.

MAKING SPACE: When drivers need space the most, they bunch up the most. In snow, instead of trying to place their vehicles so that there is more space for seeing, maneuvering, and skidding, they bunch up. The slowest drivers take the cleanest lanes and force those behind them to bunch up, or drive through the deepest snow to try to pass and get clear. One wonders who really causes accidents.

When two expressways merge, drivers slow down and bunch up instead of making space. They slow down because they have not been seeing and planning far enough ahead. The bunching up is caused by the needless slowing. Whenever there is a merging or a funneling down of lanes, space is valuable. See these conditions early and place your vehicle to make space, not to use it up.

BLIND SPOTS: Your major blind spots are here.

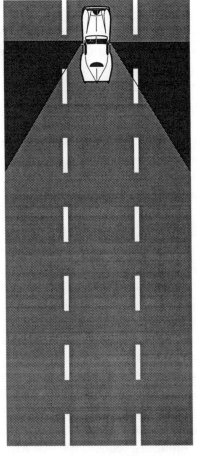 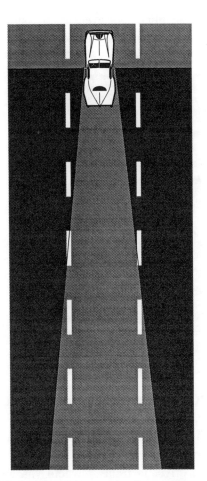

Blind spots with properly adjusted mirrors;   *Blind spots with improperly adjusted mirrors.*

Whenever you move your car more than a few inches sideways, check the blind spot on the side toward which you are moving, unless you are all alone in a wide lane. Check the proper blind spot just before pulling out of a parking space, before lane changing, before pulling over to the curb, in merging and funneling down situations, etc.

Check your blind spot to avoid *immediate* danger. Checking your blind spot lets you avoid crashing into something off to the side close behind you, something you cannot see in your mirrors. Think of checking blind spots this way. In restaurants, when one waitress passes just behind another, she says, "behind you" so that the other waitress does not step back into her. This is especially important when something like hot coffee is being carried. Check your blind spot for danger that is *RIGHT NOW*!

Checking your blind spot must become so strong a habit that you *cannot* move a car sideways without doing it.

Check your blind spot even when you are merely following your lane. You cannot count on others to follow theirs.

GET IT DONE: When merging into heavy or very heavy, urban expressway traffic, get it done. Just hanging in the merging area and fading ever so slowly into traffic is wrong. It confuses the driver in front of whom you are merging. He wonders why you do not just merge. He has seen you and made a slight adjustment in his pace to help you merge. Then you do not merge. What is he to think? He may feel that you have made a fool of him and speed up to close the space he has made for you. In extremely heavy traffic, your oozing can take

such a long time that he actually loses track of you, only to be surprised when you finally do squeeze in in front of him.

Too slow merging can also confuse the driver behind whom you will merge. He sees you behind him, but notices that you are not merging. He speeds up a bit to help you, cutting his own following distance. You still do not merge.

This too slow merging slows traffic and makes it just that much more dangerous by causing a ripple in the flow. At its best, it shows inattention on the part of the oozing driver. At its worst, it shows his attitude that everybody else is supposed to get out of his way whenever he gets ready to make his move. Each driver must work within the overall traffic flow, not expect traffic to accommodate him.

This problem is not limited to expressways. It happens often in other lane change situations in heavy, urban traffic. In merging and lane changing, once you are sure that your spot is safe and obtainable, *take it*.

SEE WHAT IS THERE: The lights are flashing and the bells are ringing at the railroad crossing. You can see well down the tracks in both directions, but you cannot see a train coming. The lights and bells must be broken — working for no reason.

Maybe, maybe not. The signals may be working because a railroad section car or a small truck with flanged wheels which can run on the railroad tracks is about to cross. Do not be fooled because you do not see the train for which you are looking. *See what is there*!

It is the same with motorcycles. Drivers miss seeing them and even crash into them, because they do not expect to see them. They expect to see cars, trucks, buses. They do not expect to see motorcycles and therefore do not see them.

Look for motorcycles, and section cars, and snowmobiles, and wheelchairs, etc.

GLIMPSES AND SUBTLE CLUES: Be alert to notice tiny clues in driving. Shadows, especially moving shadows, can alert you to possible conflicts you would not otherwise be able to notice, because the objects casting the shadows are invisible to you in blind areas. Gleams of light must come from somewhere. A red glow under the car ahead will be cast by the brake lights of the otherwise nearly invisible car in front of it. The lit headlights of oncoming vehicles will seem to flicker when pedestrians, cars, or trains are crossing in front of them. Just noticing something out of the corner of your eye or in the darkness is an excellent clue.

Early misidentification is alright. Suppose you see something off to the side in the dark at night. You think it might be a pedestrian about to enter the street. It turns out to be a road sign. You did not make a mistake. You saw *something*. The point is to see these little somethings, then recheck them to be sure about what they are, not to know instantly on the first look. If you always know what everything is as soon as you see it, you are probably not looking far enough ahead.

Glimpses are another kind of clue. Look through spaces for glimpses. Look through parked cars for heads attached to the bodies of children about to run into the street. Look through and beside the cars ahead of yours for glimpses far ahead in heavy traffic.

Look for little spaces through which to look. By looking through whatever little spaces you can find, you will be able, very early, to pick out clues to traffic events far ahead. This information will give you much more time to plan and do needed lane changes, etc. In the example below, a glimpse of motion may have prevented a crash.

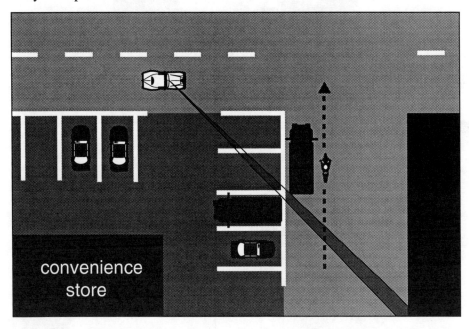

The driver of the white car caught a glimpse of motion on the side street through the narrow (perhaps one foot) space between the two vans. He blew his horn to warn whatever might pop out from behind the van. He slowed, covered his brake, and got ready to take further evasive action if needed.

The bicyclist, who had been the blur of motion, did not heed the horn and continued directly into the major cross street. He was very surprised to see the white car. He almost fell off his bike when he saw the car.

The driver, on the other hand, was not surprised at all. That glimpse may have prevented an ugly crash.

See the obvious. *Look for the nearly invisible!*

USE OFFSET AND CURVES TO AID SEEING: Not following directly behind the car ahead can aid your forward vision.

Driver of white car improves his field of forward vision by not following directly behind the car ahead.

On curves, avoid looking only at the vehicle directly ahead of yours. Use the curve to see farther ahead.

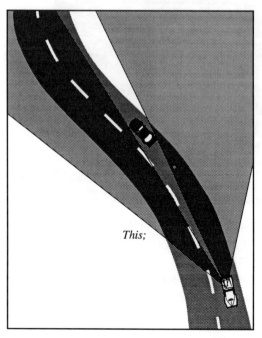

This;

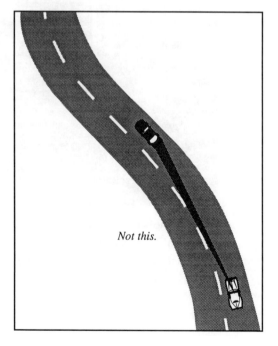

Not this.

THE DANGER ZONE: The concept of the danger zone can be valuable to drivers. The danger zone is not really an area, but an equation of time, speed, and distance with what you can see. If you cannot see beyond a certain point, you must be able to stop or swerve before reaching that point. Think of driving through fog.

LOOK WHERE THE OTHER GUY LOOKS: In traffic, find out why the other person is looking where he is.

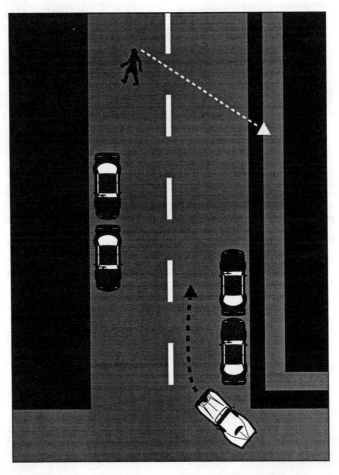

The lady j-walking across the street looks back over her shoulder. Why? Did someone call her? Will that person follow her across the street? Will she go back across the street? Check the area at which you saw her look.

DO NOT LET ROADS LIKE THESE LULL YOU INTO STOPPING SCANNING: Driving down this tree lined, two lane road is almost like driving in a tunnel. One forgets that there can be cross streets, driveways, joggers, animals, etc., along the sides. (See illustration next page.)

Drivers tend to limit their looking around on very wide roads, too. They tend to look only at their own side of the street. They are surprised by oncoming cars turning left across their path. They also neglect to check past the edges of the road onto the shoulders and into the parking lots, etc. They get surprised from those areas, too.

Six lanes is very wide.

WHAT COMES NEXT? When a ball flies or rolls into the street, what should you do? Stop, because someone may be running into the street after the ball.

What do you suppose might follow a cat running full speed across the street? A dog. What might follow that dog? Its young owner.

From between parked cars, three 11 year old boys walk calmly across the street well ahead of your car. What comes next? Just as they pass the middle of the street, the younger brother of one of them comes running after them. Afraid that he will be left behind, he is not thinking about traffic. He runs directly after his big brother without checking traffic.

DO SOMETHING ABOUT IT: One, two, or more drivers ahead of you are getting into a dangerous situation. Do more than comment to your passengers about the clowns ahead trying to drive. The clowns in traffic are not on television. They are real people with real problems, which can become your problem very quickly. Their accident can easily involve you.

Do something! Check your mirror(s), blind spot(s), etc. Cover your brake pedal, slow down, change lanes, etc.

Be smooth and subtle, though. Try to avoid sudden, vigorous evasive actions like jamming on the brakes unless they are needed. The drivers near you may not see the clowns. Even if they do see them, they might not be ready to take evasive action. If you do something violent, you may cause your own accident, while the clowns ahead drive on safely.

HE IS COMING AT ME ON MY SIDE OF THE ROAD: Traffic is forced onto the wrong side of the road. Expect it. Look for construction, double parked trucks, etc., on the opposite side of the road which might force oncoming traffic onto your side of the road.

COVER THE BRAKE PEDAL AUTOMATICALLY: Eliminate the time it takes to move your foot from the gas pedal to the brake pedal when a predictable quick slowdown or stop is needed. Make it a habit to cover the brake pedal automatically every time you release the gas pedal to coast past some problem.

DO NOT: Once you have gone past the stop bar and into the crosswalk when stopping at a red light, do not back up. Unseen by you, pedestrians may be crossing behind your car.

Do not stop immediately after making a right turn. This maneuver is sometimes done when dropping off people. It can get you rear-ended easily. If you must do this kind of maneuver, make sure that you know conditions behind your car. Give the driver behind you time to figure out what you are doing by driving smoothly and quite slowly.

Expect others to stop suddenly in front of you after making right turns, especially after right turns into parking lots.

Car stops to let out people at the store;

Car stops to look for a parking space;

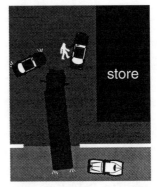

Semi stops because of traffic or to check close clearances.

LOOK FOR SPACE, ALWAYS: Look for obstacles and hazards, but *never* look *at* them while trying to steer around them. The car goes where you look. Look where you want it to go. Check clearances and developing situations as needed, but *always* aim for space. Drivers actually crash because instead of looking for space, they look directly at whatever they are trying to avoid. They look at it. The car goes where they look. They crash.

SPECIFIC VEHICLES: School buses, taxi cabs, mail trucks, ice cream trucks, driving school cars, etc., create special traffic problems. Children walk and run to and from school buses and ice cream trucks. Mail trucks pull over and pull out at mail boxes. Taxis often rush. They pull over to pick up and drop off passengers. Taxis may also do strange and illegal maneuvers. Driving school and driver education cars are usually safe, but they can do almost anything at any time.

Crippled vehicles can get into the way because they cannot get out of the way. When you must drive a crippled vehicle, try to stay out of the way and, in most situations, use your emergency, four-way flashers.

DRIVE MASTERFULLY BY STANDING STILL: Sometimes masterful driving is accomplished by standing still. Standing still does not mean doing nothing. It means *purposely* not moving.

When the traffic situation is such that other road users would expect you to stand still, stand still. Do not send confusing messages about your. intentions by creeping along, looking as if you might pull into traffic at just the wrong time from an alley, driveway, parking space, or side road.

Remember that in traffic your car is always sending messages to other road users. Send the proper message. When you should be sending, "I am standing still and will keep standing still," do not send, "I am not paying attention," or "I am going to try to bluff my way into traffic."

WATCH THE PEOPLE IN THE VEHICLES: Why watch only the vehicles in traffic? Watch the people in them, too. Drivers give all

sorts of clues about the future movements of their vehicles. See where the driver is looking: staring straight ahead, checking mirror(s), checking blind spot, etc. See his mood, too. Is he relaxed, uncomfortable, attentive, intensely searching the road ahead, sight seeing, talking or laughing or arguing with passengers, using the telephone, listening to the radio, trying to control children and/or pets, etc.

The behavior of passengers can give an idea of the mood in the car.

Finally, seeing the people, not just the vehicles, makes driving a much more human experience. You realize that almost all the other drivers — good, bad, or indifferent — are not trying to make your life miserable. They are just doing the best they can to get wherever it is they want to go.

EYE CONTACT: Eye contact is a very valuable driving tool. Once you get eye contact with the other person in a confusing or doubtful traffic situation, the problem seems to resolve itself automatically. Both people just "know" who will go first, or one will wave on the other.

TRAFFIC CIRCLES: The basic rule is the farther around a traffic circle you want to go, the more you move toward the middle and back toward the outside again. If you want to go only a short distance, stay to the outside.

Notice that a street which continues through a traffic circle may not exit directly across from the point at which it entered.

HABITS: Every time you drive, you build habits. Every time you drive, these habits get stronger and stronger. The good habits you build will keep you safe to enjoy more joyriding. The bad habits will, one day when the chips are down, hurt or kill you or someone else.

Build good habits. Try always to drive with maximum control. Be safe, and swift, and graceful, and confident. Avoid tickets. Avoid accidents. Enjoy the sincere compliments of your passengers not on your car, but on your wonderful driving. *MAKE THE WORLD A BETTER PLACE BY DRIVING THROUGH IT!*

COMMENTARY DRIVING: Commentary driving is nothing more than talking while you drive — talking about driving, of course. Just talk. Name the things you see in the overall traffic scene. Tell where these things are. Try to keep talking constantly. Look far ahead for things to talk about. Look near. Look to the sides. Look to the rear. Look inside your car at the instrument panel.

Soon you will begin to talk about how traffic events are related to each other and to you. You will begin predicting. You will explain what you are doing in traffic and why you are doing it. You will be able to keep talking about driving all the time you are driving. Even waiting at stop lights, you will find yourself analyzing traffic signals, other drivers, pedestrians, physical features, etc.

This is a very worthwhile exercise. It lets you know, by hearing your own words, what you see when driving and what you do while driving. It forces you to think about driving while you are doing it. Therefore, it forces you to learn more about driving.

You do not need to talk to anybody but yourself. Talking to your driving instructor can be very rewarding.

Try commentary driving. Go ahead, try it. It is one way to build great skill at driving. It can lead you to a wonderful relationship with driving.

Commentary driving is *not* just a great learning technique. It is an excellent review technique which you can use as long as you drive to keep your driving as sharp as you believe it is.

DESTINATION DRIVING: Destination driving is simply driving to a destination and parking *all by yourself*. You can have somebody with you, but he may not help you to see, or think, or maneuver, or navigate.

Destination driving is very good for new drivers, because it is how driving really is. Driving lessons can concentrate on specific skills, and the driving teacher will almost always give advice in the hope that he is teaching a valuable lesson. In destination driving, however, the student driver is free to make his mistakes, see their consequences first hand, and learn to deal with them.

A student driver or a newly licensed driver should do destination driving several times before being turned loose on his own in what is a very different experience from taking driving lessons.

Both destination driving and commentary driving can be very valuable.

13 *Chapter Thirteen*

Out in the Country

Exactly like urban and suburban driving, rural driving is about aiming, steering, speed control, positioning, signalling, and getting ample, correct, timely information about road, weather, and traffic conditions. There are crossroads, traffic control devices, vehicular and pedestrian traffic, blind areas, etc. Like the good

urban driver, the good rural driver must use his eyes carefully and constantly to get the overall traffic scene in plenty of time.

There are differences. Though the rural traffic scene is often much less crowded than the urban, it is frequently driven through at much higher speeds. While expressways in cities allow high speeds, they also separate fast traffic from the surrounding area. In the country, there is often little or no separation between high speed traffic and roadside hazards. Expressways are engineered to give ample sight lines, etc. The original engineering of many rural highways and roads consisted of figuring out the easiest, cheapest, shortest way to build a road between two places. On many rural highways and roads high speeds take traffic over blind hill crests, through forests filled with wild animals, around blind curves, and right past hidden driveways. Rural roads are shared with pedestrians, stray and wild animals, very slow moving farm machinery, etc. High speed, rural driving usually allows much less time between seeing and reaching hazards than high speed, urban driving.

The key is readiness. Look not only for trouble. Look for places where trouble might lurk. Search for blind areas: windbreaks, forests, hills, curves, bushes, buildings, hedges, tall crops or weeds, etc. Look for places where people and animals are most likely to be. Look into farm entrances, front yards, barn yards. Look near, across from, and up and down the road from mail boxes and stopped or parked vehicles. Finally, look for the places where people and animals are *least* likely to be. Expect and look for the unexpected — the sudden.

You are driving up a hill at 55 m.p.h. What is on the other side of the hill? Perhaps a sign tells you that there is a sharp curve. Perhaps a sign tells you that there may be a school bus stopped ahead or children waiting for the bus. Perhaps there is no sign, but there is a cow standing in the road, on your side, just past the crest of the hill. Perhaps a tractor has just pulled onto the road and is moving only seven miles per hour. Perhaps an oncoming driver is passing, driving straight at you on your side of the road. Actually, if you can see the top of a car coming toward you on its own side of the road, you can almost certainly see the top of a car on your side of the road. You might not see a boy who had just fallen off his bicycle, though.

Be prepared. Once again just realizing that you are motoring into a blind area gives you the jump on trouble. Realizing that a problem could be hiding just past the next curve will let you react much faster and better if there is one, than just cruising nonchalantly along the road. Just as in the city, if you notice blind areas early and check them properly, you will automatically adjust your car's speed and position correctly.

Be ready *every time* you drive through blind areas. You may have gone through a certain blind curve hundreds of times, thousands of times, and it has always been clear. The next time it may not be clear. We feel comfortable in familiar surroundings, so we assume that we are safe, and let down our guard. Part of being a champion is not being tricked into a mistake by the familiar.

Use the terrain. You may be able to see from the top of one hill to the top of the next.

Likewise, you may be able to see from one curve to the next.

bushes blocking
driver's view

You may be able to see parts of several hills and curves.

On gravel and dirt roads, a dust cloud on the other side of the hill or far out to the side can alert you to other traffic. Dust can also be coming from a tractor out in a field or from wind blowing across a field. You and your car are both better off if you do not follow closely through a dust cloud created by the vehicle ahead. You can see and breathe better. Your car's mechanical parts are not subjected to needless extra wear from dust particles.

PASSING ON TWO-LANE ROADS: Passing on two-lane roads requires driving on the wrong side of the road.

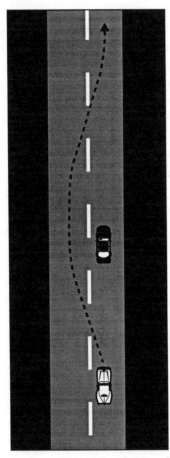

There is obvious danger in that, and two-lane passing has built-in drama. Two-lane road passing is a challenging driving maneuver. Understanding the maneuver is essential to meeting its challenge with poise.

The passing situation begins when you notice that you are catching up to the vehicle ahead. At this point, it must be assumed that: you know the speed limit; you are travelling at exactly the speed you intend; you are aware of any ongoing road, visibility, weather, and/or traffic problems; and you are conscious of the capabilities of yourself and your car. Making your initial decision about whether or not to pass is based on this information.

In deciding whether or not to pass, it is good to consider your location, too. If you know that you will soon turn off this road, the slight time advantage gained by passing might not be worth the bother of doing it.

If you decide not to pass or not to pass at this time, *do not* catch up to the vehicle ahead. Maintain a good following distance. This following distance allows you to see well and maintain the best control over your driving situation. The following distance also leaves a space which might be needed by someone trying to pass you.

If you have decided to pass, the next decision is *when* to pass. On straight, level roads with little traffic and great visibility, this decision is easy. It is often made as soon as you notice that you are catching the vehicle ahead. You will pass just as soon as you catch up enough. With more traffic, hills, curves, etc., the opportunity to pass probably will not be available so easily. You will have to wait, check, plan, double-check, etc. You may have to cancel your decision about when to pass. You may begin pulling out several times, only to find that passing is impossible or too risky. That is part of the game. It should never cause shame. Your decision to pass may not be final until you are actually next to and passing the other vehicle. Never think that a good driver must always make the pass/no pass decision instantly and correctly on the first try. There is no dishonor in changing your mind when new information is received. There is only safety.

Once you have decided to try to pass, look for a piece of road which might allow your pass. It should give you plenty of clear sight and passing distance ahead. Check or double-check that you are not entering a no passing zone. Look for barrier lines on the pavement. Look for no passing signs. Look for places where it is illegal to pass: bridges, intersections, overpasses, and railroad crossings. Look also for driveways on either side ahead. Driveways and small, hard to see crossroads or side roads can cause a lot of trouble. Traffic can move out of any of them and come right at you while you are on the wrong side of the road. The vehicle you are passing can also cut you off by turning left across your path into one of them. See what is behind you. See whether anybody is passing you. Try to see that there is a space ahead of the vehicle you want to pass for your car when you have completed your pass. Look for oncoming traffic. If there is oncoming traffic, is it far enough away to allow your pass? Is it coming at you slowly enough to allow your pass? Hilly country can both help and hinder you in gathering this information before you begin pulling out to pass.

When conditions for a pass seem adequate, recheck your mirror(s), signal, check your left side blind spot, and begin pulling out to get a better look at conditions ahead — *ESPECIALLY THE ONCOMING TRAFFIC!* Make sure that a hillcrest or curve up ahead does not block your view of oncoming traffic. Check the vehicle you want to pass. Might it pull in front of you to pass the vehicle ahead of it? You can signal the vehicle to be passed with a toot of your horn or, at night, with a flash from low to high to low beam headlights. If there is an obvious problem, cancel your decision to pass. If everything still looks good, though, continue your maneuver. Keep rechecking and re-evaluating as you catch up. If a problem comes up, do not hesitate to cancel the pass. If you must cancel the pass, check at least your right side blind spot before diving back onto the right side of the road. If time allows, check your inside mirror, too. If there is even more time, signal right.

There is no exact, step-by-step order in which to do this information gathering, checking and rechecking, speed/distance calculation, and any needed speed changes. They all overlap each other. Many are done at the same time or almost the same time. The order may change because of the specific passing situation.

Once you have completed your pass, check your inside rearview mirror before returning to the right side of the road. When you can see the whole front end of the vehicle you have just passed, you are far enough ahead of it to pull back into line without causing its driver any anxiety. Signal right. Check your right side blind spot. Pull gracefully back onto the right side of the road.

If oncoming traffic is getting close, do not wait around on the wrong side of the road, watching your mirror. Check your right side blind spot to be sure that you are clear and get back on your own side of the road. If there is time, signal. *Avoid slowing down while changing lanes!* Slowing down too soon will make your car cut off the vehicle you have just passed.

When you are back on the right side of the road, cancel your turn signal if you have not used the lane change feature and resume driving normally.

As stated earlier, understanding this maneuver is essential to your meeting its challenge with poise. Understanding the maneuver will lead you to three general rules about it. They are:

1. Almost all decisions are tentative, subject to cancellation.

2. Control of vehicle speed is very important.

3. Beginning your pass from farther back rather than farther forward gives you much more control in the maneuver.

Always keep these rules in mind when you are doing two-lane passing.

That almost all decisions are subject to cancellation has already been discussed. Indeed, the tentative nature of decision making is the essence of two-lane passing. Until your car is actually passing the other vehicle, you keep evaluating the progress and safety of the maneuver.

Speed is what gets two-lane passing done.

The idea is to get out, around, and back as quickly as possible. Adequate speed is crucial. In bad weather, on gravel roads, in extremely powerful cars, and in violent lane changes, traction can be a problem. Consider traction problems in deciding speed and accelerator use. In certain cases it is better to slow down when passing. For example, it is often wise to slow down to pass a horse or a horsedrawn vehicle, a tractor, etc. In any case, the state in which you are driving may not allow you to exceed the speed limit to pass.

Beginning your pass early enough is what gives you real control over the whole two-lane passing maneuver. It might seem that the best way to pass would be to rush right up to the vehicle to be passed, then jump onto the wrong side of the road and blast past. In rare cases, you do have to catch up, wait, swerve violently onto the wrong side of the road, and pass under full acceleration. This should not be your normal way of passing, though.

Catching up usually forces you to slow down to the speed of the vehicle you have caught. This has several disadvantages. You lose your speed advantage. You have to start your pass from a lower speed than if you had not caught up. Therefore, the actual pass must take longer, and you will be boxed in on the wrong side of the road longer by the vehicle you are passing. Slowing down forces violent acceleration. Catching up requires violent lane changing. As noted above, this combination can cause traction problems.

Catching up also gives you the problem of reduced visibility. Getting right behind the vehicle you wish to pass, especially if it is a truck, large RV, bus, etc., blocks your forward vision. Your view of oncoming traffic and overall conditions is blocked. To check these properly, you will have to pull farther out of line to the left than if you were farther back.

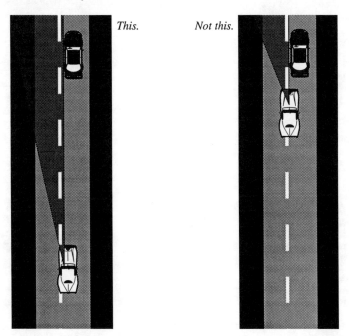

This.   *Not this.*

You have a much shorter time to be sure about oncoming traffic's speed and distance away from you.

Catching up or starting your pass later rather than earlier means that you have to rush every part of the maneuver. In addition to making sure the way ahead is safe, you will have to try to check your mirror(s), check your left side blind spot, signal, change lanes violently, and floor the gas pedal all in

a very short time. What if you made a mistake? Too bad. You are stuck with it. You are instantly boxed in on the wrong side of the road under full acceleration. Where is your escape path? You gave it up. Where is your control? You gave that up, too. You must rely on the other drivers involved to save you from the consequences of your needless mistake.

Starting your pass farther back gives you much more time to check ahead, as well as behind, and signal. It gives you plenty of time and space to double-check and triple-check your maneuver and, if need be, to duck back onto the right side of the road.

Starting your pass farther back gives you a higher starting speed, so that you will be trapped on the wrong side of the road next to the vehicle you are passing for a shorter time. You *will* be on the wrong side of the road longer, but being on the wrong side of the road is not the problem. The problem is being on the wrong side of the road and not being able to get back to the right side. The relatively long run on the wrong side up to the vehicle to be passed aids in seeing, planning, evaluating your progress, and even bailing out if you have to.

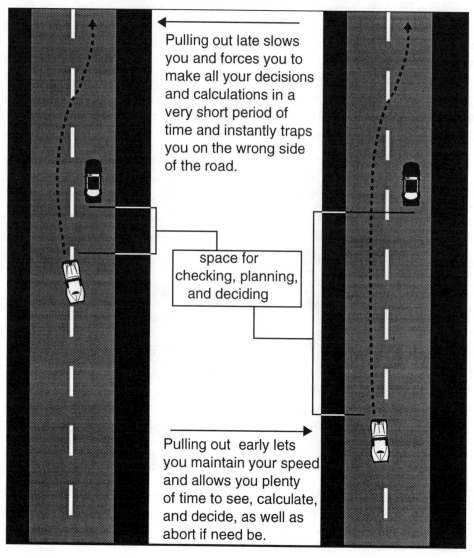

You are going to catch up anyway. What difference does it make which side of the road you are on when you do it?

In hilly country, it is good to plan your pass to begin just after you have crested the next hill. This will give you maximum distance before the next uphill no-passing zone. Get as much basic information as possible before reaching the crest. Then, if it looks safe on the other side of the hill, begin pulling out. Do not rush, though. Make sure before you commit yourself.

This pre-planning and prechecking concept is vital to two-lane passing and many other maneuvers, like pulling over to the curb, entering the expressway, lane changing, pulling out into traffic, turning into traffic, turning across traffic, etc. First locate the exact spot at which you want to do the maneuver, or the gap where you want to fit into the traffic flow. When entering expressways, find both the spot and the gap. Next, check any other factors involved in the maneuver. Check signs, signals, road markings, the law, road surface conditions, obstacles, pedestrian traffic, vehicular traffic, etc., as needed. Then, just as you reach the spot or gap, or the gap reaches you, you will be able to do your maneuver confident that everything has been checked and is ready. You will not miss the best place to do the maneuver. You will not get in the way because you are still checking when you should be doing. You will not lose your chance because you are not ready when the time comes.

When you are passing downhill, the driver of the vehicle you are trying to pass probably will not ease up on the gas. Do not be surprised when gravity accelerates his vehicle and causes your pass to take longer than you planned. Incidentally, it is illegal to speed up when being passed.

Uphill passing, on the other hand, gives you the problem of trying to accelerate while going uphill. This will also make your pass take longer. Passing just after a stoplight may surprise you,

too. The vehicle you are trying to pass will be accelerating, too. Your car's ability to accelerate will be lower when it is loaded with people, luggage, etc., than when it is carrying only you.

When there is trouble with a two-lane road pass, the oncoming driver has all the advantages, or should. If he is looking far ahead as he should, he will have plenty of warning that there is trouble. He will be able to slow down and, if need be, pull off the road to the right. Sometimes it is very difficult to tell whether the car far ahead on your side of the road is going your way or coming at you. Daytime running lights help here.

What the driver of the vehicle being passed should do when the passer gets into trouble is less clear. He has to try to judge the relative speeds of the two vehicles and their present and future relative positions. He cannot *legally* speed up, even though the passing driver might be trying to get back behind him. If the passing driver obviously wants to get back in behind, the driver being passed should cooperate in every way, including speeding up. If the passing driver thinks he is better off trying to finish the pass, the driver being passed should slow down to help him.

The trouble is that this is an emergency situation. All decisions must be made very quickly. There is little or no time for communication. The driver of the passing car is in the better position to judge whether or not he should continue the pass. If the driver of the vehicle being passed decides, on his own, to slow down, he may block the passing driver who also decided to slow down. This will only prolong the emergency.

The driver of the vehicle being passed is often the last to realize the situation. This is not all bad. If he stays uninformed, he will keep a steady speed. The passing driver can then base his decision to pass or not on that steady speed.

The driver being passed can move as far to the right as possible on his own. As a last resort, he can leave the road to the right.

The passing driver, boxed in on the wrong side of the road, should try to keep his head and do the best he can: move right, slow down and abort the pass, or speed up and finish it. He should try to avoid a head-on crash. The general rule for avoiding head-on crashes is never dodge to the left, because the oncoming driver might try to dodge you by instinctively moving to his right, which is your left. Try to reduce speed to minimize the force of impact. Try for a glancing crash instead of a direct hit.

The frustration of being unable to pass, whatever the reason, can be exasperating. The human feeling of exasperation at being needlessly held back is natural and strong. It has caused drivers to try to pass when they should not, sometimes with tragic results. When you cannot pass, show your maturity and mental control. Try to relax. Consider the challenges, the victories, the joys of the rest of your life. Decide to go with the flow and live the rest of your life.

Do not be the cause of frustration and exasperation. If you are unable to keep up with traffic, watch your mirror carefully and pull over when possible to let the jammed up traffic behind you pass. In long parades of slow traffic, leave space between your car and the one ahead for passing vehicles to enter. Allow following drivers to see the road ahead better by driving toward the right side of your lane when possible. Do this especially when you suspect that following drivers want to pass.

Watch the lines of oncoming traffic on two-lane roads. Be ready for a driver to pull out and try to pass when he should not.

School buses can hold up traffic in a maddening way. The bus stops to load or unload. You stop behind it. It resumes motion, and you want to pass. However, the long line of oncoming traffic which also had to stop for the bus blocks your pass. Just when things begin to clear up on the other side of the road, the school bus stops again.

This scenario can be repeated over and over and over and over . . . . It is another chance to show maturity. Stay cool and ride it out. Laugh at the absurdity of the situation. If you are in a familiar area, turn off and go another way. Remember to laugh again when you get stuck behind another school bus there. If the situation seems never ending, stop for coffee or gas, etc. If you get into this situation daily, change your schedule, or route, or just allow for it.

OFF ROAD RECOVERY: Suppose you drop one or two right side wheels off the road onto the shoulder. What should you do? It depends on the specific situation. If you drop a wheel or two onto a hard-packed gravel shoulder which is almost exactly level with the pavement, you merely drive right back onto the pavement.

Other situations can cause trouble though. Soft shoulders of deep sand will not support your vehicle as well as packed gravel shoulders. The right side of your car will tend to dig in and slow down when it hits the sand. This will tend to make the car difficult to control. *Stay off the brakes*! Hold on and steer the car gently to a straight ahead direction with two wheels on and two wheels off the pavement. Then slow down gently, checking your mirrors. At much reduced speed, check oncoming traffic, recheck following traffic, and turn sharply back onto the pavement. The sharp turn and lower speed keep your right rear tire from catching on the edge of the pavement and causing your car to want to spin.

A large drop-off between the pavement and the shoulder is also cause for concern. The remedy is the same as that for soft shoulders.

Why fall off the pavement at all, though? You might be forced off the pavement, but most drivers drive off all by themselves. They aim and steer incorrectly. If you aim along the right edge of the pavement, you will fall off now and then. If you aim far ahead at the space through which you want to drive, you will be fine.

Whether or not you fall off the pavement, it is worthwhile to learn exactly where your wheels are. This knowledge is very useful when driving near the pavement's edge, when dodging potholes or debris, and when pulling over to the curb, etc.

Learn where your wheels are by trying to run over things in the road. Run over things which make a noise when you hit them, or break apart, or flatten out, so that you can tell that you did hit them. Run over things like pop cans, paper cups, soft chunks of icy snow, or mud, or very small puddles. Do not run over things which can do damage like hub caps, rocks, bottles, or paper bags filled with bricks purposely left in the road.

It takes some work to get good at running over things. It is not so easy as it might sound, but it deepens your understanding of your car. Knowing where your wheels are gives you a new and different sense of confidence in your car control — a new understanding of human for machine. It can be fun too, like dart throwing, target shooting, snowball throwing, etc.

It is a good idea to know how wide your car is, too. You will get used to this just from driving in lanes and pulling over to the curb, etc. Accelerate your learning by paying close attention when pulling into and out of narrow parking lot spaces, driving close to cars, walls, etc. in tight garages and crowded driveways. Check your clearance from inside the car. Get out of the car and look at your actual clearance. Get back into the car and compare what you know the clearance is with how it looks from inside. Be careful who sees you doing this. Somebody may think you hit his car.

You can learn a great deal by following cars through tight spots in traffic, especially by following cars about the same width as yours. Watch the car ahead go through a narrow space. Look at its clearance on both sides. If you drive through the same space the same way, your clearances must be the same. If you have a place available, you can even go to the extent of setting up tight clearances with flags, or sticks, etc. and driving between them. You will think up your own variations on this exercise. In case you do hit a stick, it might be good pre-planning to pad it so that you do not scratch your car (your father's car).

Knowing how wide your car is and where your wheels are can give you a lot of satisfaction and confidence when driving in the mountains or past deep ditches next to your lane in construction zones. Knowing how wide your car is makes you more comfortable when zipping past rural mailboxes and cruising between lines of construction barricades.

In all these exercises, games, and situations, make sure that you are learning and practicing the right things. Do not use your fender tips to measure. Fender tips can be used when you are moving at very low speeds as you enter or pass through tight places to check or recheck clearances. They cannot be used when you are moving at normal speed. What you must do is internalize the dimensions of your car. Know them as you know your own body size, then use them to judge your clearances far ahead. You should know pretty well whether or not your car will fit through a tight space or past an obstacle and how to line it up well before you get to the space or obstacle.

UP IN THE MOUNTAINS: It's so beautiful up in the mountains, especially for flatlanders. Do not be distracted by sightseeing. Drive! See sights only when safe. Take the time to pull over into pull-off areas to enjoy the scenery with your full attention. Think twice about pull-offs on the left side of the road. Getting to them often involves turning left with very little information about oncoming traffic. The same is true for pulling back onto the road.

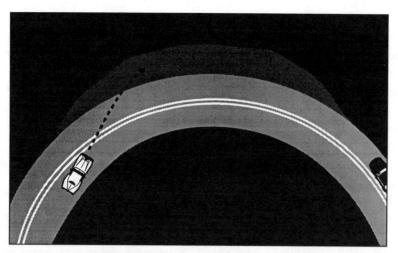

Turning left just before a blind area can cause a crash.

Attention big city people! Remember that you are more likely to meet wild animals in the wilderness than in New York City or Chicago. When you get out of your car in a deserted but stunningly beautiful place, look for a lost scorpion, rattlesnake, etc.

Runaway truck ramps are for runaway trucks. They are not for sightseeing. They are not even for emergency stopping of cars. They are like safety nets to catch trucks which have lost their brakes going downhill. An 80,000 pound truck going downhill with virtually no brakes picks up speed fast. If it hits a car, it destroys the car. If it hits the side of the mountain or goes over the side, it destroys itself. It's simple, and it's very serious. It happens, too.

When going downhill in the mountains, check your rearview mirror more frequently than in level or uphill driving. If you see a semi coming at you fast, especially with smoke pouring from its wheels, get out of its way to the right. If, by some fluke, you are just approaching a runaway truck ramp, *do not* use it. Get past it fast so the truck driver can use it.

Car brakes can fade from overheating, too. If your brakes fade, you will lose some or all of your ability to control downhill speed, slow down, or stop. Modern disc brakes cool off very fast, and cars do not weigh 80,000 pounds, so the danger is slight. In extreme downhill situations, though, use lower gears to help control gravity induced acceleration just as truck drivers must do.

Having car trouble way out in the country can be much worse than having it in a city or town. Check the car BEFORE you go to the wilderness. If you live there, keep your vehicle in the best possible mechanical condition. Take warm clothes, a first aid kit, any medicine you must take regularly, tools, even if you cannot use them — perhaps somebody else can help you with them. You might keep spare parts like hoses and belts, etc., in the car. Blankets, food, and water can be very useful, too. A knife or an axe can be worth more than its weight in gold.

After driving in the mountains for a while, your sense of uphill and downhill may begin to trick you. You might swear that you are going downhill, when you are actually going uphill. Believe the car. If it is straining to accelerate or keep a steady speed, you are going uphill. If it is tending to speed up too easily, you are going downhill.

At very high elevations, the air is thinner. This can lower your engine's ability to produce power. Your radiator may boil over more easily, too.

234

Just around the next corner there may be a fallen rock in the road. Remember that. There may be very little traffic up in the mountains, but there are many blind areas.

Be sure to aim and steer properly through curves. Look at the space through which you want to drive. Look far and near and far and near through the curve. *Be very careful to stay off the wrong side of the road*! With a mountainside on one side and a drop-off on the other side, there is little or no room for dodging.

On switchbacks or hairpin turns, see as much as possible of the curve before entering it. Do not look right down in front of your car to see more and more of the curve as you drive through it. See the end of it if possible before you enter the turn. Know where your car will end up before you start the turn.

If possible, in hairpin turns, get an idea where your car will end up before starting the turn.

This technique should be used on very sharp turns in the city, too.

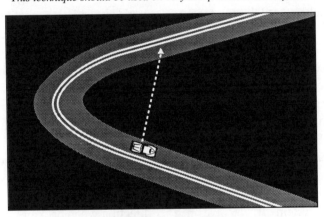

Avoid trying to aim like this

Aiming high and being sure of your vehicle's width are important in mountain driving. If you worry about driving next to drop-offs, you will look at them instead of at the road, the traffic, etc. You might get too close to the drop-offs, because your car goes where you look.

Way out in the wilderness, on *extremely narrow,* mountain roads, it is a good idea to blow your horn before entering a blind curve. Listen for an answering horn. This is standard procedure in some places. If on a one-lane road you meet an oncoming vehicle, the vehicle moving downhill must back up until there is room to pass.

THE DESERT: Take it easy. It's hot out there. Do not strain your car with overloading, very high speeds, lugging the engine (driving a stick shift car in too high a gear for conditions), etc.

CARRY WATER! CARRY WATER! CARRY WATER! Carry water for yourself and the car. *CARRY WATER!*

Using your air conditioner does add to the work of the cooling system. If you live in a desert area, order your new car with a heavy duty cooling system. An oil cooler can be useful, too, as can a transmission oil cooler.

When driving in the country, you are more directly affected by the weather than in cities. Flash floods mean exactly that, dry one minute, flooded the next. Wind can push your car sideways with gusts or every time your car comes out from behind a windbreak: house, hill, forest, etc. Wind can blow debris across the road and at your car. A sandstorm can make seeing extremely difficult and sandblast your car.

TRAILER TOWING: Trailer towing adds to the work your car's engine, brakes, clutch, automatic transmission, cooling system, etc., have to do. Take it easy. Make sure to notice whether your trailer is wider than your car. Also notice how tall it is. Remember that a trailer rides closer to the inside of a turn than the car does.

Backing up with a trailer is challenging to learn and a source of pride when you can do it well. To back a trailer straight, you have to keep your car lined up behind it. Therefore, you should know how to turn when backing a trailer. To get the trailer started turning in the proper direction when backing, you must turn the car's steering wheel in the opposite direction and then follow the trailer. It's weird when you first try it. It is fun once you have learned it.

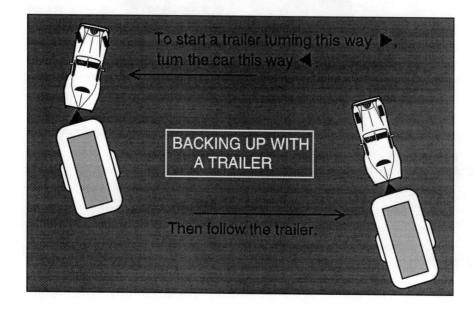

To start a trailer turning this way ▶,
turn the car this way ◀.

BACKING UP WITH
A TRAILER

Then follow the trailer. ➝

14 Chapter Fourteen

Expressways

Expressways, or freeways, are not like ordinary roads or streets upon which people park, and stroll, and shop, and sit on benches to relax. Expressways do not give direct access to houses, or factories, or stores, or farms, or parks, or drive-ins, or roadside stands. Many times they do not even give direct access to towns!

Expressways are very special roads — very pure roads. They are called "superhighways," and they *are* superhighways. Their *only* purpose is to move motor vehicles. They are especially designed and built to provide fast, safe motor travel over vast distances. While they are not the romantic "open roads" of myth and legend, expressways do beckon drivers with promises of long distance adventure and freedom.

Before you answer that call to adventure, though, make sure that there is enough gas in your tank. It can be a long walk on the expressway, along the road, and down to the gas station. The walk back can seem even longer when you have to carry a leaking can of gasoline. Speed and distance are not the only reasons to check the gas gauge. Your car burns gasoline when idling in unexpected traffic jams, too.

When travelling through cold weather,

make sure you have warm clothing in the car in case of breakdown, bad storm, etc. If you wear prescription sunglasses, make sure you take along your regular glasses. It might get dark before you get back home. ALWAYS CARRY MONEY!

Know whether your car is capable of travelling long distances at high speeds. Have you checked your oil lately? Do you know how much oil your engine burns or leaks? How are your tires? Do you have a spare? Is it inflated? Can you change a tire?

The list of suggestions and questions can go on and on. Think ahead. Read. Talk to experienced drivers. Being prepared can save your life!

PEDESTRIANS ON THE EXPRESSWAY: Because they are specially designed to carry motor vehicles, expressways are not comfortable places for pedestrians, but pedestrians *do* use them. At any time, there may be pedestrians walking and/or working near toll booths. There may be pedestrians walking fairly long distances along the shoulder to or from their disabled cars, or working on them. Pedestrians may be walking *across* the expressway to get parts or tools from a friend's car parked on the opposite side of the road. Pedestrians may be walking across the expressway to get water from the ditch in the median, or just to get to the other side.

There may be someone collecting aluminum cans along the expressway. Road crews do maintenance, construction, and repairs on expressways. Children play alongside and even on expressways. People hitchhike. After accidents, scared, confused, even angry people walk around on the expressway. After parties, people may be put out of cars when drunken disagreements occur. People have been known to ride bicycles on expressways. You'll see motorcyclists waiting in viaducts for thunder storms to stop. They should not be a safety concern, but you can be surprised when you see them sud-

denly. Most farm, pet, and wild animals do not know that they should not stand, walk, or run on expressways.

Pedestrians, bicyclists, animals, etc. may not really belong on expressways, but they *are* there. Expect them at any time and at any place. *Never drive expressways as if there were no pedestrians on them!*

Lane Characteristics

The old saying, "If you've seen one, you've seen them all," does not apply to expressway lanes. Expressways differ. Expressway lanes differ. However, most *left* lanes do share basic characteristics, most *right* lanes share basic characteristics, and most *middle* lanes share basic characteristics.

THE LEFT LANE: The left lane is intended to be a clear, easy, fast lane in which to drive. It is to be used by the fastest traffic and for passing. Often the left lane must not be used by trucks, and it is usually free of entrance and exit ramps.

The most frequent problem for drivers in the left lane is probably pressure from faster traffic behind. A good driver *never* gets in the way. If you or your vehicle cannot keep up with the speed of traffic in the left lane, leave it. If you are being passed on the right, you are not going fast enough to be so far left. Move over into a lane farther to the right where traffic is moving more slowly.

An occasional problem for left lane drivers begins on the opposite side of the expressway, beyond the median strip. In wet weather, on expressways with very narrow median strips, oncoming traffic on the opposite side of the road can blind left lane drivers with heavy splashes of water and/or slush. A rare problem that starts on the other side of expressways is not flying water but flying cars. An oncoming car can go out of control and jump the median. What goes up must come down.

Splashing water;   *flying car*

THE RIGHT LANE: Entrance and exit ramps are usually connected to the right lane. Therefore, many lane changes are made into and out of the right lane. Traffic moves into the right lane from the left to prepare to exit.

Traffic moves into the right lane from the right when it enters the expressway.

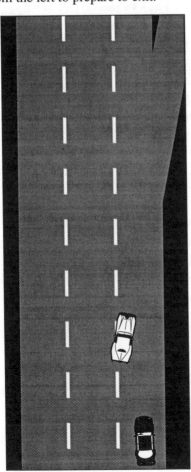 

Traffic moves out of the right lane to the right when it leaves the expressway.

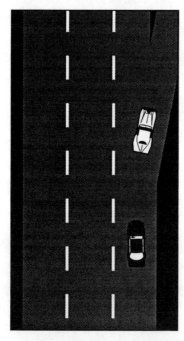

Traffic moves out of the right lane to the left to get to the faster, inner lanes.

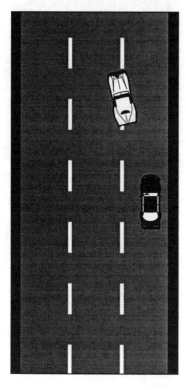

All this lane changing forces many changes in speed and following distances for right lane drivers. Usually right lane traffic is neither smooth nor fast. It is often congested and complex.

It's also full of trucks. Trucks are often restricted to the two right lanes. Trucks are big and clumsy. They block vision. They are frequently noisy and may smell bad. Trucks take up a lot of room (adding to congestion) and cannot accelerate, decelerate, or maneuver rapidly. Their drivers may have difficulty seeing your car. Trucks even drop things onto the road occasionally.

Most drivers do not like the right lane. However, the right lane is a very handy place to be when you are not sure where you must exit the expressway. The right lane is often the lane you will have to use if you are trying not to exceed the speed limit. On some expressways the right lane can be the most efficient during rush hour.

The right lane can help a student driver learn about merging. Cruising it will force him to blend with entering traffic. Because he is already on the expressway, however, the blending will be relatively easy. He will have all the advantages. He will have the logical if not necessarily the legal right-of-way. He will have the speed. He will probably have an excellent view of the entire merging event. He will not have the pressure of getting on.

He will be able to watch most of the merging maneuver as done by somebody else. Then he'll be able to analyze and criticize what he has just watched and learn from it. Finally, he will begin to overcome the fear of blending two cars onto one lane near each other at relatively high speed.

THE MIDDLE LANES: Middle lanes are not supposed to be either the fastest or the slowest, and usually they aren't. Some drivers think the middle lanes are the best lanes because they have less crisscrossing traffic than the right lane and less pressure from fast traffic to the rear than the left lane. They also provide more chances to maneuver in traffic.

When trucks are restricted to the two right lanes of three, the middle lane is the fast lane for the trucks. Apparently forgetting this, some car drivers cruise along below the speed limit and block trucks trying to run at the limit. Other car drivers run at the limit and enforce that limit very strictly on the trucks following them.

Whether other drivers obey or disobey the speed limit is *none of your business*! In all lanes, it is the job of the police to enforce the speed limit as they see fit. You must be aware of vehicles moving faster and slower than yours, especially vehicles moving *much* faster and slower, but you are not the police. Consider the case of somebody going *downhill* and purposely blocking a truck that weighs 80,000 pounds with a car that weighs 2,500 or 3,500 pounds. Is he using his brain?

LANE CHOICE: A good expressway driver does not just plow along straight ahead in his lane, no matter what, like a boxcar in a freight train. Nor is he part of a mob, with no judgment of his own. He does not act like a horse in a stampede, looking desperately only for his own, immediate right-of-way. A real expressway driver uses his brain. He plans. He makes judgments about which lane to use and how long to use it. He chooses the lane that will keep his driving its safest, most efficient, and most graceful.

Sometimes his lane choice is made fully or partly for him. When he has to exit the expressway soon, he must drive in the lane next to the exit ramp(s). If he is driving a truck, he may be legally restricted to the two right lanes. When the road splits into two or more different roads going different places, he must use the lane(s) leading toward his destination.

When travelling for any distance on a relatively open interstate, a good freeway driver will probably base his lane choice mostly on speed. He will note the speed limit and the speed of other traffic. Then he will slip neatly into the lane which is moving at the speed he judges most appropriate for himself and his vehicle in the current conditions. This will help him avoid repeatedly catching up to and being blocked by slower traffic ahead. It will also help him avoid blocking faster traffic behind.

A real driver, whether he is on an expressway or not, does not cause problems. Neither does he get mixed up in them. He always seems to be where the problems and heaviest traffic aren't. This does not happen because of fate or luck or by accident. On an expressway, it comes largely from his great skill in lane choice.

A real driver is constantly checking ahead, behind, and next to himself. He is constantly checking near and far in *all* lanes. He is always looking for an advantage, not the imagined advantage of being first for an instant. He is looking for a control advantage. He is looking for the lane that will give him maximum space, best visibility, surest traction, most comfort, and smoothest traffic flow.

He is constantly re-evaluating his position in the changing flow of traffic. He is looking for developing problems to avoid. He sees changes in flow. He sees blockages and potential blockages early and changes lanes early to avoid them. That's why he is always where the trouble isn't.

A good expressway driver does not get stuck in the slow lane. He does not get caught in the lane that is closed for repairs. He does not get pushed along by faster traffic behind him. He is not passed on the right by drivers making rude gestures at him. He is always in the right place at the right time.

There are many factors involved in lane choice. As a driver you must assign values to the various advantages and disadvantages. Then you must weigh them and decide which lane is best for you. Sometimes your choice will be clear. By changing lanes you will get all the advantages and give up all the disadvantages. At other times you will have to compromise. You may have to take on small disadvantages to get big advantages. You may have to give up some advantages to get rid of bigger disadvantages.

The point is that you *do* have a choice of lanes and you *should* use it. If another lane is moving at the speed you want and is less bumpy, why not change lanes? If another lane is moving more smoothly and steadily, why not change lanes? If another lane will let you see better and therefore have better control, why not change lanes? If you are blocking faster traffic, *do* change lanes!

Getting the Information About Advantages and Disadvantages, Traffic Flow, Pavement Condition, Trouble, and Navigation Aids

Expressways have no intersections, no stop lights, no alleys, no driveways, no shopping strips. Their traffic is carried on one-way pavements separated by median strips. They are safer and easier to drive on than regular roads.

Therefore, they encourage drivers to look around even less than usual and just follow the vehicle ahead (usually much too closely!). Because of this lack of attention to business, drivers are frequently surprised by the ordinary things that expressways *do* have: entrance and exit ramps, merging lanes, separating lanes, blind areas, road signs, road surface problems, and occasional pedestrians, parked vehicles, bicyclists, and stray animals. *Drivers are not supposed to be surprised*! Even on extremely busy urban expressways, if you are being surprised, you are not getting information early enough. You are not looking for trouble.

LOOKING AHEAD: Look as far ahead as you can see, beyond the car you are following. Do not let yourself get into the habit of just following the car ahead and never looking beyond it. The rear end of the car ahead *is not* the limit of your forward vision. You *can* see beyond it. *Do it!* Look through the car ahead. When possible, look over it. Sometimes, going uphill, you can even look under it. Look past its sides. Move over in your lane to see around it. Going around curves you can easily see past it. *(Figure 1)*

You are allowed to see beyond vehicles in other lanes, too. Look between them. Look under trucks. Look through cars.

Get an idea of where the road goes. See where your lane goes. Does it continue as far as you can see? Does it merge with another lane? Does it become an exit only lane?

Figure 1

Look for entrance and exit ramps, overpasses. Read the signs and keep track of where you are. Check traffic and the flow of traffic ahead. Try to get early warning of things like road work, slow moving vehicles, vehicles parked on the shoulder, pavement problems, pedestrians, animals, etc.

Check the road surface on your side of the expressway far and *near* for potholes, cracks, frost heaves, patches, pavement buckles, ruts, debris, snow, ice, puddles, mud, etc. Advance knowledge of the road surface will make avoiding problems easy and smooth. Advance knowledge of the road surface will also help you predict the problems of other drivers. Then you will not be caught napping when they slow down suddenly or squeeze into your lane to avoid a huge puddle or pothole. Stay aware of the lane lines just ahead of your car so that you can see their continuity into the distance ahead.

Keep aware of traffic in *all* lanes on your side of the road. Know which lanes are fast, which are slow, which are congested, and which are free flowing. Keep aware of the traffic next to you and passing you in relationship to the overall traffic flow. This will help you predict drivers cutting into your lane in front of you. Any time you have more space in front of your car than the fellow just ahead in the next lane does, he may change into your lane. (Figure 2)

This is especially true if your lane is moving faster than his. It is also true for someone passing you. (Figure 3)

Check for brake lights ahead in *any* lane. Frequently a slow down or stop in one lane will spread all the way across the expressway to include your lane.

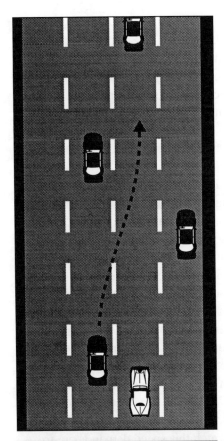

Figure 2

Figure 3

LOOKING TO THE SIDES: Look way out to the sides. Look past the right shoulder. Check for entrance ramps and traffic on entrance ramps, especially when driving in the right lane. Check the left shoulder and median strip. See what's happening on the opposite side of the road. Check for animals in the fields.

LOOKING BEHIND: Look into your mirrors. Know what is behind you far and near and out to the sides. Is there a lot of traffic or a little? Is it bunched up or spread out? Is it catching up to you, or keeping a steady distance, or dropping back, or all three? Are there any trucks back there, or motorcycles, or buses?

Here is a little test of whether you know what is happening behind your car. When someone passes you going 30 miles an hour faster than you are, are you surprised? You shouldn't be. You should have seen him coming. You should even have mentioned to your passengers to watch this speed demon about to pass.

In this situation drivers often get angry at the passer. They call him names and yell that he is a crazy fool and a great hazard on the road. Why?

They never knew the passer was coming. They were very surprised when, suddenly, "out of nowhere" he rocketed past them. They were not paying attention. They were not really in control. They got scared. They got excited and had to do something. They got angry. There was nothing else they could do.

Surprises are for birthday parties, jokes, and some gifts, not for the road. Always be on the lookout for erratic drivers and vehicles in poor mechanical condition. On expressways, just as on side streets, in alleys, in parking lots, on rural roads, on major city streets, always see as much as you can.

Cruising the Expressway With a Good Driver

A good expressway driver is not surprised. He is aware of the traffic flow and his place in it. He looks for advantages and disadvantages. He does not get stuck in his own lane rushing helplessly toward trouble. He looks for trouble. When he sees it, he reacts. He rechecks his position in traffic and decides upon his best course of action.

His best course of action is always graceful. He does not force his way out of trouble by cutting off other drivers. His pride in his ability as a driver will not let him do anything that would cause a traffic jam or could cause an accident.

On the rare occasions when he really is trapped in a traffic situation, he accepts it. He deals with it the best he can. Then he tries to figure out whether he was lax in getting information and how to do better next time.

He realizes that he makes mistakes occasionally, too. He accepts their consequences. He accepts responsibility for them, and he works his way out of them himself. He would never dream of just putting on his turn signal and waiting until some other driver noticed his problem, took pity on him, and helped him. He knows that that would mean slowdowns and jam-ups for everybody behind him and his helper. All those other drivers would have to be inconvenienced and put at risk because he couldn't take care of himself.

Finally, he realizes that there are times when there are no advantages. He is trapped in a group or wolf pack, and he must do the best he can until he can break free. By the same token, he does not assume that there is nothing he can do about being stuck in these packs. He looks for the causes of the packing — the plugs in the traffic flow, and he makes sure *he* isn't the plug.

Staying Back

Very possibly the most important expressway driving tactic is staying far enough back behind the car ahead — *at least* two seconds. Some drivers follow far enough back but do not use their following distance properly. They do not let their eyes see beyond the vehicle they are following. The reason for staying back is NOT just that you can stop in time when the car ahead stops suddenly or have enough time to see and dodge a pothole. It is so that you can have the time and space to look around and get all the information you need to drive well, the kind of information mentioned earlier in this chapter.

You need to know much more than the color of the car ahead and whether its brake lights are lit up or not. Don't maintain a good following distance only to waste it by ignorantly following the car ahead. Keep a good following distance and use it! See!

HOW TO KEEP THAT GOOD FOLLOWING DISTANCE: First, look far enough ahead to notice when you are catching up (a quarter of a mile, a half a mile, a mile). Then, *DON'T CATCH UP!* Assess the situation *immediately* and begin deciding whether you should pass the vehicle you are catching or follow it. Check what's happening behind you. Check what's happening in the other lanes ahead. Then, based on your needs and your speed, within this total traffic scene, decide whether it is better to pass or follow. By the way, check your speed. Is it still what you think it is, or have you gained or lost speed?

Suppose you are in the right lane and want to get off the expressway just ahead. Do not pass. Follow at reduced speed and *do not catch up*.

Suppose you are in the crowded, slow, middle lane and want to get off about a mile up the road. The right lane is empty. It's probably a good idea to change into the right lane and pass.

In one movement you will have improved your safety and set yourself up to exit.

Suppose you are not sure yet whether to pass or even whether you are catching up or not. Check to the rear and see how much room you have back there. Check whether traffic behind is catching up to you. With that knowledge, recheck ahead. By rechecking ahead and behind, build a picture of your total traffic situation. With this knowledge you will see exactly how you fit into the overall traffic flow. This will make your decision about how to deal with what's happening ahead much easier. You'll know whether to let one or more cars from behind pass you before you change lanes and pass. You'll know whether to make your move right now, before they catch you. You'll know whether you can just sit back and keep watching the car ahead before deciding. You'll have *control*!

Now suppose you decided to pass but caught up anyway because moderate traffic in the next lane blocked your lane change. Bad luck? Probably not. Very likely you are still not looking far enough ahead to notice things while you have time to deal with them easily.

OTHER REASONS NOT TO CATCH UP: Once you have caught up to the car ahead of yours, you'll find it difficult to re-establish a proper following distance. The car behind yours will have caught up, too. That will make slowing down very clumsy indeed.

You may find that you can't change lanes either. Following too closely can seriously affect your ability to change into a faster lane. You find a space behind the car that is just passing you. The space seems big enough. You wait for the passing car to pass. Then you recheck the space only to find that you're too late. The next car is coming up to pass you. You have to wait for it to pass, too. Then you have to wait for the next and the next, and the next....

Why? You are not going fast enough. The spaces would be big enough if you were going as fast as they are, but you're not. You need to speed up in your own lane before changing lanes, but you can't. You are following too closely. You are stuck, and you are to blame.

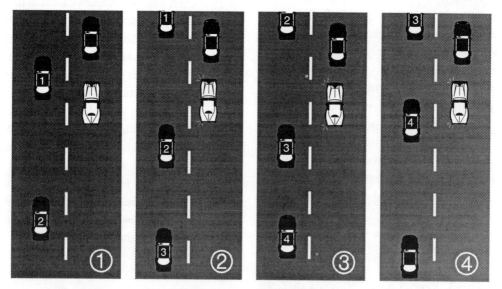

Above: Because the white car is following too closely, it cannot change into the faster lane.
After it waits for car 1, it must wait for car 2, car 3, car 4.

Below: The white car speeds up in its own lane and easily changes into the faster lane in front of car 3.

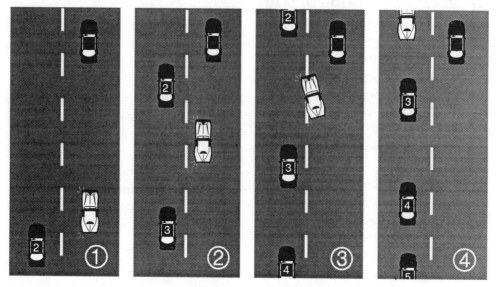

If you keep a good following distance in heavy, stop and go, speed up and slow down, urban, rush hour, expressway traffic, though, what happens? Drivers from adjacent lanes cut into your lane in front of you.

Some drivers work very hard to prevent this. They try to stay very close to the car they are following. Their driving becomes a series of short drag races. Each start becomes a leap forward, each stop a jolt and bounce. Grace and real control are traded away for passenger discomfort, vehicle abuse, and driver stress. The result is the total victory of ignorance and bad manners over efficient traffic flow.

A good expressway driver keeps his following distance. He realizes that drivers *will* cut into his lane, but he knows that only some will stay there. Others will change into yet another lane almost immediately. Still others will change right back into their old lane again.

Moreover, a good expressway driver knows that many drivers in adjacent lanes will ignore the space he's leaving. Some will be moving just as fast or faster in their own lane. Others will be so happy staring at the rear end of the car they're following that they'll never even notice the space. Still others will be listening to the radio so carefully that they can't spare the time to drive.

Therefore, stay back. Leave plenty of space. Yes, some drivers *will* cut in in front of you. You'll have to watch for them. You'll have to stay alert. Is there anything wrong with staying alert while you are driving? Leave enough distance to look around, and *look around*!

Look for drivers who are making unsuccessful lane change attempts. Remember them. They'll try again. Look for vehicles in adjacent lanes riding very near the lane line. Look for

vehicles with their turn signals flashing. Look for drivers who are looking into their mirrors and/or checking their blind spots.

When somebody does start heading for the space ahead of you, be like the good, and fair, and kindly, fairy tale king who is beloved by all his fairy tale people. Be generous. Let the poor peasant into your lane. He may even thank you with a wave. Even if he doesn't, you can thank yourself because most likely you have improved the overall traffic flow, helping not only the lane changer but yourself and everybody behind you.

Do not take this to mean that you should *always* let *everybody* into your lane. Some people have the idea that letting people in is *always* courteous and keeping people out is *always* discourteous.

This is not true. For example, suppose someone wants to change lanes in front of you, but no space exists there naturally. You could create a space by slowing drastically or stopping short. That would allow his lane change, but it would also cause needless traffic tie-ups for you and everyone behind you. It could also cause an accident behind you, right behind you — an accident involving your rear bumper and trunk.

Black car signals desire to change lanes;

white car creates space by rapid deceleration;

lane change is successful, but white car is hit in rear.

When there is no naturally occurring space, just move along and let the lane changer find someplace else. After all, he *is* responsible for *his* lane change. It is never courteous to let someone in when you can see that letting him in would work against traffic flow or could endanger him or others.

When someone does cut in and take your following distance, don't drop back too quickly. Falling back instantly and automatically every time anybody cuts in in front of you can get you hit in the rear end.

White car drops back quickly to re-establish good following distance and is hit in rear by black car changing lanes to where there had been plenty of space a moment ago.

Dropping back too quickly can also make you into a moving roadblock. It happens like this. Somebody cuts in in front of you. You drop back quickly. The fellow behind you notices that his lane is slower because of your dropping back. He passes you and cuts back in in front of you. You drop back again. The next driver behind you repeats the passing and cutting in process. You drop back again, and the next driver repeats, and so on and on.

Do not sit back and congratulate yourself on the great maturity and safe driving you have shown by dropping back over and over again. Instead, realize that *YOU* are causing all this needless lane changing and passing and, thereby, causing possible danger to yourself and everybody else.

The idea is to be aware of traffic. Think "flow". Think "blending". Think of everybody doing what he wants to do or needs to do in traffic without disturbing the overall smooth flow. After all, the idea is not to go out and sit in stopped traffic every day after work, or on a Sunday drive. The idea is to *move*! Anything that helps traffic flow is good for everybody.

BLIND SPOTS: Stay out of other drivers' blind spots. That's good advice. Keeping your vehicle visible helps you avoid getting cut-off or crowded off the road by lane changers.

How do you know when you are in somebody's blind spot, though? Usually you don't even know when somebody is in your own blind spot unless you check it. How can you possibly tell when you are in somebody else's blind spot?

Any time your car is only slightly behind the vehicle in the next lane, assume you are in it's driver's blind spot.

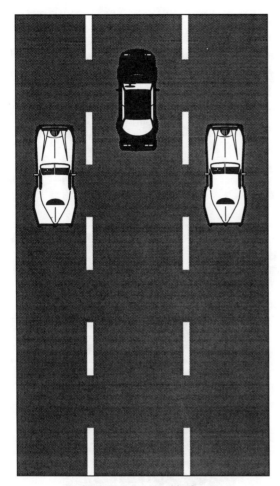

Both white cars are in blind spots.

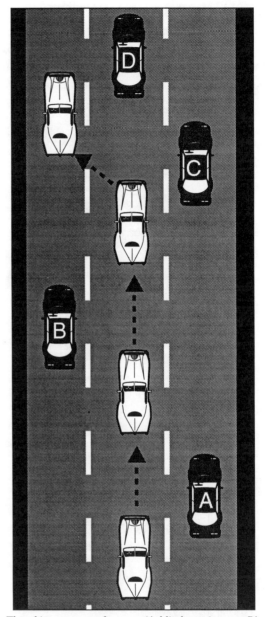

Check the mirrors of the driver you suspect cannot see your car. If you cannot see his face in any mirror, or directly, you must be in his blind spot. Once you know you're in someone's blind spot, the sensible thing to do is get out of it. On busy expressways, however, when you drive out of one fellow's blind spot, often you drive right into someone else's. (See illustration on right.)

The white car moves from car A's blind spot into car B's. From car B's, it moves into car C's. From car C's, it moves into car D's.

When you cannot stay out of everybody's blind spot, just be aware that some drivers near you may not know your car is there. Expect occasional bad lane changes. Relax, stay back, stay alert, watch traffic, and think a little about the possibilities. Based on the problems facing other drivers, predict their clumsy lane changes. Be prepared with horn, brakes, and/or a place to swerve.

You need not plan a complete strategy for *each and every* POSSIBLE mistake by *every* other driver. Many times just realizing that trouble COULD be brewing is enough to make all the difference between a timely avoidance and a crash.

STRAIGHT TALK ABOUT CURVES: Try to see the end of a curve *before* you enter it. Sometimes you can. Sometimes you can't. Sometimes you only think you can't.

Before entering the curves illustrated below, many drivers would believe that the bushes block their view and drive through at least the first curve wondering where the road goes and what is happening ahead.

A driver with better seeing habits and more understanding of driving around curves would check to *both* sides of the bushes. Looking to the *left* of the bushes would give him a very good idea of where the road goes and what is happening on it.

To be driven upon, the road must be continuous, but your vision of it needn't be. Seeing a lot of the road in unconnected sections is far better than seeing a little bit of it in one uninterrupted stretch just ahead.

Many curves are truly blind. Using the technique explained above will allow you to identify them. When you cannot see the whole curve or sections of it, you know you will be driving through a blind curve.

Never assume that the road will merely continue and be clear when you cannot see it. Take a "wait and see" attitude. Base your speed on how much you *can* see. Expect the possibility of a problem. Once again, just realizing that there could be a problem will often give you that slight jump on the situation you need to avoid trouble.

When there is a car ahead of yours in a blind curve, use it as a kind of early warning, radar system. Drive just far enough behind it to keep it in view. If anything goes wrong ahead, its driver will see the trouble and react. You'll see his reaction much before you can see the trouble. You should be quite safe.

A truck or bus close ahead can make a curve blind even when it is not in your lane.

Rounding curves on multi-lane roads like expressways, the car in the inside lane travels a shorter distance than the car in the outside lane.

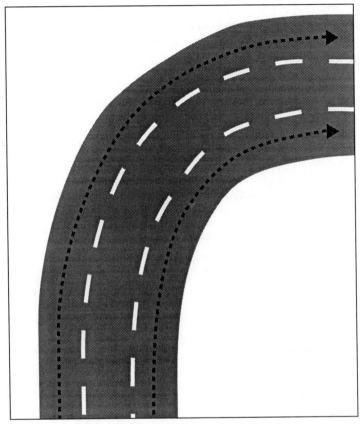

Measure the arrows if you do not believe it.

This explains why the other guy sometimes speeds up just as you begin passing him and why the fellow passing you slows down. Neither is really speeding up or slowing down. Each is just going a shorter or longer distance. This is why a jockey usually wants to run his horse along the inside rail of the racetrack.

LANE SIGNALS AND SIGNS: You may encounter lane signals on the expressway.

253

Look for them. See them early so you will have plenty of time to change lanes if necessary.

The same is true when you encounter lanes that split off to go to different towns or to join different roads. See the signs early and try to get under the proper arrow early.

Curves and hills between you and the sign combined with engineers' adding and/or subtracting lanes can make perfect and timely lance choice tricky. Do the best you can as early as you can. Make final adjustments as soon as you know exactly which lane you need. Keep looking for and checking the next sign, and the next, etc.

PAYING TOLLS: There is more to it than you might think. First, make sure you know when you are on a toll road. Plan ahead. Have money handy, even precounted. Do not have your wallet in your back pocket seatbelted to the seat between your overcoat and your pants, or in your purse on the floor somewhere in the back. It's very pleasant if you have a passenger who will take charge of the money and pass you the correct amount at the proper time.

Read the signs, the ones that tell you that you will come to a toll booth soon.

Look for the toll plazas. Check which lanes are open and closed. Pick your lane early. Don't drive well into one lane only to change both your mind and three lanes at the last moment. That is very bad manners and can cause an accident. Roll you window *all* the way down and place the car near the booth or machine. Line up your window with the toll collector's window or the basket on the machine. Use your *left* hand to pay. DO NOT THROW MONEY AT THE MACHINE. DROP IT INTO THE BASKET.

When you leave the toll plaza, check for pedestrians and pay attention to the traffic in *all* the lanes. See who is slow, who is fast, who will be clear, and who will be in your way. Do not get into anyone else's way! You will almost certainly have to change lanes or at least pick a lane after leaving the toll booth. Know what's happening ALL AROUND YOU.

GAPERS' BLOCKS: Gapers' blocks occur when drivers slow down to look at something that is off the road. There is no physical road blockage. Somebody is parked on the shoulder in front of a police car getting a ticket. Two lightly damaged cars are parked on the shoulder after a fender-bender. A tow truck is hooking up to a stalled car on the shoulder.

Historic moments all, like the signing of the Declaration of Independence or the end of World War II! Anybody getting the chance to see a pair of cars parked by the side of the road should do all he can to make sure that he does see them. After all, it's something he will remember for the rest of his life. It's something about which he will tell his grand children and even his great-grandchildren! It's an event that is almost as important as the dropping of the atomic bomb on Hiroshima or the first manned lunar landing. Think of it! In your own lifetime to see damaged vehicles parked on the side of the road!

Blood! Maybe the gaper will even see blood or somebody's severed arm lying on the pavement. Now there's excitement! Of course, the fellow who does see a head rolling along the road will wish he had never seen it. He will wish he had never slowed down.

All of the gapers will complain about the terrible traffic, the wasted time, their overheating cars. Well, who causes it? Who has to gape at what amounts to nothing, even after waiting in traffic for an hour fussing and fuming about being late for work?

Gapers' blocks are caused and continued by selfish, blood lusting, thrill seeking fools with driver's licenses. A *driver* would much rather enjoy driving than creep along for an hour so he can get to see a dented automobile. He can see smashed cars in junkyards. At demolition derbies he can watch them get smashed.

Sadly, gapers' blocks accurately show the mentality of most of your fellow drivers. Gapers' blocks show how much most drivers care or even understand about traffic flow — about what a driver is supposed to do!

Some drivers actually slow down even more as they pass the non-event, because they think they might have missed something. Well, the driver behind is gaping, too. He is not looking where he is going.

Crunch! The second car runs into the rear end of the first. Now doesn't its driver feel foolish?

Intelligence, maturity, and cooperation can eliminate gapers' blocks, saving money, time, nerves, etc. Think, evaluate, drive!

Merging and the Concept of Uninterrupted Traffic Flow

Originally, the idea was that traffic *on* the expressway should move at a relatively fast and *quite steady* pace. It should not be interrupted by intersections and stop lights. Therefore, the number of entrances and exits was limited. The entrances and exits were designed as extra lanes that gradually blended into or out of the main road. This was to give entering and exiting traffic time and distance. Using this time and distance, entering traffic could accelerate to cruising speed *before* merging, and exiting traffic could decelerate *after* leaving the main road.

There was to be no interruption of the fast, safe, modern, efficient traffic flow on the expressway.

GETTING ONTO THE EXPRESSWAY: Today, the truth is that, at least in urban areas, smooth, almost effortless expressway merging is rare indeed. The causes are traffic volume not expected by planners, outdated and poorly engineered ramp designs, drivers with outdated and incorrect ideas of how to merge and help others merge, laws which can easily confuse drivers and worsen the situation.

Regardless of these, the intrinsic logic of the expressway and the expressway entrance remains. The traffic already on the expressway *is* the reference point. It sets the standard to which entering traffic must adapt. It sets the speed that entering traffic must match. Entering drivers must perceive, plan, and act so that their vehicles *blend in* with the established traffic flow. The responsibility for getting on must be taken by the entering driver. It cannot go to anyone else. The intrinsic logic of the expressway entrance makes that obvious.

Accept it. Then learn to enter properly. Do not be one of those drivers who spend their entire driving lives, 10, 20, 30, 40, or 50 or more years, getting scared every time they have to merge onto an expressway. Don't worry every time you get on whether there will be a space into which to fit your car. Don't be forced to hope that somebody will *let* you in. Don't wonder whether your car will accelerate fast enough. Don't clog up the flow. Don't fight the logic!

Accept the task of entering expressways for what it should be, a challenge, not a threat. Take the responsibility for getting on and learn the right way to do it. Be what a driver is supposed to be — IN CONTROL!

MERGING: Merging is not a ragged, stumbling, surging, turbulent, haphazard mixing together. Merging is a smooth, graceful, easy, *planned* blending. The vehicles merging into the traffic flow already on the expressway should fit right in without causing even a ripple.

GETTING ONTO THE EXPRESSWAY IS MAKING A LANE CHANGE: Getting onto the expressway is making a lane change. *Getting onto the expressway is making a lane change*! However, this lane change is different from most others. Unlike regular lane changes, merging *must* be done at a *specific place*. It must be done where the entrance ramp blends into the expressway, and it MUST BE DONE. It cannot be done in the next block, or the one after that, or right now, or not at all because of traffic, inattention, distractions, whim, etc. It *must* be done, and it *must be done at a certain place*.

Keep that concept in mind. It gives you the basic framework for the whole maneuver. EVERYTHING YOU DO MUST LEAD TO MAKING THAT LANE CHANGE HAPPEN NATURALLY AT JUST THE RIGHT PLACE!

We will discuss merging from a straight entrance first. It is the simplest type and allows the clearest explanation of proper merging technique. All else being equal, you should practice merging from a straight on entrance first.

LOOK AHEAD: Look as far ahead down the ramp and onto the expressway as you can. Do this as early as possible. If you can, do it even BEFORE you get onto the ramp. As soon as possible, try to see the place where the lane change *must* happen. Try to get an idea whether the ramp is clear and look at the traffic ahead on the expressway. The traffic into which you will be merging will be more or less the same density and moving at more or less the same speed as what you can see ahead on the expressway now. Begin setting up the lane change to happen at the right place now.

GET GOING: Once you can see that the ramp is clear and traffic is moving, and you have an idea where the lane change will have to happen, get going! Accelerate hard. Your best friend in getting onto an expressway is speed. Get the speed. Get it early. Get as much speed as you can as early as you can. Get it BEFORE you can see the exact situation into which you will be merging.

What? Just a minute here! Common sense and all I know about driving tell me not to do that. Remember when little Kenny ran over his neighbor's foot because he forced his scooter through a blind corner too fast? Remember that in blind and semi-blind situations your speed must ALWAYS be determined by your stopping distance and how much you can see?

True, but this situation is completely different. When getting onto the expressway you can almost always see ahead well enough. You can

see your stopping distance and any problems ahead on the ramp and/or expressway. The reason people don't want to accelerate hard early enough has nothing to do with safety or visibility ahead. It has to do with fear of the unknown. It has to do with fear of the traffic into which they must merge, but cannot see yet, because it is back there somewhere, behind them on the expressway.

People worry that when they get to the place to merge, there will not be a space for them. That's why they hesitate to accelerate hard and early. They want to know exactly what conditions will be when they reach the end of the ramp before they speed up. This ruins the whole maneuver, though. It's like waiting to brake for a red light until after you have reached it. You are absolutely certain that it is still red when you get there, but it's too late to stop. It can't work. It's the same when getting onto the expressway.

257

You need to be going fast enough when it is time to change lanes, not a quarter of a mile later. Accelerate! Accelerate EARLY!

Suppose you are trying to merge into expressway traffic which is going 60 m.p.h. If you are going only 35 m.p.h., the traffic into which you want to merge is passing you at 25 m.p.h. It is very difficult to figure just how you will fit into it. Every time you see a space, it passes you quickly. Space after space passes you. While these spaces keep passing you, you are running out of both time and distance ahead. You are way behind in planning. You are way behind in speed. You are in a pinch. You have to go somewhere, but you have nowhere to go. You need to speed up but are afraid you'll run out of distance ahead before you can find a place to enter traffic. You might end up moving even faster with no place to go. In the end, you force your way into traffic, cutting someone off because your speed is so low.

This is how many people merge onto the expressway. No wonder they're afraid!

Now suppose that instead of going 35 m.p.h., you go 60. The spaces will *not* be passing you. They will be staying in just about the same position relative to your car. It will be quite easy to figure and execute a good lane change. Adequate speed makes any lane change easier.

Having enough speed early gives you all these other advantages:

You'll already have plenty of speed. You will not have to worry about whether your car will accelerate fast enough later. This is especially important in slow accelerating and heavily loaded vehicles.

You will not have to figure your acceleration rate into your merging plan.

You will have speed in hand. You can always slow down or even take to the shoulder if you need to, but you cannot always speed up in time.

A side benefit is smoothness. Instead of several sudden bursts of hard acceleration interrupted by harsh slowdowns, you'll have a single, long, solid, smooth, fully controlled run of steady, brisk acceleration ending in a perfect blending into expressway traffic.

ACCELERATION IS NOT SOMEHOW EVIL, IT IS A CONTROL FUNCTION!

Get the speed *and the information* as early as possible, so that you can *plan* the lane change well *before* you must execute it. That way your merge will be easy, safe, smooth, and satisfying. You have no control over what the traffic conditions will be when you get to where you must merge. Therefore, set up everything you can in your favor. Get the speed, and get the information *EARLY*!

GET LOOKING: Start looking *early* for a space to enter. Immediately after you have checked the ramp and the expressway ahead and are accelerating hard down the middle of the ramp, start looking *back over your shoulder* for a space to enter. *Look back, not across!*

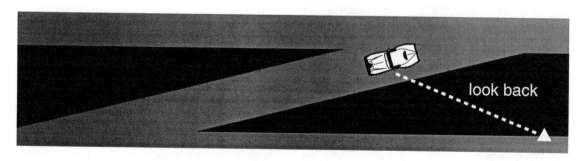

look back

NOT across

Looking across is wasted effort. Traffic you see straight out to the side will be far ahead when you reach your merge point. You must see what is coming FROM BEHIND. You must see the traffic into which you will be merging.

Look for a *space*. Don't see a lot of cars and trucks. See *spaces*! See spaces that are *in front* of cars or trucks, etc., not behind them. This is important. Thinking about merging BEHIND a vehicle is thinking *WRONG*. It will doom you to a lifetime of awkward merges. It is much easier to judge whether you will be able to fit in front of a vehicle than behind it. It's also the way you are used to making other lane changes. Planning to get in front of a vehicle gives you a definite reference point. You can figure and check your lane change against the approaching vehicle. The entire feeling of the maneuver is one of speeding up to fit confidently into the flow.

By contrast, trying to get behind a vehicle gives the maneuver an out of control feeling. You wait for the first car to pass. You hold down your speed to help it pass sooner. You check the space behind it only to find that the next car is bearing down upon you and you still haven't enough speed. You wait again with the same result. Finally, running out of space ahead and still at too low a speed, you have only one choice. You squeeze onto the expressway. You clog up traffic on the ramp and on the expressway. Your maneuver has been clumsy and dangerous. You are scared.

In most other lane changes you plan to get into a space IN FRONT of some other vehicle. You usually speed up to avoid cutting it off. You are used to changing lanes this way. You know it works. Do not change everything just because this lane change happens at the end of an expressway entrance ramp. See spaces IN FRONT of other vehicles! Plan to enter spaces IN FRONT of other vehicles!

There will be times when you will have to slow down and merge BEHIND another vehicle. Fine, just do not make a habit of *planning* it that way.

When finding spaces and planning and checking your entry, do not look back over your shoulder for a long time. Take several quick looks rather than one or two long ones. Looking several times gives your brain a dynamic understanding of how the traffic is moving and how your car relates to it. A long look will probably scare you. If what you see on the expressway doesn't scare you, what you see on the ramp might. When you look ahead again, after a long look back, you might find that you have veered well off to one side of the ramp.

When you look ahead, do not just aim. Recheck the ramp and the expressway ahead for slowdowns.

When checking rearward again, check at least the two lanes nearest the edge of the expressway, not just one. That way, you are sure you are looking at the proper lane and have an idea about who might be changing lanes into the space you plan to enter.

Keep checking *way* back over your shoulder as you accelerate down the ramp. Some students look way back at the expressway *once, early* and then just drive down the ramp. When they get ready to merge and look at the expressway again, everything has changed, their speed is too low, and there is no longer a space into which to merge. *Keep* aware of what is ahead of you and your relationship to the space into which you want to merge. It should keep looking better and better until you're in! If it doesn't, or somebody else already on the expressway fills the space you wanted, you'll have to change your plans — so have *speed* and *keep* taking *many glances far back* over your shoulder.

PLAN: Don't forget to plan. Sometimes students accelerate and look, but do not really see and plan.
   Begin planning early. Begin planning even before you are on the entrance ramp.
   Plan the lane change/merge to happen early.

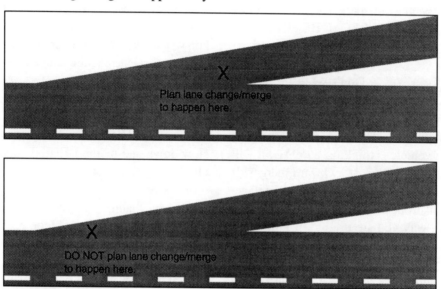

If you plan your merge to happen at the very end of the merging area, as many people do, you will have no margin for error if you do make a mistake. Plan to merge into expressway traffic at the earliest point possible. That way, if anything does go wrong, you'll have all the rest of the acceleration lane and merging area to make adjustments and enter.

Never wait to begin accelerating, looking, and planning until you get here.

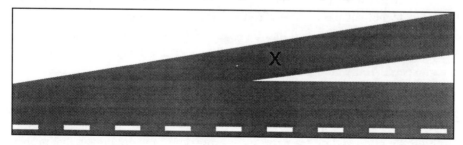

On many expressways this is much too late. Begin *accelerating, looking,* and *planning* as early as possible, and keep doing it. When you get here you should already have the speed and the information you need. You should be ready to change lanes CONFIDENTLY.

Let the challenge of each expressway entry be an opportunity to prove and polish your driving skill.

1. Check traffic ahead, down the ramp, and onto the expressway. Begin planning your lane change to happen at X.

2. Begin serious acceleration as soon as safe.

3. As soon as possible, begin checking traffic.

4. Keep accelerating, checking traffic, and planning.

5. By the time you reach this area, you should have everything figured out and you should have enough speed. Always make a last blind spot check just before merging.

6. On. Fully merged. Moving at expressway speed. Make any small speed and position adjustments that may be needed.

7. Safety zone. Use if any problems arise.

8. Shoulder is escape road.

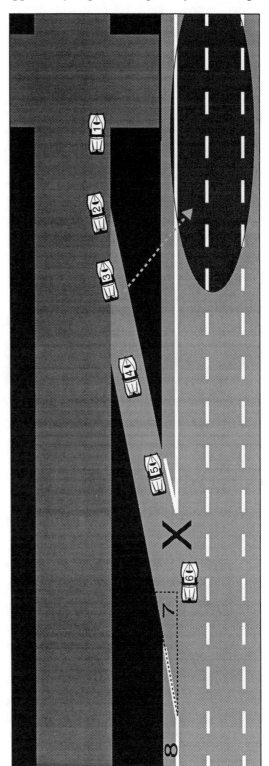

INCORRECT EXPRESSWAY ENTRANCE CONCEPTS: *Do not* memorize this concept of expressway entrance structures.

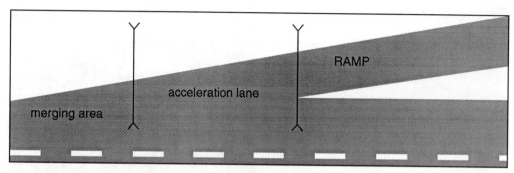

It may be the concept that engineers use in designing expressway entrance structures. It is *not* the concept drivers should use in entering expressways. Its sections are arbitrary and, from a driver's point of view, plain wrong. Think of entrance structures this way.

It is your responsibility to get onto the expressway. Never *expect* anybody to make room for you. Once in a while, when you are in trouble, someone may help you. That is a kindness from him, not a duty.

Do not think of speed or acceleration as evil, irresponsible, socially unacceptable, or a sign of immaturity. Speed is merely how fast something is moving. Acceleration is the rate of upward change in speed. Speed and acceleration can be appropriate or inappropriate. Neither can be good or bad.

Problems

TRAFFIC AHEAD ON THE RAMP: Almost always, the driver ahead of you on the ramp will accelerate too late, will begin checking traffic too late, and *will* begin planning too late — if he plans at all. Moreover, he will probably plan to enter a space BEHIND some vehicle instead of IN FRONT of it. He may believe that it's up to the drivers already on the expressway to *let* him onto it. Very often the result of all this is that he slows down or stops at the end of the entrance ramp.

His lack of information, his indecision, his low speed, and his possible slowdown or stop at the end of the ramp will make it impossible for you to plan and execute a perfect merge. Do not just give up and follow him into a situation you are not controlling. Keep as much control as you can.

Stay back! Stay WAY BACK! As early as possible, begin moving at an extremely low speed to let him pull far ahead of you.

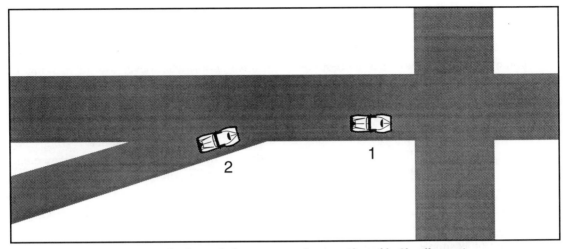

*Begin moving slowly even **before** you get to the ramp, if possible. If traffic permits,*
*begin moving **extremely** slowly at position 1. If not, begin at position 2.*

This will give you some open space ahead on the ramp. Use it to see, to accelerate, and to plan the best, safest, smoothest, most efficient merge you can.

Because his slow, clumsy merge maneuver directly affects yours, keep watching his while you plan yours. His slowness and clumsiness in merging will also affect the traffic on the expressway. It will slow down and bunch up. Therefore, you will have to plan and execute a lane change into a space which is slowing down and getting smaller. However, because the traffic is slowing, the reduced size of the space is not a very serious problem.

Planning and executing a good merge maneuver despite the problems caused by the clumsy, slow driver ahead of you will mean that at some point on the ramp, you will be travelling faster than he is. If your car is moving faster than his, it cannot stop as quickly as his. Remember this. Plan an escape route in case he does slow drastically or stops. Either have plenty of space to stop or know that there is enough room to pass him.

Sometimes the slow accelerating vehicle ahead will be a heavy truck. Drivers on the expressway will see the truck, and somebody will make space for it. At times, you will be able to enter the expressway in the extra space made for the truck.

NEVER let the driver ahead control your speed and merging maneuver! Never *wait* for him to get on first! Keep an eye on him, but *get your car on*! *Once you are on*, you can deal with him.

THE DRIVER BEHIND YOU: While you are moving extremely slowly to build up some space between your car and the one ahead, what is happening behind you? If there is anybody back there, he is probably tailgating you. He has no idea what you are trying to do. He has no idea that what you are doing should benefit him, too. All he knows is that you are moving very slowly and blocking him. Unless you are driving right down the middle of the ramp, he may even pass you. Then, when he reaches the end of the ramp with no plan, he will slow down or even stop in front of you! Speed up a little to pacify him, but do not let his ignorance and impatience ruin your safe merge.

PROBLEMS FROM HAVING PLENTY OF SPEED EARLY: What if you are really rolling and when you get to the end of the ramp there are six semi-trailer trucks in a line next to you on the expressway, and there are no spaces among them?

What if you get into the same situation while you are moving slowly? Do the best you can. Don't forget about your safety escape route, the shoulder. You will not outrun the line of thundering trucks. However, if your speed is high enough, you may find a place in that line.

A rare problem actually caused by good speed early is this. Your obvious speed on the ramp outrages some driver approaching on the expressway. He accelerates to keep you, the "crazy" man, from getting on ahead of him.

The solution is simple. Relax and watch the drag race. If he beats you, he will have opened a huge gap behind his car. Just pull right into it. If you beat him, there is no problem, is there?

Finally, what if there is a big puddle or patch of snow, ice, etc. at the end of the ramp, but the rest of the ramp and expressway are clear? Hitting a puddle etc. at high speed can cause VERY SERIOUS control problems. Think. Analyze the whole merge situation. KEEP CONTROL! Entering the expressway spinning is spectacular, but it is neither safe nor graceful. It could, however, be lethal!

ADJUSTING TO TRAFFIC: Many drivers entering expressways apparently do not accelerate, do not look, do not plan. They never actually perform the very satisfying maneuver of merging. They get on somehow, anyhow! Some force their way into a space already being used by another driver. Some wait until another driver helps them onto the expressway. Others ooze into traffic like a root slowly growing down through the ground toward moisture, making no decisions, shunning responsibility, and taking no positive action whatsoever toward merging — just letting it happen in a slow confusion.

After these non-merging drivers have crowded, cut-off, slowed down, confused, angered, and endangered other drivers, they "adjust to traffic". Leaving the mess they created behind them, they accelerate and join the merry flow ahead.

"Adjust to traffic" means to make *fine* adjustments to your position in traffic. It means to fit in, to establish a space cushion, to get the new overall traffic scene, etc. It does not mean to do the acceleration you should have done 3/4 of a mile ago, before you got onto the expressway.

GET ON: In heavy, urban traffic, when the space is available for your merge, do it! Make a definite move. Get in and have it finished. Do not use the entire length of the acceleration lane and merging area to merge if you do not have to. Get your spot and allow all the other drivers around you to get on with their business. Waiting around and just sort of floating listlessly into position confuses and irritates drivers behind and even ahead of you.

LINES OF VEHICLES ON THE RAMP: When a line of vehicles comes down the ramp, drivers on the expressway will often change lanes to let it on or plan to merge into it rather than expecting the line of vehicles to try to merge with them.

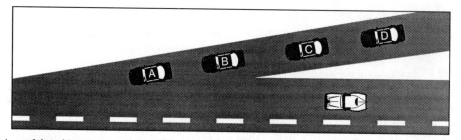

The driver of the white car may well change lanes or control the merge by planning to fit between cars B and C.

MAINTENANCE AND REPAIRS CAN CAUSE EXPRESSWAY ENTRANCE PROBLEMS: When the lane into which entering traffic must merge is being repaired, it may be closed to traffic by barricades. However, entrances are not usually closed and are set up like this.

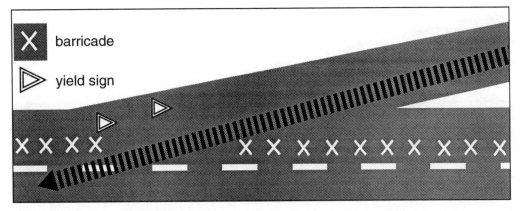

The space the entering driver has to make his lane change is much shorter than normal, and his vision is frequently restricted by construction, machinery and barricades. In the same way, the vision of drivers approaching on the expressway is also restricted.

The best thing for drivers on the expressway to do is keep out of the lane into which entering drivers must merge. If they can't, they should be very watchful for merging traffic, and do all they can to help.

Entering drivers should be extremely careful in planning their merge. The situation will be confusing. They will probably face a yield sign. Unless they are absolutely certain that they will merge *perfectly* and that normal merging is the safest course, they should slow down, even stop, yield, and wait for a safe space to enter.

STOP LIGHTS ON THE ENTRANCE RAMP: During rush hours on urban expressways stop lights may control traffic flow on entrance ramps. When operating, they show red until a vehicle stops at them. They change to green for a very short period to let only one vehicle through at a time.

When these stoplights show steady red, stop and wait for green. When they show steady green or are not lit at all, ignore them.

GETTING OFF: The intrinsic logic of the expressway exit is that drivers should slow down AFTER they have left the main road without disturbing its traffic flow. The exit maneuver itself is usually quite simple, but still enjoyable. Make it a demonstration of perfect speed control and aiming technique.

For explaining the basics of exiting the expressway we will again use a straight ramp.

First, make sure you know where you want to exit. *Before beginning* the trip, check maps, ask for directions, etc. It's a very good idea to know the names or numbers of one, or two, or three exits before yours. That way you run less risk of being surprised. Have your passenger make the trip safer and share in the enjoyment of "automobiling" by helping find the way.

Make sure you are in the proper lane to exit. Not all exits *(or entrances for that matter)* are on the right.

Check traffic ahead, behind, and up the ramp.

Signal.
Aim.
Leave the expressway as early as possible.

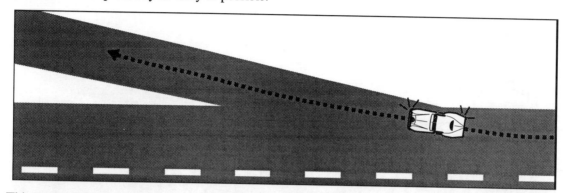

This assures you your place on the off ramp. You cannot be blocked by a car behind you exiting first.

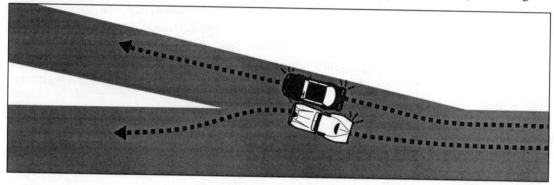

Exiting as early as possible also keeps the traffic situation as simple as possible. By signalling your intention to exit and then exiting promptly, you leave no doubt for your fellow drivers about your course. This certainty about you helps them make and execute their own plans.

Aim again.

Immediately after exiting, check your outside mirror and/or blind spot for vehicles getting off late and cutting ahead of you in the process.

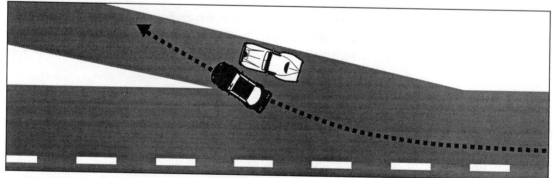

Gray car, exiting late, cuts off white car.

Aim and check ahead again.

Check your inside mirror to see what is happening behind you on the ramp.

Aim.

Prepare to do whatever you will have to do at the end of the off ramp. Notice whether traffic ahead seems to be staying in the middle of the ramp or forming two lanes before turning left and right. Look for direction signs, stop lights, stop signs, yield signs, cross traffic, pedestrians, blind areas, merges into one-way traffic.

Merging into one-way street traffic is done just like merging onto the expressway. Look and plan early to have adequate speed. Do not simply lose speed as soon as you leave the expressway. *Keep your speed until you know that you will not need it any more.* It is much harder and takes longer to speed up than to slow down. Plan ahead and keep just enough speed to stay in control of whatever conditions appear ahead and over your shoulder.

In general, drive down the middle of both off and on ramps.

1. *Maintain speed. Know what is ahead of and behind your car. Plan to exit at X.*

2. *Exit.*

3. *Check left for someone getting off late who might cut you off.*

4. *Check ahead. Check inside rearview mirror. Center your vehicle in lane and begin reducing speed.*

5. *Check traffic ahead and behind on road onto which you will merge. Plan to merge early. Keep enough speed to stay in control of situation.*

6. *Merge check and adapt to all conditions ahead. Check mirror.*

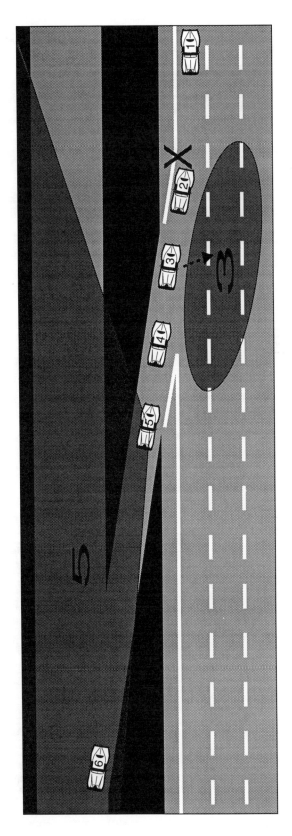

Crossover Ramps

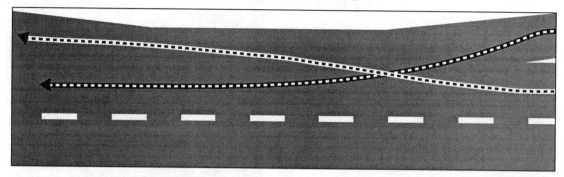

Whether entering or exiting on this type of ramp, use the same basic procedures outlined above. As the arrows in the illustration show, do it as early as possible. This gets you the space/lane you want/need and gets you out of the way. Everybody else on the ramp can then do his maneuver without having to wonder about you. Hanging around and looking indefinite about what you are doing will only confuse the situation, lead to last moment lane changes, and add needless danger to the situation.

Drivers entering on this type of ramp will need no new procedures. When entering, get speed early, start looking early, and plan early. Merge as early, safely, and efficiently as possible.

Exiting drivers will find that they do not have much to worry about in merging with entering traffic if they keep speed and begin looking and planning early. Because they are ON the expressway, they have all the advantages. They can see the entering traffic more easily than it can see them, and they have the speed. They will find it relatively easy to pick and merge into a gap in entering traffic if they look and plan early and keep speed.

Exiting drivers should eliminate doubt and leave themselves extra space by planning to change lanes as early as possible.

Cloverleafs

EXITING: When exiting onto a cloverleaf, stick to the basic procedure of getting off as early as possible. Getting off on a cloverleaf can be easier than getting off on a straight crossover ramp. Often you will be able to see entering traffic while it is still quite a distance back on the curve.

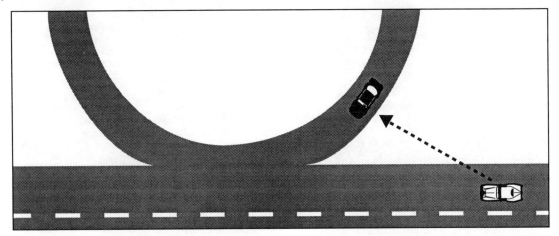

This will make planning your exit quite easy.

Make sure to slow down for the curve and aim toward its inside.

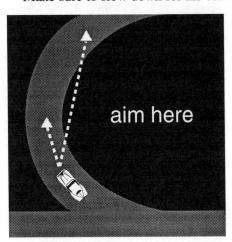

Aiming at the outside of the curve will make you steer toward the outside of the curve. Because you are looking straight off the edge of the road instead of at the middle of the space through which you want to drive, your control will be *very unsure*. It will look as if your car wants to run right off the outside edge of the curve. It will feel that way, too. You will scare yourself.

No matter how advanced the driving situation in which you find yourself, you must ALWAYS AIM, and you must ALWAYS AIM PROPERLY!

Very little traffic uses the outside edge of the cloverleaf curve, so debris builds up there — little pebbles, etc. Traction is not good on these "marbles." Stay away from them. *AIM!*

On some cloverleaf exits, if you take a moment just as you exit, you can see all the way around the curve before you actually enter it. This can prevent the rare truck parked half way around the curve from surprising you.

269

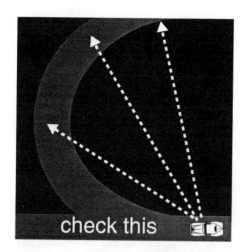

ENTERING FROM A CLOVERLEAF: Some cloverleaf interchange structures are much better than others. In all cases, though, using them to enter traffic is clumsy. The ramp's curve limits your acceleration, speed, and vision. Therefore, your planning *must* be done very late in your trip along the ramp.

Keep plenty of distance between your car and the one ahead. Drive around the curve at a speed which makes perfect car control easy. At about half distance around the curve, you may be able to see the road onto which you will merge.

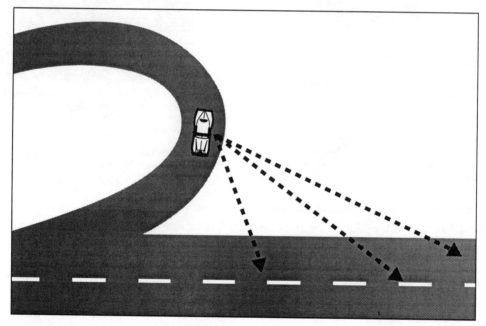

Tear your eyes off the curve and take a quick look or two. Try to get some advance information about traffic on the expressway.

Aim ahead on the ramp.

Look ahead to where the merge area is. Locate it.

Locate the merge area.

Avoid this by checking for exiting traffic.

Now, with some idea about traffic and the location of the merge area, your subconscious will be able to do some pre-planning while you aim and continue around the curve.

Just before reaching the merge point, make sure you know where the road continues ahead, and stay to the INSIDE of the curve. You must not enter expressway traffic before you are ready.

Finally, staying to the inside of the curve, aim, accelerate, look, and plan as early as possible, using whatever space you have ahead as you would use a straight crossover ramp. Your merge will most often happen toward the end of the ramp or merge area. Some newer cloverleaf ramps have better curves. They get wider at the end instead of sharper.

Stay to the inside of the curve.

At this point it is also extremely important to check for exiting traffic.

ONE LAST PROBLEM: Some drivers have found that they can have fun by taking a curved ramp (usually a cloverleaf) fast. However, they forget that their fun is not the purpose of the ramp and the expressway. They forget that they have to merge.

They use all their ability to control the car on the curve and have no chance to pre-plan or set up the merge maneuver. They come tearing through the curve, then slow drastically to figure out how to enter expressway traffic. Needless to say, this confuses other drivers on the expressway. It also marks these drivers as selfish, foolish babies.

15 *Chapter Fifteen*

Physics

Photo courtesy of The Jerry Murawski Collection.

Every material thing in the universe acts or works according to natural law. Every material thing in the universe *must* act according to natural law. *Nothing* can act contrary to natural law. When you drop a book, it falls —natural law. When water gets cold enough, it freezes, and when it gets hot enough, it boils —natural law. An airplane flies because its designers understood and used natural law to make it fly. Your car works according to natural law. Even your body works according to natural law. Natural law is *not* something unusual. It is everywhere all the time. It cannot be broken or changed. It can only be understood and used.

Physics is the study of natural law. The word "physics" is also used to mean natural law.

The word "physics" scares many people. It should not. Every physical thing we do involves physics, so we all know a great deal about physics. Drop a glass; it will probably shatter. Drop a ball; it will bounce. Drop a wet rag; it will just stay where it falls. Ice is slippery. Sandpaper is rough. Syrup is sticky. Physics is all around us all the time!

It should be no surprise then that physics is all around us when we drive. Our cars operate according to physics. Our tires grip the road according to physics. The weather and light work according to physics. The speed laws are based on physics. Our own bodies work according to physics. Driving is about physics. Driving is a great way to explore physics, to *feel* physics at work through car control.

Gravity

Gravity pulls *everything* on Earth toward the center of the Earth. In other words, it holds everything down. It holds your car on the road. It holds you on the driver's seat. It holds your feet on the car floor.

Drivers do not generally think about gravity except on hills. Just as walking uphill is harder than walking on a level surface, driving uphill is harder for your car than driving on a level surface, because going uphill is working *against* the pull of gravity. Driving uphill, you will have to feed more gas and maybe even shift to a lower gear. (See Chapter 4 and Chapter 13.)

In downhill driving, gravity works *with* your car to accelerate it. Going downhill, your car will pick up speed very easily. You will need to feed less gas or no gas going downhill. You may have to use your brakes to control your speed going downhill. You might also shift to a lower gear to help hold back the car. (See Chapter 4 and Chapter 13.)

Stopping when driving uphill can be done in a shorter distance because of the pull of gravity. For the same reason, stopping when driving downhill can take a longer distance.

Trying to stop on ice when driving downhill can take an amazingly long distance. Flatlanders especially can very easily misjudge how very much space their cars will need to stop when travelling downhill on ice.

Skidding

Skids are not well understood. People insist on putting them into a special category outside "normal" driving. Many drivers, driver education books, and even racing movies seem to consider "normal" driving and even "normal" racing as "like being on rails". According to them, skids *interrupt* "normal" driving and even "normal" racing suddenly, without warning, and for mysterious reasons beyond our ability to understand.

NONSENSE! There is nothing abnormal or mysterious about skidding. Even the relatively few skids caused by mechanical failures or sudden, possibly unpredictable changes in traction, obey natural law perfectly. They must. *It is impossible to disobey natural law.* The trick to predicting, controlling, and preventing skids is understanding them.

For every driving maneuver, in every vehicle, in every set of conditions, there is a certain amount of grip or traction between tires and road available to be used by the driver. If the driver tries a maneuver which needs more traction than is available, he skids. *THE DRIVER CAUSES THE SKID!* The ice is there. The rain is there. The design and compound of the tire are there. The sharpness of the curve is there. The power of the car is there. The *driver* is the fellow in charge. It is his job to balance *all* factors in driving. The skid is not imposed from outside. *The driver causes virtually all skids.*

Combining the facts that drivers cause skids and that skids must follow natural law leads us to the answers about having, controlling, and avoiding skids. Stripped of their mystery, skids should neither frighten nor ambush us.

INERTIA: Inertia is the tendency an object has to remain in its current state of motion. If an object is not in motion, it tends to stay at rest unless an unbalanced force puts it into motion. Books, or bananas, or bandannas, or suits of armor do not move by themselves.

If an object is moving, it tends to keep moving at the same speed and in the same direction. To make a car speed up or slow down or turn, the driver must apply an unbalanced force to the car by feeding more or less gas, stepping on the

brake pedal, or turning the steering wheel.

FRICTION: Friction is the resistance to sliding of one surface on another. While gravity pulls you down into your driver's seat, friction keeps you from sliding out of it. Friction is what allows you to hold your car keys between your fingers. Friction is what allows you to push the gas, brake, and clutch pedals without sliding off them. Friction is what allows you to hold and turn the steering wheel. Friction is what allows your car's tires to grip the road. Without friction between the tires and the road, your car could not accelerate, decelerate, or turn.

We call the friction between tires and the surface on which they are operating traction. Traction changes for many reasons. For example, a properly inflated tire in good condition has more traction on dry concrete than on ice. Traction is the amount of grip your car's tires have at any moment.

CENTRIPETAL FORCE: Centripetal force makes a moving object take a curved path or move toward the center. When you turn your steering wheel, you apply centripetal force to your car. You make it turn.

CONTACT PATCHES: Basically, all car control is control of the car's inertia. All this inertia control happens where the tires meet the road.

The area of a tire which is actually touching the road at any one time is called a contact patch. A four wheeled car has four contact patches. At rest, each is about the size of a man's open hand with the fingers spread. However, the size of the patches changes often as the car moves. For example, braking pitches weight forward, increasing the size of the front contact patches while reducing the size of the rears, affecting traction. As long as the contact patches maintain enough traction, control is no problem. When any maneuver requires more traction than is available at the contact patches, a skid begins.

THE PHYSICS OF SKIDDING: Virtually all skids start because a driver tries to change the inertia of his car too forcefully. He does this with his brakes, his engine's power, his steering wheel, or some combination of these.

A driver steps on the brake pedal *hard*! He wants to slow down or stop, that is, he wants to lower his car's forward inertia. A car's brakes slow or stop the car's wheels. Because the car is attached to its wheels, slowing the wheels slows the car. As long as the tires have enough traction to allow the slowing force of the brakes to reduce the car's forward inertia, everything is alright. The car slows or stops. When the traction needed to slow the car is greater than what is actually available, the tires begin to slide. The car is skidding.

Another driver steps on the gas pedal *hard*! He wants to accelerate, that is, he wants to increase his car's forward inertia. (If the car is standing still, the driver wants to overcome his car's resting inertia and give the car forward inertia.) As long as the tires have enough traction to allow the turning force (torque) of the drive wheels to raise the car's forward inertia, everything is alright. When the traction needed to accelerate the car is greater than what is actually available, the drive wheels begin to spin. The car is skidding.

Still another driver drives through a curve *very fast*! He wants neither to increase nor decrease his car's forward inertia. He wants to change the direction of his car's inertia. He turns the steering wheel. By doing this he applies centripetal force to the car.

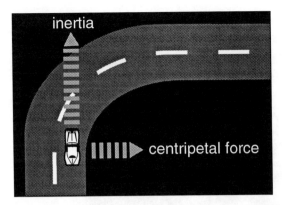

inertia

centripetal force

Like the other control functions, this happens under the car, where the tires meet the road. As long as the tires have enough traction to allow the centripetal force to overcome the car's forward inertia, everything is alright. When the traction needed for the centripetal force to overcome the car's forward inertia is greater than what is actually available, the tires begin to slide sideways. The car is skidding.

Once more now, *a driver causes a skid when he tries to make his car do a maneuver needing more traction than is available. This maneuver can be accelerating, decelerating, turning, or a combination of turning with accelerating or decelerating.*

Actually, a skid resulting only from cornering too hard is very rare. Cornering skids generally result from the driver's trying to accelerate or decelerate while cornering. The amount of traction needed to accelerate or decelerate added to the amount of traction already being used to turn exceeds the amount actually available.

SKID CONTROL: As a driver, you are interested not so much in understanding the physics of skidding, but in dealing with skids successfully on the road. The basic rules for correcting all skids are very simply: 1. *Steer the car where you want it to go* (where it was going before it started to skid). 2. *Release whichever pedal, gas or brake, you stepped on too hard.* Because a

spinning tire has very little traction and gives little or no directional control, and because a sliding tire has very little traction and gives no directional control, you must get spinning or sliding tires rolling again.

When operating near the limits of adhesion (traction), rear wheel drive and front wheel drive cars often respond quite differently to the same control inputs by the driver. The drive wheels (front or rear) are the wheels which apply the car's power to the road to move the car.

First, we shall examine the common skids which result from specific control inputs as they happen in rear wheel drive cars. Then we shall examine the common skids which result from those same control inputs as they happen in front wheel drive cars.

Before we begin, let us assume that in all of these examples, we are driving on a uniform layer of snow which covers the entire road surface.

COMMON SKIDS AS THEY OCCUR IN REAR WHEEL DRIVE CARS: On our lovely layer of snow, drive a rear wheel drive car through a curve or turn. Remember now that when you turn a car with its steering wheel, you are applying centripetal force at the tires' contact patches to change the car's course, that is, to overcome the car's natural, inertial tendency to keep going straight. Your tires need a certain amount of traction to do this.

As you begin coming out of the turn, you feed gas as you would on dry pavement. This will cause the rear wheels to spin, reducing their traction. The front tires (not spinning) will still have enough traction to keep turning the car, but the rear tires (spinning) will not. The skid *must* happen at the end of the car with less traction. Inertia will overcome centripetal force at the rear end of the car, which will begin to slide straight ahead. The resulting skid feels as if the rear end of the car is sliding toward the outside of the corner. It looks like this.

To correct this skid, release the gas pedal. This will stop the rear wheels from spinning, restoring some traction. At the same time, keep aiming at the space through which you want to drive and steer the car to align it properly with the road again. In the skid illustrated above, steer left.

Next, wait. The car will begin to stop skidding and align itself properly. As the car comes back on course, keep aiming far ahead and straighten the steering just as the car gets pointed straight ahead again.

This skid is the classic rear wheel drive skid. It is the skid which defines our concept of a car going through a corner fast. It is the skid which is the most fun to learn to control. It is the reason many driving enthusiasts consider rear wheel drive cars more fun. It is the skid out of which grows the race driver's love of going through corners at the very edges of physics. Learning to control it has always been the beginning of confidence and safety in car control under slippery conditions.

This kind of skid can end in a counterskid. The rear end of the car may continue moving past the straight ahead alignment.

counterskid
begins here

In the counterskid illustrated above, merely steer toward the right. If another counterskid develops, steer left again. Just repeat corrective steering until all counterskidding has stopped.

The thing is to avoid the counterskid. Often, this can be done by reacting early enough and fast enough to prevent a serious skid which requires a great deal of corrective steering.

A second kind of skid comes from tying to stop. To induce this skid in a rear wheel drive car, drive along in a straight line and hit the brakes hard! (Check the mirror before you do this.) What normally happens in this situation is that at least the front wheels lock (stop turning), and the car slides straight forward. The car is not stopping as fast as if the wheels were still rolling (more traction), but it is stable and stopping. If there is room to stop without crashing, this skid may not require any corrective action.

Quite often, though, the car begins to turn sideways. The rear end may start to catch up with the front.

On a crowned road, gravity will tend to pull the front end of the car downhill toward the right curb.

In either case, control the skid. Restore rolling traction by releasing the brakes and steer. As soon as directional control is regained, re-apply brakes to resume stopping. Use less pressure to prevent causing another skid.

In real world conditions, there is always some reason you are trying to stop. Often that reason is an intersection where another vehicle is already stopped in front of yours.

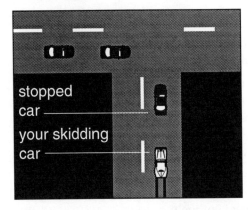

In this situation, your goal is not merely to stop or maintain steering control. Your goal is to avoid hitting something. Because of the intersection with its cross traffic, releasing the brakes and neatly swerving around the stopped vehicle will probably not be a choice.

Pump the brakes. Just keep hitting and releasing the brake pedal hard and fast. This is the standard way to stop a car after a brake induced skid. Properly done, it will get the car stopped faster than continuing the skid and it will allow some directional control. It is a very basic form of what an anti-lock braking system (ABS) does electronically.

To induce our next rear wheel drive skid, with the car pointed straight ahead, step on the gas pedal *hard*! The rear wheels will spin. The rear end of the car will probably skid sideways. It will probably skid toward the right.

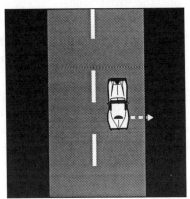

To correct this skid, release the gas pedal, restoring rolling traction to the rear wheels, and steer the car straight.

COMMON SKIDS AS THEY OCCUR IN FRONT WHEEL DRIVE CARS: Drive a front wheel drive car through an icy turn. As you begin coming out of the turn, feed gas as you would on dry pavement. As you feed gas, the front wheels spin. This reduces their traction. The car's forward inertia must take over at the end with less traction. The front end of the car begins skidding straight ahead toward the outside of the turn.

In a rear wheel drive car, these same control inputs would cause the rear end of the car to skid, because the rear wheels were spinning and therefore had less traction. With the front wheel drive car, however, it is the front wheels which are spinning and therefore have less traction. The skid must happen at the front.

To control this skid, release the gas pedal. This stops the front wheels from spinning, restoring some traction. At the same time, keep aiming properly and steer the car to align it correctly with the road again. In the skid illustrated, steer toward the right.

Next, wait. The car will begin to stop skidding and align itself properly. As the car comes back on course, continue aiming far ahead and straighten the steering.

Induce the next front wheel drive skid by driving along in a straight line and hitting the brakes *hard*! This skid is often much more interesting in a front wheel drive car than in a rear wheel drive car. Front wheel drive cars have so much of their weight over the front wheels that the front tires have better traction than the rear tires. The forces of braking will pitch even more weight forward, reducing the load on the rear wheels even more. Because of the light load on the rear wheels, the rear brakes may lock before the front brakes. This reduces the rear tires' traction even more (sliding tires). Inertia keeps pushing the car straight forward. Because there is so much less traction at the rear than at the front, the rear end may slow down less than the front end. However, the two ends are connected. The only thing that can happen is that the rear end will try to catch up with and pass the front end. In other words, often a front wheel drive car under extremely severe braking will not slide straight ahead. It will try to spin or slide down the road sideways.

To regain control, once again, restore traction and steer. Release the brakes and aim properly. The rear may not always slide to the same side. It can go either way depending upon the exact conditions in any single skid. Therefore, although you can expect a possible sideways skid, you may not be sure which way the rear end will go.

Once again, pumping the brakes fast and hard will give you the most control in trying to stop after controlling a skid induced by braking.

For our next front wheel drive skid, while pointed straight ahead, step on the gas pedal *hard*! Spin the front wheels. If the car does not go straight, more often than not its front end will skid to the right. It may skid either way, though. Be ready, and control the skid by steering and releasing the gas pedal.

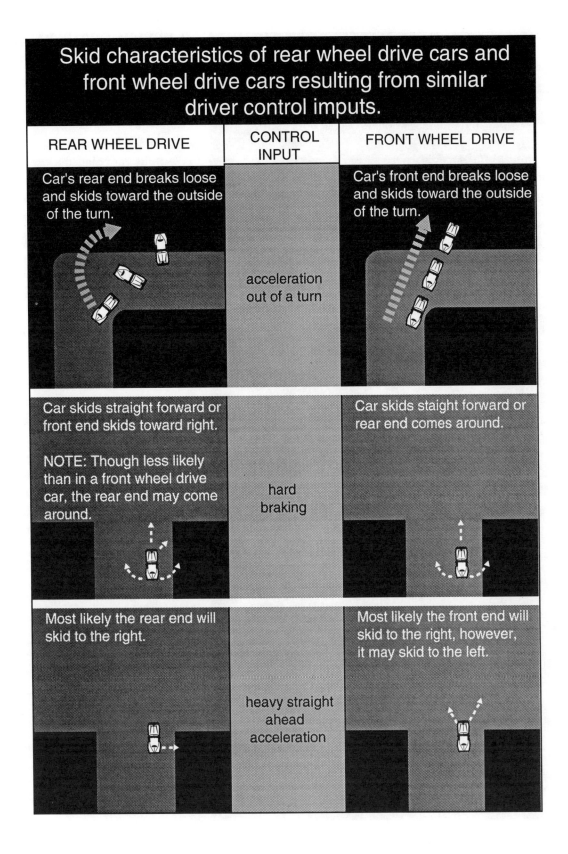

Skid characteristics of rear wheel drive cars and front wheel drive cars resulting from similar driver control imputs.

REAR WHEEL DRIVE	CONTROL INPUT	FRONT WHEEL DRIVE
Car's rear end breaks loose and skids toward the outside of the turn.	acceleration out of a turn	Car's front end breaks loose and skids toward the outside of the turn.
Car skids straight forward or front end skids toward right. NOTE: Though less likely than in a front wheel drive car, the rear end may come around.	hard braking	Car skids staight forward or rear end comes around.
Most likely the rear end will skid to the right.	heavy straight ahead acceleration	Most likely the front end will skid to the right, however, it may skid to the left.

UNDERSTEER, OVERSTEER, AND NEUTRALSTEER

The terms understeer, oversteer, and neutralsteer are very handy for describing skids. These terms also describe vehicles' basic handling tendencies when driven hard through corners.

UNDERSTEER: As it approaches the limit of adhesion in a corner, an understeering vehicle will tend to turn LESS than the driver has turned the front wheels. The vehicle *under*steers. When an understeering vehicle begins to slip, it will tend to go straight ahead even through its front wheels are turned hard into the turn.

Front wheel drive cars and most rear wheel drive cars tend to understeer. Vehicles with more of their weight at the front tend to understeer. Vehicles carrying less air pressure in their front tires than in their rear tires tend to understeer. Engineers purposely design most cars to understeer, because understeering cars are more stable, like arrows which carry most of their weight in front.

OVERSTEER: As it approaches the limit of adhesion in a corner, an oversteering vehicle will tend to turn MORE than the driver has turned the front wheels. The vehicle *over*steers. When an oversteering vehicle begins to slip, instead of its front end pushing straight ahead as in

Continued next page

A REVIEW OF THE BASICS OF SKID CONTROL:

1. If the brakes lock, release the brake pedal.

2. If the wheels spin, release the gas pedal.

3. If the car points the wrong way, steer to point it the right way.

Those are the rules. They are simple. They are perfectly natural. They work. They must work, because it's physics. Any action must have only certain specific results. Skids must follow the laws of physics. That means that skids are not only controllable, they are *predictable*! Skids do *not* come "out of the blue." If a driver knows that his control inputs may cause a skid, he also knows which kind(s) of skid may be caused. If he knows ahead of time that he may skid and how he may skid, obviously he also knows ahead of time what to do about the skid. The mystery is gone. The surprise is gone!

GO SKIDDING: You need to see that all of this theory really does work. You need to *feel* it work. You need to *feel* skids. You need to *feel* skids ending because of your control inputs. You need to *feel* skids starting because of your control inputs. You need to *feel* (and hear) your tires spinning. You need to *feel* (and hear) them sliding. Once you *feel* these things, once you *know* these things, skids and skid control become just another part of the wonderful hobby of driving, like parallel parking.

Begin learning about skidding in the safest, most isolated area you can find. The idea is to learn about skidding, not to damage anything or get into trouble. Use a surface slippery enough that very low speeds (5 to 15 m.p.h.) will allow lovely skids. Ice is terrific. Use a place which gives you plenty of room — PLENTY OF ROOM! A large parking lot without curbs or concrete bumpers is excellent. Go at a time when the place you use is deserted if possible. If the person in charge of the place you are using or a policeman asks you to leave, do not argue. Be polite and leave.

People living in the north have the advantages in finding snow and ice covered parking lots. People living in warm climates will have to be much more patient when searching for good, safe skidding places. Gravel, mud, grass, especially wet grass, are slippery. Sand on pavement is slippery. Wet asphalt can be quite slippery, especially during the first few minutes of rain. During days, or weeks, or months of dry weather, oil and rubber residues build up on pavements. Until they are washed away by relatively long periods of rain (usually more than half an hour), these residues mix with the water to form a lovely, slippery goo on the pavement.

understeer, its rear end tends to swing around toward the outside of the turn.

Some rear wheel drive cars tend to oversteer. Vehicles with more of their weight at the rear tend to oversteer. Vehicles carrying less air pressure in their rear tires than in their front tires tend to oversteer.

NEUTRALSTEER: As it reaches the limit of adhesion in a corner, a neutralsteering vehicle will tend to turn exactly the same as the driver has turned the front wheels. It steers neutrally. When it begins to slip, it will tend to move straight sideways.

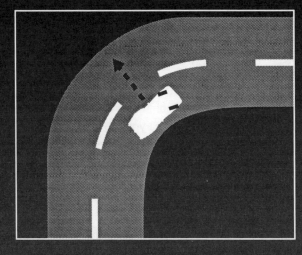

Continued next page

DRIVER CONTROL INPUTS: The control inputs of the driver can also induce, increase, and decrease both understeer and oversteer. High performance driving schools teach how to do this kind of thing correctly. It is a refinement of skid control technique. A driver with extremely high skill and great sensitivity can make a car dance on the very edge of control. He can save a bad situation. On the other hand, the control inputs of an oaf can force a crash when none should happen. An oaf's incorrect control inputs will unbalance the car and make it less able to hold the road and perform properly. Rather than achieving the best control possible in a given situation, the control inputs of an oafish driver can easily FORCE his car out of control! Warning: Oafishness is rampant among today's drivers!

UNDERSTEERING, OVERSTEERING, AND NEUTRALSTEERING SKIDS: Understeering, oversteering, and neutralsteering skids are merely gross exaggerations of the basic handling tendencies described above. Typical understeering, oversteering, and neutralsteering skids are illustrated below.

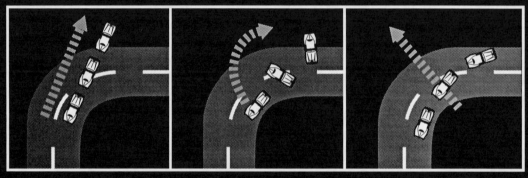

SKIDS: Understeering (left); Oversteering (middle); Neutralsteering (right)

Drizzly weather can keep pavements slick for days.

Wherever you go skidding, be very careful to keep paying attention to looking for any kind of traffic anywhere near the area you are using.

A smooth, flat surface is always better than a bumpy or sloping one for skidding practice.

Just flinging cars around, doing doughnuts, looking for *thrills*, are not learning about skidding. Learning about skidding is actually more rewarding, because you are learning, growing, achieving, controlling. You are developing sensitivity, building a master touch.

You need limits. There must be a course for your car to leave before you can put it back on course. Suppose you have the best of possibilities. Your family owns a big parking lot. It has just snowed. It is five o'clock on Sunday morning. Arrive at the lot and drive around it to make a course for yourself by leaving tracks in the snow. Go around several times to establish an obvious path. Then skid. Stop hard. Start hard. Accelerate hard coming out of corners. Get the *feel*! Begin predicting. (You will do that automatically.) Polish your technique. Learn to skid *smooooooothly*!

Then try to do this skid. Brake and turn at the same time. Do this by rushing up to the corner, leaving braking until too late. Then brake fairly hard, but try to avoid skidding. Arrive at the beginning of the turn still on the brakes and still going too fast. Stay on the brakes and turn. Your car will skid toward the outside of the curve.

Try this skid a few more times. You will find it virtually impossible to control. You will find that the thing to do with this skid is avoid it. Slow down earlier so that you do not get into this skid. You will have found the traditional advice given to both racers and street drivers, "Slow down *BEFORE* entering the turn". "In slow, out fast." There is very little one can do to control this skid, so one must *PREVENT IT*!

Especially on dry pavement, people often mistake this skid for one caused by merely going through a corner too fast. This skid is caused by a combination of trying to go around the corner fast and trying to brake at the same time. There might be just enough traction for the car to get around the corner alright if all the tires had to do was turn it. The trouble is that the driver, by trying to turn and brake at the same time, is forcing the tires to try to turn the car and slow it down at the same time. There is not enough traction to do both. The car skids.

This leads us to the next major rule about skidding. When skidding, *STAY OFF THE BRAKES*! In the overwhelming majority of skids, using the brakes will just make matters worse — often *MUCH WORSE*!

Along this same line of thought is the advice to shift to neutral in an automatic transmission car or simply to step on the clutch pedal in a stick shift car when you are skidding through a corner. Doing this cuts engine power or engine drag to the drive wheels. This lets the car just coast. Coasting helps the car to regain and keep its balance. It also allows the tires to use *all* their traction to steer the car.

This technique should not be necessary in any but the very worst skids, and shifting to neutral while skidding can be clumsy.

Finally, do not tell your driver education teacher that your friend did this and this in such and such a skid, and it didn't work. Physics works! Although he may not have known it, your friend did something else, or he was skidding some other way.

THE FOUR WHEEL DRIFT: The four wheel drift is a state of traction in a curve which is between being "on rails" and skidding. In a four wheel drift, the tires are partly rolling and partly skidding. The car is at the limit of adhesion and *is controllable*! The four wheel drift is the state in which most race cars take most corners. *IT IS A RACING TECHNIQUE*! LEAVE DRIFTING TO THE RACERS WHO KNOW HOW TO DO IT OR UNTIL YOU CAN LEARN IT AT A HIGH PERFORMANCE DRIVING SCHOOL OR RACING DRIVER SCHOOL AFTER YOU HAVE A LOT OF DRIVING AND SKIDDING EXPERIENCE! DRIFTING IS MENTIONED HERE TO SHOW THAT THERE *IS A STATE BETWEEN "ON RAILS" AND SKIDDING*. This fact is intended to be the final nail in the coffin of the "MYSTERIOUS SKID". The sudden, "mysterious," skid generally comes from insensitivity, ignorance, and lack of attention.

A driver who really has the *feel* of skids can predict approximately when and how his car will skid. He knows what to expect. Therefore, he knows ahead of time what to do and can take corrective action early, before the skid becomes serious, and while control inputs can be minimal.

Good skid schools and high performance driving schools are extremely valuable in learning amazing car control at the limits of adhesion. A good school will take you far beyond the EXTREMELY BASIC techniques in this book.

Books and videotapes on advanced driving and racing technique will introduce you to understeer, oversteer, neutral steer, threshold braking, cadence braking, trail braking, four wheel drifts, slip angles, weight transfer, slipstreaming, adjusting tire pressures, anti-roll bars, high performance tires and shock absorbers, ground effects, etc.

Sanctioned motorsports competitions also open the door to a world of car control unknown, even unimaginable, to the vast majority of drivers. The very best race drivers ordinarily perform absolute wonders of delicate sensitivity in controlling their race cars on the razor edges of physics.

PREVENTING SKIDS: The old advice to slow down in slippery conditions is not enough. Preventing skids is not done by a mathematical formula like slowing down 5 m.p.h. for rain, 10 m.p.h. for snow, and 15 m.p.h. for ice. Preventing skids is not done by going the speed of traffic. Preventing skids is not done by an act of will or by just deciding not to have skids. Preventing skids is not done by good intentions.

Preventing skids is done by learning about and mastering them. Preventing skids is done by making skids, and controlling skids, and finally by smoothing skids into graceful dances by FEELING THE TRACTION.

Knowing how slippery it is lets you know how fast you can go, how fast you can turn, how quickly you can stop, how quickly you can accelerate, how much following distance to keep, and how much earlier you need to begin braking.

A sports car racer racing in the rain is not driving the way he does in the dry. He is not exploring the limits with a sophisticated dance of threshold braking, drifting and wheel spin. He is out there *skidding*! He gets away with it, though. Lap after lap, he slips, and slides, and gets sideways, but he does not "lose it". Why?

He is dealing with a limited stretch of road. He is going over the same road again and again. He is slipping and sliding at the same places. He *KNOWS HOW SLIPPERY IT IS*!

The road driver does not have this advantage. That is why it is so easy for him to think skids are mysterious. The road driver drives along at well below the limit of adhesion. Then he tries to turn or stop and suddenly finds himself way beyond the limit.

The trick is to *keep aware* of the limit of adhesion by continually testing it. In slippery conditions, whenever you can, skid A LITTLE. Approaching a stop sign, for example, slow down to a very low speed well before the place where you must stop. Get the speed low enough and leave enough space to ensure a safe stop even if you should skid badly. Then, based on your current knowledge of the traction, hit the brakes just hard enough to cause a slight skid.

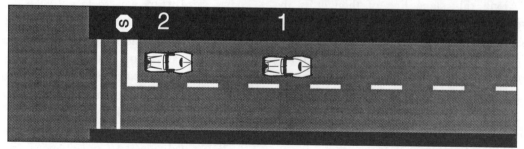

Have speed way down and try a gentle skid at position 1, not position 2.

If you skid exactly as you intended, you know how slippery it is. If you do not skid, it is less slippery than you thought. If you skid more than you expected, it is more slippery than you thought.

As you leave the stop sign, feed just enough gas to induce a little wheel spin. Once again, if your wheels spin just as much as you expected, you know how slippery it is. If they spin more, or less, you do not know.

Your body will use this information automatically, and you will drive accordingly. Your body cannot use information it does not get, though. Keep informed about the limit of adhesion through tiny, safe skids whenever possible.

Sometimes it is so slippery that the skids happen by themselves. You needn't force them. In these conditions, simply do all you can to maintain traction. *Be extremely gentle with all control inputs.*

Checking traction in traffic can be difficult or impossible. You scare other people, look dangerous or irresponsible to the police, and if you make a mistake, you can cause a crash. Therefore, be very careful about inducing skids unless you are sure there is plenty of space, so that you do not worry or endanger anybody.

Driving along at 30 m.p.h. on the expressway through snow for miles and miles can be frightening, because you are stuck in a tight pack of vehicles and therefore cannot check traction. You know that if anybody else makes a mistake, you will be part of a chain reaction crash. It is even more important to stay out of packs in bad weather than in good.

Never base your speed, following distance, etc., on what other drivers are doing. Most American drivers, at their current state of development, are poor judges of traction. Moreover, with technical advances like ABS and automatic traction control, there may be quite a large spread in the capabilities of modern cars in slippery conditions. Also consider other differences like tire width, tire tread depth, car power, rear wheel drive versus front wheel drive or four wheel drive, driver skill, etc.

You do not get to be an expert on skidding by driving through one snow storm, or one winter, or by practicing skids for an hour. It takes a great deal of experience. Show your maturity. Be careful. Do not make what should be a rewarding and inspiring driving and learning experience a needless and silly crash.

Center of Gravity

The center of gravity of a thing is the point around which all of its weight is evenly distributed. More weight lower down in an object gives the object a lower center of gravity. More weight higher up in an object gives the object a higher center of gravity.

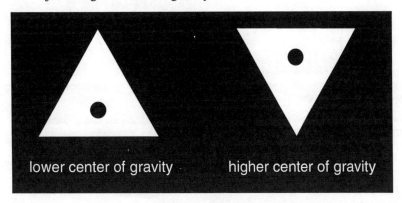

lower center of gravity   higher center of gravity

The lower the center of gravity of an object is, the more stable the object is. Stability is a good thing in cars. A car with a lower center of gravity "hugs the road" more than a car with a higher center of gravity. It is very important for a race car to have a low center of gravity.

In general, trucks, school buses, and four wheel drive utility vehicles (SUVs) have higher centers of gravity. They are not as stable as cars. Think of them as being top-heavy. Top-heavy objects tend to fall over easily.

Driven through corners fast or forced into extremely quick lane changes, cars, having relatively lower centers of gravity, tend to keep all four wheels on the road and begin to slip and slide sideways. They do not tend to turn over. A car, sliding sideways, tends to keep sliding sideways unless it "trips" over a curb, etc.

Vehicles with relatively higher centers of gravity driven through corners fast or forced into extremely quick lane changes *DO NOT* tend to keep all four wheels on the road and slide. They tend to go up on three or even two wheels and finally topple over. The wheels on the inside of the turn tend to lift off the road because the higher center of gravity gives the vehicle a greater tendency to topple over.

Some people have tipped over four wheel drive utility vehicles during relatively violent turning or lane changing maneuvers. Once a vehicle is up on two wheels, get it back down

by widening the arc of the turn and easing off the gas.

For most people, driving a four wheeled vehicle on two wheels is quite unusual. Unfortunately, the first few times one drives on two wheels, he may not realize that he is doing it. It feels strange, but one is not sure until after he has felt the two wheels which had been off the ground drop back down onto it forcefully. Obviously, if you do not know that you are on two wheels, you will not take corrective action. Here again, one's *feel* for physics, one's sensitivity to his vehicle becomes very important.

Just as some crashes are blamed on the car that came out of nowhere and others on the skid that came out of nowhere, still others are blamed on the rollover that came out of nowhere. All vehicles must be driven within their limitations. A real driver understands the physics of driving and is very careful about learning the limits. A real driver does not blame a crash on physics. He avoids crashes because he understands physics. When he doesn't know, he is mature enough to admit it and take it easy.

Adding weight higher in or on a vehicle raises its center of gravity.

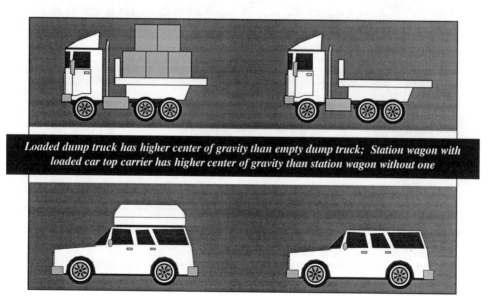

Loaded dump truck has higher center of gravity than empty dump truck; Station wagon with loaded car top carrier has higher center of gravity than station wagon without one

Hydroplaning

In driving, hydroplaning and aquaplaning mean the same thing. "Hydro" comes from Greek. "Aqua" comes from Latin. Both refer to water. "Plane" comes from French and has to do with soaring, gliding, or skimming. As a hydroplane is a boat designed to skim along the surface of the water at high speed, automotive hydroplaning is skimming along the surface of the water in a car.

The grooves in the tread of a car tire are there mostly to allow water on the road to flow out from under the tire's contact patch. Basically, if the grooves are shallow enough, the water is deep enough, and the car's speed is high enough, there is not enough time and space for the water to flow out from beneath the tire. The tire loses contact with the road. It begins to float or plane on the water. For all practical purposes, a hydroplaning tire has no traction. A car riding on hydroplaning tires *cannot* be controlled.

If your car hydroplanes, release the gas pedal. Your car will slow down, and the tires will come back in contact with the road surface. Like skidding, hydroplaning should not be an either or situation. You should feel it happening before you get into a serious situation. Hydroplaning does not feel like skidding. It feels just about like what its name means, skimming along the top of the water. Once again, *feel* what your car is doing! Develop sensitivity to your car and its relationship with the road.

Prevent hydroplaning by keeping your tires properly inflated. More air keeps your tires' tread grooves open better. Check your tires. Tires with very worn tread hydroplane much more easily than tires with deep tread grooves. Incidentally, very wide tires have more tendency to hydroplane than narrow tires. Think of water skis or snow shoes.

When there is a choice, do not drive through standing water at higher speeds. Drive where the standing water isn't. For example, on worn pavements, water collects in the ruts worn into the surface. Drive on the higher parts of the pavement if possible.

Realize that hydroplaning can begin at speeds as low as 30 m.p.h. Avoid hydroplaning particularly on curves.

Front wheel drive cars put a new spin on hydroplaning —literally. Because they are not just rolling through the water, but being turned to propel the car and leading the way through the water, the front wheels of front wheel drive cars may spin when they hit puddles at relatively high speeds. When they do, the car jerks around on the road, the speedometer needle jumps to amazing heights,

and the engine roars. One can avoid this by choosing the lane with fewer puddles, avoiding most puddles, and mostly by just slowing down.

Kinetic Energy

Kinetic energy is also called energy of motion. Kinetic energy or energy of motion is the energy an object has *because* it is moving. Energy was needed to get it moving, so energy is in it while it is moving.

To stop a moving object, one must do something about its kinetic energy. When one stops a car, he changes its kinetic energy into heat energy with the car's brakes.

Brakes work by rubbing two surfaces together. The friction between the rubbing surfaces creates heat. Disc brakes rub pads against a disc (rotor). Drum brakes rub linings on brake shoes against the inside of the brake drum. The friction from the rubbing changes the car's kinetic energy into heat energy, which is given up to the surrounding air. Indeed, the reason disc brakes are better than drum brakes and have virtually replaced them in modern automobiles is that disc brakes release heat better.

When a car crashes, its kinetic energy is used up in the damage done to the car and whatever it hits. It takes energy to crush the front end of a car and knock down a tree.

When a car skids or spins to a stop, its kinetic energy is used up by the skid or the spin.

When you are riding in or driving a car, your body has kinetic energy. When the car was set in motion, it got kinetic energy. When your body was set in motion in the car, it got kinetic energy, too. If your car crashes, it stops. Its kinetic energy is used up in the crash. Unless you are wearing a safety harness when you crash your car, you keep going until something stops you. The things which will probably stop you are the steering wheel, the windshield, and/or the dashboard. When you hit the steering wheel, the windshield, the dashboard, etc., your body's kinetic energy is used up in the damage done to those things and *your body*!

If you are wearing a safety harness, though, your kinetic energy is transferred by the harness to the car. The car then uses up that added kinetic energy by doing a bit more damage to itself and whatever it hit.

Finally, doubling a vehicle's weight doubles its stopping distance, but doubling its *speed quadruples* its stopping distance. Doubling a vehicle's weight means it will hit something twice as hard, but doubling its *speed* means it will hit something *four times as hard*. As they say, "A word to the wise is sufficient."

Total Stopping Distance

It is fairly easy for a driver to get some idea of how fast he can stop his car and make the mistake of thinking that that distance in his *total stopping distance*. The distance it takes a car to stop after the brakes have been applied is called its braking distance. The total stopping distance is the braking distance added to the reaction distance and the perception distance. Before you can hit the brakes, you must notice something is wrong and decide to stop. The distance your car travels while you are doing that is your perception distance. Then you must move your foot to the brake pedal and use it. The distance your car travels while you are doing that is your reaction distance.

Your perception distance can vary enormously. How early you see trouble is dependent on terrain, lighting, weather, obstructions to your view, and how you use your eyes, etc. Matching your speed to visibility as you always must is the key here.

Your reaction distance is dependent on the complexity of the situation, how many control choices you have, your physical condition and, to some extent, the distance your must move your foot to and on the brake pedal.

Your braking distance can vary with the road surface condition, type and condition of brakes, tires, and the driver's skill at using the brakes to their maximum. A car is stopped fastest by its brakes when enough pressure is used so that the wheels are just about to stop turning, not when they are locked. A rolling tire has more traction than a sliding tire.

Of course, perception distance, reaction distance, and braking distance are all very dependent on the car's speed.

Perception distance and reaction distance can easily be longer than braking distance.

Photo courtesy of Peter and Heather Donnelly.

16 *Chapter Sixteen*

Conditions

Driving is done in sunlight, darkness, rain, snow, wind, fog, etc. These conditions are all quite natural. A real driver accepts natural conditions not as threats, but as challenges to his driving skill. He does not blame natural conditions, he deals with them. He is properly proud of the safety and grace with which he is able to control his vehicle even in very bad conditions. He has achieved his skill through study, analysis, and practice.

He is prepared for adverse conditions. He carries necessary equipment. He maintains his car properly. He understands conditions and never underestimates them. He does not take foolish chances. He does not believe that he is invincible. He knows when he is overmatched. He knows when to quit.

He knows how to use time to his advantage. For example, he might start a trip one day earlier or later to avoid a predicted serious storm. He might stop for dinner rather than keep driving into a blinding sunset. Knowing that a thunder shower lasts only a short time, he might find a *safe* place to wait until it ends.

There are so many ways, both simple and sophisticated, to deal with conditions. This chapter contains some of them.

FOG: Huge, chain-reaction crashes (the largest on record involved some 300 vehicles) happen because drivers routinely underestimate the danger of driving in fog. Fog makes it hard to see, and seeing is *fundamental* to driving.

Turn on your headlights in fog. Even if this does not help you see, it will make your car more visible to others. Do not use your parking lights. Driving day or night with only your parking lights lit is illegal. The idea is that parking lights confuse other drivers who think they are seeing headlights. Things are bad enough in fog. Do not add to the problems by confusing other drivers.

Use your low beam (regular) headlights in fog, not your high beams (brights). Fog is made up of millions of droplets of water. Water often reflects light; it sparkles and shines. Because your high beams are aimed higher than your low beams, they throw more light almost straight out ahead of your car. This is like shining a flashlight straight into a mirror at eye level. The light is reflected right back into your eyes. Fog reflects the light from your high beam headlights right back into your eyes. This makes the fog look like a curtain or wall through which you cannot see. Because your low beams are aimed lower, their light tends to shine through the fog onto the road instead of being reflected straight back into your eyes. Occasionally, at night, in light, patchy fog, your high beams may work better.

A fog light's lens is designed differently from the lens of a headlight. A headlight's lens allows quite a bit of light to stray upward. This light bounces back off the fog into the eyes of the driver. The lens of a fog light lets virtually no light stray upward to be reflected back into the driver's eyes.

Fog lights are mounted low on the car. The driver's eyes are farther above the fog lights than above the headlights. Therefore, there is even less tendency for their light to be reflected straight back into the driver's eyes.

The advice to follow a semi in fog or other conditions of poor visibility has been given. The idea is that watching the truck's lit tail and clearance lights will give you a good idea of where the road goes. While that is true, there are problems with the technique.

First is a form of highway hypnosis. In conditions of poor visibility a driver can easily let himself concentrate only on the lights. If he does, his gaze can get fixed on them. His eyes can stop moving and seeing all that they should. Without noticing it, the driver can stop driving and simply follow the lights.

People have followed lights which were not moving and crashed into stopped vehicles. Accident investigations have shown no skid marks. The drivers had not tried to stop. By the time they realized that they were following a stopped vehicle, it was too late.

Second, to keep the truck's lights in view, you may have to follow too closely for the speed at which the truck and you are going. If the truck stops quickly or crashes, you hit it.

Finally, following the lights on a semi is one example of a *very common, very dangerous* mistake drivers make *very easily* in conditions of poor visibility. When visibility is very poor, just seeing enough to aim and steer becomes a big job. A driver concentrates on figuring out where

the road goes. He forgets all about looking for pedestrian traffic, cross traffic, following traffic, disabled vehicles, potholes, road signs, normally blind areas, etc. He just aims and steers. He thinks that he is driving, but he is not.

That mistake makes him go too fast. A properly operating car can always be aimed and steered at a higher speed than it can be driven, if by driving we mean guiding the car along the road under full control based on a full awareness of road surface, weather, traffic, and light conditions; pavement markings; the laws; etc. When the brain has been working so hard on just aiming and steering, it comes to believe that aiming and steering are the only job. It gives up trying to drive and just aims and steers. Then it automatically lets the car move along at a speed which is appropriate for aiming and steering, but too high for driving. In fact, that high speed makes real driving, real control, impossible!

Through it all, the driver stays unaware of the truth. He continues his brave battle against the elements. He gets to wherever he is going *completely* by luck!

When he gets there, he talks about how bad the fog, etc., was, how he couldn't see past his hood ornament. Then, he explains how he just followed the edge line of the road or straddled the center line of a two lane highway and went the 55 m.p.h. speed limit.

He thinks he is telling us how brave and clever he is, what a great driver he is. What he is really telling us is that he hasn't a clue. He is boasting that he does not know the difference between driving and aiming. He is bragging about playing Russian roulette with his life and the lives of everyone else who might have been in his path. He is telling us not to ride with him.

Probably because so many drivers do not know what they should see when driving, they underestimate fog. Therefore, never just go along with the crowd in fog. Most often, the crowd has no idea what is a safe speed!

In darkness, in blinding sun, in fog, in rain, snow, dust, etc., remember what driving is. Remember all the things you need to see when you are cruising along in conditions of perfect visibility. Remember that any or all of those things can be hiding in the fog, etc. to ambush you. Never be satisfied with just barely being able to see where to go. See what you *need* to see to DRIVE! Move your car at the speed which lets you DRIVE! A real driver knows where the limits are, and he does not ignore them.

Check your mirror *often*. If you are travelling at the correct speed for conditions of poor visibility, you will probably be going slower than most other traffic.

What should you do if you do see somebody coming up behind you fast? You would like to become more visible. The only way to do that is to show brighter light to the rear. You could light your brake lights by using your brakes. Of course, that would also slow you down, decreasing the distance between your rear end and the front end of whatever is bearing down on you. You might switch on your hazard lights (four-way flashers). They might get the attention of the driver behind you. The trouble with hazard lights is that they can be very confusing to drivers trying to follow you through fog, heavy rain, etc. Anyone behind you who is trying to control the situation by keeping you in view and still staying as far back as possible, is all keyed up to see brake lights. He may slow down when he sees a flash through the thick fog, only to lose sight of your tail lights. He may then try to re-establish visual contact by speeding up a little, only to see what he thinks is another brake light flash. The situation becomes absurd. The driver following you keeps losing track of where you are exactly because of the way in which you are trying to show him where you are.

On the other hand, flashing hazard lights could cause someone who really is catching up to believe that you are parked on or off the road.

He might then drive onto the *wrong side of the road* to avoid you.

Whenever you *do* use your hazard lights to warn other drivers that you *are* parked, turn on your car's dome light, too. Cars are not generally driven with their dome lights lit. A driver seeing a car with its interior lit up in conditions of poor visibility will expect it to be stopped. He should also look carefully for pedestrians in the area.

Driving at the proper speed can be dangerous because of a speeding aimer-and-steerer behind you. A semi driver, believing that he *must make time*, may be unable to stop before hitting your car because of the difference in speed. WATCH YOUR MIRROR!

You can be tricked into thinking that the fog is getting thicker when it is not. The inside of your windshield may begin to steam up. When you think this might be happening, wipe the windshield with your fingertip. Touch the windshield in some corner through which you virtually never look.

Open your windows to eliminate steam on glass, or turn on defrosters or air conditioner. Outside temperatures affect how these tactics work. Use the one which works the best and is most comfortable to you. Have something handy with which to wipe the insides of the windows: a clean rag, paper towels, a squeegee, a clean blackboard eraser. A fine mist can cover the outside of your windshield, too. Use your wipers and/or washers.

DARKNESS: For many centuries people have done sneaky things at night because it is DARK at night. Darkness hides things and makes them harder to identify.

For the same reason, people do not do outdoor activities which require seeing well at night. They do not mow the lawn at midnight. They do not paint the house, or wax the car, or wash the windows in the dark. When the sun

sets, people stop playing catch and looking at beautiful mountain scenery.

Many drivers, though, ignore darkness. After all, it comes every night. What's the big deal? The big deal is that it is much harder to see at night.

Cars have headlights so drivers can see at night. Headlights, like all artificial lights, help, but they are not as good as sunlight. Their coverage area is limited. They glare. They cast harsh shadows.

The real problem is that the seeing habits of so many drivers are so poor. These drivers have no idea how much they are missing, even in broad daylight! How can they know what they are missing at night?

With a great deal of effort and practice in actively "looking for trouble," you can build seeing habits which automatically protect you in conditions of poor visibility. Your brain will know when you cannot see enough and will automatically lower your speed. You will habitually and automatically base your speed on your visibility.

Often other drivers will pass you when visibility is bad. You will wonder how they can see enough to DRIVE at their speed. THEY CAN'T! They are not "driving". They are aiming and steering. It is easy to be swept up into their high speed club. Avoid that if possible. Try to stay out of their way and just let them go.

Headlights, in addition to helping you see, *help others to see you!*

Even headlight glare can be useful. Headlight glare above the crest of a hill tells you that an oncoming car is approaching on the other side. Often headlight glare can be seen through the trees on curves and through the windows of parked cars. It can give early warning of cross traffic at intersections. Headlight glare can make you aware of the presence of another vehicle in a blind or semi-blind area BEFORE you would be able to see it in daylight.

For best performance, headlights should be kept clean and properly aimed. All lights should be kept clean and in good repair. If your windows and mirrors are dirty, so are your lights. Carry and use a rag. Make use of the glass cleaning equipment at the gas station.

The inside of your windows should also be kept clean. A film of dirt does build up on the inside of your windows. This film can come from vapors given off by the plastic upholstery, smoking, etc. The film spreads glare. Looking at oncoming headlights through a clean windshield or side window, you will be able to see the lights *and the darkness surrounding them.* Looking at the same lights through a dirty window, you will see a window filled with glaring light. Your vision into the dark areas will be seriously reduced. Your ability to judge the distance and speed of oncoming vehicles will also be reduced. Keep fingers, dog noses, etc. off windows and mirrors. They leave marks. Try to use clean, lint-free cloth or paper to clean glass.

Do not overdrive your headlights. Speed is limited by visibility. Do not go so fast that you cannot stop in the distance you can see with your headlights.

Use your high beam (bright) headlights when it is dark and there is little traffic. Remember to dip your headlights (change to low beam) when approaching oncoming traffic and when following. When an oncoming driver forgets to dip his lights, flash your brights, but do not try to blind him by keeping your brights lit. There is no advantage in your both being unable to see.

Keep your eyes used to the dark. You will see what is in your headlight spray. Look beyond it. Look also to the sides of your headlight spray. Look into the darkness for movements, shadows, gleams of light, and areas of contrast. Look for objects, people, and animals in and near the road.

Do not look directly into the high or even the low beam headlights of oncoming vehicles.

Look toward the right and beyond the headlights. You can also block out oncoming bright headlights with your carefully positioned left hand.

The time you can see the least when passing an oncoming vehicle at night is just *after* you have passed it. Your eyes are still dazzled by the light. Your pupils have closed down a great deal. You are back in near pitch darkness. It takes time for your pupils to open up again and for your eyes to recover from the glare.

Try to see what is beyond the oncoming vehicle *before* passing it. Use its headlight spray to study your side of the road *before* your vision is reduced.

Notice the times when other cars' headlights blind you. Then use that information to avoid blinding other drivers. When waiting to turn left at night, keep your car pointed straight ahead. When the driver ahead of you wants to back into a parallel parking space, switch off your headlights while you wait for him to park. He will be able to see. Therefore, he will get out of your way sooner. Sometimes you can be legally parked on the left side, facing traffic. Switch off your headlights.

When you signal another driver that he is running without his headlights, or is running with his brights, etc., switch your lights to exactly what he has wrong. Do not just flash your brights. If he is running with only his parking lights lit, he will check the high beam indicator on his instrument panel and see that he is not using his brights. He will keep using only his parking lights.

Day or night, a flash of your brights into the mirror of the car ahead in the fast lane asks its driver to speed up or move over and let you pass.

When being passed by a semi, flash your lights when its trailer is clear of your front end. Check other traffic, though. Do not tell the truck driver that he can pull over into your lane when someone else is about to block it. When in

doubt, do not signal. Also be aware that any headlight flashing may be illegal.

Adjust your instrument panel lights according to the outside light. When in a brightly lit city, turn your dash lights up so you can see the instruments easily. When you are out in the country and it is very dark, turn down your dash lights to cut the distracting and needless glare inside the car.

Do not drive with your dome light lit. Keep it dark inside your car at night. Light inside the car makes it much harder to see outside.

Adjust your inside rearview mirror to the night position at night.

When driving at night, look for trouble the same way you do in the day time, and drive at the speed which lets you.

DUSK: Dusk is the time of day just before dark. At dusk everything seems to turn gray. Colors are less bright. Contrast is reduced.

Because it is not dark at dusk though, it is easy to assume that you can see as well as you can in the bright sunlight of noon. You can't. You must take special care in looking for trouble. You must also realize that, just like everything else, your car is less visible at dusk. Incidentally, car colors do affect cars' visibility. Light colors are more visible than dark colors, hence school bus yellow, fire engine greenish yellow, and international orange. Red is *not* a highly visible color except in bright light. White would be difficult to see in snow. Finally, lit headlights make your car more visible at dusk.

SUNRISE AND SUNSET: Seeing, when driving into the rising or setting sun, can be *extremely difficult*! Because the sun is so low on the horizon, it shines directly into your eyes, blinding you. A clean windshield helps, but not much. Your car's sunvisor, your billed cap, brimmed hat, sunglasses, etc., will also help. However, your hat, sunglasses, etc., will *not* help if you leave them at home. Do not let your sunglasses get dusty and/or scratched by knocking around the car. You can shield your eyes with your hand. It is clumsy, though. People have taped newspaper, etc., to their windshields. Whatever method you use to shade your eyes, block only as much of your view as is necessary to keep the sun out of your eyes.

When using the sun visor, make sure that its edge points away from your face in case of a crash.

THIS

NOT THIS

When you are driving out of the sunrise or sunset, your car can be extremely difficult for oncoming drivers to see. Expect mistakes from oncoming drivers who cannot see your car, mistakes like left turns just in front of your car. Pedestrians will also have trouble seeing your car. Lighting your headlights may help.

Sun behind your car will shine blindingly into your inside rearview mirror. Use the night adjustment. Sun behind your car will make traffic signals look as if all their lights are lit. Knowing whether you have a red, yellow, or green light can be next to impossible.

Low angle sunlight can make it impossible to see through dusty windows, especially severely raked windows.

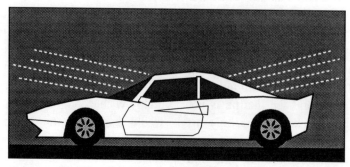

GLEAMS, FLICKERS, AND BLACKOUTS: The blinding gleams from windows, chrome trim, and shiny body panels can make it very difficult to see. These gleams can also be very irritating and tiring to drivers. Sometimes the road itself can glare. Polarized glasses may help.

Driving through the flickering light that one finds under elevated railroad tracks and when light filters through the leaves on trees is very tiring. These kinds of light also make seeing tricky.

Finally, there is driving into a viaduct in bright sun. Just as you enter the dark viaduct, you will not be able to see. Be prepared. Keep your windshield clean and try to see into the viaduct BEFORE you enter it.

WIND: You are driving along the interstate across the great American prairie. As you enter an underpass, your car dodges to the right. You correct. Then, as you leave the underpass, your car dodges to the left. You correct again. At first, you do not think about it. At the next underpass, the same thing happens. Your car dodges right as you enter and left as you leave. Then it happens again at the next underpass and the next. There seems to be something about underpasses. There is. They block the wind.

   In the example above, this is what is happening. The wind is blowing from the right, across the prairie and across the road on which you are driving. To keep a straight course, you steer slightly right without realizing it. When you enter the underpass, the underpass blocks the wind. Your car moves to the right, because you are still steering slightly right. You stop steering slightly right. Then, when you leave the underpass, the wind hits your car again and moves it to the left. You correct by steering slightly right again. (Read captions below from bottom to top.)

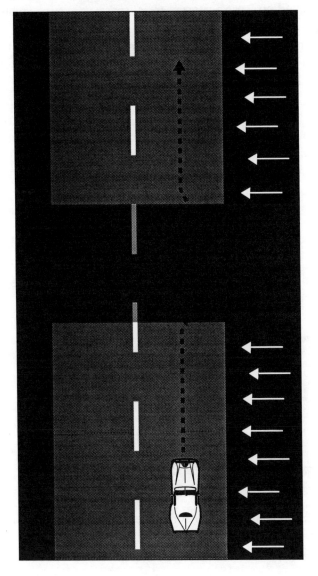

6. *Driver keeps steering slightly right.*

5. *Driver corrects.*

4. *Car dodges left when wind hits it again.*

3. *Car dodges right. Driver corrects.*

2. *Underpass blocks wind.*

1. *Constant wind from right causes driver to steer slightly right.*

This small disturbance of your driving path can become greater and much more interesting if the road is covered with ice.

Wind does affect your driving. Gusty cross winds move your car around sideways on the road. Headwinds cause you to push harder on the gas pedal to maintain speed. Gusty headwinds interrupt your forward progress with jerks and lurches as the gusts alternately hold back and release your car. Tailwinds make your car go forward more easily.

Crosswinds are the biggest problem. They affect some vehicles more than others. Most at risk are buses; large, box-type trucks; travel trailers; house trailers; motorhomes; and vans. These vehicles give the crosswind more side surface to push against. Indeed, in very windy conditions, house trailers may be banned from certain roads. In cars most crosswinds are merely noticeable or annoying. In vehicles with a lot of "sail area" though crosswinds can be dangerous.

Know what to expect. Look to the side from which the wind in blowing. Look for windbreaks: buildings, forests, hills, embankments, etc. Look also for open areas, spaces between windbreaks including cross streets in cities, where the wind is not blocked.

The wind also blows things onto and across the road. The wind breaks limbs off trees. It even uproots trees. The wind blows trash cans into and across streets. It blows all sorts of dust and debris around. It blows pedestrians around, too. Picture a pedestrian crossing in front of your moving car on ice in a strong, gusty wind.

When the wind blows rain or snow against your windshield, your vision can be very seriously reduced. Your wipers may not be able to handle the amount and force of water or snow. In blizzard conditions, snow may build up on your windshield so fast that your defrosters may not be able to melt it. Your wipers will wipe an ever smaller area. The inside of your windshield may fog up despite your defroster's best efforts.

Be careful when opening your car doors, trunk lid, and hood in strong winds. The wind can easily slam them open and cause damage.

The high and low pressure areas created by tractor semi-trailer trucks moving at high speed can also move your car around on the road. When meeting an oncoming truck, expect your car to be moved toward the right by the air shoved aside by the truck's front end. When passing a large truck, expect that air to slow you down just before you pull even with the truck's front end. A flat nosed, cab-over-engine (c.o.e.) truck will create a bigger air wave than a conventional truck.

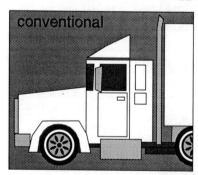 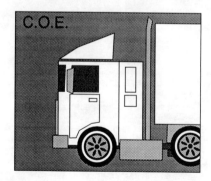

Air behind a truck is unstable. It can buffet your car. You may sometimes feel your car pulled toward the side of the truck you are passing. A truck can also block crosswinds. However, do not use a truck as a mobile windbreak by driving next to it. If the wind is so bad that it makes trucks noticeably unstable, stay away from them.

RAIN: Rain has bad effects on both your ability to see and your car's traction.

Every drop of rain on your car windows works against your being able to see well. Rain water streaked and smeared by your windshield wipers also lessens your ability to see. Heavy, hard-driven rain and the heavy spray from trucks going fast can make seeing almost impossible.

If your windshield wipers streak the windshield, the blades are probably worn out or just too old. The cure is to replace the wiper blades or the blade refills. It is more comfortable to do this in good weather than in bad. Do not forget all about your wiper blades just because the sun is shining today.

If your wipers smear, either there is something on the windshield, or the blade is not pressing against the glass hard enough. As cars age and windshield wipers are used over and over, they can get out of adjustment and sweep less of the windshield than they should. Readjustment is usually easy, as is most wiper maintenance. Carefully washing your windshield wiper blades and windshield in dishwashing detergent can reduce many streaking and smearing problems.

A rear window wiper can be very useful.

To avoid scratching your windshield, make sure that it is wet enough to use the wipers. Do not just let the wiper run regardless of how wet or dry the windshield is. Running your wipers on a dry windshield is hard on the little electric motor which runs them and can scratch the windshield or leave a film on it. Avoid using the windshield washers to clean away dust, mud, etc., unless you are fairly sure that there is some washer fluid in the bottle. Running the wipers on dust, dried mud, or dried road grime is very rough on the glass. A leaf or seed stuck under the moving wiper blade can also do damage. A scratched windshield makes it harder to see *every time you drive*!

Rain, just like fog, dust, smoke, etc., blocks your view even before it hits your windshield just by being in the air. Very heavy rain can reflect light from your headlights back into your eyes just like fog.

Rain makes the road wet and shiny. Wet pavements reflect street lights, store lights, headlights, tail lights, brake lights, turn signals, moonlight, sunlight, etc. Especially at night, reflections can make aiming very difficult by obscuring lane lines, etc.

Rain forms puddles. Driving through puddles causes splashing. The splashes can hit pedestrians, other vehicles, even your own windshield (This is useful when you have run out of washer fluid.)

It takes a good deal of practice to identify which puddles are shallow and which are deep before you hit them. Some puddles hide potholes.

Hitting puddles slows the car. Hitting puddles with only one side of the car slows one side of the car. This can be tricky at high speed.

When other people hit puddles, they can splash your car. When a splash hits your car, it makes a lot of noise. It surprises and blinds you at the same time. Sometimes your wipers will be running because of rain or snow when the splash hits your windshield. Some splashes hit when your wipers are off because it is not raining or snowing. These tend to be more surprising. They are also more dangerous, because you need time to react and switch on the wipers. Sometimes you will be able to see the splash coming or predict it. Spray from large trucks can be predicted, and the wipers can be switched on or turned to high speed at just the right time to avoid being blinded. If the spray is muddy, turning on the *washers* just before it hits helps. When slush hits your windshield, it can hit really hard and loudly. It can be very thick so it takes quite a while to get cleared away. Whenever you predict getting splashed, be ready with the wiper switch. When your window is open and you predict getting splashed, roll up your window... fast!

If extremely heavy, wind-driven rain makes it impossible to see through your side window, open it. Do not be surprised when you get wet. If you wear glasses, this tactic may be of very limited usefulness, because just as you get rid of looking through the wet glass window, you will be looking through wet glasses.

Opening your window works when it is steamed up, too, or very dirty. If necessary, a passenger can open a window for you. A steamed up power window in a tailgate can be lowered when backing into a parking space, etc. Finally, yes, if you open a window in the rain, your car will get wet inside.

Do not cut off other drivers by seeing and swerving around puddles at the last moment. See puddles early, and identify those that look really deep. Doing this will let you check your mirror(s) and blind spot *before* driving around puddles. Remember that the driver in the lane next to yours was there first. If you need to use his lane, you must not endanger or inconvenience him, except in an emergency.

The same thinking applies to slowing down for puddles. Check your mirror as early as possible.

Driving through puddles or any standing water can cause hydroplaning (See Chapter 15).

When driving through deep water, go very slowly. The idea is to avoid making waves or splashes. Waves and splashes can get your ignition system wet and stall your engine right there in the deep puddle. Your engine's cooling fan can also catch splashed water and blow it back over the engine, shorting out your ignition system. Diesel engines, because their fuel is burned by compression rather than by electrical spark, can make splashes much less worrisome.

Off-road technique is to ford just fast enough to cause a bow-wave. This wave in front of the front tires causes a lowering of the water

under the fan. That is the idea anyway. Without a lot of experience at fording, calculating the speed needed to do this without too much splashing may be impossible. Moreover, your wave and wake can cause problems for other drivers. Finally, do watch out for waves, wakes, and splashes of other vehicles.

Ford puddles with one foot on the brake pedal and one foot on the gas pedal. The idea is to keep the brakes as dry as possible. Modern disc brakes are not affected as much by deep water as drum brakes were. Water could wet the brake linings of drum brakes. It could also get between the linings and the inside of the brake drum. When a driver came out of a deep puddle and tried to stop, he sometimes had no brakes. Keeping your foot on the brake pedal helps keep the brakes dry. Keeping your other foot on the gas pedal helps keep the car moving.

As soon as your drive out of a deep puddle, try your brakes. If they are not stopping your car very well, just keep driving with one foot on the gas pedal and one foot on the brake pedal. This will generate heat and dry out the brakes.

You can ford a puddle, stream, etc., as long as you keep your ignition system dry, your air intake clear, and your exhaust clear. Keeping your foot on the gas pedal forces exhaust out the tailpipe to keep it clear. Without enough exhaust pressure out the tailpipe, water could get into the pipes and cause the engine to stall.

Driving through deep water may wet your car's floor. Water leaks in right under the doors. This is probably not a driveability problem, but it is not good for your shoes, carpets, car floor, and any electrical wires under the carpets.

Do some serious checking before driving into deep water. People have driven into water more than ten feet deep in flooded underpasses.

Flood water might have a current. Stream water does. A current adds the possibility of being swept away to driving through water.

A sudden thunder shower can steam up the

inside of your car's windows very badly almost instantly. Wipe them or squeegee them. Turn on the defrosters, or the air conditioner, or open the windows. Do whatever it takes to be able to see. Get passengers to help if needed. If the problem continues, get out of the way to a *safe* place in a *safe* manner.

Do not look at the rain drops on the windshield. Look *through* the windshield and the raindrops on it.

Rain does make roads more slippery, especially asphalt roads.

Pedestrians get silly in rain and icy wind. Watch out for them more than usual in rainy weather.

In one way, rain is like darkness. Both are common in most places. Therefore, people do not take rain as seriously as snow. They should. It is often harder to see through rain than snow. It is also easier to *speed* through rain than snow. Rain and darkness together can add up to one really good challenge to your driving ability. Remember that!

SNOW: Snow can turn the countryside into a winter wonderland. Snow can make driving extremely difficult, even impossible. Most often, though, snow should be taken by drivers as a chance to learn, practice, and enjoy a special kind of driving. Snow brings the opportunity for driving with an unusually light touch, an increased sensitivity, and a deeper relationship among driver, vehicle, and road. Snow brings drivers a chance to fine tune their driving. It gives many and varied opportunities to show either dazzling driving skill or stunning clumsiness, ignorance, and lack of desire to drive well.

Start the fun of snow driving with the work of cleaning the snow off your car. Clean off *all* windows completely! Do not jump into the car and rely on the defrosters and wipers to clean the windows while you drive. All windows should be as clean as possible *before* you begin driving.

Brush off deep snow. Scrape off ice and frozen snow. Squeegee for the finishing touch. Squeegeeing will rid glass of any clinging snow, ice, or water. If the snow is wet enough, squeegeeing gives your windows a free wash job. Squeegeeing after a rain also gives an easy window washing.

Your windshield wiper blades may be frozen to the windshield. Free them before switching on the wipers. If ice is frozen onto the blades, remove it. Ice on wiper blades can make the wipers streak and skip.

Clean any air vent just in front of the windshield. This vent supplies air to blow through your heater and defroster. Clean snow away from the grille or other engine air intake.

Clean off *all* lights. Remember the tail, brake, and turn signal lights. Clean your outside mirror(s).

When you get under way, dry, powdery snow left on the hood will blow off and cool your already warm windshield. The inside of the windshield may fog. Wet snow on the hood will melt off eventually. Deep snow left on the hood will make it harder to see and judge distances. You will feel as if you are trying to drive while sitting way down in a bathtub.

Dry snow left on the roof will blow off and cause a miniature blizzard for drivers behind you. This snow can also pile up on your rear window. Wet snow left on the roof will melt off eventually. If you get the inside of your car really warm on a long drive, the deep pile of snow on the roof can fall across the windshield and onto the hood when you make a hard stop.

Deep snow on the truck lid blocks your view to the rear.

You need not put snow covered scrappers into your car. A well-placed whack against a handy tire will knock off most of the snow.

Letting your car's engine warm up while

you clean the snow off the car will make driving easier. There will be enough warm air for your defroster. If you turn on your defroster immediately after starting the engine, it will probably be somewhat warm in the car when you finish cleaning. If you leave the heater and defroster turned off until you finish cleaning, the engine will warm up a bit faster. In either case, though, *always choose defrosting before heating*! Make sure that you are able to see before you start worrying about being uncomfortable. If your car runs well, switch on electric wire defrosters on the rear window just after starting the engine. In *extremely cold weather,* having it too warm in the car can cause window fogging when the cold, outside air blasts against the windows at highway speeds.

People who wear glasses can warm them up to end their fogging by placing them on the dashboard and letting the warm air from the defroster duct blow on their lenses.

Snow makes seeing harder to do. It blocks your view like rain and fog just by being in the air. Blizzard and "white out" conditions make seeing virtually impossible. Snow also melts on your windshield, forcing you to use your windshield wipers. It piles up on your windshield, forming blind spots. It piles up and/or melts on your other windows, tool. It can stick to your outside mirrors. Freezing rain and sleet can freeze onto outside mirrors. Finally, snow turns everything white. Out in the country, deep snow can cause real problems in staying on the road. Vehicles ahead of yours leave tracks. Follow them, but be careful that they do not stray onto the shoulder. When there are no tracks, staying on the road can be extremely difficult. Familiarity with the area helps a lot, because it might give you some idea how wide the road is.

At night, on the other hand, snow can sometimes make seeing easier because it reflects so much light.

Snow, ice, and slush are slippery. Packed snow is slipperier than undisturbed snow. Ice is slipperier than snow. Ice is slipperier at relatively warm temperatures than at very cold temperatures. Slush is very tricky. Sometimes your tires cut right through slush down to the pavement. At these times traction is quite good. At other times, although the slush still looks the same, the traction is poor. A very thin coating of slush can be very slippery. Slush may cover and hide *ICE*!

As vehicles roll over snow, their tires pack it down in the wheel tracks. This makes wheel tracks slipperier than the surrounding snow. At intersections, especially stop intersections, the effect is greater. Approaching a stop sign, for example, some cars skid as they stop. The skidding polishes the packed snow, making it even slipperier. Also the heat created by the friction of the skid melts a small amount of the snow, which refreezes into ice. The same thing happens when cars spin their wheels as they leave the stop sign. The snow is polished, melted, and refrozen, getting slipperier with each passing car.

Such a solid coating of ice can build up on the approaches to stop intersections, that it remains after the snow and ice on the rest of the street have melted away completely. This makes those intersections very interesting.

Driving on dry roads with occasional patches of ice is the most treacherous kind of cold weather driving. Miles and miles of snow, or slush, or ice may offer poor traction, but that poor traction is pretty uniform. A driver can get a feel for the surface conditions and drive accordingly. When the roads are mostly free of ice and snow, though, he drives as if traction were very good, then suddenly hits a patch of ice. With the improved snow removal of today, this is exactly the kind of cold weather driving one experiences more and more often. Most of the snow is plowed and melted away in short order, leaving only sneaky ice patches on curves, at intersections, etc. These patches may remain for days.

Skidding across a patch of ice is quite different from skidding on a completely ice-covered surface. *Very small* ice patches can almost be ignored. They will cause slipping, but are too short to cause full-fledged skids. Just as the car starts skidding, it passes the ice patch and stops skidding again.

Being ambushed by an ice patch when trying to stop, especially when trying to stop going downhill, can cause a crash.

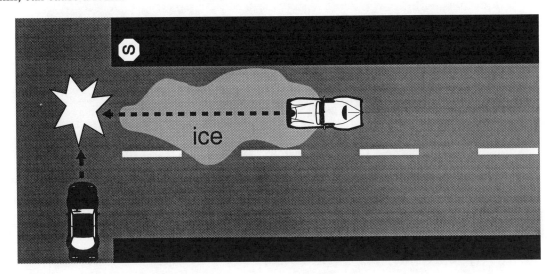

Car stopping at intersection hits ice patch and crashes into cross traffic;

Car stopping at intersection, hits ice patch and stopped car.

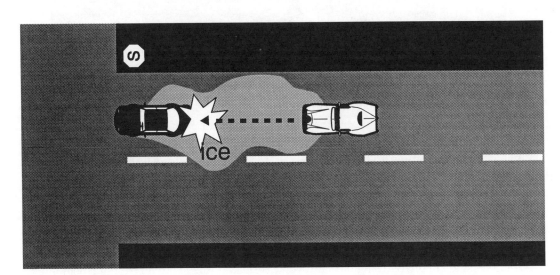

Being ambushed by an ice patch while in the classic, rear wheel drive cornering skid can cause severe control problems. In the following illustrations, a driver is trying to recover from the skid caused by feeding too much gas to a rear wheel drive car exiting a turn on a patch of ice. He has applied full opposite lock. (He has steered as far as possible in the direction he wants the front of the car to go in hopes of correcting the skid.)

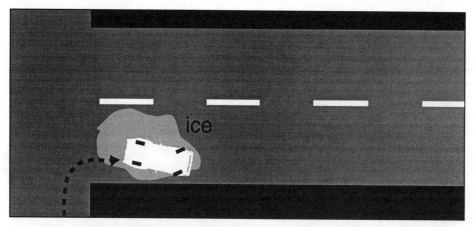

When the front tires hit the dry pavement again, they will GRIP! The front of the car will turn left VIOLENTLY! The rear end of the car, with almost no traction on the ice, will WHIP VIOLENTLY RIGHT! The car will be in a VIOLENT counter-skid.

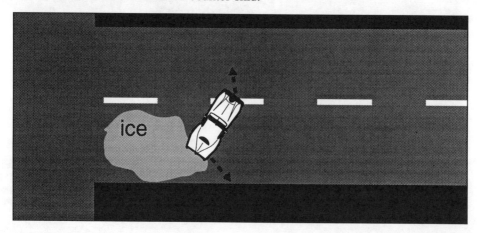

Snow, slush, and ice are all slippery. However, whereas we drive *on* ice, we drive *through* snow and slush. Our tires run on top of ice, but they must push aside or pack down snow and slush. In other words, snow and slush (and mud and deep sand) add resistance to movement to their slipperiness.

Light, dry, powdery snow gives almost no resistance. Deep, heavy, wet snow and slush give a lot of resistance. Very cold, semi-solidly frozen snow and slush give even more resistance.

This resistance to motion can be an advantage. Suppose your car is skidding in icy wheel tracks as you approach a stop intersection. Release the brakes to end the skid. Then steer into the deep snow between and on each side of the wheel tracks. The snow will resist your car's forward motion. That resistance, added to the better traction of snow, will help greatly in getting stopped in time.

Avoid this skid simply by using the snow route instead of the ice route from the beginning.

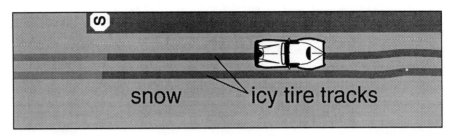

snow   icy tire tracks

The disadvantage of this trick is that the deep, thick snow piled up in front of your tires can make getting back into motion again difficult. It might be necessary to pull back into the icy wheel tracks just as you stop.

Those deep piles of heavy snow and/or slush between wheel tracks can make lane changing tricky. The higher your speed and the deeper and thicker the snow/slush piles, the trickier the maneuver gets.

When you change lanes, each tire has to go through two strips of snow/slush. Each tire may cross each strip at a different time. Each tire, along with the particular corner of the car to which it is attached, will experience slowing down and possible directional instability as it is forced into each of the snow/slush strips it must cross. Any slipperiness in the wheel tracks will add to the lack of stability. The car may want to get sideways or spin more than once in each lane change maneuver.

The most important part of your defense against spinning when changing lanes through strips of deep, heavy snow and/or slush is to understand and remember that loss of control *can* result. With that in mind, put your kinesthetic sense on full alert, and *ease* the car gently but firmly through the snow/slush into the next lane. Do not cut over sharply. Take a long, gentle angle. If possible, do this maneuver well ahead of following traffic. That will give you space to recover if a skid does happen. Whenever you drive through heavy snow/slush, your tires may follow the path of least resistance instead of the path you are trying to steer.

When your right front tire enters the deep, heavy snow/slush piled up along curbs or next to parked cars, your car may be forced farther into the snow/slush toward the curb or the parked cars.

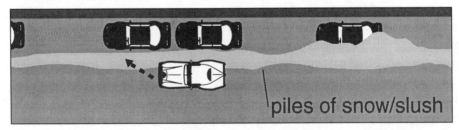

piles of snow/slush

Resistance to forward motion and directional control problems can also be caused by snow blown onto the road. Check areas of blown snow well before you enter them. Check for snow depth, and condition of tire tracks. If the tire tracks are straight, and you are sure that you can keep your tires in them, go on through. Expect the possibility of a sideways skid. If the tracks are crooked and/or criss-cross each other, take it easy. If there are no tracks, and you steer a perfectly straight course through the snow, you will probably be alright. Be ready for the shock of slowing down when you enter the snow, though. Remember that blown snow can hide ice or ruts, either of which can cause control problems. Snow depth can vary. One drift of blown snow may be an inch deep, while the next is a foot deep. When you see snow blowing across the road, expect a cross wind.

Sometimes you will be able to see the pavement right through the light snow blowing across the road. This is no problem. Beware, though. There may be a thin film of very slippery ice under the blowing snow. This film can be extremely difficult to see. Be *sure* whether the light snow through which you are driving is blowing across dry pavement, wet pavement, or *ice*!

Sometimes icy ruts form in hard, frozen packed snow or frozen slush. It can be quite difficult to get out of these ruts. Low speed will allow your tires to grip better to climb out of ruts. Low speed will also allow you better control once you get out of the ruts. On urban side streets, cars going toward each other have been caught in the same ruts.

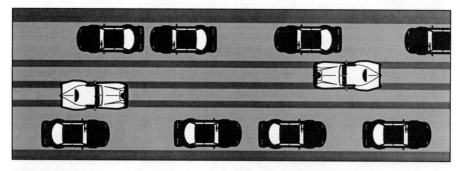

THE GENERAL PHYSICS OF GETTING STUCK, GETTING UNSTUCK, AND AVOIDING GETTING STUCK: Cars get stuck *in* snow, sand, mud, and slush. The slipperiness and resistance to movement of snow, sand, mud, and slush provide the conditions for getting stuck.

Cars get stuck *on* ice. Ice does not offer resistance to movement. Ice is merely very slippery. The resistance to movement can come from a slightly uphill slope, just the weight of the car, a small indention in the ice, a hole, snow piled up in front of the front tires because of a sliding stop, etc. Of course, these factors can also add to the resistance to movement of snow, sand, mud, and slush.

To get unstuck and to avoid getting stuck, drivers have three weapons: a) reducing resistance to movement, b) increasing traction, and c) getting outside help in the form of a push or tow.

Drivers can reduce resistance to movement by clearing away snow, digging out the hole, avoiding areas of deep snow, keeping moving by using momentum, getting moving by using gravity, keeping the front wheels pointed straight ahead when possible (turned front wheels add resistance to movement).

Drivers can increase traction by not spinning their wheels; choosing, using, and maintaining tires properly; putting something between tires and slippery surfaces; and making use of weight.

Finally, drivers can get outside help — a tow or push out of a ditch or through a mud field, etc.

In any case, remember that YOU ARE ALWAYS IN TRAFFIC! It is very easy to get so involved in trying to get unstuck or avoid getting stuck that you forget to check traffic. *Be aware of your surroundings! Time* your attempts to get unstuck or avoid getting stuck so that they do not interfere with traffic, just as you do when turning, changing lanes, etc. Keep checking traffic all during your attempts to get unstuck. It is much better to stay stuck than to cause a crash.

ROCKING THE CAR: Rocking is the time-proven way of getting unstuck by using nothing but your car and rhythm. It will not always work alone. You may need to add gravel under the tires, or do some digging, or get a push. Rock the car by moving it rhythmically back and forth. Do this until you have built up enough momentum in either direction to roll out of the hole.

Here is how rocking works: shift to drive. Move the car forward as far as it will go by itself. Do not try to force more forward movement with the gas pedal. Do not use the brakes either. Instead, just as the car stops moving forward and begins to roll backward by itself, shift to reverse, and back up as far as the car will go by itself. As it stops and begins to roll forward again, shift back to drive. Continue this. Rock back and forth in the natural rhythm of the car until you build up enough momentum to roll out of the hole. Never use the brakes. Never let the car stop. Shift just as the car begins rolling in the opposite direction by itself. Feed gas to get more momentum on each roll until you roll free. Try to avoid spinning the wheels. Obviously, conditions may force you to set your car rocking by shifting to reverse instead of drive first. Fine. It makes no difference which way you roll first.

As in virtually all maneuvers designed to get unstuck or avoid getting stuck, SPIN THE WHEELS AS LITTLE AS POSSIBLE! A spinning tire will dig a deeper hole! A spinning tire gets less traction than a rolling tire. A spinning tire will polish the ice. A spinning tire will melt the ice, which will refreeze almost instantly into slipperier ice.

There is a variation on rocking which can be done with a stick shift transmission. Using either first or reverse only, move the car as far in one direction as it goes by itself. Disengage the clutch and let the car roll all the way in the opposite direction. When the car begins to roll in the first direction again, engage the clutch and feed some gas. Repeat this to set up the rocking motion. Obviously, because power is applied in only one direction, this method may be less effective.

RAMMING OR CHARGING: Ramming or charging deep snow is similar to rocking. Trying to get out of a driveway covered by deep, wet snow, for example, charge the snow until the car stops by itself. Do not try to force more forward progress with the gas pedal. Spinning the wheels will get you stuck. Instead, shift immediately to reverse and back up in your tracks. Stop, and get a running start and charge the snow again. Keep backing up and charging until you break through.

The best thing to do as soon as you get stuck is to get out of the car and look over the situation. See how badly you are stuck. Is only one drive wheel stuck or both? How deep is the hole? How steep are its sides? Is deep snow blocking the path of the front wheels? Is the bottom of the car dragging on deep snow under it? Is deep snow blocking the path of the rear wheels? Is a snow drift rubbing against one side of the car? Are the front wheels pointed straight ahead? (They should be. Having the front wheels turned will add more resistance to movement.)

Rocking, especially frantic and/or prolonged rocking, can damage your car and not get you unstuck. Keep a sturdy shovel in the car and use it. Dig a path for the car if it needs one. Clear snow off the underside of the car. Make the sides of the hole less steep. Make the hole longer to get more momentum in your rocking. Make sure that you dig deep enough around the stuck tire(s). If possible, leave no lip of ice or snow touching the tire.

Do not leave these lips.

On the other hand, do not dig so far down that you make an even deeper hole in which to get stuck.

do not dig too deep

Improve the traction of the drive wheels by putting something as far under the stuck tire(s) as possible. Carry gravel, cinders, sand, kitty litter, oil dry, old Christmas tree branches, etc., for this purpose. If you do not carry things to improve traction, use your floor mats, rags, whatever you can find inside or outside the car to give your tires a better grip.

PUSHING, PULLING, TOWING, AND WINCHING: Do not drive another car right up behind a stuck car and expect to be able to push the first car free. You will just get the second car stuck. Pulling or towing is a much better idea. Keep the assisting car on solid ground or pavement. This will allow it the best traction available and keep it from getting stuck. Winching is the same. Keep the assisting vehicle on the best surface available. A vehicle with a winch can winch itself out of a hole. Attach the winch to a very sturdy tree, etc., and winch carefully. Check sources on off-roading for winching information and safety practices.

Pushing by hand is the most common form of assistance to stuck vehicles. Pushers should push in time with the rhythm of the rocking car. Pushers should be careful not to fall or get run over, or get splattered with slush or mud.

AVOID GETTING STUCK: Because *not* getting stuck is so much better than getting stuck, do things to avoid getting stuck in the first place. Avoid getting stuck by driving with great sensitivity, understanding the physics involved, and equipping yourself properly.

Use weight to your advantage. Drive a front wheel drive car. Front wheel drive cars have most of their weight over the drive wheels. Because most of their weight is pressing down on their drive wheels, front wheel drive cars have very good digging-out ability.

Rear engined cars also have good digging-out ability, and for the same reason — most of their weight is pressing down on their drive wheels.

Front engined, rear wheel drive cars have most of their weight in front, where it does not press down on the drive wheels. Front engined, rear wheel drive cars are the easiest to get stuck. Front engined, rear wheel drive cars can be helped to dig out better by adding weight in their trunks or back seats. One hundred pounds of sand in a bag placed in the trunk over the rear axle will do wonders for the traction of front engined, rear wheel drive cars. However, the more weight added and the farther back it is added, the more the car will tend to oversteer on icy corners.

Four wheel drive cars are best for not getting stuck and getting unstuck.

Snow tires help. Put snow tires on the rear wheels of rear wheel drive cars and on the front wheels of front wheel drive cars. Studded snow tires are excellent on ice as well as on snow. They are illegal in many places, because when there is no ice or snow, the studs do too much damage to the roads.

Tire chains are excellent for snow and ice. In certain snow conditions, cars not equipped with tire chains are legally stopped from using some mountain passes. Chains make driving on clear roads unpleasant to say the least. They cause bad vibrations. They seriously reduce traction, because much of the time your car is running on steel chains, not rubber tires!

If you are using your regular tires in the snow, keep them properly inflated. Newer tires with deeper treads are better than old, nearly bald tires. All season tires (tires with a more aggressive tread pattern) are better in snow, slush, rain, etc., than ordinary and high performance tires. Special rain tires are available.

Finally, narrow tires cut through water, slush, and snow better than wide, high performance tires. In fact, extremely wide tires are used in sand, because they do not sink into the sand.

Drive to avoid getting stuck. Use momentum. If possible, get a running start when trying to climb an icy or snow-covered hill. Try to avoid stopping half-way up the hill. Charging through deep snow in your driveway, get a running start on the dry garage floor. (Watch those blind areas!)

Using momentum can be tricky. It's great for charging uphill and smashing your way through deep snow, but momentum can make stopping at the proper place impossible. The speed needed to use momentum can add to your directional control problems. Take everything into account. See the total situation. Use momentum. Keep steering control. Be able to stop. Watch traffic. Do not, for example, blast uphill through deep snow or on ice only to be confronted by a sharp turn, stop sign, or downhill slope at the top.

Be careful where and how you park. Look for parking places with the least snow in them. Look for parking spaces with snow that is not icy, bumpy, and full of holes where other cars have already been stuck. Try to park in either the first or the last space on the block. That way you will be able to move straight into and out of the parking space, instead of having to turn sharply into and out of it. You will not lose momentum to turned front wheels which resist movement.

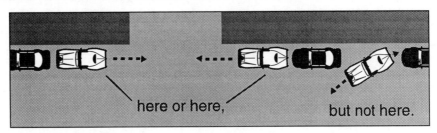

here or here, but not here.

If you must park in a bumpy, icy, holey place, pay attention to exactly where you stop. As you move slowly into position, feel the car moving up and down over the holes and bumps. Stop and park on the up-roll or on top of a bump. This way you will be able to use gravity to get a running start when you want to get out of the parking space.

If you need to back up once or more to get into or out of a parking space, use the same technique. Stop on the up roll or the top.

In extremely tough going, avoid stopping at all if possible. With the same delicate touch and perfect timing you use in rocking, shift into the opposite gear just as the car stops by itself. Convert forward motion almost directly into rearward motion and vice versa.

In virgin snow, back up in your tracks a couple of times when parking to make paths for your exit. Always choose to park in virgin snow rather than chewed up, holey, icy snow.

In angle parking spaces, *do not* pull all the way in and rest your tire on the curb or concrete bumper.

When doing maneuvers in close clearances, if possible, get moving with the front wheels pointed straight ahead to get some momentum before turning as needed. Use the most gentle turn angles possible.

Remember, when the going is heavy: use momentum. Stay straight as much as possible. Keep moving. Do not spin the wheels. Maintain directional control and stopping ability. Watch traffic. Stay very alert to kinesthetic information from your car. Use a delicate touch.

MISCELLANEOUS: When driving a stick shift car in extremely slippery conditions like sleet falling on glare ice, put the car into motion using second gear rather than first. This will require a bit of fancy clutch work, but using the higher gear will reduce wheel spin. Some automatic transmissions allow starting in second gear.

It is recommended that one shift to a lower gear to get engine braking when slowing in either a stick shift car or an automatic on very slippery surfaces. It does work, but when the lower gear takes hold, the increased drag on the drive wheels can cause a skid. Expect this and be sure that the extra slowing ability is worth the chance of skidding. With a stick shift, minimize the chances of skidding by engaging the clutch very gently and slowly.

When stuck with an automatic transmission car, be sure to take the transmission out of gear when you get out to look or dig. If you do not, the wheel(s) will keep spinning slowly and make things worse. If you are throwing sand, etc., under the stuck wheel, it might be a good idea to let it spin slowly to drag the grit under itself.

When a skid starts, the driver must release the gas pedal or the brake pedal and steer *immediately*! New drivers take longer to notice a skid beginning. Practice and try to be sensitive.

Do not keep your windshield too warm.

Salty road spray will dry very quickly on a hot windshield. It will smear and make seeing very difficult. Reduce defroster fan speed and/or heat. In very dirty going, truck spray can sometimes be used to wet your windshield when you have run out of windshield washer fluid. Sometimes you can splash your own windshield by driving through a puddle.

Bridges, because they are up in the air, are super-cooled in the winter. Therefore, they may have ice on them when pavements on the ground do not. Frost may not melt away in shaded areas.

Black ice is thin, clear, very slick ice which is very hard to detect. It can look just like ordinary wet pavement. Be alert for black ice when the temperature hovers near the freezing point. Water on the road will make a swishing sound as you drive through it. Black ice will not.

When almost stopped on extremely slick ice with a rear wheel drive, automatic transmission car, you may find that the car just keeps going very slowly instead of stopping completely. This is because the front wheels are locked and sliding, while the rear wheels are still driving the car forward. Shift to neutral. This will cut the power to the drive wheels and the car will stop.

If you cannot keep up with the traffic flow in slippery conditions, do not take the best lane and block everybody else. Check your mirror for congestion caused by you.

After the snow and ice have been melted off the streets by salt, a salt residue can remain. Look for light colored stuff on the pavement. This residue can be surprisingly slippery and treacherous.

Finally, the main thing to remember about driving in slippery conditions is that you are operating much closer to the limit than usual. Therefore, stay aware of just where the limit of adhesion is.

17 Chapter Seventeen

The Driver

Tazio Nuvolari.

Photo provided by the Klemantaski Collection.

The driver manipulates and balances the very forces of nature to control his automobile in all weathers, on all roads, in all kinds of traffic. The driver is the most important factor in driving. Without the driver, driving could not exist. The driver is the wizard who animates the magic carpet, the sorcerer who controls the powerful genie. The driver is the person who makes the magic that we call automobile travel.

Every driver, every single driver, is unique! There never has been another driver exactly like you. There never will be another driver exactly like you. Your perceptions, your knowledge, your skills, your identity and performance as a driver, and every one of your drives, are unlike those of any other driver who ever has or ever will live. Your concept of driving is unlike that of any other driver. Your point of view as a driver is unique. Remember that.

Everything about you: your genes, your personality, your physical condition, your experience, your understanding, your attitudes, your aptitudes, your emotions, your body, and your mind are yours and yours alone. Others may drive on the same roads. They may even drive the very same car you do on those roads. However, they do not do it in exactly the same way you do it.

You do not see a driving situation exactly as the driver behind you does, or the driver in front, etc. Each driver is in a different place with a different point of view. Each driver is also a unique individual.

A new driver will not see a given driving situation in the same way as a very experienced driver. An older driver, a sick driver, a confident driver, an excited driver, a sleepy driver, a drugged or drunken driver, a distracted driver, an overconfident driver, a frightened driver, a professional driver, a racing driver, a police driver, a student driver, and a driving teacher will each see the same driving situation in his own way. In fact, you yourself will probably see the same driving situation you saw today quite differently 15 years from now.

Your vehicle will make a difference. Its condition, abilities, driving position, visibility characteristics, designed purpose, controls, size, weight, etc., will affect your point of view as a driver.

The road, the weather, and time of day, will affect your point of view. Your destination, your passengers, your cargo, the other traffic, will all affect your point of view. NEVER ASSUME THAT ANY OTHER DRIVER'S POINT OF VIEW IS THE SAME AS YOURS.

Do not underestimate the importance of point of view! Adam and Eve are married. He is six feet tall. She is five feet one inch tall. Their refrigerator is five feet three inches tall.

In an attempt to lose a few pounds, Eve has decided to stop eating their favorite pastry for a month or two. Adam has no need to lose weight. In fact, if anything, he should probably gain a few pounds. Adam wants to keep eating the wonderful pastry, but he does not want Eve to be tempted by seeing it in the house. He wants to hide the pastry, but where can one hide food? Not in the kitchen cabinets, not in the pantry, not in the refrigerator …

The refrigerator — of course!

Adam gets a great idea! He will place the pastry on top of the refrigerator. Because of his height, he will be able to see it, but because of her lack of height, Eve will not.

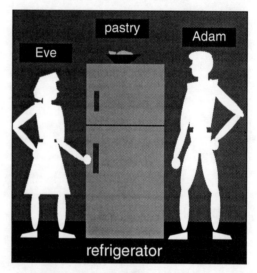

Point of view solves the pastry problem for Adam and Eve.

You feel a tickle on your left arm. Without thinking about it, you casually reach over with your right hand and brush the tickle.

The tickle was caused by a bee. The bee is not casual about the situation, because it has quite a different point of view. It thinks that it is about to be killed. It stings you.

Now, suppose that you are allergic to bee stings. You might even die from an allergic reaction. This gives you a different point of view. The sting is not just a pain and an annoyance. It might be life threatening.

You will rush to a hospital to get treatment. How will you drive? How will you see minor traffic delays? *Point of view*!

Your point of view in driving and your overall ability to drive are affected by your mental, emotional, and physical states. We tend to think of a normal driver as a person who is physically fit, has a brain which works properly, and who most often can control his emotions. "Normal" covers a broad range though.

Even for an individual, normal covers a broad range. Take, for example, one person who is young and in great condition. He has just obtained his first driver's license. He hasn't much experience. His reaction time is terrific. He may react quickly to an emergency, but he may also react improperly because of his lack of experience.

What if he has a head cold? The cold may affect his ability to hear and see. He will not feel very good either. He may be drowsy. His reaction time will probably be slower than usual.

What if he is angry? He may take chances he would not dream of taking in his normal emotional state. If he gets extremely sad or very excited and happy, he may not pay enough attention to driving.

As he ages and keeps driving, he gets more experience. He should make wiser and quicker judgments of emergency situations. He may have somewhat slower reaction times, but the quantity and quality of his driving experience will allow him to take perfect evasive action, despite his slightly slower reaction time.

As he gets even older, his body may start giving him trouble. His eyes may not see as well at night. His brain may take more time to make decisions. His body may not work as easily and quickly as when it was younger. He may have built up so much experience driving without having accidents that he has gotten overconfident. He takes driving for granted, paying less attention than he should. He is still in the normal range, though. He has changed a lot over the years, but he has always remained in the broad normal range.

Everybody drives differently for all sorts of reasons. What is normal for one driver may not be normal for another. What is normal at one time may not be normal at another. Everybody's driving skills; knowledge; physical, mental, and emotion condition; motivations; etc., are different from those of everybody else. Do not expect all other drivers to share your point of view.

Because we see driving, ours and everybody else's, from our own point of view, it is easy to notice everybody else's mistakes and faults, while we ignore our own. Always keep alert for changes in the quality of your own driving!

What *really* happened in that situation last Wednesday? Did you see the *whole* thing develop, or were you suddenly in the middle of it, fighting for position with the other guy and trading rude gestures with him? Were you *really* right, or was *he* actually right? Did he do the first clumsy thing, or did you?

Unless you *know*, unless you saw the *whole* episode develop and play out, you have only your point of view, not the actual facts of the traffic situation. Remember that every time you do not *know* how or why something happened on the road, you were not in charge, you were not paying attention, you were not driving!

Notice how *you* drive! The other guy will drive the way he drives. You are not in charge of his car. You are in charge of *your* car. Drive *it*. Pay attention. Notice how *you* drive. Develop good habits and hold the highest standards of performance for yourself. Check yourself each time you drive to see whether your really are as good as you think you are.

Analyze your driving not from the point of view of proving yourself right, but from the point of view of good driving. Analyze your driving as if you were watching tapes of a football game, etc, and looking for your weaknesses — places where you can improve. After you have made it through some sticky driving situation, think about it and try to figure out whether there was something you missed or whether there might have been a better way to handle it.

Bad habits can replace good habits so easily. They can do it without your even noticing. Suppose you were tired last night. You probably replaced at least some driving with just steering. This morning, you did not feel very well. Again, you replaced driving with steering. In heavy, stop-and-go, rush hour traffic, you just went whenever the car ahead went and stopped whenever the car ahead stopped. You forgot all about looking to the rear and sides. You did not try to improve whatever traffic flow there was; you ignored it. Then, you got all caught up in listening to a really interesting discussion on the radio. You drove by automatic pilot.

Look at what is happening. You are losing several good driving habits. You are replacing driving with steering, and you are replacing aiming and steering with following. Worst of all, you are not even noticing it!

You have a backache, so you cannot twist around as far as you know you should when you back up. The backache lasts for a month. If you are not very vigilant, you can build the habit of backing with insufficient rearward vision. You may not even notice this unless you have a close call or back into something you never even saw. Then, instead of realizing and correcting your mistake, you might rationalize it. "That garbage can was never there before." "What a silly place to leave a bicycle!"

Be very careful to notice accommodations to sickness, injury, pain, aging, etc. Then make sure that temporary accommodations do not become bad, lazy habits. If a disability continues, remember that you are no longer able to

drive the *best* way. Find a second best way and remember its limitations.

It is easy to forget rules of the road and to neglect learning new ones.

If driving is one of your hobbies, you will get great personal satisfaction out of getting better at it all the time. You will watch and analyze your driving and you will keep finding new ways to improve it — to polish it! If you take driving for granted, you will get lazy, sloppy, and see only the mistakes of others. Your driving will *not* be something to enjoy and be proud of; it will just make you and everybody else on the road less safe!

There are many physical, mental, and emotional factors which can affect your driving ability. Injuries, diseases, genetic factors, and aging can cause problems in driving. Some of these things are temporary. Others are permanent. Some things keep getting worse. Others get better by themselves. The effects of some may be lessened or overcome through therapy. The effects of others may not.

Arms, hands, feet, legs, shoulders, necks, hips, backs, fingers, etc. can become stiff and/or painful. Range of movement may be reduced. Sense of touch may be reduced. Quickness may be reduced. Balance can be affected. Ability to stay awake may be lessened. Physical endurance may be reduced. Ability to concentrate may be reduced. Drowsiness or dizziness can be problems. Physical coordination may be impaired. Ability to remember may be reduced. Some conditions can result in uncontrollable body movements or sudden loss of consciousness.

Worry, tension, anger, ecstacy, fear, hate, sorrow, depression, euphoria, grief, embarrassment, can affect your concentration and/or judgment.

When you are in a rage, pull over and settle down or scream, or do not get into the car at all. Your anger is very strong and real, but if you kill someone because of it, it will lose its importance. You will feel guilty for your loss of control for the rest of your life!

Feelings of guilt can actually make you unconsciously want to punish yourself by crashing.

Laughing, crying, coughing, sneezing, choking, etc., can affect your ability to drive.

Some things can cause confusion, delusions, hallucinations, inability to reason, loss of touch with reality.

You might suffer hearing loss. Many things can go wrong with your eyes: nearsightedness, color blindness, poor depth perception, night blindness, poor glare recovery, glaucoma, cataracts, tunnel vision, etc.

Falling asleep at the wheel is amazingly easy. It is so easy that people do it while driving in the city at night, not just out on the road.

The best thing to do is stop driving if you get very sleepy. Go to a motel. Pull into a gas station and ask whether you may sleep there for an hour or two. Let your passenger drive. Then do all you possibly can to make sure he stays awake!

If you must drive, drink coffee — plenty of strong coffee! Have plenty of fresh air in the car. Especially in the winter, open the window and get a nice blast of freezing air in the car. That will wake you up! Chew a whole pack of gum. Sing at the top of your lungs. Talk to yourself, the radio, or your passengers. Do not let your passengers sleep. Make them keep you awake! If you have a car phone, call somebody. Listen to something you dislike intensely on the radio —loud! Change the position of your seat. Try to drive the very best you can. Do not settle for okay. Make sure that your eyes stay open! Do whatever is necessary to stay awake! Remember that there is nothing glorious about falling asleep at the wheel and crashing. Even if you do not kill or injure yourself or somebody else, you will still look very silly!

Some things may disqualify a person temporarily or permanently from driving. Some things cannot be treated or overcome. However, many things can be treated, repaired, replaced. Some can be dealt with through therapy, special training or retraining. Some can be overcome with mechanical aids, some by changing behavior.

18 Chapter Eighteen

Your Choice

Driving is the most complex psychomotor activity in which human beings engage. Driving is physical, mental, and emotional *control*. Driving well is a natural high, a natural high with no resulting lows or bad after effects.

Each successful driving experience, each high, builds confidence and skill and leads to ever greater achievements. Each success, each high, each transcendent achievement strengthens a driver's character, making it a fortress from which to meet life's many other challenges and overcome them with intelligence and grace. Driving can be the foundation upon which to build a beautiful, positive life of honesty, success, joy, and love.

This book is about the grace, the control, the satisfaction, the beauty, the work, the accomplishment, the pride, the freedom, the status, and the joy of driving well. Apparently drugs can contribute NOTHING to any of that! Therefore, this chapter is the shortest one in the book. After all, you already know quite a bit about drugs. You already use them, or you don't. You want to use them, or you don't. You will use them, or you won't. And nobody on Earth but YOU can make that choice.

Remember that prescription and over-the-counter drugs *are* drugs. Use them wisely.

Finally, when you think about mixing recreational drugs, including alcohol, with driving, ask yourself this question, "You some kinda fool?"

19 *Chapter Nineteen*

Oops

Photo courtesy of the National Highway Traffic Safety Administration

He is about seven years old. He is crying. He is crying so hard! You have never heard anyone cry like that before. Certainly you never cried like that — so hard!

There is blood. There is blood all over his clothes. He is sort of kneeling next to and at the same time lying half on top of his mother in a puddle of her blood, and he is crying a heavy, choking, moaning cry. His tears wash clean streaks through the blood smeared on his cheeks and chin.

A highway patrolman bends down near the boy. His uniform is so clean. It has such perfectly pressed creases. Talking softly to the boy, the policeman tries gently to pull him away from his dead mother's body.

"No!" screams the boy as he wrenches himself from the policeman's grasp. Then he pleads with the dead woman, "Wake up Mommy! Please Mommy, wake up!" He kicks wildly at the policeman. He cries harder. He holds so tightly to his mother's torn and blood-soaked clothes that red oozes between his small fingers. He shakes her. He almost lifts her up off the pavement. He shrieks, "Mommy! Wake up!"

You are witnessing all of this from the back seat of a police car. Emergency lights flash crazily around the scene, reflecting off the broken glass and smashed cars. Your left arm, your face, and your chest hurt. They hurt so much, but most of the time you hardly notice the fierce pain. You are too scared. You see, YOU caused the crash. Your arrogance, your inattention, your foolishness, caused the crash, and you are so scared!

You want it not to be true. More than anything else in the world, you want it not to be true. You want that dead woman to wake up as much as her son does. You want a miracle, but that dead woman will not wake up. No wishing can fix this, no excuses, no apologies, no promises, no bargaining. This is real. This happened, and you are to blame.

Everything had been okay. Then suddenly, the screaming tires, the thunderous crash — for a long moment then, there was quiet —seeming peace. You were alright. Everything was going to be okay. Then there were the wrecked, steaming cars, then the pain, the crying, the blood, the screaming, and the panic!

It does not end. You go to trial. You suffer fear, sorrow, embarrassment, guilt. Accidentally, your eyes meet those of the dead woman's husband in court. You want to apologize. You want to fix everything, but you can't. You want to disappear or die.

You have to testify. The questions their lawyer asks tear at your soul. You hate it! You want only one thing. You want it all to be over.

It is never over! You will remember and carry the guilt every day for the rest of your life. You will see that little boy desperately kicking the policeman. You will hear his screams. You will see the blood ooze between his fingers. Every pleasure will be spoiled by a sudden memory of the crash. Every moment of joy will be ruined by your relentless guilt.

DO NOT CRASH! Avoid accidents by skill, not luck. Love driving! Work at driving! Drive beautifully! *Drive safely*! Realize that the convenience, the freedom, the mobility, the control, the prestige, the fun of driving, are all balanced against the risk —the *very real risk*! It *can* happen! In the wink of an eye, it can happen … to *you*! YOU! Never doubt that. Understand completely that there is always risk. Acknowledge that driving is dangerous. Never drive in fear, but always MINIMIZE THE RISK!

There are some unavoidable crashes, some real "accidents," but they are rare. Most crashes *are* avoidable. They are *not* "accidents." They are caused by poor training, bad habits, letting things go, inexperience, and not paying attention. They happen because each driver and/or pedestrian involved either does something which is wrong, or does not do something which is right.

"He was going too fast." "He took the right-of-way when he didn't have it." "He didn't stop for the stop sign." "He took a reckless chance."

"I wasn't paying attention." "I never thought that he would do such a dangerous thing." "I *assumed* that he saw me." "I took a chance and relied on him to take care of me."

"He was drunk."

"I was drunk."

It has been said that most crashes could have been avoided if the driver had had one second more time in which to see and react to the situation. Follow far enough back. Do not stare at and follow the rear end of the vehicle ahead. Look much more than four or six seconds ahead. See the myriad details of the overall traffic scene. Look for blind areas — ambushes. Drive according to weather and road conditions. Know and obey the laws. Keep your car in good condition. Do not drink or take drugs. PAY ATTENTION! Have that vital one second and more when it counts.

We have all heard about accident avoidance techniques, how to handle a car in an emergency situation. That is wonderful stuff. It is the stuff of driving legends. By all means, if you can go to a high performance driving school, do it! Learn vehicle control far beyond what you think are the limits. Do not fantasize about your ability to control a car; go to a high performance driving school and learn how to do it!

Do not, however, get the idea that safe driving or superior driving is driving out of emergency situations every day. Do not get the idea that the only way to save yourself from all the bad drivers is through brilliant car control in very dangerous situations. If you are taking violent, emergency, evasive action every day, or every week, or even every year, you are not driving well. You are not a hero driver. You are taking wild chances, driving as if you were the only one on the road, being totally selfish, unrealistic, immature, and plain foolish.

One should be able to drive for years without needing to take violent, emergency, evasive action. That kind of driving ability is based not only on knowledge, but on experience — lots of experience! It is unrealistic for a brand new driver to believe that he can drive like that without a great deal of experience. Only with much

study, much dedicated practice, much refining of technique, can one realistically expect to drive for years without needing to take violent, evasive actions. Even then, one can do it only if he pays attention. Driving is very complex. It takes a long time to mature as a driver. Of course, one may avoid accidents and even accident situations by luck too. Never confuse luck with masterful driving skill!

On the other hand, do not believe that you must crash to learn. Do not think that a new driver cannot drive well. He can. Mastering the fundamentals will go a long, long way toward accident proofing your driving from the very beginning.

Reviewing the fundamentals from time to time is also a very worthwhile activity. After you have driven for a year or two, after you have put on some miles, re-read the fundamentals in this and other books. Your driving experience will give you a different point of view, a deeper understanding. You will understand things better, remember things you had forgotten, and notice things you hadn't noticed before. Your review will force you to re-evaluate your driving and to set higher standards. Keep thinking about and checking up on your driving for as long as you drive.

Not having accidents is *NOT* the main reason for driving well. If you want to guarantee that you will never drive into a car crash, do not drive! It's that simple. The reason to drive well is *to drive well*! Driving well is a very worthwhile and rewarding end in itself! Safety is one extremely valuable by-product of driving well.

Not driving into accident producing situations starts with plain old good driving. The better you drive, the more trouble spots you will notice. The more trouble spots you notice, the more control you will have. Your driving will be graceful, efficient, economical, comfortable, and rewarding. Your motoring will be fun, and your motoring will be safe!

First, know the laws. Have a deep, working knowledge of the rules of the road. Understand how the laws affect traffic flow. Keep up with changes in the laws. Obey the laws, but realize that others may not obey them.

Aim and steer properly. To steer well, you need to aim well. To aim well, you need to pay attention. There is another reason for making good turns and maneuvers besides the personal satisfaction of perfect control. There is safety. You will always find yourself in the right place at the right time, going the right speed, not hoping that the other guy can save you both. Your driving will be easily predictable. It will not confuse others. Your masterful car control will free you to pay more and better attention to road, weather, and traffic conditions. Being well informed early about these things is what lets you see, predict, and avoid accident-producing situations early. It works the other way, too. Knowing the details and changing interrelationships of the overall traffic scene early will allow you to make perfect maneuvers and ensure that your speed and position are always appropriate.

Driving safely comes from driving well. Driving well comes from driving as a hobby. The reward of a hobby which is an activity, like driving, is getting better and better at the activity. Driving as a hobby will make you strive to keep learning and improving for as long as you drive. Driving well for the great satisfaction and pure fun of driving well will force you to pay attention. Your pride in and commitment to your personal driving performance will yield safety. Your record of safety will, of course, add to the pride you take in your driving.

What is the most important single factor in driving safely? There is NO SINGLE FACTOR! *Every* single factor is important. Take care of your car, your body, your emotions. Consider the road, the weather, the traffic, your vehicle, your strategic position in traffic, the signs, the signals, EVERYTHING! Any one of a million little things that you might let slide can cause an accident.

The price of safety and real pride in your driving is continuing, honest self-evaluation. Without it, bad habits *will* creep into your driving and lower your performance without your even noticing. Driving *is* control! The more things you let slide, the more "little errors" you allow, the more "little chances" you take, the less control you have. Giving up control on purpose or through laziness raises the odds that you will crash. Drive intensely! Drive with the love and care, pride and attention, you give to any hobby.

Where Danger Lurks

Danger lurks *everywhere*. People run over their own children while baking out of their own driveways! Almost anything can cause an accident. Here are some obvious hazards to be aware of when driving.

KNOW WHAT IS BEHIND YOU WHEN SLOWING AND STOPPING: Make it a habit to check your mirror(s) before every slow-down and/or stop. Even when there is just the possibility that you will have to slow down or stop, check your mirror(s) — especially when the possible slow-down or stop could be quick. As soon as you notice something ahead which could cause you to slow down, stop, or swerve, check what is behind you. Conditions behind you do affect what you can do about things ahead of you. Check mirror(s) as early as possible. See what evasive actions are open to you *before* you find yourself driving into a fully developed problem.

When slowing for a conflict ahead, try to slow down early and smoothly to alert drivers behind you early. Try not to surprise them by jamming on your brakes at the last moment. Do not surprise them by slowing when it is not nec-

essary either. Some drivers overreact when they imagine that they are being cut off.

SPEEDING UP: Never assume that accelerating traffic ahead of you will keep accelerating. Drivers make false starts at stop signs. Drivers sometimes slow or stop suddenly just after pulling away from green traffic signals. In stop-and-go traffic, the car ahead may accelerate briskly only to slow down or stop suddenly.

LANE CHANGES: Every lane change is a chance to have an accident. Whether you are pulling over to the curb, pulling out into traffic, entering or exiting an expressway, moving into a turn bay, or just changing to another traffic lane, plan, check, and do your lane change carefully. Check blind spots. Know what is ahead or behind, and next to your car. Try always to change lanes early, when there is still plenty of space.

Look for places where the lanes move around on the pavement in confusing ways. Watch traffic carefully in these areas. Be aware of other drivers' intentional and unintentional lane changes. Make no unintentional lane changes yourself.

Look for places where lanes merge. Be as careful with merging lanes as you are with lane changes.

TURNS: Turns are really quite complex maneuvers. Make sure that you give yourself enough time and space to check traffic and road conditions, notice signs and/or signals, position your car, adjust its speed, and aim *before* beginning to turn. Think of *all* left turns as dangerous. Think of right turns on red as dangerous. Always look for others who are either turning into the same place as you are, or are crossing your path.

Turning your vehicle around can be more clumsy and complex than you think. *Pay atten-*

tion when turning around and try not to rush.

NOTICE THE "OTHER" THINGS IN TRAFFIC: Expect pedestrians in traffic, and motorcycles, and bicycles, and horses, and dogs, and skateboards, and wagons....

PASSING: Be very careful when passing on two-lane roads.

BEELINES: Do not make beelines. Watch for pedestrians and other drivers who are making beelines. (See Chapter 12.)

INTERSECTIONS: Accidents happen where paths cross. Look for intersections. Find them early enough that you can check them carefully *before* you cross them.

BLIND AREAS: Do not be ambushed. Look for blind areas. You must know that you are entering or passing a blind area before you can deal with it properly. Keep learning. Keep finding new types of blind areas. You will be amazed at how varied they are, and how common!

BLIND SPOTS: Before moving your vehicle sideways, *always* check the appropriate blind spot(s). Recheck if needed. Remember, too, that you cannot see the road close to your vehicle. This is especially important when backing.

THE OTHER GUY: Make sure that the other guy really is going to do what he has signaled. Likewise, make sure that he sees and knows what you are trying to do.

SIGNAL: Time your signals beautifully and make them obvious. Make your vehicle look as if it really is going to do what it is signalling.

TAKING CHANCES: Do not take chances. After you take a chance and crash, the police officer will ask you why you didn't just wait longer or find another way to get where you wanted to go.

AVOID SEIZING AN OPPORTUNITY BEFORE YOU HAVE CHECKED IT COMPLETELY: You are coming to that bad corner, the one where there is always so much traffic from so many directions, the one where it is so hard to see, the one where turning is always so tricky. But what is this? It's all clear! Better rush. Make your turn right now! Seize the opportunity, otherwise you will have to wait a long time and still struggle to make your turn.

Oops! Where did he come from?

Avoid seizing an opportunity before you have checked it *completely*. An opportunity which seems too good to be true probably is.

GO ANOTHER WAY: You do not like this intersection. There is something wrong with it. You cannot figure out exactly what it is, but you feel funny every time you go through it. Do not use it! If you think that there is something wrong, there probably is. If you are frightened by a place, road, etc., avoid it. Go another way.

Sometimes you know exactly what is wrong with a certain place, but you continue to use it. Are you proving something by taking this needless risk time after time? Yes!

CLUMSY MANEUVERS: When doing a maneuver has put you into an awkward or dangerous position, learn from it. Analyze what you did wrong. Figure out how you could have done it better. Next time a similar situation comes up, try to avoid danger and/or awkwardness by thinking ahead and planning a maneuver which is easy and safe instead of clumsy and dangerous.

PARKING: Parallel parking is often quite a complex maneuver done in close quarters.

Accept parking's challenges and expect success. Plan and perform a masterpiece of precision car control with perfect safety every time you parallel park. Pay very close attention and keep track of EVERYTHING when parking.

PARKING LOTS: Parking lots can be very challenging. Once again, use perfect placement in the overall traffic scene. Notice all the blind areas. Avoid making beelines.

AVOID RUSHING: Rushing is an attempt to make up time, often by ignoring details. Details are what keep you safe, though. Never give up details. Never give up complete planning and careful execution. Never put your safety into the hands of some stranger who may not even know you are there. Never be the driver who charges into a half-known situation and crashes, then offers as an excuse, "I thought I could make it."

EXPRESSWAY ENTRANCES AND MAJOR INTERCHANGES: Help the flow by seeing the overall driving scene early, *making* as much space as possible, planning ahead, and using speed properly.

HILLS AND CURVES: In certain places, hills and/or curves make it easier for you to see. In other places they make it harder. Know which places are which.

SPEED: Always go at the speed which is right for the entire set of conditions in which you are driving.

VEHICLE CONDITION: Do not expect to turn the key and go without ever thinking about vehicle maintenance. Your car can save your life. Take good care of it.

MASTERMINDING: Do not let your experience and skill make you mastermind. Always predict, but always continue gathering evidence. Do not assume that your first judgment of a traffic situation *must* be correct. It may not be, and if you act on it, you may make a serious mistake.

What some person or animal does in a traffic situation is not up to you. How and when the person or animal does it are not up to you either. Those things are up to the person or animal. Remember that.

TRACTION CHANGES: Turning onto a gravel road from an asphalt road involves a change in traction. Realize that BEFORE you begin turning. Pay attention to traction all the time, not only in the snow.

ENTERTAINMENT: "Yikes! Look at those two clowns!" Two drivers ahead seem to be heading for an accident. It is so easy to sit there, looking through the windshield and feeling so safe and so superior, when other people are making driving mistakes. It is almost like watching television.

What if the two clowns do not avoid the crash? You might drive right into it. Anybody can be a clown.

DO NOT MISS OR IGNORE CLUES TO TROUBLE: It is easy to miss the beginnings of an accident situation and therefore be caught off-guard, because such things do not happen to us all the time in traffic. A driver can easily get distracted or bored. He can begin to do many other things while driving, instead of paying as much attention as possible to his hobby of driving.

NAVIGATE: Plan your trip ahead of time. Read signs, etc. Avoid having to make last moment lane changes, turns, etc.

AVOID OVERCONCENTRATION: Do not let your attention be taken by one hazard. Keep track of the overall driving scene while dealing with individual hazards.

CONSTRUCTION: Accident rates are higher in construction areas. Pay attention and drive at the proper speed.

EMOTIONS: Anger, fear, extreme joy, euphoria, etc., can make you a dangerous driver. Control strong emotions or do not drive!

DRUGS AND ALCOHOL: The idea is to lower the odds of having an accident, not raise them! Avoid drugs. Avoid alcohol. Remember that even taking medicine can make you a less safe driver.

DISTRACTIONS: Friends, relatives, the radio, worry, navigating problems, scenery, lighting a cigar, trying to read a map, a bee in the car, etc., can all distract one's attention from driving and contribute to a crash. Do not be distracted, DRIVE! Handle other things when it is safe. Pull over if you must to make it safe.

ETCETERA: Virtually anything can contribute to or cause a crash. Limbs fall off trees in wind storms. Trash cans blow into the street. Boulders roll down mountainsides. There are flash floods, earthquakes, etc. Things fall off trucks. Boats fall off trailers. Trailers disconnect from cars, etc., etc., and etc.

Do the best you can. Part of the game of driving well is avoiding accidents. See as much as you can. Pay attention to driving. Think about your driving. Use your experience to improve your driving; do not just brag that you have been driving for 40 years. Make those 40 years count for a great deal of learning. The better you drive, the more accident-producing situations you will spot. Therefore, you should be able to drive more and more safely.

Escape Routes

Look for escape routes, but *see them as parts of the overall scene*. If you are aiming through spaces, and keeping good following distances, and trying always to be in the position which gives you the most control over the most factors, you will automatically be aware of some escape routes. Spaces and surroundings are always part of the overall driving scene to a real driver.

Be aware of shoulders, ditches, and embankments alongside the road. Look for fences, guard rails, buildings, culverts, fire plugs, lampposts, etc. Know what is growing alongside the road. Purposely driving through a shallow ditch at a 45 degree angle into a corn field is much better than having a head-on crash with a bus. Purposely driving into bushes to stop your car safely or grinding along a steel guard rail are much better than plowing through a post and rail fence into an oak forest. By keeping surroundings in mind, by making them part of your overall driving scene, you will be able to take better evasive action more quickly than drivers who do not.

Ever wonder why a driver dodges away from a car which is cutting him off only to get crushed under a following semi? Ever wonder why a driver drives across the sidewalk, over a fire plug, across a lawn, up the front stairs, across the porch, and through the front door of a house after dodging another vehicle?

He was probably merely following the car ahead like an elephant holding the tail of the elephant ahead, or he was watching the road a few yards ahead and nothing else. He was unaware of his surroundings. The surroundings were there. The escape routes where there. He simply chose to ignore them.

Would he ever dream of playing football without knowing the location of at least the goal lines, the sidelines, and the line of scrimmage? Would he try to play baseball without knowing at least where the bases and foul lines were? Would he try to play chess or checkers using only the pieces and not the board? Of course not, but he habitually chooses to drive without knowing the boundaries, the fair and foul territory, etc. Every day, he chooses to move a car through traffic with less information about where it is than he has when he moves his Monopoly™ piece!

Do not, however, think of your lane, or the pavement, as the absolute limit to your movement in crash avoidance situations. Your car *can* run on the shoulder. It *can* run on grass. It *can* stop gently in bushes, haystacks, snowbanks, etc. Do not give up when your car leaves the road. Drive it until it stops. Keep trying to do the best no matter what the situation! If you must crash, choose the best, softest, slowest, most survivable crash you can get.

Finding a good escape route to avoid a specific *potential* hazard is an excellent game in relatively simple driving situations. However, in fast, heavy traffic, it is distracting. It focuses all of a driver's attention on one POTENTIAL hazard in one part of the overall driving scene. Therefore, he might miss a real hazard in another part of the traffic scene. More important, focusing on one potential hazard causes fear.

Seeing the possibility, predicting the mistake, and making an escape plan can lead you to *expect the mistake*. Then you will wait for the mistake and get more and more scared while you wait. You will worry. Instead of staying alert, aware, and relaxed enough to drive well, you will get tense. Driving will become a nerve-wracking experience. You will see your fellow drivers as deadly enemies. Predict trouble, look for escape routes, but do not use your skills in these areas to scare yourself.

Playing the game of "What if...?" can be challenging, fun, enlightening, and frightening. What if that car does not stop at the intersection? What if that truck squeezes into my lane? What if there is a car on the wrong side of the road coming at me on the other side of this hill? Questions like these can make you think about escape paths and escape maneuvers and ways of avoiding similar, real situations in the future. Unfortunately, thinking this way can also scare you. Play and enjoy the game, but do not let it scare you.

When you spot a dangerous driver or traffic situation, do not just accept it as part of your driving environment. Get away from it as early as possible. Get as far away as possible by passing it and leaving it far behind you. Staying behind it would keep it a constant threat to you. You would pay too much attention to the problem and drive at less than your best. Moreover, you would yield control of your car to incompetent drivers near you. Whatever you do, do not stay next to or right inside of an obviously dangerous traffic situation. If you cannot pass it, you may be able to drop back behind it. This will lessen the danger until you can pass it.

If you spot someone else's accident situation developing, do not just let the drivers in it handle it all by themselves. You may be able to help. If you can help, do it!

Safety Harnesses

Safety harnesses do more than protect your body in a crash. They force you to sit up in a good driving position. They also keep you behind the wheel when the car starts skidding violently, or bouncing, or flying, etc. You must be behind the wheel to have a chance at controlling the car.

Safety harnesses anchor you to the car. You can not steer if you are using the steering wheel as a grab handle. The belts hold you in place so you can use the steering wheel to steer the car.

Not wearing your safety harness, or wearing it wrong, is just as foolish as drinking and driving.

What to Do After Saying "Oops!"

Despite all your best efforts to see and stay clear of hazards, you are caught up in a crash situation. What should you do? TRY TO AVOID THE CRASH! Slow down. Swerve. Speed up. Stop. Slow down, then swerve. Swerve as you speed up. Do something! However, do not try to slow down fast and swerve hard at the same time! Remember that your tires have only so much traction. They can slow you fast, or they can swerve you hard. They cannot do both at the same time! Four wheel ABS does make swerving while stopping hard possible.

Cars and tires are better in emergency handling situations than most drivers think they are. Indeed, cars are better than most drivers are in emergency situations. Every control input by a driver has the ability to upset a car's balance. An unbalanced car works against its driver. Giving proper control inputs which keep the car balanced allows the car to do its best rather than its worst in emergency maneuvers.

Giving proper control inputs and developing sensitivity to a car's balance are what a high performance driving school teaches. A driver who learns those lessons can take much better advantage of his car's emergency maneuvering capabilities than the average driver, who knows virtually nothing about this kind of car control. While an average driver might stand on the brakes and slide into the crash, the trained driver might simply swerve violently but controllably around the crash in safety.

SWERVING: Do not misunderstand swerving. Swerving is *not* turning away from an obstacle. Swerving is intentionally driving around and past an obstacle along a specific, planned route.

There is a big difference.

The driver who swerves properly sees the obstacle, then looks for open space through which to bypass the obstacle. He aims through that space. He plans a *path*. He knows exactly where he wants to go.

Basically, swerving may be thought of as changing lanes violently. When you change lanes, you know where you want to go. You aim there. If you need to aim to be able to make an ordinary lane change, certainly you need to aim to be able to perform an emergency swerve, which is violent, unexpected, and clearly out of the ordinary.

The driver who does not know how to swerve merely tries to turn away from the obstacle. He does not visualize a path. He has no plan. Very likely, he looks right at the obstacle. As a result, the car crashes right into the obstacle or swerves out of control.

Do not *try* to swerve. Do not swerve out of control. Swerve past the problem. Think of swerving *not* as turning away from something, but as passing it and keeping control.

In some situations, swerving may be your only hope. When a pedestrian runs in front of your car, for example, you might be able to swerve even though you cannot stop.

PANIC BRAKING: When facing a potential crash, the first thing virtually any driver will do automatically is hit the brakes. Hitting the brakes without throwing the car into a wild skid can give you time. Do not waste that time by sitting there, sliding into a crash. Use the time to re-assess the situation. You might find an escape path. You might find that just slowing and stopping will not keep your vehicle out of the crash, but that you can still swerve. Your lower speed will make the swerve more controllable. The time saved in slowing might allow you to check your blind spot to make sure that you are swerving around a crash, not into

one. Panic braking with ABS will not result in a skid.

Too Late to Buckle Up Your Safety Harness

What if you cannot avoid the crash? It's too late to buckle up your safety harness. Do whatever you can to lessen the seriousness of the crash. Just as you try to minimize the risk of having an accident, try to minimize the risks *in* an accident. Do not just plow into something. Pick the best crash you can get. Never give up. Drive that car the best you can for as long as you can. Keep looking for a way out or a better crash.

There are standard procedures to use in trying to avoid or minimize accidents, but each accident is different from all others. The trick is to KEEP YOUR HEAD, assess your particular situation, and then do the very best you can.

First, of course, try not to crash at all. If that is impossible, try to crash at a lower speed and/or to strike a glancing blow rather than a solid, direct hit. It may be possible to hit something else entirely, something which will stop you more gently. It is better to hit bushes, new snowbanks, haystacks, mud fields, rather than brick walls, concrete abutments, trucks, railroad trains, etc.

Choose the best crash you can get. For example, minimize the force of impact by hitting a car going the same way as your car rather than one which is standing still. Hit a car which is standing still rather than one coming at you. Avoid the head-on crash at virtually any cost! When trying to avoid a head-on, the standard rule in America is do not dodge to the left. Suppose the oncoming car is on your side of the road. It seems to make sense to dodge to the left. However, if the other driver can dodge at all, he will try to get back on his own side of the road. If he does, and you are dodging left, you will still be in a head-on situation. If you can see that the oncoming driver has collapsed and that his car seems to be on a stable course, dodge left, unless there is more head-on traffic right behind his car. In countries where people drive on the left side of the road, obviously the preferred dodge is left, not right.

If possible, blow your horn and/or flash your headlights. The idea is that the other driver may have fallen asleep, and the noise and/or flashes might awaken him. Once awake, he might be able to help avoid or lessen the severity of the crash. Any time you think the horn or lights might help, use them.

Crash into vehicles, bushes, etc., rather than pedestrians. Hurt or kill animals rather than humans. Damage the least valuable property.

Go off the road on purpose, rather than hit something really hard. Try to find the best place to go off the road (between trees rather than through them, for example).

Do not give up trying to control your car just because it has left the road. Traction will certainly change when you start driving on wet grass instead of dry pavement, but that is no reason to give up.

Do not jam on the brakes! Skidding with the wheels locked is *not* the fastest way to stop a car with the brakes. The fastest way to stop a car with the brakes is to hold the brakes at the point just before the wheels lock up. Learn to do this at high performance driving school. With ABS, just STAND ON THE BRAKE PEDAL and KEEP STANDING on it. *DO NOT PUMP ABS BRAKES*! Practice with your ABS to get the feel of it in a safe area with no traffic behind your car.

Whatever you do, do not jam on the brakes once you are already skidding. This will make your fight for control virtually hopeless. If there is any time, try to control the skid and drive out of trouble.

Do not slide your car sideways into a curb

or run into a ditch at a sharp angle. These kinds of things can trip a car and make it roll or flip.

Race drivers have been known to spin cars intentionally to avoid crashes. The idea is that the car will use up its kinetic energy by spinning and stop sometimes almost in its tracks. Obviously, an intentional spin should be attempted only by a race driver or a stunt driver who KNOWS EXACTLY WHAT HE IS DOING, HAS DONE IT MANY TIMES BEFORE, AND IS WILLING TO GIVE UP CONTROL TO TRY TO AVOID THE ACCIDENT. Furthermore, a miraculous spin to avoid an accident will not help the drivers behind you avoid hitting your car when you suddenly spin it to a stop right in front of them.

When dealing with side impacts (T-bone type crashes), the choices are, as usual, to speed up, slow down, turn, or some combination of these. Do whatever you think will avoid the crash or minimize the impact. *Do not swerve into a head-on!*

Sometimes turning to go the same direction as the car you will crash with can minimize the force of impact.

Driver of white car should do this;

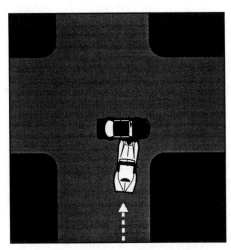

Driver of white car should not do this.

There is not much you can do to dodge a rear-end crash. Your head restraint is there to keep your head from being snapped back and causing whiplash injuries in rear-end collisions. If your head restraint is adjustable, it should be adjusted so that its top comes up at least to the tops of your ears or half way up your head. This should be done BEFORE you drive! It may be possible to speed up or move your car forward to give the driver about to hit you more room to swerve or slow down. Standard advice is to release the brakes to lessen the force of impact, then to re-apply them to avoid crashing into the vehicle ahead or cross traffic. They say that holding the brakes on during a rear-end crash increases the chances of being hit twice by the car behind.

Finally, in a crash involving a large car and a small car, the large car will survive better and probably keep its passengers safer. The small car might avoid the crash entirely, through. The small car might be better engineered and built to protect its passengers.

After the Crash

After the crash, there are still many things to be done. Do whatever you can to keep things from getting worse. This starts with *keeping your head*!

There is a racing story about a driver who crashed and came to a stop off in the grass. Finding himself uninjured, he assumed that the danger was past. He relaxed. He just sat in the car for quite a while before he noticed people waving frantically and screaming at him. They were trying to tell him that his car was on fire! KEEP YOUR HEAD — AND USE IT!

The first thing to do after crashing is to stop. It is the law, and it seems obvious. In fact, we tend to think all crashes end with all the vehicles stopped. Think about hitting a pedestrian, though. You hit him, and he flies away, but you keep going. You get scared and want more than anything to *keep* going, and going, and going — to drive away and leave the trouble behind you. *Force yourself to stop!*

In crashes which are more than fender-benders, shut off the ignition switch as soon as possible to minimize the risk of fire set by electric sparks.

Get out of the car and look around the area. Quickly get the most complete picture you can of the crash scene. Do not think of the few seconds needed to do this as wasted time. Time is wasted by running hither and yon without knowing the situation.

Avoid further damage! Do not get run over or cause more crashing by acting without thinking. Make sure that the most serious dangers are controlled. Look for living people in burning cars or lying in the road where they can be run over easily, etc.

When using a fire extinguisher, aim at the base of the flames. Look for electrical power lines on the ground or on top of cars —especially cars with people in them. People in cars which are touching power lines should stay inside and not touch anything they are not already touching. Touching the wrong thing or trying to exit the vehicle might cause electrocution. Do not try to move power lines yourself. Wait for skilled help. Try to notice any gasoline leaks.

Give first aid if needed. It is a very good idea to carry a first aid kit and a first aid book in your glove compartment. A first aid course is an excellent investment. If you are the only person available to help seriously injured people and do not know what to do, you will very likely panic. You might then easily do more harm than good.

The priorities in giving first aid are: first, stop arterial bleeding; second, restore breathing; and third, treat other injuries and shock.

Do not give drinks to unconscious or semiconscious people. Keep people conscious by talking to them. Do not move injured people. Moving a seriously injured person can paralyze him, puncture his lungs with his own broken ribs, etc. If a seriously injured person wants to move by himself, insist calmly that he stay in place. Explain that he might hurt himself much more by moving.

Organize the efforts of any people who stop to help. At least tell them what you know that is of immediate importance.

Send someone for paramedics, police, etc. Make sure that this messenger knows the location of the accident, so that he can give it to the emergency people. It is against the law to leave the scene of a serious accident in which you are involved.

Warn approaching traffic (in both directions, if necessary). Use flares, flashlights, lanterns, white cloths, etc. Do not light flares near vehicles which might be leaking flammable or explosive liquids or vapors.

In fender-benders, the first thing the police will tell you to do when they arrive is to move the cars out of the way to get traffic moving. In very serious accidents, the scene should be left untouched for the investigators.

Give paramedics and/or police the most important information first. Tell the police what happened. Do not take or assign blame. Just tell what things happened. Give your name, address, telephone number, driver's license number and state, license plate number and state, to the police officer. Give this information to the other drivers involved in the crash. Give them the name of your insurance company. Get this information from them, too. Get the names and addresses of everybody involved in the accident. Get the names and addresses of *all* witnesses. If any car involved is owned by someone other than its driver, get the name and address of the owner. Do not discuss blame. Just gather and give out needed identification information.

Make a drawing of the scene. Take notes. If you have a camera, take pictures of the scene. This sort of thing can be valuable in lawsuits resulting from the crash.

Do not argue with anyone. People have been shot while arguing after accidents.

Phone home. Make arrangements to get your car removed from the crash scene. Call your insurance company. Make out accident report forms for the state and your insurance company.

You may get a traffic ticket. That ticket has no bearing on your liability in a lawsuit resulting from the accident. Likewise, the result of a lawsuit has no bearing on your guilt or innocence on the traffic charges.

If you are dead, none of this will matter to you.

Keep Actively Interested in Driving Safely

You feel quite safe in a car. You do not get into your car with the idea that you have only a 50% chance of getting where you want to go. You believe you have a 100% chance. Crashing and dodging accidents are not daily activities, like changing lanes, entering the expressway, and parallel parking. The average driver might encounter an emergency driving situation once in years, or once in decades, or even once in his life! Because he practices accident avoidance so seldom, he is not ready to perform properly with grace and lightening speed in an emergency. In an emergency, he will think with surprising slowness. If he survives, he might still get new ideas about what he should have done weeks, months, etc., after the crash.

A race driver, on the other hand, will respond better and more quickly to a driving emergency because he encounters driving emergencies relatively often. Emergencies and emergency actions are always fresh in his mind.

The trick, the way to get the edge on handling emergency situations, is to keep your mind prepared for them. That means think about safety! Do not be content with reading an article once every five years about the 10 most common highway emergencies and what to do about them. Do not take one high performance driving course and expect it to protect you for the next 40 years. Do not play "What if…?" *once.* Do not relax in your easy chair or lie on the grass and make up emergency situations and figure out things to do about them *once.* Do not read *a* driving book.

Just as you should review the rules of the road from time to time, just as you should keep a constant check on your driving performance, you should think about crashing and emergency maneuvers and techniques from time to time. Just sit back and think about these things now and then. Keep techniques for avoiding accidents and lessening damage fresh in your mind. When a real emergency does happen, your brain will not have to sort through dusty, 20 year old memories of high school driver ed. trying to remember what to do. It will have a relatively fresh supply of remedies from which to choose. It will figure out the situation and what to do about it faster. Just as with aiming and steering, let your brain know what you want it to do and give it practice. Let it think about emergencies from time to time. Memorize escape actions and priorities. Play "What if…?" Do not just read about emergencies or try to pass a safe driving test in the newspaper once every seven years. *Make* your brain *stay* interested in saving its life. To save its life, your brain will have to save your life, too.

Other Emergencies

This idea of being ready to deal with crash situations carries over to other road emergencies. Do not just *read* about emergencies, *learn* about them. Learn to prevent them. Memorize things to do about them. Think about and review these things as recreation from time to time. Make up imaginary emergency situations and figure out what you could, should, would do in them.

When your own, unique emergency situation does happen, try to keep your head, try to analyze the situation, and try to apply those remedies which fit it. You may not need to apply all the remedies you have learned. You may need to apply them in a different order. The important thing is that your brain has remedies ready to apply to the situation the instant you recognize it.

CAR ON FIRE: Get out! Keep your head, though. Do not jump out of the car and get run over just because of a bit of smoke.

It is a good idea to carry a fire extinguisher INSIDE THE PASSENGER COMPARTMENT, *NOT* IN THE TRUNK. Make sure that the fire extinguisher is safe for all kinds of fires. Learn how to use it. Make sure it is fully charged.

A small, engine compartment fire can flare up when you open the hood to fight it. Opening the hood will give the fire a better draft. Air from under the car will rush to feed the flames. Suddenly, a small fire can become much bigger.

It can also flare right at you when you open the hood. The hood and outside hood release may be hot.

Aim the fire extinguisher at the base of the flames. Shut off the ignition. Never "test" a fire extinguisher.

Car upholstery can give off poisonous fumes when it burns. Also, plastic melts. It is better not to get molten, flaming plastic sticking to your skin or clothing.

If the car must be left to burn, get everybody well away from it, in case the gas tank explodes.

HOOD OPENS: If the hood opens while you are driving, it will block your view of the road. In almost all cases of hoods flying up, the driver can look through the space between the open hood and the dashboard.

If this is impossible, open the driver's side window and put your head out to see. Check traffic, signal, pull over and stop. Have passengers help you.

ACCELERATOR OR THROTTLE LINKAGE GETS STUCK: Sometimes kicking or pulling on a stuck gas pedal will work. Sometimes it will not. What if you kick a stuck accelerator and instead of coming unstuck, it sticks farther down? What if you reach down to pull up the accelerator, lose control, and crash? People have crashed reaching to the floor to pick up cigarettes, etc.

A floor mat can jam the accelerator. Other things which should not be on the floor can jam the accelerator.

The brakes can overcome the engine's power. Use them.

The throttle can stick wide open (gas pedal flat on the floor). A broken throttle return spring will make this happen. Do not panic. Look for open space and steer. Use the brakes. Make sure that you are pushing the brake pedal, not the accelerator. Shut off the ignition switch. Sometime before you actually have to do this, check the operation of your ignition switch. It should not lock your steering wheel so long as the transmission is in gear. In any case, it is worthwhile to practice shutting down before an emergency requires it. Do this away from traffic, especially traffic behind you.

Pushing the clutch pedal down (stick shift) or shifting to neutral will cut off power to the drive wheels. The trouble with this technique is that the engine will speed up instantly. It can ruin itself very quickly. Still, if the choice is a bad crash or a blown engine, choose the blown engine. If you do shift to neutral or disengage the clutch, shut off the ignition immediately but avoid locking the steering.

ENGINE STALLS: Your car is stalled on the railroad tracks. What should you do? LOOK FOR A TRAIN! If you can see that there is time, try to start the engine. Try calmly. Flooding the engine will not help. If the car does not start immediately, get your passengers out of it. Make sure that they do not get run over by other street traffic.

You might be able to push the car off the tracks. A stick shift car can move itself even when the engine will not run. The starter can move the car. Put the transmission in first or reverse. Let the clutch pedal up. Turn the key. The starter will turn the engine. The turning engine will move the car.

If the train is coming, get out of the car. Get away from the car. Run away somewhat *toward the train*. When the train hits the car, the car and pieces of it will fly in the same direction the train is moving. Run *away* from the debris.

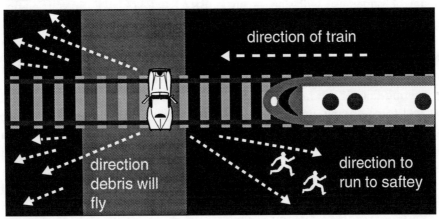

When your engine stalls while the car is in motion, just shift to neutral and turn the key. You do not have to stop and shift to park to restart the engine. Often a stick shift car in motion can be restarted merely by leaving the ignition on and shifting to the next lower gear. The engine should start as you engage the clutch.

Stick shift cars can be push-started. This should *not* be done in traffic. Move the car which will do the pushing into position behind the car needing to be pushed. Check bumper heights. Bumpers can lock together or miss each other completely and damage either or both cars. Get into the cars. The car needing the push start should be in second gear. The ignition should be turned on. The clutch pedal should be pushed down. The car doing the pushing should be in first gear. When everything is ready, the driver needing the push should signal for the pushing to begin. When being push-started, do not expect or wait for a great deal of speed. Ten miles per hour is plenty and about all you will get. Engage the clutch. The engine should fire. Wave off the pusher. Do not stop suddenly.

A stick shift car can be started by being *hand* pushed, too. The ignition should be on, the transmission in first gear, and the clutch pedal down. In this kind of push-start you will get almost no speed. Do not wear out the pushers. As soon as you get rolling, pop the clutch.

It is illegal to coast down a hill. However, a stick shift car can be started by letting it roll down an incline a bit (ignition on) and popping the clutch as in the push-start.

Push-starting should be used when the starter will not turn over the engine and a jump-start is not available. There is nothing magic in pushing. All that the pushing does is get the engine to turn over when the starter cannot do it. If there is something wrong with the engine and no amount of starter use will start it, no amount of pushing will start it either.

STEERING FAILURE: Drivers tend to take their steering system for granted. They ignore it. Happily, steering failures are rare. Consider how it must feel to be driving along and suddenly have no steering control. Then remember to have your steering system checked from time to time — especially in an older or high-mileage car.

If your engine stalls, your power steering will lose its power assist. You will still be able to steer, but the effort needed will be MUCH higher. As long as you are going straight when your engine dies, steering is not much of a problem. If your engine dies just as you begin to turn, though, the sudden heaviness of the steering can be a real problem. You might not have time to react to the problem with more muscle.

A tie rod end can break loose. This will disconnect one wheel from the rest of the steering system. One wheel will react properly to your steering inputs, but the other will go wherever the physics of the situation force it. Especially on older and high-mileage cars, have tie rod ends and ball joints checked.

Total steering failure is rare. It would mean that the steering wheel would have no effect whatsoever on the car's direction of travel. Trying to stop and riding it out might be the only thing you could do. If what were ahead looked really bad and you were going *exactly straight*, you might try to STAND ON THE BRAKE PEDAL SUDDENLY AND WITH ALL YOUR MIGHT to lock all four wheels at the same time to make the car slide to a stop in a straight line. This could leave you open to being rear-ended. Standard advice is to try to warn other drivers of your problem with your four-way flashers, horn, lights, etc. If your steering binds, feels loose, or has excessive play, *have it repaired*!

BRAKE FAILURE: If your engine stalls, the power to your power brakes will fail. However, there is a built-in reserve. You will get at least one good stop from your power brakes after your engine stalls. Even after this reserve is used up, your brakes will still work, you will just have to push the pedal extremely hard!

Total brake failure is rare today because modern brakes have two separate hydraulic systems. If one goes, you still have the other. Your brake pedal will go lower and a light on your instrument panel will tell you that your brakes have failed, but the car *will stop* — eventually.

If you lose your brakes completely, go for the parking brake. It works independently of the hydraulic brake system. It is worked by a cable under the car. The parking brake (emergency brake, hand brake) works on the rear wheels only. Be careful not to lock the rear wheels when you apply it. Locked rear wheels cause a rear-end skid (see Chapter 15). *Be sure to keep the release handle or button activated. If you* merely step on the parking brake pedal or pull up the parking brake handle, you will lock on the brakes. Again, this will cause a rear wheel skid. This time, though, you will not be able to release the brakes instantly.

Practice using your parking brakes to stop your car. Do it in a quiet area with nobody behind you. Remember that your brake lights will not be activated by your parking brakes.

If your brake pedal goes to the floor, you will probably automatically pump the brakes. This is good. Some brake fluid may be left in the system and might stop the car.

Aim and steer. Swerve around things. Look for a place where you can use up momentum until your car stops. Look for something which will stop you: bushes, mud, a snowbank, etc.

It is recommended that you rub your tires against a curb to reduce speed. This can work, but be prepared for the car to begin doing acrobatics as soon as a tire contacts the curb. You will have to do some serious steering to keep your tires rubbing the curb. It will be a rough ride, not like dragging your feet to stop a bicycle.

Swerving the car from side to side will scrub off some speed.

Turning off the ignition and then flooring the accelerator will slow you down.

Shifting to a lower gear will also slow the car, especially with the ignition off. Shifting to a very low gear or reverse in a stick shift car or shifting to park or reverse in an automatic transmission car might ruin the transmission, but it might stop the car — VERY SUDDENLY WITH THE WHEELS LOCKED.

CAR GOES UNDERWATER: This is very unusual. It would also be very frightening.

You should have been wearing your safety harness. That would make it less likely that you would be knocked unconscious in the crash.

Your car should float for a short time. At night it will be dark underwater. The car might end up on its side or upside-down. Releasing the safety harness in an upside-down position can drop you on your head. Be careful. The air pocket might be in the rear of the car. The engine will pull the front end downward. *TRY TO KEEP YOUR HEAD*! Get air. Check the situation.

The door probably will not open because of water pressure outside it. You will have to open a window and let the car fill up with water to equalize the pressure before you can open the door. You might be able to get out through a window. Try not to rush. Power windows may not work because of an electrical short circuit. You might have to try to break a window. A spring loaded center punch can save your life by breaking a window for you. Check with your hardware store.

ROADSIDE BREAKDOWN: One standard signal of distress is a white cloth tied to the antenna or door handle. Another is an open hood.

Pull as far as possible off the road. Set up reflectors or flares. Get passengers out of the car in case of a rear-end crash.

You want the police or highway emergency truck to stop. If a motorist stops, make sure that he is not trying to rob you, etc. If you really do not trust him, tell him that the police are already on the way.

When going for help, think about whom to leave with the car or child, etc. If everybody goes for help, leave a note for the police. Let the good samaritan go for help while you stay with the car.

20 *Chapter Twenty*

Vehicular Variations

Motor vehicles have many very different images, images we understand and recognize quite well: the racy, devil-may-care sportscar; the tough, independent cowboy's pick-up truck; the huge, powerful tractor semi-trailer rig which evokes the romance and adventure of rolling along the open road; the cheap econobox; the rusted, dented junk; the elegant luxury car; the sensually gratifying motorcycle; the noisy, colorful, and exciting fire truck; etc.

As the images of motor vehicles vary, so do their functions. The purpose of a hearse is not that of a dump truck or motor scooter. Motor vehicles are carefully designed and constructed to perform their specialized functions. They vary greatly in shape, size, weight, power, seating capacity, cargo capacity, etc. We easily understand differences in both vehicle image and vehicle purpose.

What we do not understand so easily is how the variations in vehicle design and construction which give different vehicles their images and fit them to their purposes affect the act of driving them. The problems and joys of driving sports utility vehicles are not the same as those of riding motorcycles, or driving semis or vans or family sedans, etc.

We all act and react based upon what we know. If we have driven only the average, front-wheel-drive, four door sedan with automatic transmission and four cylinder engine, our whole concept of driving is based on driving that kind of vehicle. We have no idea of the joys and problems of motorcycle riding, or bus driving, or sportscar driving, etc. Our limited experience makes it easy for us to assume that all types of vehicles must act and react and be driven in exactly the same way as our vehicle.

This is not true. Different types of vehicles *do* require different things from their drivers. Our ignorance of this fact can cause us to misunderstand the maneuvers and motives of those who drive vehicles different from ours. It can make us cause problems for those drivers without realizing it. It can even make us cause problems for ourselves which we mistakenly blame on the drivers of other types of vehicles. To share the road with drivers of various kinds of vehicles, we must understand some things about driving those vehicles.

TRUCKS: Big trucks cannot accelerate quickly. They lag behind when pulling away from stop lights and in heavy, stop-and-go traffic, creating long gaps in front of themselves. Car drivers frequently take advantage of these long gaps to change lanes.

Unfortunately, car drivers also change lanes in front of big trucks when traffic is slowing or stopping, and the gaps are getting shorter, not longer. These car drivers do not realize that their lane changes into shortening spaces in front of trucks in slowing traffic can frustrate and annoy truck drivers and endanger themselves. Moreover, they do not realize that each car which cuts in front of a truck has the effect of moving the truck backwards in the traffic stream. To the helpless truck driver this too, is frustrating and annoying, because his job is to make time, not lose it.

When truck drivers need to change lanes in heavy traffic, they are once again victimized by car drivers. Car drivers seem not to realize that because of their length, trucks need long spaces into which to change lanes. Likewise, car drivers seem neither to notice nor look for turn signals on trucks in adjacent lanes. They just float along with the traffic and block the trucks next to them, although often they could easily speed up or slow down a bit to make a space for a truck.

Remember that a lane change in heavy traffic is quite a bit more work for a truck driver than for a car driver. The truck driver cannot accelerate or decelerate his vehicle as easily as the car driver. He has much more vehicle to maneuver, and he has to rely on mirrors to do his checking.

Do not get impatient with truck drivers trying to change lanes. Cooperate with them. Stay out of their way. Even if your help to a truck driver does put you into a disadvantageous position now and then, it is not that bad. In your maneuverable car, you can easily move to a section of clear road, and cooperating to keep the traffic flow smooth helps everybody.

Remember that you can signal a passing or lane changing semi driver that the rear of his trailer is clear of your front end by flashing your headlights.

Car drivers get impatient with semi drivers backing into loading docks from the street. Loading docks can be narrow and quite clumsy to enter. Car drivers blocked in the street by truckers backing into docks may not realize that the truckers are doing the best they can.

A truck driver backs part way into a dock. This opens up some space on the street in front of the truck. As soon as he sees this space, the car driver at the head of the line rushes through it. The drivers behind him follow. Then, something up ahead forces traffic to stop. At least one car has to stop right in front of the truck. Of course, the trucker needs to pull forward one more time to be able to back all the way into the dock. The stopped traffic blocks him. The jam-up lasts longer, involves more vehicles, and annoys more people.

Car drivers also rush across in front of backing trucks just as the truck drivers, trying to

prevent the situation above, rush to pull forward for another attempt at backing into the dock. These car drivers are surprised to see the massive front end of the semi coming right at them as they try to dash past it. The truck driver is also surprised — and annoyed.

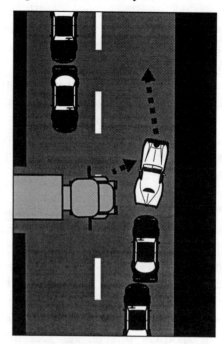

Be patient. Let the truck driver have the benefit of the doubt, and think about how fast you could back a truck (which bends) into a narrow dock using only mirrors to aim.

Car drivers get into the way all the time when semis are turning. Often, on right turns, the semi must move left before turning right because of its great length. The truck is simply too long to be able to turn using only one lane. The truck driver clearly signals right, then swings left and cuts back right only to find some car driver trying to pass him on the right and driving under his trailer.

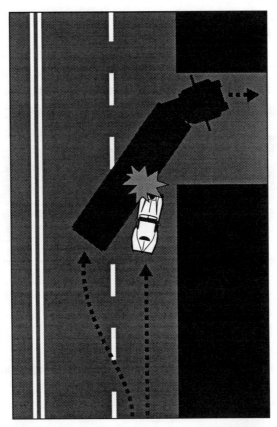

Believe the turn signals a semi driver gives!

Approaching intersections where semis are turning right into their street, car drivers neither slow down nor stop short to give the trucks room to turn, but rush right up to the intersection and block everything.

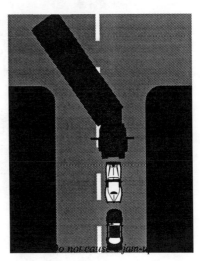

Trucks are tall. Car drivers do not have to figure whether their vehicles are too tall to fit through viaducts. Truck drivers have to do this all the time in city driving.

Upon getting into a truck and trying to drive it, one of the first things an alert car driver should notice is that seeing out of a truck is much different from seeing out of a car. In many trucks the driver cannot see straight back at all. He can see to the rear only through outside mirrors.

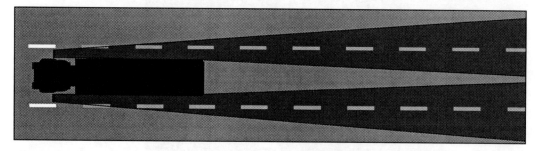

These mirrors leave a huge blind spot directly behind the truck. When you follow a truck, if you cannot see the driver's mirror, he cannot see your car.

Truck mirrors also leave long blind spots alongside the truck. Unlike a car driver, a truck driver cannot simply twist around and check his blind spot. The rear of the truck's cab blocks his view. When a truck driver signals and changes lanes, cutting you off, he most likely is not trying to push you around. He just cannot see your car.

These convex mirrors (below) are added to trucks to give better vision.

The convex mirrors are used to supplement the west coast mirrors for side vision.

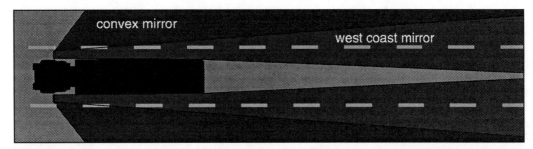

Because of their fish eye shape, these mirrors give a distorted and often small image. A truck driver, using his convex and west coast mirrors together, can get a pretty good idea about what is near his truck. However, he can still miss seeing a car, especially a small, low car, riding in either of these positions.

The tall west coast mirrors cause blind spots in forward vision to both sides of the cab.

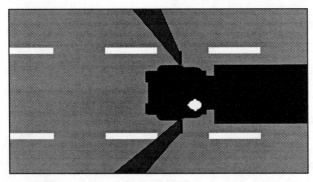

It can take quite a while for a semi to pass a car. While the truck is passing him, the car driver can easily speed up to match the truck's speed without realizing it. When this happens, it is easy for the truck driver to think that the car driver is speeding up to stay ahead. He may then drop back behind the car again, only to have the car driver notice his own increased speed and slow down again. At this point, the truck driver thinks that the car driver is harassing him by speeding up to block his pass only to slow down again. Watch your speedometer!

Though he has serious blind spots behind, next to, and ahead of his truck, the truck driver, because he sits so high, can see much farther straight ahead than a car driver. This is a great advantage to truckers who use it.

Driving vehicles of different heights gives very different views of the road.

View from an average car.

View from a semi in exactly the same place on exactly the same road.

There are advantages and disadvantages. For example the view from the truck is much better *over* the parked cars, but gives almost no chance to see under them. Very often it is much more difficult to see into parked cars from a truck than a car.

Medium height vehicles like vans, pickup trucks, and SUVs have their own vision advantages and disadvantages. Often they may compromise the best and worst of taller and shorter vehicles.

It can be very noisy in the cab of a truck. The truck driver cannot hear traffic sounds as well as the car driver. Because of size, weight, and noise, a truck driver can sideswipe a car or hit a pedestrian, etc., and not even know it.

Trucks carrying various dangerous materials have to stop at railroad crossings. Do not let this surprise or confuse you.

Shifting a big truck's transmission requires more work than shifting a car's stick shift transmission. Moreover, the truck will probably need a different gear for even a relatively small variation in its speed. Therefore, the truck driver wants to roll steadily, not keep speeding up and slowing down.

Going down gentle hills the truck driver will want to get up some momentum to help carry him up the next hill. Do not block trucks on downhill stretches.

Finally, remember that the truck driver is being paid to get his cargo somewhere, not just to put in hours. He wants to roll and to make time, not to be blocked by a bunch of ignorant car drivers. The simplest, safest rule is just try to stay out of the way. Let the trucks roll. Think flow. If a truck driver wants to pass you, let him.

Driving large trucks or buses as part of their training would give driving students the opportunity to learn several worthwhile lessons easily. The great forward sight distance over the tops of cars would let them experience seeing many seconds ahead easily. It would give them a stunning example of what they should try to see from their cars. Having to deal with the clumsiness of trucks caused by their large size would help them learn a lot about perfect placement. Driving a long vehicle forces a driver used to short vehicles to learn the importance of planning and achieving proper placement of the vehicle *BEFORE* beginning a maneuver. If you do not start from the right place in a long vehicle, often you will not be able to complete the maneuver. If you do complete the maneuver, it may be needlessly difficult. In smaller vehicles, achieving perfect placement BEFORE beginning a maneuver is rarely that important. However, placing any vehicle perfectly to begin a maneuver does yield easier maneuvering; better check of traffic; and all around more graceful, safe, and satisfying performance. It shows others seeing the apparent effortlessness with which you achieve perfect results the great depth of your driving ability.

Coupled with the greater sight distance ahead, the slow acceleration and deceleration available in trucks would make a student driver much more aware of traffic flow. From his lofty perch, a truck driver cannot only see how drivers confound the free, safe, efficient flow of traffic, he can learn techniques for improving flow. THE SMOOTHER THE FLOW OF TRAFFIC IS, THE FEWER CHANCES FOR CRASHES THERE ARE!

Experiencing first hand the difficulties of seeing certain parts of the traffic scene through a truck's mirrors would make driving students appreciate the all around visibility available from their cars. It would encourage them to take full advantage of the seeing possibilities offered by the clean, unobstructed windows of their cars, to maximize the usefulness of their mirrors by painstaking adjustment, and to twist well around when backing, parking, etc, to take full advantage of the view out the rear.

Finally, the added involvement needed to drive a big truck or bus would raise a student driver's appreciation of the amount of attention which can and should be applied to the demanding and rewarding psychomotor skill of driving.

MOTORCYCLES: Riding a motorcycle can be a lot of fun. It can be dangerous. If you want to ride a motorcycle, learn how from a good school/instructor. Learn to ride well. Then, keep riding better … and better! Take pride in your riding abilities. Don't just talk about how good you are, be good. Be *very* good!

Get the best equipment you can, and take good care of it. Remember that if you crash or have to get off the bike before a crash, your only protection is your helmet, gloves, boots, and heavy clothing. Light, bright colors and reflective materials will help other road users see you, especially at night. At night, a motorcycle can easily fade from view among the multiple bright lights on each of the cars surrounding it. Make sure that your bike meets your needs. A huge, luxurious touring bike will not be at its best in desert sand or trying to cross a fallen tree.

Car drivers should try to remember that motorcycles are more complicated to ride than cars are to drive. They are also more sensitive to road and weather conditions. They can be extremely quick. They can be hard to see, although often riders' heads can be seen sticking up above the tops of cars. Motorcyclists have the same rights on and to the road as drivers. Share the road with motorcyclists. Try to understand their special problems.

The motorcyclist has to keep his vehicle balanced on two wheels. This can get tricky in the wind, the rain, and other conditions of poor traction. Rain also makes it harder for the motorcyclist to see. Rain and cold can make the motorcyclist uncomfortable. When it is cold and raining, and you see a motorcyclist from your cozy car, do not just laugh at the poor guy because he is getting wet. Realize that he may be uncomfortable, and that any discomfort he feels will probably affect his riding performance negatively. Realize that he has to balance his vehicle on only two wheels in slippery conditions. Realize that he probably cannot see as well as you can. Then give him a break, and next time don't laugh.

Do not crowd motorcycles, especially from the rear. Picture what would happen if a motorcyclist fell down right in front of your car.

In some places it is legal for motorcyclists to ride between lanes in heavy traffic. Watch for this *wherever* you drive. Idling in heavy traffic on a hot day can overheat a motorcycle's air cooled engine. The rider will want to get moving and may be tempted to take to the shoulder or ride between lanes.

In northern states, motorcycles are used very little or not at all in the winter. Therefore, by spring, car drivers have forgotten about looking for them. Remember that each spring the motorcyclists return.

It may be difficult for a motorcyclist to hear traffic noises. Pavement irregularities and wind affect motorcycles more than cars.

Look out for beginning motorcyclists who are unsure of themselves. They are often easy to spot. They may ride with unusually jerky movements. They may keep their feet down a long time when pulling away from a traffic signal or other stop. They may check and recheck too many times before making lane changes. They may wobble. They may be slow. They may kill the engine or rev it very high when starting from rest. See whether the motorcycle itself has a license applied for sticker instead of a license plate. This can indicate a new rider on a new bike.

If driving students had to ride motorcycles, they would certainly appreciate weather and road surface conditions more. Just as when they drove the trucks, they would learn that much more attention can and should be given to driving. They would see that extra effort pays off in more driving safety, efficiency, and fun.

VANS: Vans are very popular. Vans are often thought of as very versatile and, sometimes, very big cars. They are *not* cars, though. They are vans, and thinking of them as cars and trying to drive them like cars lead to trouble.

Vans can be much bigger than cars. Even though vans offer the same kind of forward sight advantages as trucks due to their high seating position, they also have blind spot disadvantages similar to trucks. Even in window vans, parking, backing, and other close maneuvers are clumsier to do than they are in cars. New van drivers especially must keep this in mind and not do these maneuvers as casually as they do them in cars.

CARS: There are surprising variations among cars, too. A person used to driving a front wheel drive car in snow will not understand the traction problems experienced by the driver of a rear wheel drive car in snow. A driver used to a low powered car may not understand that a high powered car can cause certain problems for its driver as well as move him along very rapidly. Likewise, he may not expect the burst of rapid acceleration the driver of a high powered car might use to cut through traffic. This might cause him to drive right into the path of the fast car. On the other hand, a driver used to powerful cars can easily forget that not all cars are as fast as his. He can feel annoyed at being needlessly blocked when traffic accelerates at what seems to him to be an abnormally slow rate.

Vision from very low cars is generally worse than vision from cars of average height. In traffic, drivers of low cars see mostly the rear end of the car ahead. Watching traffic, avoiding trouble, and planning and executing maneuvers are more difficult in low cars. The problem of blind areas caused by rows of parked cars lining urban side streets is worse for drivers of very low cars. Even out in the country, the driver of the very low vehicle encounters vision problems. His view down the road is more limited by hill crests. Certainly passing on two-lane roads in hilly country is more difficult.

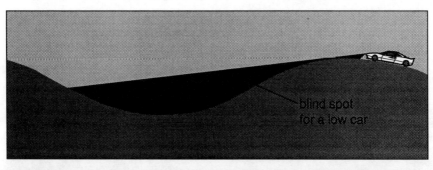

A very real problem for drivers of low cars (or drivers who learn to drive in very low cars) is that they can easily get used to the seriously restricted vision and come to believe that it is normal. Accepting reduced vision, reduced information, and reduced maneuvering ability as normal instead of trying to compensate for them dooms one to a lifetime of poor or at best mediocre driving.

Cars with swoopy body work make close maneuvering clumsy because the driver cannot see the corners of his vehicle. Judging clearances becomes guess work.

A low seating position inside a car causes similar problems. The lower the driver sits in a vehicle, the larger (wider and longer) the vehicle appears to him. His vision near the vehicle is also restricted.

Windows with extreme rake make vision difficult.

Mild rake   *Photo courtesy Peter and Heather Donnelly.*

Severe rake

They collect dust easily. When the dust or other dirt reflects light, it becomes nearly impossible to see through the windows.

Some cars have large c and b pillars.

They create big blind spots which make lane changing and backing maneuvers difficult.

Modifications made to cars to suit them better to racing, off road travel, etc., often lessen their abilities as street vehicles.

Some variations are not easy to spot on other vehicles in traffic: worn out wiper blades; bald tires; carbon monoxide leaking into the passenger compartment; malfunctioning brakes, steering, engines, etc.

CARS AND THEIR DRIVERS: The kind of vehicle a person drives can easily affect the way he drives. The semi driver, high up in his cab, far above the crowd, can feel secure, even superior. These feelings, added to the truck's ponderous way of moving, may allow the semi driver to stay relaxed and be generous to other drivers.

Motorcyclists and drivers of very small, underpowered cars can easily think that they are being pushed around by the drivers of the bigger vehicles. They can easily feel threatened and become very aggressive.

Drivers of high performance and sports cars may feel unfairly blocked by the needlessly slow driving of others. Feeling cheated out of the joy of really using their high-spirited vehicles, they may take chances to get ahead to clear space.

Just as "You can't tell a book by its cover," though, you can't tell a driver by his car. While it is true that the vehicle driven affects the way its driver drives, it is equally true that one may not expect all motor vehicles always to be driven according to their image. Indeed, some drivers buy images and never drive in accord with them.

Do not assume that the driver of a high performance car will use its high performance all the time. In fact, do not assume that the driver of a high performance car is a high performance driver. He may have the car, but not the skill. Likewise, do not assume that the econobox or luxury car will never be driven flat out in a great rush.

Do not assume that the driver of a taxicab must be an absolute master of making time in impossible traffic, or that he will cut off as many people as he can.

Do not assume that a driver education car is being driven by a student. The instructor may be doing those clumsy maneuvers.

By the way, this seat was not invented for the first driver ed. teacher.

YOUR DREAM CAR: With driving experience, you will find that there is no perfect car. The car you drive should fit your real needs, not just some fantasy you have about yourself and your vehicle. An absolutely wonderful, powerful sportscar may be a real handful in the snow. Moreover, the salt used to melt the snow will attack the steel body of your very expensive dream chariot, turning it into junk in no time. You cannot haul many friends around in a two-seater. A huge engine will burn huge amounts of gasoline. Can you afford that? A fast car will probably cost more to insure. A sport-utility vehicle may not have as much everyday utility as you expect, and it may be a very uncomfortable vehicle in which to ride. Your smooth riding boulevard cruiser will not give ultimate cornering performance. Your stick-shift can be a real inconvenience in stop-and-go, city traffic. A big van or a very long car may be hard to find a parking space for in the city. Very low slung cars usually have ground clearance problems.

Think about the most important things you need your car to do. Think about the things your car will have to do most often. Think about just exactly what kinds of pleasures you insist upon from your car. Then think about trade-offs and compromises. Decide what you will not sacrifice. Research the market. Choose the car which best meets your unique driving needs.

Someday, when you get rich, you can buy several cars to fulfill your automotive needs. Choose them carefully. Pick each to do a particular hauling, driving, travelling, etc., job perfectly.

21 *Chapter Twenty-one*

Wonderful Machines

In the beginning, cars were toys for the young, wealthy, and daring. They were dirty, noisy, impractical, socially unacceptable, expensive, and...*wonderful*! In the beginning, *all* cars were sportscars!

In the beginning, cars needed amounts of care and repair that would seem unbelievable to us today. Even with all the maintenance they got, they broke down often. The early motorist had to be a mechanic or have one at his disposal.

Cars are still wonderful and, by horseless carriage standards, they are virtually maintenance and trouble free. Today, many drivers have almost no idea about how cars work and how to keep them working. Today, the skills of a mechanic are not required of a driver.

Mechanical Knowledge will give a good driver a better understanding of what his car has to do when asked to accelerate, stop, take bumps, turn, etc. Mechanical knowledge will allow him to understand exactly what the lights and gauges on his instrument panel are and are not telling him. It will help him deal with the people who *do* work on his car. It will let him do some of the work on his car himself. It will let him understand the need for proper maintenance. It will give him some idea of how serious his car's problem might be even before he talks to a mechanic. Actually getting dirty and working on a car can be a very rewarding experience. It is also a much more educational experience than one might at first think. Learning to work on a car under a really good mechanic, one delights in seeing how the principles he learned in high school physics apply to real machinery.

This book about driving cannot hope to give any more than the most basic information about automobile mechanics. Many whole books have been written about auto mechanics and about very small areas of auto mechanics: engine rebuilding, suspensions, carburetors, ignition systems, transmissions, etc. Finally, technology is expanding so rapidly today that it is impossible to cover all the variations on the basics.

The Engine

Cars have been powered by gas and diesel internal combustion engines, steam engines, electric motors, jet engines, etc. This chapter will deal only with the most common automobile engine, the four cycle, gasoline engine.

Engines have cylinders. You have probably heard of engines with one, two, four, six, eight, or 12 cylinders. Some engines have three, five, 10, or 16 cylinders. What is a cylinder? A cylinder is a tube. In the case of an automobile engine, a cylinder is usually a tubular hole bored through an iron engine block. For now, think of the block as just that, a big block of iron with some cylinders bored through it.

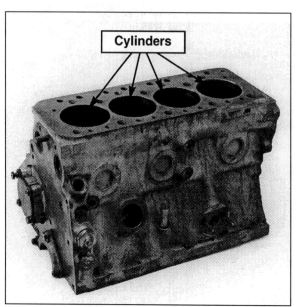

Cylinders

Combustion chambers are where the gas is burned to make the power. The sides of the combustion chambers are formed by the walls of the top ends of the cylinders. The top of the combustion chamber is formed by a lid (the cylinder head or head) attached to the top of the block. The bottom of the combustion chamber is formed by a piston. The piston can be thought of as similar in shape to a straight sided water glass turned upside-down.

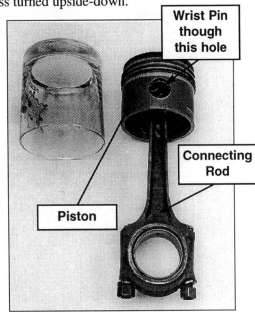

Through the piston is a wrist pin. This pin allows the piston to be connected to the crankshaft by a connecting rod.

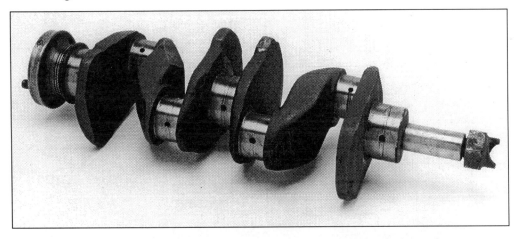

The crankshaft is bolted to the bottom of the engine block at its main journals.

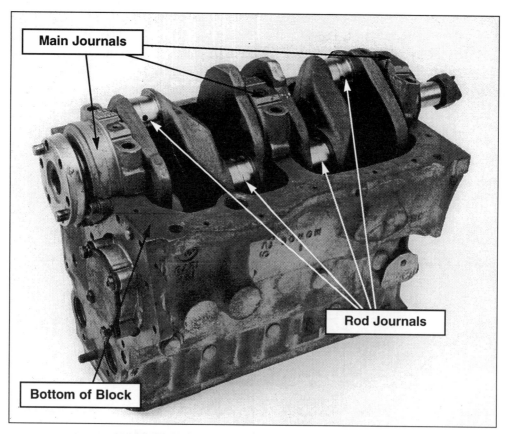

The crankshaft is free to turn, because its main journals run in bearings.

The pistons are connected to the crankshaft's rod journals by the connecting rods.

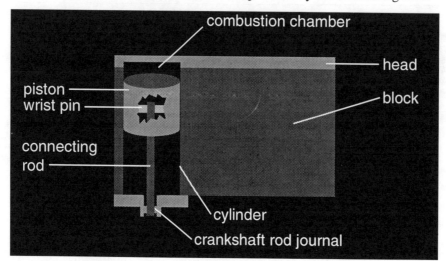

Every time gasoline is burned in a given combustion chamber, that combustion chamber's piston is forced down and turns the crankshaft, just like the bike rider's feet and legs push down and turn the crankset of a bicycle sending power to the rear wheel.

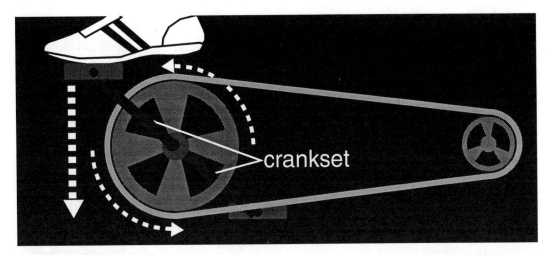

The crankshaft sends power to the clutch in a stick shift car or the torque convertor in an automatic transmission car.

Both the automobile engine's crankshaft and the bicycle's crankset change the direction of power from straight down to twisting.

Just as pushing down one pedal in a bicycle's crankset pushes the other pedal up so that it can be pushed down again, the power stroke of one piston pushes the other pistons up through their compression and exhaust strokes and down through their intake strokes to get ready for their power strokes.

The gasoline gets into the combustion chambers through valves. The exhaust gases get out through valves. The valves are usually stuck through holes in the cylinder head and kept closed by springs.

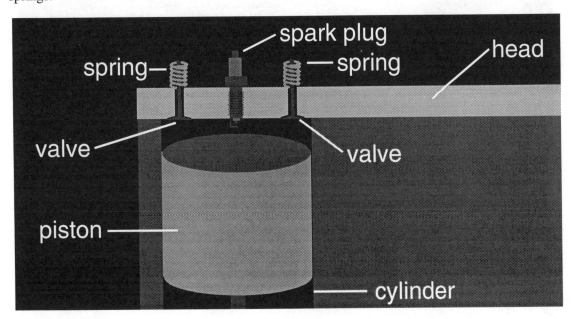

The valves are opened by a camshaft. The camshaft has cam lobes on it.

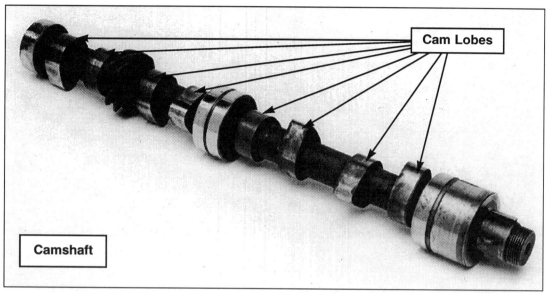

Cam Lobes

Camshaft

As the camshaft turns, the cam lobes force open the valves, either directly (overhead cam) or indirectly through a system of pushrods and rocker arms. Valve springs close the valves when the cam lobes release them.

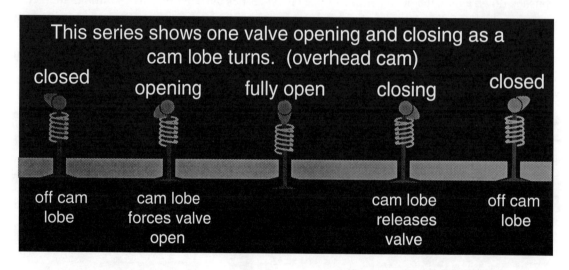

This series shows one valve opening and closing as a cam lobe turns. (overhead cam)

closed — opening — fully open — closing — closed

off cam lobe — cam lobe forces valve open — cam lobe releases valve — off cam lobe

Altogether, it works like this:

THE FOUR STROKE OR OTTO CYCLE

1. Intake

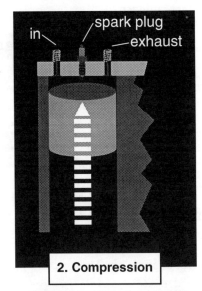

2. Compression

1. INTAKE
On the intake stroke, the piston is moving down. The intake valve is open to let in fuel;

2. COMPRESSION
On the compression stroke the piston is moving up to squeeze the fuel mixture together. Both valves are closed;

3. POWER
On the power stroke the spark plug fires and burns the fuel. The expansion of the burning fuel forces the piston down to turn the crankshaft and make power to run the car. Both valves are closed;

4. EXHAUST
On the exhaust stroke the piston moves back up to push out the exhaust gases. The exhaust valve is open.

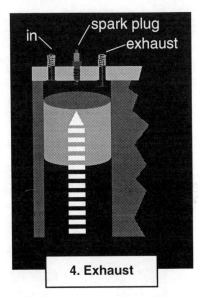

3. Power

4. Exhaust

The cycle keeps repeating. The valves open at the right time because the camshaft is connected to the crankshaft by timing gears. These gears may be connected directly or by a timing chain or timing belt.

That is how the engine makes power by burning gasoline. There is much more going on under the hood, though. Several other systems are needed for the engine to operate properly.

FUEL SYSTEM: Gasoline is pumped from the gas tank to the engine through a tube (fuel line) by a fuel pump. Along the way, the gas is filtered. Gasoline cannot burn without oxygen. Oxygen is one of the gases in air. Gasoline is mixed with air by either a carburetor or a fuel injection system.

The air is actually sucked into the engine on the intake stroke of each piston. As each piston moves down on its intake stroke, it creates a partial vacuum in its cylinder by increasing the volume of that cylinder.

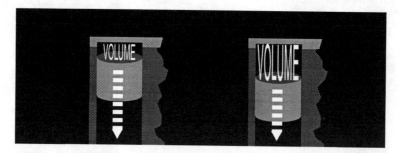

During the intake stroke of each piston, that cylinder's intake valve is open. Ordinary air pressure outside the car forces air into the cylinder to fill the partial vacuum.

First, though, this air goes through an air filter. Then, in a carbureted engine, it goes through the carburetor. In the carburetor, gasoline is sprayed into the moving air to form a cloud of gas droplets surrounded by air. This mixture moves through pipes (intake manifold) to the intake valve of each cylinder.

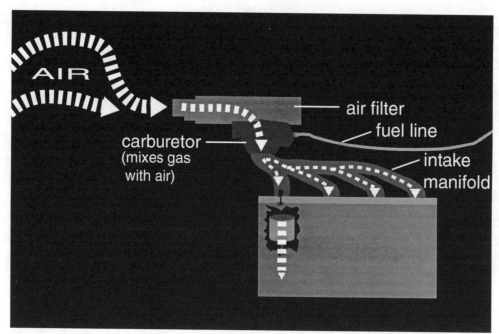

Number one piston on intake stroke, moves down, creates partial vacuum, which sucks air in through air filter, carburetor, intake manifold, and intake valve

A fuel injected engine does not have a carburetor. Gasoline is sprayed into the intake manifold just above each intake valve (port injection) or at the beginning of the intake manifold, where the carburetor would have been (throttle body fuel injection).

EXHAUST SYSTEM: After the fuel mixture has been burned, forcing the piston down on its power stroke, the exhaust valve opens as the piston moves back up to force out the exhaust gases.

356

These gases move through pipes (exhaust manifold) into the exhaust pipe. Then they go through the catalytic convertor, where they are cleaned. Another pipe takes them to the muffler, which quiets them. They leave through the tail pipe.

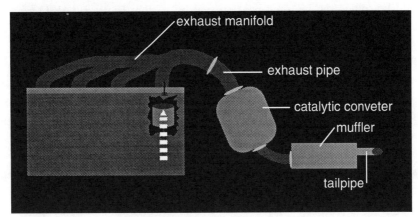

Piston moves up on its exhaust stroke, pushing exhaust gases through the exhaust valve and through the rest of the exhaust system

IGNITION SYSTEM: The ignition system is what sets fire to the air/gasoline mixture. Actually, a spark at the tip of the spark plug sets fire to the air/gasoline mixture. The ignition system makes and delivers that spark.

Low voltage electricity (usually 12 volts) flows from the battery through the coil to a switching device. This switch used to be the breaker points in the bottom of the distributor. Breaker points have been replaced in modern electronic ignition systems. The switching device breaks up the electricity into little bits. Each interruption of the flow of electricity causes the coil to increase the voltage greatly (from six, 12, or 24 volts to many thousand volts). Then the high voltage electricity is sent back to the top part of the distributor. There, another switching device (this used to be the rotor) distributes these high voltage bits of electricity through wires to each spark plug at just the right time to fire the mixture in each cylinder. The spark arrives on time, because the distributor is run by a gear off the camshaft which, you remember, is connected to the crankshaft by other gears. The design of an engine makes each engine part do the right thing at the right time.

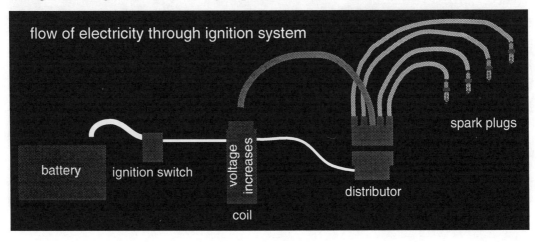

357

LUBRICATION SYSTEM: But for an amazingly thin film of oil, many parts of an automobile engine would rub directly against each other. They would scratch and wear each other. Without lubrication, the engine would wear out soon after it was started. Even before it could wear out, though, it would be ruined by the great heat created by all that friction. *Lubrication is vital to an engine!* Oil lubricates. Oil also cleans, cools, and seals.

A cover is bolted to the bottom of the engine block. This cover is called the oil pan. An oil pump sucks up oil from the oil pan and pumps it under pressure via passageways throughout the engine to keep everything properly lubricated. The oil is also pumped through a filter to help keep it clean. After lubricating whichever engine parts it is sent to, the oil drips down into the oil pan to be used again. Actually looking at the parts of an engine and learning how cleverly the lubrication system is designed is a delight.

COOLING SYSTEM: There are engines designed to be cooled directly by air. Most engines, however, are water cooled. The engine block not only has cylinders bored through it, it is full of oil passages and large, water passages. The head, likewise, has oil and water passages.

Heat from a running engine is picked up by the water circulating through the water jacket (the large, water passages in the block and head). The hot water is circulated by a water pump to the radiator. The water moves through small tubes in the radiator and is cooled by air passing over the tubes. The cooled water is then pumped back into the engine to pick up more heat.

The air gets to the radiator through the car's grille or cooling air intake, because the car is moving. When the car is not moving or not moving fast enough, the air flow is provided by a fan.

Hoses connect the radiator and engine. Hoses also connect the engine and heater. Yes, the heat from your car's heater comes from the water which was heated by the engine.

An engine should not run too hot, but it should not run too cold either. A thermostat controls engine temperature by opening and closing to let more or less water flow through the radiator.

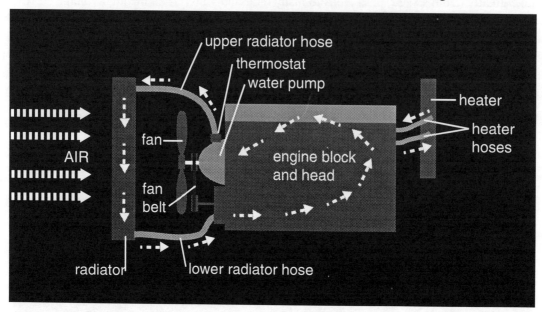

ELECTRICAL SYSTEM: The car's lights and all other electrical accessories need electricity. The engine needs electricity to run. The engine needs electricity to start.

When you turn the ignition key, you close an electric switch. Electricity from the battery, where it is stored, flows to the engine and the starter. The starter is a small electric motor. Its job is to turn the crankshaft. The turning crankshaft then forces everything in the engine to operate. The pistons go up and down, the valves open and close, etc. Air, gasoline, oil, water, and electricity all flow to and through the engine as they should. When the spark plugs begin to burn the gas, the engine has been started. You let go of the ignition key, and the engine is running on its own.

The electricity to fire the spark plugs, work the starter, and power all the electrical accessories comes from the battery. The battery is kept charged by an alternator (older cars used a generator). The alternator makes electricity. It is driven by a belt connected to the engine by pulleys. A voltage regulator keeps the battery from getting overcharged.

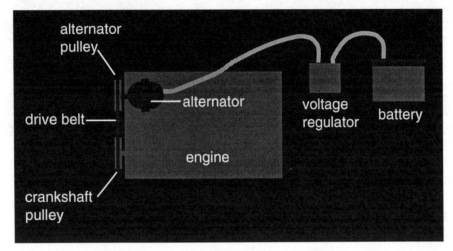

ENGINE LAYOUT: The two most usual engine layouts are V as in V-6, V-8, V-12, and straight or in-line as in straight 6 or in-line 4. What is a V-8 engine, or a straight six? The number tells how many cylinders an engine has. Straight or V refers to the way the cylinders are laid out — the shape of the block.

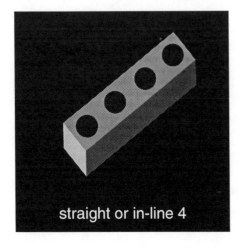

straight or in-line 4

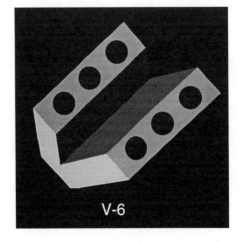

V-6

Drive Train

The drive train delivers the engine's power to the drive wheels. The drive train is a series of mechanical devices connected together like the cars of a train.

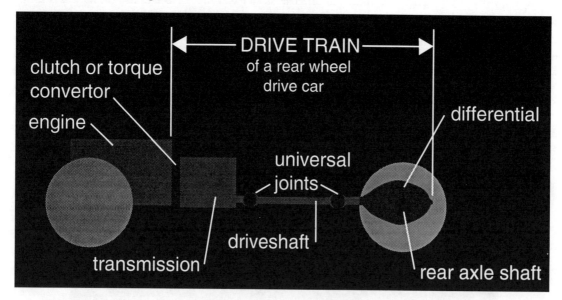

CLUTCH/TORQUE CONVERTOR: These are the connecting/disconnecting links between the engine and transmission. (See Chapters 4 and 22.)

TRANSMISSION: The transmission is a system of gears which are shifted either by the driver (stick shift), or automatically (automatic transmission). The transmission gives the car forward and reverse capability, neutral capability (the engine runs but cannot move the car), and, with several forward gear ratios, matches the engine's power to the wide range of acceleration and speed needs of driving. (See Chapter 4.)

DRIVESHAFT: Rear wheel drive cars need a driveshaft to get the power from the front of the car to the rear, where the drive wheels are.

UNIVERSAL JOINTS: The driveshaft connects the transmission to the differential. The transmission is mounted solidly to the car's frame. The differential, however, is in the rear axle housing. The rear axle housing is mounted on springs so that the rear wheels can move up and down with road irregularities. This presents a problem. As the car moves, the rear end of the driveshaft is constantly moving up and down, while the front end stays in the same relative position to the rest of the car. Without universal joints, it would be impossible for the driveshaft to turn and deliver power to the differential under these conditions. Universal joints, due to their clever design, can flex at the same time they are rotating. A universal joint at each end of the driveshaft allows it to work properly even though the rear axle housing is being bounced around by the road surface.

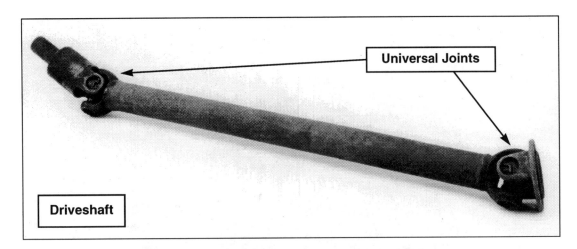

DIFFERENTIAL: Inside the rear axle housing is the differential or rear end. It is a set of gears which does two remarkable things. First, the ring and pinion gears turn the rotating power from the driveshaft at right angles to be used by the rear drive wheels.

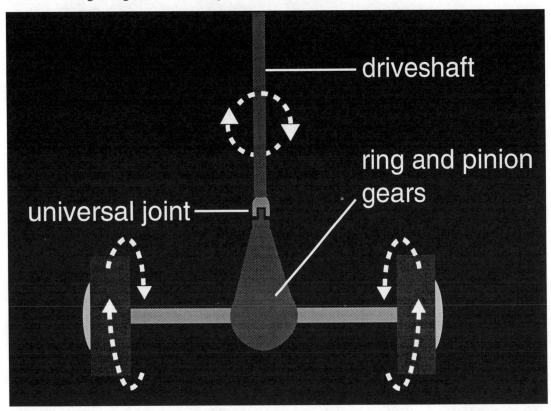

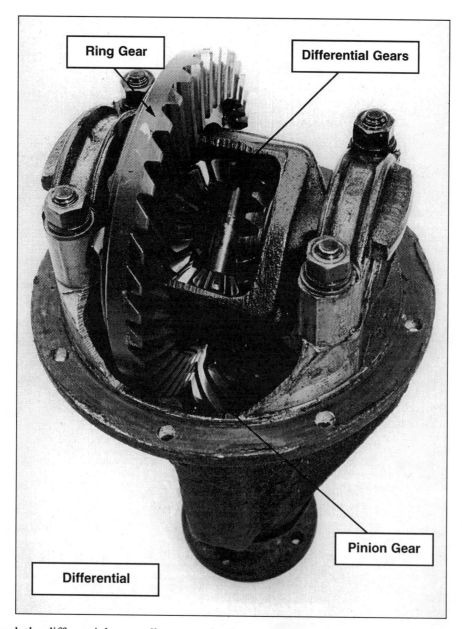

Ring Gear

Differential Gears

Pinion Gear

Differential

Second, the differential gears allow one wheel to go faster or slower than the other even though both wheels are connected to each other. When a car goes around a corner, the outside wheels travel farther than the inside wheels.

The problem is that both the inside and outside wheels must travel their different distances in the same amount of time. Therefore, the inside wheels must turn slower than the outside wheels. This is no problem at the front, because the front wheels roll independently of each other. The rear wheels are *both* driven indirectly by the driveshaft. It turns at only one speed —whatever speed the driver dictates through the engine and transmission.

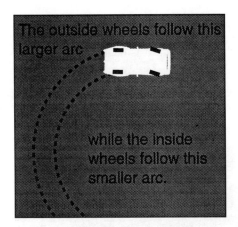

The outside wheels follow this larger arc, while the inside wheels follow this smaller arc.

The problem is solved by differential gears. The two rear axle shafts (one to each wheel) are connected to differential gears in the differential. The differential gears allow the inside wheel to coast while they feed power only to the outside wheel. Therefore, the inside wheel can roll as slowly as needed, while the outside wheel powers the car through the turn.

If not for the differential gears in the differential, the rear end of the car would skip around on turns.

On front wheel drive cars, the differential does its wonders for the front wheels. On front wheel drive cars, the rear wheels just roll free.

LIMITED SLIP DIFFERENTIALS: Part of the reason cars get stuck is differential gears. They keep sending power to the wheel which is moving faster. When your car is stuck in snow, one drive wheel is getting all the power because it has less traction than its mate. It keeps spinning. Therefore, it keeps getting the power. The other drive wheel just stands still. Locking differentials or limited slip differentials eliminate this problem. They are also useful in racing and offroad use.

REAR AXLE SHAFTS: The rear axle shafts connect the differential to the rear wheels. The rear axle shafts turn the rear wheels to move the car.

FRONT WHEEL DRIVE CARS: Front wheel drive cars do not have a driveshaft or its universal joints. They do have a clutch or a torque convertor, a transmission, a differential, and axles. These are all in the front end of the car. The axle shafts are connected from the differential to the drive wheels by constant velocity or c.v. joints. They are based on the idea of the universal joint.

Suspension

The tires of your car stand on the ground. They are mounted on wheels which are connected to axles which are connected to the car by springs. The springs hold up the rest of the car. The car is suspended on its springs. It stands on its springs. Springs give cars a smoother ride by allowing the wheels and tires to ride up and over bumps and down into and out of holes without the whole car having to go up and down. Without springs, the whole car would tend to bounce and leap into the air on bumpy surfaces, making control at modern speeds very difficult.

Springs cannot do the whole job themselves, though, because they tend to keep bouncing and bouncing after each bump. If not controlled, this bouncing would make the car very unstable, because the tires would not be pressed into firm contact with the road surface, and the car's weight would be thrown around all over the place. Shock absorbers control the springs' bouncing, keeping the car's weight under control and pressing the tires against the road.

The British call shock absorbers dampers. That term describes their job much better. Springs absorb shock. Shock absorbers dampen the action of the springs. Springs give a comfortable ride. Shock absorbers keep the tires on the road.

Many modern cars' suspensions combine springs and shock absorbers into one unit — the MacPherson strut.

Steering System

The most common type of steering system today is rack and pinion. It is beautifully simple. When the steering wheel is turned, the pinion gear turns, moving the steering rack left or right. The rack is attached to the tie rods. They move left or right, forcing the front wheels to turn left or right. The tie rod ends pivot to allow for the up and down movement of the front wheels as they run over surface irregularities.

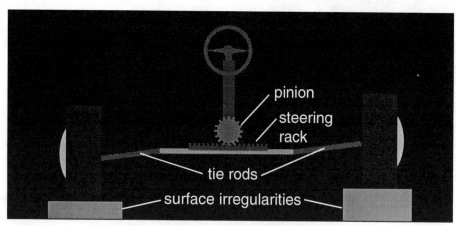

Brake System

When you step on the brake pedal, a piston in the brake master cylinder pushes against hydraulic fluid in brake lines (tubes) connecting the master cylinder to slave cylinders at all four wheels. Liquid cannot be compressed. Therefore, applying force to brake fluid in the brake lines is just like applying force to levers or cables. Wherever the tube goes, the brake fluid goes, carrying the force with it.

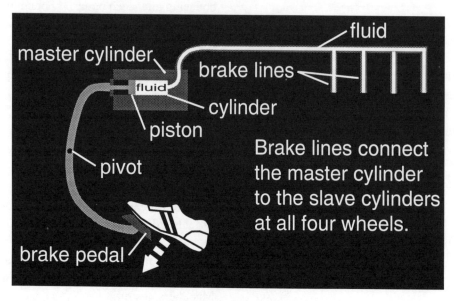

Modern cars have disc brakes. At each wheel there is a disc (or rotor) and a caliper. Inside the caliper are pistons in slave cylinders. The brake fluid applies a force to the pistons in the slave cylinders. The pistons move, forcing brake pads against the discs, slowing them. Because the discs are attached to the wheels, this slows and stops the car.

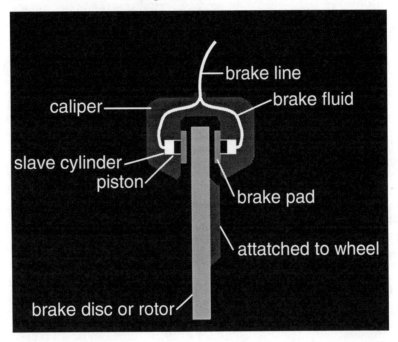

Some new vehicles may still have drum brakes on their rear wheels. Drum brakes are less effective than discs.

Up to the slave cylinders in the wheels, everything in the drum brake system is about the same as in the disc brake system. What happens at the wheels, though, is this: the pistons in the slave cylinders push against brake shoes. The brake shoes move, rubbing their brake linings against the brake drums which are attached to the wheels. The friction slows and stops the car.

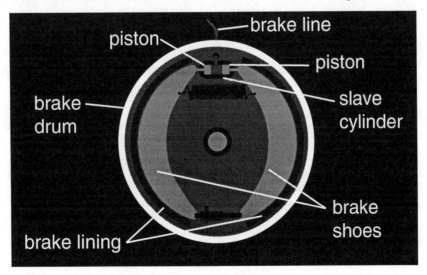

Instrument Panel

The lights and gauges in your instrument panel give you information about how your car is working. *Notice them*!

When you turn the ignition switch to the "on" position, the warning lights light. This lets you know that they are working.

Auto manufacturers are experimenting with heads up displays. These displays show information on the windshield instead of on the instrument panel.

SPEEDOMETER: The speedometer tells you how fast the car is going.

ODOMETER: The odometer shows the mileage on the car (how far it has gone). Many cars also have re-setable trip odometers.

OIL PRESSURE GAUGE/WARNING LIGHT: Oil, to do its job properly, must be pumped all through the engine *under pressure*. If the pressure falls too low, the engine will not be lubricated properly. Running an engine with little or no oil pressure will destroy the engine. If your oil pressure falls to zero while you are driving, think of it as an emergency for the engine. *IMMEDIATELY pull over and turn off the engine! Do not drive the car again until the oil pressure has been restored!*

Low oil pressure can be caused by low oil level. The oil pressure gauge or warning light does not tell you how much oil is in your engine. To find that out, you must check the oil dipstick under the hood. If your oil level is low, add oil and recheck the oil pressure.

As an engine is used, it wears. Wear causes the very narrow clearances at engine bearings to widen. Engine bearings must be lubricated under pressure. The wider the bearing clearances get, the lower the oil pressure falls. Low oil pressure readings are common on very worn engines. They mean that the engine must soon be replaced or rebuilt. If the engine is not replaced or rebuilt, it will eventually destroy itself.

The oil pressure in a worn engine may drop to nearly zero at idling speed, but return to a more or less normal reading at driving speed. The problem is the same as above, increased bearing clearance. Do not expect long service from this engine.

The screen over the oil pickup in the oil pan can clog. This can also cause low oil pressure.

Finally, the oil pump itself can wear. The most likely cause of low oil pressure, however, is wear on engine bearings.

The oil pressure warning light is designed to light up at about three pounds per square inch of oil pressure. This is virtually nothing. *Do not drive with the oil pressure warning light lit*! The oil pressure warning light may light up or flicker at idle, but go out at driving speed. This means the same thing as the serious falling off of the reading on the oil pressure gauge at idle means. The engine is almost worn out.

TEMPERATURE GAUGE/WARNING LIGHT: Your car's engine is designed to run between certain temperatures. If your engine runs too cold, it may give poor performance and eventually develop problems. Your heater will give little heat if your engine runs too cold. If an engine runs too hot for any length of time, it can destroy itself. Your temperature *gauge* tells you whether your engine is running in the correct temperature range. Your temperature *warning light* tells you that the engine is running too hot.

One obvious cause of a hot running engine is lack of water in the cooling system. In modern cars, coolant (anti-freeze and water) level is checked by looking at the coolant recovery bottle. This is a plastic bottle connected by a hose to the radiator.

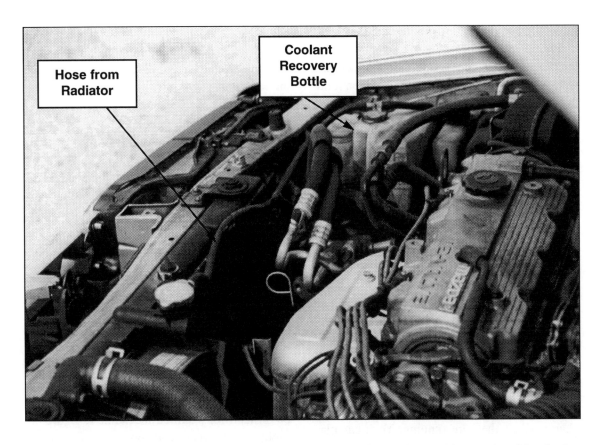

If the bottle is empty, add water and/or anti-freeze to it. The liquid will eventually be sucked into the radiator. In older cars, coolant level is checked by taking off the radiator cap and looking into the radiator. This can result in steam and boiling coolant being sprayed on people. Today the radiator or radiator cap has a warning on it not to open the radiator when the engine is hot. First thing in the morning before you have started the engine, you may open the radiator, take a look, and add coolant with no danger to yourself or the engine. Notice when you open the radiator cap that it seems to unlock twice. It does. This is a safety feature. When the engine is hot, open only to the first lock to let the steam escape. When the steam stops, open all the way. For both openings, cover the cap with a heavy rag to control heat and spray.

Summer or winter, your car should run a 50/50 mix of anti-freeze and water. Remember that anti-freeze has nothing to do with whether your car will start in winter. Anti-freeze keeps the water in the cooling system from freezing. Freezing water expands. Engines have been cracked by freezing water expanding inside them. One hundred percent anti-freeze is *not* better than anti-freeze and water.

Your car may overheat in heavy traffic on a very hot day. Stuck in traffic, your car will not be moving much. Therefore, very little air will blow through the radiator to cool the coolant. The coolant will just keep picking up heat from the engine and get hotter and hotter. First, turn off the air conditioning. This should lower the coolant temperature. Next, open the windows and turn on the heater. The heat from the heater comes from the hot engine coolant. By putting some of that heat into the passenger compartment, you are taking it away from the engine. If you can get out of the traffic and move the car, do it. This should cool things off nicely.

The temperature gauge and temperature warning light get their information from a sending unit attached to the engine. If this sending unit is bad, it can send a hot reading back when the engine is actually running at a good temperature. If your car's warning light comes on too often, replace the sending unit. That may solve the problem.

A blocked grille or air intake, or a radiator all plugged up with rust inside or ice, bugs, or mud outside can also lead to overheating.

Finally, your radiator cap may have failed.

Overheating is not an emergency. Get to a service station immediately or pull over, shut off the engine, open the hood, and call for help.

AMMETER, VOLTMETER/BATTERY DISCHARGE LIGHT: An ammeter is a gauge which shows whether the battery is being charged. Modern cars should show a slight charge when they are running. Your car may have a voltmeter. It serves the same basic purpose. The warning light may say: "volts," "batt," "discharge," "alt." Whatever it says, if it lights up, it is telling you that your battery is not being charged. The trouble may be with the alternator, voltage regulator, battery, the belt which drives the alternator, or an electrical connection. Battery discharge is not an extremely serious problem like no oil pressure, or even a serious problem like boiling engine coolant. It is a problem which can wait a while to be repaired. In other words, you can probably drive home or to your own service place with no trouble. While driving there, though, use as little electricity as possible. For example, do not use the radio or air conditioner. If the temperature light comes on just after the battery discharge light, probably the fan belt which drives both the alternator and the water pump has broken. Modern cars have one serpentine belt to

drive *all* engine ancillaries. If your serpentine belt breaks, your engine will overheat, your battery will discharge, and your power steering and air conditioner will stop working.

GAS GAUGE: This gauge tells you how much gas is in the tank. "E" means <u>e</u>mpty not <u>e</u>nough.

TACHOMETER: Sportscars have tachometers (tachs). They tell you how fast the engine is running in revolutions per minute (R.P.M.).

BRAKE WARNING LIGHT: This comes on when the engine is running and the parking brake is engaged. It also comes on to warn of partial brake failure.

Driver Inspections and Simple Maintenance

The modern automobile is very complex. It can be difficult for a skilled mechanic to figure out problems. A driver with no mechanical background may fear trying to do any automotive checking or maintenance by himself. There are, however, quite a few things which can be checked and maintained by a driver with just a little training.

WINDOWS: Clearly, windows can be kept clean by just about anybody.

LIGHTS: It is easy to check your car's lights. You can even check your brake lights and back up lights by stepping on the brake pedal while the car is in reverse and its rear end is reflected to you by a window or the glass in a shop door.

TIRES: Buy a tire gauge and learn how to use it. Then learn how to use the air pump at the gas station. These are two very useful things for a driver to know how to do. Once you know them, you will be amazed at how simple they are.

Check your tire pressure at least once a month. If possible, check it before driving when the tires are cold. Heat generated in the tires by driving increases their air pressure. Even the sun's beating on the tires on one side of your car can raise the pressure in them above that of the tires on the shady side.

Before checking tire pressure, release just a bit of air. This will blow away any dirt which might be on the air valve. Dirt should not be blown into the tire gauge. Dropping a tire gauge may affect its accuracy.

Look at your tires, too. Tires with cracked, dried out sidewalls should be replaced. Look for cuts, etc. If you find any, have them checked by a competent, honest mechanic. Tires with bubbles on the sides should not be used. Look at the sides of the tires which are under the car, too.

Check sides of tires under the car, too

Check your tires' tread. Tread depth gauges are very inexpensive. Lacking a gauge, you can use a penny. Put the penny into the tread grooves with the top of Lincoln's head toward the tire. If you can see all of Lincoln's hair, the tire is worn too much to be legal.

With a bit of practice, you can depend on just your eyes to judge the general safety of a tire.

Modern tires have tread wear indicators. These are bands of rubber which appear across the tire tread in several places when the tire is reaching the limit of its legal tread depth. Wear indicators are easy to notice if you look at your tires regularly.

When using a tread depth gauge or penny, use it in several places around the tire to avoid a false reading caused by measuring right on top of the tread wear indicator. Use the gauge or penny all across the tire, too, to check for uneven wear.

Varying tread wear patterns mean different things. Probably the most common type of wasteful tread wear is this.

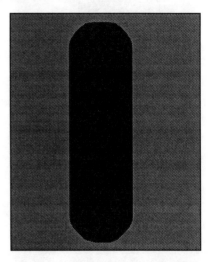

The tread is worn at the edges, but still good in the middle of the tire. This problem is caused by under-inflation, simply not keeping enough air in the tire. An under-inflated tire runs like this.

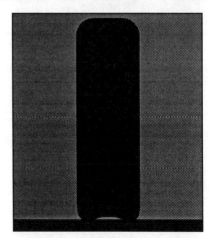

Middle of tire touches road very little

Therefore, it wears out like this

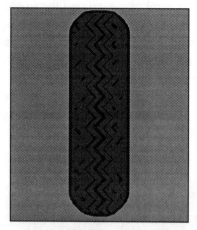

A properly inflated tire runs like this.

Tread runs flat on the road

Therefore, its wear is even all across the tread.

On the other hand, an over-inflated tire would run like this.

The middle of the tire bulges and carries most of the weight

Therefore, its wear pattern would look like this.

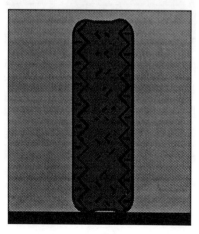

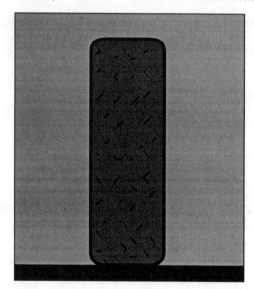

Tires with worn tread are less efficient in gripping on snow; icy, muddy, wet, etc. roads. Tires with less tread hydroplane more easily.

On dry roads, slicks (racing tires designed to have no tread) grip the best. Racing tires are *not designed to be used on the road*, though. The best street tires are designed to be the best street tires. Do not try to outsmart the tire engineers.

There is quite a lot of information about tires available in magazines, in books, from tire dealers, etc. Proper inflation pressure and other information are printed right on the sidewall of the tire.

CHECK THE OIL: To check the amount of oil in the engine, pull the dipstick. Wipe it off. Put it *all the way* back into the slot. Pull it out again and see how far up the stick the oil is. This stick is marked.

If you check the oil first thing in the morning, before starting the engine, you do not need to wipe off the dipstick, because the oil is all settled in the oil pan. MAKE SURE THAT THE CAR IS SITTING ON A LEVEL AREA AND THAT THE ENGINE IS NOT RUNNING WHEN YOU CHECK THE OIL!

You do not need to wait until the oil level is down to where the dipstick says to add one quart. You can add a cup, etc., whenever necessary. NEVER OVERFILL! Add engine oil through the oil filler opening.

Do not let your half-full container of oil get contaminated. Resealable plastic oil bottles make this easy. Do not knock dirt into the engine's oil filler or the dipstick slot.

CHECKING THE AUTOMATIC TRANSMISSION FLUID: On a level area, with the engine *running* and the transmission in park, check the automatic transmission fluid. Check your owner's manual to find out whether the car should be completely warmed up or not. Pull the transmission oil dipstick and wipe it. (Use lint-free cloth or paper to wipe dipsticks.) Replace the stick and pull it back out again. The oil level will be shown just as it is on the engine oil dipstick. Notice, though, that the "add" mark will probably be at one pint, not one quart.

NEVER OVERFILL! This is even more important with the automatic transmission than the engine. Add transmission fluid through the dipstick tube using a funnel.

BATTERY: Look at the condition of the battery terminals and cables. They should not be corroded. With batteries which are not sealed, you can open the vents in the top and look inside to see the electrolyte level. If it is low, fill with distilled water. *Do not overfill!* Find out how far to fill. Check each vent because each battery cell is separate.

Batteries contain acid. Be careful, especially about putting your soiled finger into your eye or splashing your eyes!

POWER STEERING FLUID: Unscrew the cap on your power steering fluid reservoir. There is a dipstick attached to it. Read it. Use power steering fluid in your power steering, not automatic transmission fluid. They are *not* the same.

WINDSHIELD WASHER FLUID RESERVOIR: Keep this full, especially in very dirty driving conditions like melting snow. Windshield washer fluid will not freeze at normal cold temperatures. Be sure to use it in the winter. In the summer, water may be used, but windshield washer fluid will clean bugs off the windshield better.

Make sure that you do not add engine antifreeze to the windshield washer bottle or vice versa.

DRIVE BELTS: Look at the belts which drive your power steering, alternator, fan, air conditioning, etc. Look for fraying and/or glazing.

HOSES: Look for leaks around hoses. Look for cracks or bubbles on hoses.

LEAKS: Look under the car for leaks. Start by parking on a clean area, or you may be checking somebody else's leaks. See what color the leaked liquid is, and note where under the car you found it. Color and location of leaking fluid help you learn which part is leaking. Look for leaks in the engine compartment. Look for leaks at the wheels.

Like any other liquid, gasoline can leak. A gas leak is obviously the most dangerous.

Common Problems

The automotive technology explosion has lead to great variation in technical details among modern cars. As a result, much of the standard, general advice given about handling many common problems has become less standard and less general. It has, however, gotten easier to give: *read your owner's manual.* Read other books and magazines on the subject. Call an expert. Join a motor club (an organization which gives roadside assistance).

CHANGING A TIRE: Changing a tire is *not* a great cosmic mystery. The instructions are given in your owner's manual and/or some place in the trunk. Jacking instructions may be on the jack. Some standardized, general advice can be given, though.

Park the car to be jacked up on the best surface available, on the most level ground, and as far away from traffic as possible. Jacking a car on mud or sand can be very frustrating, or very funny, depending on how you look at it: You jack up the car and take off the flat tire. You return with the spare tire and find that there is not enough clearance between the bottom of the spare and the ground. The jack has sunk into the soft surface, lowering the car. On a very soft surface, the car may never rise at all. The jack may just work itself into the ground. A wide, stout board under the jack's base may help. Another surprise reason for not being able to fit the spare tire is that the old tire had just stayed flat on the bottom, even after it had been raised off the ground. A car jacked high enough to remove this flat-bottomed tire is not jacked high enough for the new, circular tire to clear.

Use the most level area available, because cars fall off jacks. Cars fall off jacks not only forward and backward. Very high crowned streets can cause cars to fall off jacks sideways.

Get the car away from traffic, especially fast highway or expressway traffic, because people can get hit by cars while changing tires.

Make sure that the jack is situated properly and that it is standing solidly on its base. Check for stability before, during, and after jacking and before removing or replacing a tire. *Do not think that holding or leaning on your car will keep it from falling off a jack*! Jack the car only as high as necessary. Place chocks in front of and behind the wheel diagonally opposite to the one to be changed.

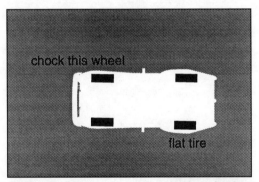

Chock the wheel diagonally opposite the one to be changed.

Chock both front and rear of wheel

Get everything you'll need out of the car BEFORE jacking. If the car falls, the trunk lid will slam shut. If you are reaching into the trunk when the lid slams …. Get what you'll need from the passenger compartment before jacking, too.

Use the lug wrench to break loose the lug nuts BEFORE jacking up the car.

Make sure that the spare wheel is seating properly before, during and after hand tightening the lug nuts.

Do not sit with your feet or legs under the car while working on it. The car can fall. Try to hold the tires in a way that keeps your hands and arms in the safest position, in case the car does fall.

This

Not this

Along the same line of thinking, do not stick your head under the fender.

While changing the tires, do not lose the lug nuts. When cars commonly had hubcaps, the idea was to put the nuts into the upturned hubcap. The next idea was not to kick over the hubcap and spill the lug nuts down the sewer.

After snugging down the lug nuts with the lug wrench, lower the car until the spare tire is touching the ground and some of the car's weight is on it. Then finish tightening the lug nuts with the lug wrench. Tighten them hard, but do not try to break them off. Use a criss-cross pattern for tightening lug nuts.

When you are finished, stow everything again. Before leaving, recheck the area for tools, parts, etc. Do not forget to have the flat tire repaired. When the job is finished, it is nice to have something with which to clean your hands.

If your car has a space saver spare tire, it is a good idea to carry a truck tire gauge. Space saver spares are designed to run at air pressures higher than can be measured by automobile tire gauges.

Note: when working *under* the car, place the car on jack stands. *NEVER rely on just a jack to hold up a car under which you are working!*

CAR WILL NOT START: Check the owner's manual. Call for help. The best way to deal with breakdowns is to be signed up with a roadside assistance plan.

In very humid weather, the starter may crank the engine well, but moisture on the distributor cap, coil, distributor, spark plugs, or spark plug cables prevents the engine from firing. Try to dry them with silicone spray. Spray thoroughly. Then wait for the silicone to work before trying again to start the engine.

A car which is out of gas will not start — period.

JUMP-STARTING: A jump-start may help if your car's starter will not function or operates very slowly, because of a dead or weak battery. To jump-start, you'll need jumper cables. *Do not buy cheap ones!* They might work once and never again. Get high quality cables. Use them carefully. Take care of them and protect them from theft. Do this with *all* tools!

Check battery locations of both cars. Place cars so that the distance between their batteries is the least possible. Park the assisting car near *but not touching* the non-starting car. Turn off the assisting car's engine. Turn off ignition and all accessories on non-starting car. Attach one end of the *red* cable to the positive (+) terminal of the dead battery. Attach the other end to the positive (+) terminal of the assisting car's battery. Do not let cable ends touch each other or either car while attaching them. Attach one end of the *black* cable to the negative (-) terminal of the assisting car's battery. Attach the other end of the black cable to the engine or frame of the car to be started, not to its battery. This is because there will always be a spark on making or breaking this last connection. Attaching this cable to the engine or frame will keep that spark away from any explosive hydrogen gas which may have escaped from the battery. Batteries do explode, injuring even mechanics.

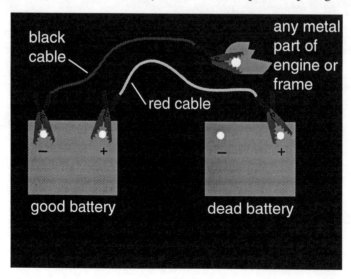

Check that the cables are clear of fan blades, etc. Start the assisting car. Try to start the other car. Remove the cables carefully in the reverse order from which they were attached. Remove the black cable from the engine or frame first. Once again, do not touch cables together or to either car.

376

Do not shut off the engine until you get home or to help. Assume that the engine will not start again until the battery and charging system have been checked and the problem put right.

DRAGGING EXHAUST SYSTEM: Usually, you can stop a broken tailpipe, muffler, etc., from dragging by tying it to the car until repairs can be made. Use wire. String might burn. Make sure that you do not tie the broken piece to something which moves. Expect the exhaust system part to be hot. Use gloves or a rag to protect yourself. Watch out for sharp edges and rust.

Any time you are doing anything under a car, be sure to protect your eyes. It is very easy to get things into them. *Do not put your head and especially your eyes directly under your work*! Be careful in the engine compartment, too. Do not get burned. Do not get an electric shock. If the engine is running, be very careful to avoid moving parts.

Pay Attention

In addition to paying attention to the road, the traffic, the signs, the signals, the weather, the laws, etc., pay attention to your car! Listen! Feel! Smell! Look!

Pay attention to how your car sounds when it is operating properly. That way you will notice unusual sounds. When you do hear something unusual, try to notice when it is happening: when accelerating, when starting the engine, when braking, etc. Try to figure out whether the sound is in the car, under the car, in the engine compartment, etc. Is the sound a grinding, tapping, thumping, growling, moaning, rattling, squeaking, etc? Is it rhythmic, constant, intermittent?

As you encounter various noise causing car problems, you will learn how they sound. Remember the sound for the future. You might also ask a very knowledgeable driver or mechanic you know the causes of the sounds you hear together from other people's cars.

A loud, rumbling engine sound under the car means a bad exhaust system. A puffing, chuffing, or hissing sound under the car may also mean a bad exhaust system.

A jingling, tinkling, or ratcheting sound on acceleration is probably ping. Sometimes ping can be properly cured by using gasoline with higher octane. Sometimes ping requires mechanical attention. The pinging sound is made when the gas mixture is being fired at the wrong time. Any pinging is bad for an engine. A lot of pinging will shorten engine life.

Valve lifter noise is a tapping sound common on worn engines. A noise similar to lifter noise, only louder and heavier, is rod knock. Rod knock means that the engine is on its last legs.

A moaning sound when you turn is probably caused by low power steering fluid level.

Shrieks and squeaks on starting or revving the engine come from loose drive belts.

Pay attention to how the car rides, accelerates, handles, brakes, shifts, etc. Many problems can be felt by your kinesthetic sense. Pay attention to how the controls feel.

Pay attention to how things look, too. Take smoke, for example, Exhaust leaving the tailpipe may be blue, black, white, brown, or invisible.

Invisible is what you want. Blue means the engine is burning oil. This is probably a serious condition. White is not smoke, but water vapor. It may be just steam from condensation left in the muffler, or it may indicate a serious engine problem: cracked block, cracked head, blown head gasket. Black smoke is usually not much of a problem. Black smoke comes from too rich a mixture (too much gas and not enough air in the mixture being burned in the combustion chambers). Black smoke is normal from diesel

engines in certain conditions. Brown smoke is what comes out the tailpipe when you "burn out the carbon" with flat-out acceleration runs.

Look for leaks, dents, loose parts, things dangling under the car, etc.

Pay attention to smells. Your car should not smell as if it is burning. You know how gasoline smells. You can learn to smell the differences among engine oil, gear oil, and anti-freeze.

Carbon monoxide *DOES NOT SMELL!* Exhaust gases may smell several different ways, but none of those smells is carbon monoxide. Carbon monoxide is odorless, colorless, tasteless, and *deadly!* Carbon monoxide can seep into your car's passenger compartment and kill you.

Do not run your engine in a closed garage, etc. Pay attention to the condition of your exhaust system. Pay attention to holes in the floor of your old junk car. In heavy traffic, carbon monoxide from the vehicle ahead can enter your car through the air conditioning, heating, or defroster ducts. It is recommended that in the winter you always drive with one window open at least a crack to make sure of getting fresh air.

If you get sleepy or feel sick while driving, you may be getting carbon monoxide poisoning. If you let it continue, you might pass out and crash or suffocate. GET FRESH AIR!

Features

Once upon a time, the self-starter was a new and wonderful convenience for motorists. Today, few people ever think about hand cranking engines to start them.

Automatic transmissions meant not having to deal with a clutch pedal and shift gears for yourself.

Power steering took most of the effort out of turning the steering wheel when parking, etc.

Today, there are so many new features it is hard to keep up with them. Some will become standard. Others will be tried and discarded. More will appear in the future.

FOUR WHEEL STEERING: Some people believe that four wheel steering may be the answer to the question nobody asked.

ANTI-LOCK BRAKING SYSTEM (ABS): This will probably become standard equipment. ABS prevents the brakes from locking the wheels under very hard braking. When a sensor in a wheel detects imminent lockup, the brake on that wheel is released for an instant and re-applied. It is the same idea as pumping the brakes for yourself, but much faster. Four-wheel ABS allows directional control when stopping hard and prevents sliding stops. It allows swerving even during panic stops.

Rear wheel only anti-lock brakes are very useful in front wheel drive vehicles and other vehicles with very lightly loaded rear axles like empty pick-up trucks and vans. They keep the rear end behind the front end in panic stops.

ANTI-SPIN FEATURE: Think of anti-spin as the opposite of ABS. Sensors detect wheel spin. The system eliminates it. This gives better traction.

ANTI-SKID FEATURE: The anti-skid feature uses anti-spin technology to help avoid skidding when turning by slowing individual wheels which are losing traction.

ACTIVE SUSPENSION: An ordinary car suspension system reacts to road irregularities. It does the best it can to keep the car under control and give a good ride. Active suspension has sensors which read the road. Then suspension pieces are actually powered to deal with each road condition as it is encountered, giving even more control and a better ride.

Maintenance

Your car will not just keep operating forever without maintenance. Engine and transmission fluids must be changed. Filters must be replaced. Tires, spark plugs, etc., must be replaced from time to time. Worn out parts must be replaced. Mechanical adjustments must be made. Check your owner's manual and read at least one book on the subject of car maintenance.

Finally, this chapter is extremely limited in its coverage. Learn much more about taking care of your car. Take care of your car; it will take care of you. Get to know your car. You will want to drive it better!

22 Chapter Twenty-two

Stickshifting is More Fun

Driving a stickshift car *is* more fun than driving a car with an automatic transmission. It's more fun because it forces a driver to develop a closer relationship with his car, to understand it better, to use it better, to work *with it* rather than against it. It's like the difference between sitting on the bench at the championship game and helping to win it by playing. It's like the difference between turning on a radio and making the music yourself.

A stickshift car requires more work and more involvement from its driver, but it rewards him by helping him improve his driving performance. A stickshift car makes its driver use the clutch pedal and the gearshift lever. At each shift, the feedback from the lever and the car as a whole gives the driver more understanding and appreciation of what his car does and has to do — of how it works. This "feel" for the "machine nature" of his car allows the driver to work or cooperate better with it. That's driving. That's good.

Once the stickshift driver begins to develop this understanding of his car, this feel for it, the car responds with smoother, quicker, more economical, more sensually satisfying performance. Then, the car seems to demand even more finesse from its driver, but it keeps on helping him to get better. It lets him know when he's shifting well by obeying his commands so smoothly, so quickly, so easily, and so gracefully that shifting is not a chore or a struggle but a joy!

If you care enough and if you are sensitive enough, a perfect shift can be magical. Really! It can give you that very special feeling described as "being in harmony with the universe." It's a feeling completely different from anything in the daily routine of ordinary life. It's not just a good feeling or a happy feeling. It's that feeling you get when you know, ABSOLUTELY KNOW, from objective evidence that, at least for an instant, you did everything perfectly! It's the reward nature gives you for a masterly performance!

The wonderful thing is that you can get that feeling driving your car to work in the morning. You can get it from a perfect shift. You step on the clutch pedal, release the gas pedal, and move the gearshift lever to slip the transmission out of gear with perfect timing. You feel no lurch of the car, no resistance in the shift mechanism. It's as if everything is happening on frictionless ball bearings in a vacuum. Then you *ease* the lever so smoothly and lightly but so quickly into the proper position for the next gear. You release the clutch pedal and feed the gas again. The return from shifting to solid acceleration cannot be felt. There is no lurch, no drag between clutch engagement and gas feed. There is no revving of the engine a moment before clutch engagement; only a perfect shift; only a clean, beautiful break in the sound of the exhaust.

It takes study and plenty of practice, and it's worth it!

Another thing a stickshift car does is require a better grasp of road and traffic conditions. A stickshift driver must choose the proper gear for each different road and traffic condition. If he doesn't recognize these conditions *before* he drives into them, he will find his car in the wrong gear. His driving will be clumsy, and he will be frustrated. Therefore, he *must* pay attention, analyze, synthesize, and predict constantly. That's driving, and that's good.

Someone may tell you that there is nothing to stickshifting, that he learned it in a day or an hour. Bunk! He got a very basic idea of it. He managed to get the car moving and stopped several times without killing the engine. He *did not master* stickshifting, and he probably never will! Like driving itself, stickshifting can be studied and perfected for a long, long time. It can be a rewarding part of a very rewarding lifelong hobby — driving well!

Doing It

Happily, doing it is much easier than explaining it. Explaining it in a stickshift car is much easier than explaining it in a textbook. Nonetheless, here goes.

THE CLUTCH: The clutch is the *necessary connecting/disconnecting link* between the engine and the rest of a stickshift car's power train. It fits between the engine and the transmission. When the clutch pedal is up, the clutch is engaged, connecting the engine and transmission. Power can get through the car's entire power train from the engine to the drive wheels to move the car. When someone steps on the clutch pedal, the clutch is disengaged, disconnecting the engine from the transmission. Power cannot get to the drive wheels to move the car.

Got it? When you step on the clutch pedal, the clutch opens. Then engine and transmission are disconnected from each other. That's when you shift.

After shifting, you let the clutch pedal back up again. The clutch closes. Everything is connected again, and the car rolls along. That's it.

If that's "it," where does all the fun come in, and what is all the fuss about?

The fun comes in when you get the feel of the whole process of stickshifting and start developing a new skill. The fuss is about the *friction point*, the point at which the clutch is engaging or closing. Some of the fun and almost all of the problems come at the friction point.

THE FRICTION POINT: To understand the friction point, think for a moment about a car with an *automatic* transmission. You can hold the car in place with the brakes even though its engine is running and its transmission is in gear (D, R, D1, or D2). This is because instead of a clutch connecting the engine and transmission,

there is a fluid coupling. This fluid coupling is *always* connected, but the fluid in it allows slippage. It's like stirring soup in a pot. The spoon stirs the soup, but the pot does not spin around on top of the stove. The soup, a fluid, allows the spoon to *slip* through it. That's why the pot can stand still even though the spoon is stirring the soup.

The engine of an automatic transmission equipped car can run without moving the car because the fluid in the fluid coupling allows slippage. However, when you release the brakes, the fluid does offer enough resistance to transmit the engine's power to the transmission and move the car. It's as if the soup had frozen in the pot with the spoon still in it.

In a stickshift car, it's as if the soup were *always* frozen. The clutch makes a solid connection between the engine and transmission. Therefore, if the engine is running, the transmission is in gear, and the clutch is engaged, the car *must* move.

Suppose the pot were kept from turning around by a vise. If the pot could not turn, you could not move the spoon frozen in the soup. You'd have to stop trying to stir.

It's the same with a stickshift car. If the engine is running, the clutch is engaged, and the transmission is in gear, but the car can't move, the engine *must* stop trying to move it. It can do that only by stalling.

However, when the clutch is *disengaged* or the transmission is in *neutral*, it is as if there were no soup in the pot at all. Moving the spoon around inside an empty pot would never move the pot, because there would be no connection.

The friction point is the point at which the clutch makes the connection between the running engine and the transmission to begin moving the car. For the engine it's like going from stirring an empty pot to stirring a pot with the soup frozen in it, from no connection to a solid connection.

What makes it possible for the car to start moving is the slippage in the clutch at the friction point as it closes or engages. This slippage allows the engine to keep running as it *gradually* takes on the work of moving the car. Controlling this slippage in the clutch at the friction point is the hardest part of learning stickshift driving.

CONTROLLING THE CLUTCH AT THE FRICTION POINT: Suppose you are at the wheel of a stickshift car. The engine is running, the transmission is in gear, the way is clear, and you are holding down the clutch pedal. You let the pedal up a little. Nothing happens. You let it up a little more. Still nothing happens. That's because the friction point is just a very short part of the full travel of the clutch pedal. You keep letting up the pedal slowly. Finally the car begins to move. You have found the friction point. Delighted, you take your foot off the clutch pedal, but the car doesn't go. It bucks and stops. The engine stalls.

Why? The friction point is not really a point. *It is a SHORT DISTANCE.* That's the key to clutch control. YOU MUST EASE THE PEDAL ALL THE WAY THROUGH THAT DISTANCE BEFORE TAKING YOUR FOOT OFF THE PEDAL.

GAS FEED: Many people believe that one MUST feed gas as he engages the clutch. This belief causes the problem of coordinating the actions of two feet on two pedals. More importantly, it is *not* true! On level ground, you *can* make any regular stickshift car that is running well start moving without feeding gas. You can make it move just by *EASING* the clutch *carefully* through the friction point.

It is essential to know this and to master it because it gives you confidence that the car *will* move smoothly exactly when you want it to. It's like knowing and proving to yourself that your body *will float before* you try to learn to swim.

Do this simple exercise. WITHOUT FEEDING ANY GAS, put the car into motion by carefully easing completely through the friction point. Then let the car go a little distance with or without gas and stop. Repeat until you *KNOW* just where the friction point begins and how long it is.

Knowing that, you can begin trying to coordinate gas feed with clutch engagement. Learn to begin feeding gas as the car just begins to move, at the beginning of the friction point. Sort of let the gas take over from the clutch. That's the perfect way, the beautiful way, the way that shows that you are a master of the friction point. Feed exactly the right amount of gas just as you ease through the friction point, not too little, not too much, not too soon, not too late. That's beautiful! That's driving, and that's good!

Another technique is purposely using too much gas. In a way it's cheating, but it can be very useful in a tight spot. Suppose you are at the green light waiting to make a left turn in very heavy traffic. The light turns yellow. You must go RIGHT NOW! You can't afford to stall the car in the intersection. You're nervous. Feed more gas than you'll need *before* you get to the friction point. Keep the gas on and *EASE* through the friction point. The extra gas will cause the engine to run faster, make more power and torque, and not stall if you do not engage the clutch perfectly.

SHIFTING GEARS: Before you try to drive a stickshift car, get the feel of where the gears are. Push the clutch pedal all the way down and move the gearshift lever into the proper position for each gear several times. The shift pattern may be shown on the gearshift knob or on a plate near it. It will be shown in your car's owner's manual. Here are some common shift patterns.

383

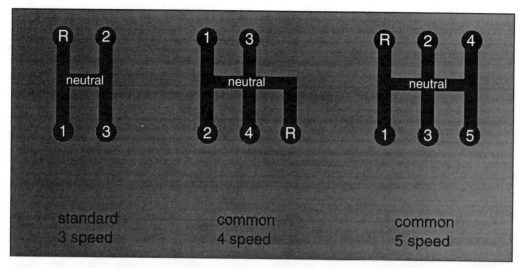

You'll notice that if you move the lever more or less in the proper direction, it will guide itself. Let it. Never force the gearshift lever! Work *with* it when shifting gears.

In each gear position, the lever will feel as if it has locked in place. It should. Make sure it does.

Neutral will not lock in place because neutral is not a gear. A transmission in neutral is OUT OF GEAR. No power can get through the transmission to turn the drive wheels when the transmission is in neutral. It's the empty pot again. This time, though, the power goes through the engaged clutch but stops in the transmission, which is OUT OF GEAR. In neutral, the gearshift lever just flops around.

Play around a bit finding the various gear positions. Get a feel for where they are and how the lever moves.

Never force the gearshift lever! *Never force the gearshift lever*! If it doesn't go, put it somewhere else, somewhere it will go. Then try again to put it where you want it. If it still doesn't go, put it somewhere else again and engage the clutch at least part way. Then disengage the clutch again and put the lever where you want it. *NEVER FORCE THE GEARSHIFT LEVER*!

DRIVE IT: Now, with some idea of where the gears are and the engine running, use your left foot to push the clutch pedal all the way to the floor. Always shift with the clutch pedal all the way down to the floor. Move the gearshift lever into position for first gear. Check traffic and begin releasing the clutch pedal. Nothing will happen. Keep releasing *slowly*. When the pedal gets halfway or more up, the clutch will begin to engage. The car will try to begin moving. You will have found the *friction point*. Don't rush. Feed some gas with your right foot, and KEEP EASING THE CLUTCH PEDAL UP until the clutch is *fully engaged* and the car is accelerating solidly.

Good! Now get a little speed and shift to second. Push the clutch pedal to the floor as you release the gas pedal. Move the lever out of first, through neutral, and into second gear. Release the clutch pedal. Feed gas as you ease through the friction point.

Now get more speed and shift to third gear. Clutch pedal all the way down, shift out of second, through neutral, into third. Feed gas as you release the clutch pedal. Fun?

MOVING THE LEVER: At each shift, the transmission should slip out of gear so smoothly that you can't feel it through the gearshift lever. If it drags, it's most likely your fault. You may be moving the lever before the clutch is completely open, or you may not be pushing the clutch pedal *all* the way down to the floor.

Never slam the lever into the next gear position. Just as you begin moving the lever into position for the next gear, you'll feel resistance. You should. It's the synchronizers working. You'll find out more about them later. Ease through the resistance. *Never force the lever.* Once you get the feel of things and develop a good rhythm, you may stop noticing the resistance because you handle it perfectly.

Don't try too hard to be gentle. Shifting timidly or too slowly will not work. It will destroy the natural rhythm of shifting. Your shifts will never be smooth, or easy, or satisfying. Be sure of yourself and really mean it when you move the lever, but always work *with* the car. Remember, the car cannot feel, or think, or adapt, but you can.

WHICH GEAR SHOULD YOU USE? People who have not driven stickshift vehicles wonder how they'll know which gear to use. It's really not much of a trick. First, your car's owner's manual tells you which gears to use for which speeds. Second, your car may have a tachometer. This gauge tells you how fast your engine is turning in revolutions per

PROPERLY STICKSHIFTING A 3 SPEED

TO ACHIEVE	CLUTCH	GAS	SHIFT LEVER
Get Transmission into First Gear	Down		
			Shift into First
Get into Motion	Up to Friction Point.		
	Ease through Friction Point and Release	Feed as Required	
Accelerate			
Shift into Second Gear	Down	Release	
	Up to Friction Point		Shift to Second
	Ease through Friction Point and Release	Feed as Required	
Accelerate			
Shift into Third Gear	Down	Release	
	Up to Friction Point		Shift to Third
	Ease through Friction Point and Release	Feed as Required	
Accelerate and Cruise			

minute (RPM, also called revs). When accelerating very hard, shift just before the tachometer needle gets to the red area. That way you will not over-rev the engine (run it too fast) and possibly damage it. Third, your car will tell you. You'll develop a feeling for which gear the car needs. In may cars, when just cruising at the normal speed of traffic, you'll probably be able to use your car's highest gear. However, when accelerating back up to cruising speed after slowing for traffic, a slow corner, a yield sign, etc., you will probably need to downshift to a lower gear. You'll know, because your car will tell you, like this:

Suppose you are driving a three speed stickshift car. Slow down and make a right turn. Try to accelerate out of the corner in third gear. The car accelerates *very slowly*. The engine seems to be having trouble making the car go. It is. The engine is running too slowly to make enough power (too few revs). This condition is called "laboring" or "lugging" the engine. It is to be avoided, because it is bad for the engine. Avoid it by raising the revs. Raise the revs by shifting down to second gear. Because second gear is a lower gear than third, it forces the engine to turn faster at the same vehicle speed. That makes the engine much more comfortable, and it produces all the power needed to accelerate the car smoothly and easily.

Be Prepared. Always downshift BEFORE you actually need the lower gear. Using the example of the right turn again, you know you'll need a lower gear to accelerate out of the turn. Downshift just before starting the turn. That way the car is all set up to go through the turn and out of it properly with no fuss. If you wait until you are making the turn, you will have to shift right in the middle of trying to steer or after you have steered and should be accelerating. Both are clumsy and unsatisfying.

In general, when regaining speed, use a lower gear rather than a higher one. Downshift-

ing is guaranteed to handle the power requirements. You'll be able to accelerate briskly.

Many situations will give you a choice of downshifting or not downshifting. There is a fairly large area of overlap, so don't worry too much. With a little experience, you will handle most situations very well. If you decide to get by without downshifting, you'll have to accept slower acceleration. You'll also have to feed the gas very gently and keep alert for signals that the engine is starting to labor. Heavy or abrupt gas feed can cause the car to buck.

Just as with automatic transmissions, you can shift to a lower gear to hold the car back when going downhill. Going uphill may also require a lower gear, as may passing on a two-lane, country road. Anytime the engine is having a hard time (laboring), you need a lower gear.

STOPPING A STICKSHIFT CAR: To stop a stickshift car use the brakes of course. However, just before the car stops, push down the clutch pedal. Remember that soup pot. A stickshift car CANNOT stand still with its engine running unless the transmission is in neutral or the clutch is disengaged. If you stop without disengaging the clutch, the car may buck, the engine will shake and stall. EVERY TIME YOU STOP A STICKSHIFT CAR, PUSH DOWN THE CLUTCH PEDAL!

What you do next depends upon the situation. If you stopped for a stop sign, just shift to first gear and go again when it's your turn and traffic is clear. If you stopped and need to back up, shift to reverse, check everything and go. If you stopped for a red light and must wait, shift to neutral and let the clutch pedal back up again.

The higher the gear in use when stopping, the higher the speed at which the engine will begin shaking. Don't worry about this. You'll learn very quickly when to disengage the clutch. You'll find that in first and reverse, the car can move quite slowly indeed without stalling.

LEAVING A STICKSHIFT CAR PARKED: In hilly areas, people are quite careful about how they leave their cars parked. They don't want them to roll away. People in flatlands, though, tend to shift their *automatic* transmissions into park and just walk away.

With a stickshift car, there is a little more to it. Even on nearly flat surfaces, if you leave the transmission in neutral and walk away, the car may quite easily roll away. Use the parking brake to hold a stickshift car in place. Instead of using the parking brake, many people just leave the car parked in first or reverse. This makes it hard for the car to move, because whatever is trying to move it must overcome the engine's compression. Trucks are usually parked this way. Some people leave the car parked in gear *and* apply the parking brake. Whichever method you choose, stick with it, because you can fool yourself when you restart the engine after leaving the vehicle parked.

STARTING THE ENGINE OF A STICK-SHIFT CAR: It is wonderfully easy to fool yourself and possibly crash when starting the engine of a stickshift car. When you turn the key, the starter motor (a small electric motor) turns the engine. If the transmission is in gear and the clutch is engaged, the starter motor *will* move the car. Immediately! The instant you turn the key, the car will move. It will be quite a surprise. If the engine should start very quickly, the surprise will be even bigger.

BEFORE STARTING THE ENGINE OF A STICKSHIFT VEHICLE, ALWAYS STEP ON THE CLUTCH PEDAL, CHECK THAT THE TRANSMISSION IS IN NEUTRAL, AND BE SURE THAT THE PARKING BRAKE IS APPLIED. This is especially important when starting a vehicle parked by someone else!

You may start the engine with the clutch pedal up or down. In most cases, pushing it down makes starting easier, because the engine is separated from the transmission. Therefore, the starter has to turn only the engine, not the engine *and* the transmission. If you start the engine with the clutch pedal down, be sure that the transmission is in neutral before letting the pedal up again. Newer vehicles will not start unless the clutch pedal is down.

It is best to apply the brakes or engage the parking brake before you do anything else in starting the engine. If the parking brake is disengaged, the vehicle may roll as soon as you push down the clutch pedal.

FANCY FOOTWORK: You can make a car with an *automatic* transmission creep ever so slowly by gradually releasing the brakes just enough to allow motion. Can you make a stickshift car creep that slowly too? Of course you can, but *not* by using the brakes. You have to use your old friend the friction point.

Yes, after you get control over it, the friction point does become a very good friend. To make a stickshift car move ever so slightly and ever so slowly, just let the clutch pedal up to the friction point and hold it there. Use a little more or less clutch engagement to control car speed. It's called "slipping the clutch." You might need a little gas. You might need the brakes to stop, but most of the control is in using the clutch's friction point.

FANCY FOOTWORK II, PUTTING THE STICKSHIFT CAR INTO FORWARD MOTION FACING UPHILL: You have had to stop at a stop sign on your way up a hill. You have checked traffic, etc., and you are ready to roll again. Your left foot is holding down the clutch pedal. Your right foot is holding down the brake pedal. You take your right foot off the brake pedal to feed gas, and immediately the car starts rolling backwards! It's the pot of soup once again. With the clutch pedal down, there's no soup. With the clutch pedal down and the brakes off, the car *must* roll backwards because of gravity.

There are several ways of avoiding rolling backwards when starting forward uphill. The nicest is to let the clutch pedal up to the friction point and *keep it there* while your right foot releases the brake pedal and begins feeding gas. Keeping the clutch at the friction point will hold the car in place while you move your right foot to the gas pedal.

Another way is to hold the car with the hand operated parking brake while moving your right foot to the gas pedal.

In the very old days, when cars had hand throttles, drivers could use them to feed gas while using the brakes to hold the car.

Finally, in some situations, one can use a wheel chock.

Every time you stop uphill, remember that the car stopped ahead of you may have a stickshift. Stay back. Give it room. Don't put pressure on its driver by crowding him from behind.

Of course, putting a stickshift vehicle into forward motion facing *downhill* is no problem at all. Gravity works with you to get the car moving.

In parallel parking places, etc., on hills, fine adjustments can be made in the downhill direction (forward or backward) by using gravity. Just leave the transmission in neutral and use the brakes to control the car as it rolls slowly backward or forward downhill. The opposite of this is having to use power to move backward or forward *uphill* in a very tight spot. Plan ahead. Try to leave yourself some room in the *downhill* direction in case you do roll downhill before you can get going *uphill*.

GOOD FORM: Except when shifting or creeping, KEEP YOUR FOOT *OFF THE CLUTCH PEDAL!* Many people waiting at a red light habitually shift to first gear and then sit there holding the clutch pedal down until the light changes to green. Bad form! Holding the clutch open any longer than necessary causes needless wear on a clutch part called the throw-out bearing.

Many stickshift drivers waiting at a red light on an uphill slope do not hold the car in place with the brakes. Instead, they slip the clutch (hold it at the friction point) with the transmission in first gear. One supposes that these drivers believe this trick is a very sophisticated and classy bit of driving. It isn't. It is brutal abuse of the clutch. It wears the clutch disc, throw-out bearing, and the friction faces of the pressure plate and flywheel.

Never "ride" the clutch. "Riding the clutch" is slipping the clutch any time it should not be slipped. The clutch pedal is *not a footrest*! Riding the clutch not only damages the clutch disc, throw-out bearing, pressure plate and flywheel faces, it marks you as an unskilled driver or an insensitive brute who just doesn't care about the machinery — like someone who rides a horse hard until it drops dead right under him. Except when shifting or creeping, KEEP YOUR FOOT OFF THE CLUTCH PEDAL!

Always keep the clutch properly adjusted! Step on your clutch pedal. You should feel less than one inch to about two inches (see owner's manual) of free play before you feel the clutch starting to open.

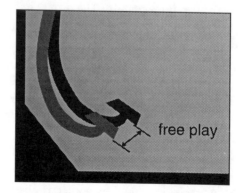

Hydraulically operated clutches adjust this by themselves once their master cylinders have been set up properly. Mechanically operated clutches must be adjusted periodically.

If you allow the free play to disappear, the clutch will never close completely. It will slip whenever the engine is running, and it will wear out with amazing speed.

CRUNCH! That little resistance you feel when you shift is the transmission's synchromesh working. Synchromesh gets everything in the transmission going the proper speed when you change gears. It makes crunchless shifting easy. Most cars have synchromesh on all forward gears, but not on reverse. Some older cars do not have synchromesh on first gear either. Many drivers shifting into non-synchro gears grind gears and believe that there is nothing they can do about it. That is *not* true! To select a non-synchro gear correctly, merely push the lever toward any synchronized gear enough to get the synchromesh working — feel the resistance. Then shift into the non-synchronized gear. Presto! No crunch!

SLICK STUFF: You will notice that when shifting to a lower gear, engaging the clutch causes the car to lurch as the engine revs up. Engage the clutch gently and try to use the right amount of gas so that the engine is running the proper speed when you engage the clutch.

SLICK STUFF II: Double clutching can be very helpful when downshifting, a lot of fun, and very rewarding to your ego. It helps the synchromesh do its job. In vehicles with worn out synchromesh, proper double clutching can substitute for it. It works like this. Suppose you want to shift down from 4th to 3rd:

- Press clutch and release gas
- Shift to neutral
- Release clutch
- Feed gas to rev up engine and transmission
- Press clutch and shift to 3rd
- Release clutch

The whole thing should be remarkably slick and delightful. There should be no drag on the lever, no lurch of the car, just an incredibly smooth downshift. It takes work, and you should be very good at regular shifting before you attempt it. You'll need to do it quickly and surely with *perfect* timing. Remember, if your double clutched downshifts are not unbelievably smooth, you are doing them wrong! If you are double clutching improperly, you may be doing much more harm than good.

Try stickshifting. It is more fun!

23 Chapter Twenty-three

We Are Not Lost

Many people do not know how to use maps. Some seem to fear them. However, maps give many kinds of information which cannot be given in any other way. Maps can teach. Maps can give pleasure. Maps can fascinate. Do not fear maps. Pick up an atlas and relax with it. Just sit back and look at the maps. Soon your curiosity will be aroused by something on one of the maps. The next thing you know, you will find yourself studying the maps. You will learn what the lines, and symbols, and numbers, and colors mean. As you learn how maps work, you will find that they are not to be ignored or feared, but to be used and enjoyed.

Drivers need to know how to get from here to there. They want to know the fastest way, the shortest way, the prettiest way, the northern route, the southern route, etc. They want to know what sights they can stop to see along the way. They want to know roughly how long the trip will take. Often to estimate costs, they may want to calculate how many nights they will have to spend in motels, how many meals they will have to eat on the road, how much gasoline their vehicles will burn, etc. To do these things, drivers need maps — road maps.

As with other kinds of maps, a great deal of information can be found on road maps. The main use for a road map, though, is to find out how to get from here to there.

THE BASICS OF USING ROAD MAPS: Completely unfold a road map and look at it. See the evenly spaced letters and numbers along its edges.

Notice how lines between the numbers and letters run completely up and down and across the map, dividing it into little, square sections or boxes.

When you want to find a town on a map, you do not just search the entire map for it. You look in the little box which contains the town. How do you know which box contains the town? You look

in the map's alphabetical index for the town. The name will be followed by a number and a letter. The number and letter are map coordinates. They refer to the letters and numbers along the map's edges. Find the number and the letter. Then find the box indicated by the intersection of the coordinates. For example: look up Villagetown Heights in the index. Its coordinates are D-5. Find D and 5 on the map's edges. Then find the place where they cross. That is the box in which you will find Villagetown Heights.

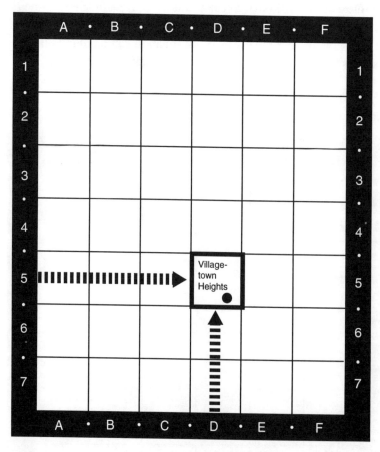

To plan a route to Villagetown Heights, you must also find the town in which you are now, Oakforest Springs. Find Oakforest Springs the same way you found Villagetown Heights. Find its coordinates in the index. Then locate the proper box on the map and find Oakforest Springs.

When you know where both towns are on the map, look for the roads which connect them. Try to find several routes. One may be shorter than another. One may be more scenic. One may run on the interstate all the way. One may pass near some point of interest at which you would like to stop along the way.

The lines which represent the roads will be of different colors and thicknesses, etc. Find the "legend" of the map. The legend is the key to the map. It explains the map's symbols. It tells you how to use the map, how to get the information you want from the map. The legend will tell you what kinds of roads connect the two towns. A heavy, red line may be an interstate. A thin, gray line may be a gravel road. A medium, black line may be a four-lane highway, etc.

The lines which represent the roads will also have numbers on or alongside them. The numbers in which you are interested at this point are the route numbers — the numbers which identify the roads, the numbers which are posted on signs along the roads. Check the legend. It will show what symbols are used to indicate interstate route numbers, state highway numbers, U.S. highway numbers, county road numbers, etc.

It is easy to make mistakes when using road maps. Look carefully, and check several times. Make sure that the road at which you are looking really is the road at which you are looking. sometimes two highway numbers run along the same strip of pavement. That is, the same road has two or more different highway numbers on it. This can lead you astray. You may think that you have to change to another route number when you really do not. Look farther along the road for the original route number. If it is there, that number does go right through. Sometimes the original route number turns off in another direction at an intersection. It is easy to assume that the number just continues along with a certain line on a map. This can lead you off course. Look beyond your destination and along your intended route to double check exactly where which route numbers actually do go. Double check where they intersect, too. Do not just see a line which goes from here to there and assume that it keeps the same route number for its entire length. It may not.

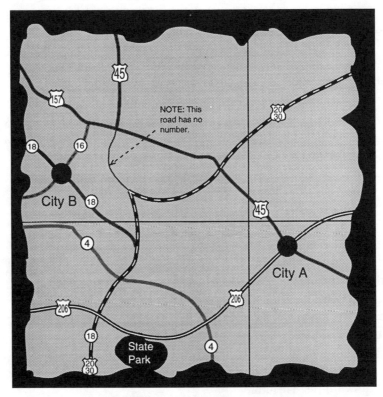

In the illustration above, for example, to get from City A to City B, you cannot just take Route 45 to Route 16. Route 45 does not connect with 16. It connects with 157, which connects with 16. An alternate route would be 206 to 4 to 18/20/30 to 18. There are other possible alternate routes. For example, if you would like to stop at the state park along the way, take 206 to the state park, then take 206 to 18/20/30 to 18.

You may find other numbers along the roads on a map. These are probably mileages between certain points. Road maps will also have mileage charts showing the distances between major towns on the map.

Make sure that there really are intersections where you want to turn off one road onto another. Study the map carefully. Roads may come very close to each other, but not cross. Superhighway interchanges are usually shown by little, white boxes. Unusual or incomplete interchanges may actually be drawn on the map. If a superhighway just crosses another road on a map, you may assume that there is no way to get from one road to the other. With no indication of an interchange, the crossing at which you are looking is an overpass or an underpass.

Experience and navigating skills come into play in finding these tricky, little things on maps and in not getting confused when trying to relate the map to the real road. Learn by doing. you will make mistakes. Learn from them.

Learn navigating by being the navigator instead of the driver on a trip. Keep rechecking the map as you roll along the road. Stay just ahead of the car on the map. Predict to the driver what the next town, etc., will be. Keep rechecking the long haul, too, for traps. It is fun, and you will learn a lot. Your driver will appreciate good navigation, too.

It should be possible to travel the interstates just by reading the big, green signs to keep track of route number, direction, and the next big city on the route. This is frightening to the old time map reader, because he cannot bring himself to trust signs without double-checking his good quality, current road maps. If you know, though, that I-90 will take you from Chicago, Illinois to Seattle, Washington, you can merely follow the signs and stay on I-90 West.

THE LEGEND: Look at the legend of the map. The legend explains all the codes and symbols on the map. It also gives a mileage scale. This is usually based on an inch. One inch on the map equals 25 miles on the road, or one inch on the map equals 10 miles on the road, etc.

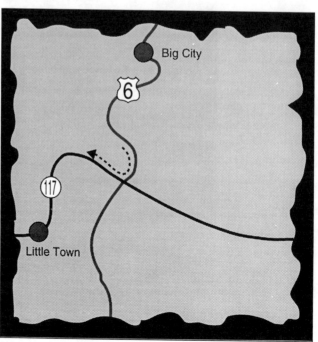

ORIENTING THE MAP: "When we get to Route 34, we turn left. No! I mean right. No! I mean left. Oh, wait a minute! Left!" All you have to do is look at the intersection and see whether the turn is left or right. In the illustration below, you are travelling along Route 6 from Big City. When you get to Route 117, you must turn right to get to Little Town.

It might look like a turn to the left, because 117 goes toward the left, but you have been going down on 6. Therefore, the turn onto 117 must be to the right.

Another way of figuring this is to orient your map. Turn the map so that you are always travelling up the map. This makes the lines on the map go the same way you are going.

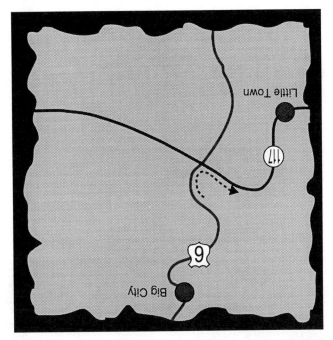

This makes it obvious that the turn is to the right. With practice you should be able to overcome the need to turn the map every time you turn the car. Since maps are easier to read when they are right side up, you should learn to recognize right and left turns even though the map is not turned upside down or sideways.

Somewhere on the map is an arrow which usually indicates north. Make sure that you are reading the map the right way. Usually, you want north to be up.

CITY STREET MAPS: Street maps of cities and/or towns work the same way as other road maps. They have alphabetical indices. They have coordinate systems. They have legends.

MAP CARE: Some people must always refold their map correctly. Others seem not to care about this. An improperly folded map is bulky and subject to being torn and otherwise mistreated when not in use. When in use, a map may be easier to handle when folded into a small, handy section. Once a map is folded incorrectly, though, it will be difficult (sometimes seemingly impossible) ever to fold it correctly again.

When unfolding maps for use, be patient with the creases. Do not pull the map to force unfolding. This can tear the map, shortening its useful life and, sometimes, making it impossible to read just the tiny area you need.

24 Chapter Twenty-four

Insurance

Photo courtesy of the National Highway Traffic Safety Administration.

To insure is to protect against loss. Your automobile insurance protects you against loss in matters related to your car. Insurance works like this: many people get together, and each puts some money into a common fund. If one of these people suffers a great loss, the money from the fund is used to pay that one person. It is called sharing the risk. Each person pays a little money to insure against losing a lot of money.

Insurance companies do the paperwork, calculate the risks, and handle the money. To make a profit, they make sure that more money is collected than is paid out.

Liability insurance is the important kind of automobile insurance. It protects you against lawsuits resulting from your liability in a car crash. It pays people who were hurt because of you. It also pays for things which were damaged because of you. In many states it is illegal to drive without liability insurance.

Buy the most liability insurance you can get for what you can afford to pay. Do shop around for insurance.

As part of your liability insurance, you will probably be sold *uninsured/underinsured motorist insurance* and *medical payment insurance*. Uninsured/underinsured motorist insurance pays you for your injuries and damages when they are caused by another driver with little or no liability insurance. Medical payment insurance pays for injuries suffered by people in your car. As with liability insurance, buy as much of these two kinds of insurance as you can afford.

Some states have *no-fault insurance*. This takes the place of liability insurance. *Your* no-fault insurance pays for *your* injuries and damages regardless of who may be at fault.

Collision insurance pays for damage to your car resulting from a crash. If your car is financed (paid for on time payments), the financier (bank, credit union, loan company, etc.) will require you to have collision insurance. It works like this: you buy a $20,000 car by making a down payment of $5,000. You borrow the other $15,000 from a bank. The bank pays off the dealer. You owe the bank $15,000 plus interest. Then you total the car. The car is worthless. The bank could then lose the $15,000 plus interest. The collision insurance, however, pays off the bank.

If your car is worth a good deal of money or is financed, have collision insurance. If you own an old beater, do not bother with collision insurance. It is not worth paying to insure a car of very little value.

Collision insurance insures your car against collision damage. *Comprehensive insurance* insures your car against everything else: fire, flood, theft, vandalism, etc. The same rules apply with comprehensive insurance as with collision insurance. If you drive an old beater, do not waste money on it.

Some insurance agents work for one insurance company. That company's name is on their business cards, their office, and all the policies they sell. Other agents, independent agents, have their own businesses. They handle several insurance companies and match up customers with insurance companies.

Those are the basics. Study, ask questions, learn, shop, and *have liability insurance*.

25 *Chapter Twenty-five*

Motoring Moods

Photo courtesy of Rob and Debbie Pulsidski.

"Motoring," such a happy word, such a likable concept! The lure of the open road, the adventure of the trip, the freedom, the feeling of control, the roar of the exhaust, the wind in your hair, the sun on your skin, the songs of the birds in the air, the feeling of movement along the road, the camaraderie, the just plain fun!

To too many of us motoring is something wonderful that used to be, or might have been, but no longer is. Motoring was a very special relationship with an automobile. The Sunday drive and picnic, the automobile excursion to the beach — they were *events*! They were care-

fully planned. They were eagerly awaited. They were fondly remembered. Getting there *was* half the fun. Motoring was a thing to be enjoyed for itself. Motoring was an activity, a sport, a passion. The motorist was a hero: brave, skilled, knowledgeable, fit, self-reliant, adventurous — a man or woman far beyond the ordinary.

The concept of motoring lingers on in our memories and in our imaginations. Its magic still touches us on driving vacations: the planning, the maps, the travel folders, the packing, the anticipation, the camera, the film, getting the car serviced for "the trip," loading the car, locking the house and making sure we have the keys, driving away, getting "on the road," wondering what we have forgotten, seeing new places, navigating, snacking in the car, talking, joking, singing, playing games, stopping for gas, washing the bugs off the windshield, checking the oil, getting back into the car and driving off again, calculating the gas mileage, staying at the motel, having breakfast along the road, getting back into the car and driving off again and again, that very special relationship with the car because everything in the whole world that matters is ourselves, the car, the road, and the trip — then being "almost there," arriving, unpacking, a different relationship with the car — using it for short, casual rides to nearby but still excitingly unfamiliar places and, of course, taking the trip home, and being home again after "the trip" — after "the adventure," setting about familiar tasks, seeing friends, telling them about our adventures, looking at the pictures, and finally, one day realizing that "the car trip" has become a cherished memory.

So often today, though, driving is not motoring. We ride in a closed car, the air conditioning annoying us with chill drafts of stale air. We hear the radio or the tape, not the sounds of the car, the road, the countryside. We pound along endless miles of boring interstate. We eat at national chain restaurants.

Worse yet, in our daily commuting, we fight traffic. We wait in construction zones. We get late. We are forced to conduct business on car telephones. We worry. We cuss. We cut off other drivers. We make rude gestures. We RUSH! Driving has become rushing, rushing to make up time we no longer seem to have. Driving is no longer a sport; it is a trial, a burden, a torture. People actually hate to drive!

For so many people there seems to be only one driving mood nowadays — a mood of tension and frustration. Driving is *always* a

desperate jamming and forcing one's way to the front of the pack, only to catch another pack. Speeding is as natural as breathing. Fun? Control? Mastery? Personal growth? These are rare in driving today. For too many people, the wonderful activity of driving has become, at best, a chore.

We come across people on country roads who are neither stimulated by the challenge of the road, nor relaxing and enjoying the sounds, the sights, and the smells of the countryside. They are just rushing. They are like electrons inside atoms, rushing around mindlessly in their orbits. Electrons never get to a destination. They never get ahead of schedule or save time. They never enjoy the trip. They just rush. Driving that way is not motoring. Motoring is feeling the movement, enjoying the ride, celebrating the driving.

Sanctioned racing certainly is a form of motoring, but racing is not mindless rushing. Racing has a goal. Racing has rules. Racing demands achievement. Racing is a wonderful sport. Racing fosters growth. Racing rewards intelligence, skill, discipline, determination, planning, work, patience, and speed under perfect control.

There are many other motoring moods. What a truly delightful thing it is just to grind along in first gear (or maybe second) in an open sports car along a quiet country lane, or up and down hills through woods, feeling the car climb uphill and hold itself back downhill, while you actually *see* the scenery, *feel* the air, and *hear* the sounds. Is that hard to believe? Try it.

Parks and preserves are not places through which to rush like electrons. "Gotta get there!" Where? You ARE there. You are in the park; enjoy it. You didn't really go there to rush desperately through it, did you? There is something wonderful about going slowly in a car, especially an open car.

Caution! Slowly and in a relaxed manner

do not mean getting in the way. Real drivers *NEVER* get in the way! Watch the mirror and let the soulless electrons pass.

Rain — rain not only makes it hard to see and slows you down, it provides a motoring mood. Feel the mood. Enjoy the concept of driving through drops of water. It is different from driving through sunshine. Rain hits the windshield. The wipers sweep it away. The road seems to swish as the tires cut through the water. The puddles splash. All moving motor vehicles are surrounded by a fine mist of road spray. Everything looks cool and in soft focus.

Drive through light rain with the top down. You probably will not get wet — or not very wet anyway. You *will* enjoy the experience, though. Take the open car out after a morning rain shower. Feel the sun begin to warm and dry the cool damp. See the road steaming and the clouds making beautiful pictures as they block, reveal, and reflect the sunlight. Feel the reduced traction. Gently frolic with it in perfect safety through masterful control.

Fog isolates you from almost everything outside your car. It is so cozy to drive through fog if you are not an electron. Rain can make motoring very cozy, too.

On a cool morning or evening, drive with the windows open or even with the top down and the heater on. Try it.

A snowy landscape is absolutely beautiful all by itself. Try driving through it with the windows open, or the top down, and the heater roaring! Snow gives all sorts of opportunities to enjoy motoring, meeting its challenges and enjoying one's self behind the wheel.

Rush hour traffic as a steady diet is unpleasant. It is mostly *not driving anyway*. For rush hour, you need a *very* comfortable car with excellent air conditioning and heating, power everything, and an absolutely terrific stereo. It is very good to have a friend with whom you can have fascinating conversations. Still, expressway driving at rush hour is a motoring mood. Take it for what it is. Go along with what it is. Become part of it. Read the vanity license plates. Look at the cars, the people, the trucks, the buildings along the road. Feel the city at its most congested. Enjoy the not going.

Rolling up miles is a motoring mood. Cleverly making time and being where the traffic isn't are motoring moods.

Going out to breakfast on Saturday morning can be a very happy motoring mood. Taking someone somewhere like a taxi driver is a friendly thing to do and another motoring mood. Hauling and towing are motoring moods.

Trips to auto races, car shows, car museums, etc. are totally about cars and driving. They are the pure essence of motoring like racing, slaloming, rallying, etc.

Driving along the river, the lake, the ocean — driving through the mountains, the desert — dirt biking, off-roading, skid school, high performance driving school — motoring moods all —

Driving on a date, riding in a funeral, driving or riding in a wedding, riding or driving in a parade — these are motoring moods you will probably remember for the rest of your life.

At this point, think again about the idea of "the trip." Think of that feeling that the only things that matter are all right there on "the trip." The cares, problems, sorrows, and triumphs of the whole world fall away into insignificance. For us, there is only "the trip." We are free. We are travelers. We have only that role, only that responsibility. We are visitors who witness and momentarily touch the lives of others. We are "passing through." We carry that special aura of *travelers*, of people of the road, of heroes on their hero journeys.

Think about *all* trips. Each trip to the grocery store; each trip to the gas station, or the post office, or the next town; each trip to work, to school, or home is different. Each is its own story.

Some days your driving is nearly perfect. Everything you do works right. You are always in the right place at the right time. You make all the green lights. Even the mistakes you make turn out alright, as if they had been tactics planned by a master driver.

Other days, everything goes wrong. Every brilliant move you plan is spoiled by the incredibly clumsy or unpredictable maneuvering of others. Every yellow light catches you at the point where stopping or not stopping is a toss-up. Every time you change lanes, your old lane begins moving briskly, and your new lane stops.

Some days you will get stopped by the police. Some times you will be given a warning and let go. Other times you will get a traffic ticket.

Some days you will even crash.

Each drive, you see, is a little story, a little piece of your driving life. See your drives that way. See each and every drive as one unique chapter in the lifetime story of your driving career, as an individual part of your life's work as a driver. Each drive, each chapter, will have its own mood. Do not see all your driving as rushing.

What if you rushed and never got there? Are you really that important? Whoever you are, and wherever you are rushing, what if you died on the way? Some people would be inconvenienced. Perhaps their plans would be set back a few days. Some people would go to your funeral, and the *whole world would go on without you*! The whole world cares very little whether you rush. It cares not at all whether you enjoy driving.

Put as much motoring as you can into your driving! Experience as many motoring moods as possible. There must be as many motoring moods as there are roads, motor vehicles, and people. Do not rush and make every drive a torture test. Look at your driving as a life-long body of work of which to be proud. Drive according to conditions. Drive according to moods. Expect variety. Expect different challenges and rewards. Try to make each and every drive a chapter in your personal history of driving enjoyment, accomplishment, ever increasing mastery, and satisfaction in personal growth! Try to make each and every drive a *JOYRIDE*!